FOOTPRINTS IN NEW YORK

Tracing the Lives of
Four Centuries of New Yorkers

JAMES NEVIUS AND MICHELLE NEVIUS

LYONS PRESS
Guilford, Connecticut
An imprint of Globe Pequot Press

Lyons Press is an imprint of Globe Pequot Press.

Maps by Design Maps Inc. © Morris Book Publishing, LLC
Project editor: Meredith Dias
Layout: Kirsten Livingston

Library of Congress Cataloging-in-Publication Data

Nevius, James.
  Footprints in New York : tracing the lives of four centuries of New Yorkers / James Nevius and Michelle Nevius.
     pages cm
  Includes bibliographical references and index.
  ISBN 978-0-7627-9636-6
  1. New York (N.Y.)—Biography. 2. New York (N.Y.)—History. I. Nevius, Michelle. II. Title.
  F128.25.N48 2014
  974.7'1—dc23

                                                                              2014001590

Printed in the United States of America

10 9 8 7 6 5 4 3 2 1

To the world's librarians, without whom this book
—and most others—
would never have been written

Contents

Preface vii

Chapter 1: Shadows of Shadows: Peter Stuyvesant
and the Dutch Frontier. 1

Chapter 2: The Dissenters 15

Chapter 3: The DeLanceys and New York's Lost Century 27

Chapter 4: Alexander Hamilton: The Life and Death
of a Patriot 43

Chapter 5: DeWitt Clinton and the Making of the
Modern City .63

Chapter 6: Gertrude Tredwell: At Home in
Greenwich Village 77

Chapter 7: "A Ghastly Poverty": Edgar Allan Poe 91

Chapter 8: The Birth of Central Park 105

Chapter 9: Abraham Lincoln and the Civil War 121

Chapter 10: Boss Tweed 137

Chapter 11: Mrs. Astor and Mrs. Wharton: Tales of
the Gilded Age 155

Chapter 12: How the Other Half Lived. 171

Chapter 13: Seth Low: From the Brooklyn Bridge to
the Big City. 184

Chapter 14: The City of Morgan 199

Chapter 15: The Liberators: Harlem, Greenwich Village,
and the American Left 213

Chapter 16: Peace through Trade: The Rockefellers
and the Modern City. 225

Chapter 17: The Battle for New York: Jane Jacobs vs.
Robert Moses 239

Chapter 18: "City Like a Web": Bob Dylan and
MacDougal Street 255

Chapter 19: New York Stories: Martin Scorsese and
Woody Allen 265

Maps 279

Acknowledgments 288

Notes on Sources 290

Photo Credits 305

Index 306

PREFACE

THE CONCEPT OF THIS BOOK IS SIMPLE: We wanted to build a time machine. Since our grasp of particle physics is weak, we decided on the next best thing, to tell the story of New York City by having each chapter transport the reader to a distinct historical era, from the Dutch village of New Amsterdam to the modern city of skyscrapers that's been built along the very streets the city's Dutch founders once walked.

As our goal is to, literally, follow in the footsteps of the New Yorkers who've come before us, each chapter is linked to a person (or, sometimes, a group of people) whose story is emblematic of that era. Some people—like Edgar Allan Poe and Abraham Lincoln—are universally famous. Others, such as Gertrude Tredwell or Stephen DeLancey, will only be familiar to a few. But all of them played an important role in the story of the city.

New York is so chock-full of intriguing sites that it's a historian's dream. We've been leading walking tours of the city for nearly fifteen years, and in that time we've searched out forgotten byways and journeyed to unexpected corners of the city. It's those places—from the city's oldest house to a small synagogue on a stretch of Broadway that most people don't even know exists—that paint a vivid portrait of New York. We talk about famous sites in these pages too, but we hope that when you're reading about some of the more off-the-beaten-track sites, you may want to seek them out yourself.

The greatest joy of leading tours is the moment when a client—often someone for whom history has always been dry recitations of names, dates, and battles—makes that real, personal connection with the city of the past. It can happen in unexpected places—a walk down the streets of Little Italy can evoke childhood memories. Examining gun placements in the old fort in Battery Park can suddenly illuminate the importance of the War of 1812 to someone who'd never before been able to get a handle on it. Simply walking from Battery Park to Soho—the same path that Alexander Hamilton walked during the Revolution with his artillery company—can do more to reveal the contours of the war for American independence than any textbook. It's our hope that the New York stories in these pages will uncover some of those hidden histories, too.

—◦—

This book is the work of two people, but from this point forward, we are writing as a single, first-person "I" instead of the second-person "we." In part, this better reflects that some experiences apply to only one of us—for example, in Chapter 1, it is James's ancestor who was New Amsterdam's city secretary; later, it's Michelle who visits the Plymouth Church in Brooklyn Heights. More often, we are experiencing places together, but rather than switch back and forth—or write in a more distant, royal "We"—we've stuck with a more accessible, approachable "I."

A slightly fanciful view of New Amsterdam, ca. 1650.

CHAPTER 1

Shadows of Shadows:
Peter Stuyvesant and the Dutch Frontier

"I've never even heard of Peter Stuyvesant."

I'm in the East Village, at St. Mark's-in-the-Bowery, one of the city's oldest churches, with a client who has just realized he's standing on Peter Stuyvesant's grave. Though the tour I'm leading is called "Peter Stuyvesant's Bowery" (*bowery* being the English corruption of the Dutch word for farm), the client has just now—an hour into the walk—worked up the courage to confess that he doesn't know who I'm talking about.

He's certainly not alone.

Peter Stuyvesant was the longest-serving director-general of New Netherland, the Dutch colony on the American frontier, an area that, at its peak, included parts of Connecticut, New Jersey, and Delaware. Stuyvesant served from 1647 until 1664, when the English stole the place right out from under him. Stuyvesant's headquarters were in New Amsterdam, or as it is known today, New York.

The man's wife chastises him. "You know—Peg-leg Peter Stuyvesant."

The man keeps shaking his head.

Peg-legged. Hard-nosed. Irascible. Anti-Semitic. Old silver nails. If you have ever read about Stuyvesant, you've likely seen these terms bubble to the surface. He isn't a person, but a cartoon character: Big, Bad Peter Stuyvesant.

Of course, if you live outside the United States, you may be more familiar with Stuyvesant's name, but only because he's lent it to a popular brand of cigarette. Emblazoned on the cigarette pack is a regal-looking coat of arms, the cross of St. Andrew topped by a furry little rodent.

That rodent is a beaver and it's the reason New Amsterdam existed at all.

Standing in the heart of old New Amsterdam—today's Financial District— trying to picture what it would have looked like in Peter Stuyvesant's time takes a vivid imagination. Not a single architectural artifact remains in Manhattan from the Dutch period. What we have left isn't even ephemeral—it's shadows of shadows.

Those shadows have spread over my entire life. I am a Knickerbocker— a descendant of one of the settlers of Manhattan. My ancestor was named Johannes Nevius, and he arrived in the colony sometime around 1652 (his first recorded appearance is March 3, 1652, when he served as a witness at a baptism). This was about five years after Stuyvesant had taken over as director-general of New Netherland, and nearly thirty years after the first permanent residents established roots on the island of Manhattan in 1625.

Not long before coming to the New World, Johannes had graduated from the University of Leiden. To indicate his educational status, he styled his names—first and last—in Latin. (In Dutch, the name would have been Jan Neeff—"John, the cousin" or "John, the nephew.")

Presumably, Johannes came to New Amsterdam to make money, though his motivations are lost to us. A history of New York published in 1853 says he was "engaged in mercantile pursuits," but that tells us little. Back then, who wasn't?

At the time of Johannes's immigration, tensions in Europe were running high between the Netherlands and England. On May 29, 1652, the Battle of

Goodwin Sands sparked the First Anglo-Dutch War. Many men Johannes's age fought in the conflict. It's possible Johannes came to Manhattan to avoid serving in the Dutch navy, but it wouldn't have been an easy choice. Consider the "low and ruinous condition" (as lawyer Adriaen van der Donck labeled it) of New Amsterdam when Johannes emigrated: poor sanitation; garbage-eating pigs loose on the streets; brackish wells and contaminated water cisterns; hostile natives; and the ever-present threat of the English encroaching on their territory. Though Johannes might not have been better off going to war, New Amsterdam was a long way from easy street.

But, back to the beavers.

There would have been no New Amsterdam for Peter Stuyvesant or Johannes Nevius to immigrate to if not for Henry Hudson, the explorer who sailed into New York Harbor in September 1609, in search of the Northwest Passage. A navigator-for-hire for the Dutch East India Company, Hudson had assured his employers that he could find them a shortcut to the spice-filled East Indies, even though he'd tried and failed twice before. Hudson failed this time, too, but he did discover that the Hudson River Valley was teeming with beavers. Spices were the most important luxury import into Europe at the time, but furs were almost as valued. It was like Hudson had struck gold.

As Hudson's first mate, Robert Juet, observed in his diary, the local natives were willing to part with animal pelts at a bargain price: "knives, hatchets, copper kettles, trivets, beads, and other trifles." Juet was amazed that they would even trade with the French for "red cassocks," though it isn't clear whether this jibe is aimed more at the French or the natives.

In Hudson's wake, navigators and fur traders verified his claims, including Adriaen Block who, in 1613, circumnavigated Manhattan and Long Island for the first time. In 1621, to regularize trade—and keep the English in Virginia and Massachusetts at bay—an official Dutch West India Company was founded. In 1624, two ships of settlers under Captain Cornelius Mey arrived to create permanent company-run settlements up the river at Fort Orange (modern-day Albany) and on Governors Island in New York Harbor.

In 1625, those Governors Island settlers, mostly Walloons (French-speaking Protestants from what would one day become Belgium), moved to Manhattan and began building a fort. A year later, the colony's new director, Peter Minuit, paid sixty guilders of trade goods to one or more of the local Lenape tribes to purchase Manhattan.

When I tour New Amsterdam—sometimes with far-flung Nevius cousins who've tracked us down on the Internet—I often start in Battery Park at the Netherlands Memorial Flagpole, a 1926 commemoration of Minuit's purchase. Not only does the flagpole feature a handsome version of the city's coat of arms—replete with the iconic beaver—it also shows Minuit in the act of handing over a string of beads. There's something compelling about this image, though I know it to be a myth.

Even if you've never heard of Peter Minuit, the purchase of Manhattan for "twenty-four dollars of beads and trinkets" is probably familiar to you. However, almost every element of the story, from the dollar amount to the trade goods used, is either wrong or misleading. The figure we have (third-hand, since the deed of sale was lost) is sixty Dutch guilders. Sixty guilders of what? It could have been red cassocks for all we know. The twenty-four-dollar figure—a nineteenth-century, back-of-the-envelope calculation—makes it seem incredibly cheap. But what would sixty guilders have bought you in 1626? If you were lucky enough to have that much money in your pocket—and many poor Dutchmen would never see such a large sum—it would have bought you 2,400 tankards of beer.

One day, while I'm standing at the flagpole thinking of this, I wonder how much a tankard of beer would cost today on the island that Peter Minuit bought. According to my smartphone, the closest pub is Murphy's Tavern on Stone Street. This seems highly appropriate: Stone Street was probably the first paved street in New York, laid with cobblestones in 1655 to lessen the dust and mud churned up by horses from the local brewery. That brewery, owned by Oloff Stevenson van Cortlandt, stood near the spot Murphy's Tavern occupies today. Beer was central to life in New Amsterdam; when Peter Stuyvesant arrived in 1647 to take over the colony, he found "one full fourth of the City of New Amsterdam has been turned into taverns." Men, women, and children drank beer every day, often at every meal. Even today, in places of poor sanitation, beer can be healthier than water.

It's a rainy evening when I finally stop by Murphy's. The place has an odd dissonance. The barkeep's Eastern European accent is about as far from a Murphy as one can get. The drink special involves doughnut-flavored vodka.

Since there are no more Manhattan breweries, I order the closest thing, an ale from the Brooklyn Brewery, headquartered across the river in Williamsburg. It sets me back $6.50. At that rate of exchange, Manhattan Island today would cost $15,600. Still a bargain, but not twenty-four bucks.

A few days later, I'm guiding some Nevius cousins through Lower Manhattan and we pass by Murphy's. The same barkeep is out front, smoking a cigarette and yelling into her cell phone in what I think is Russian. Maybe this is the perfect evocation of old New Amsterdam. After all, Peter Stuyvesant's predecessor, Willem Kieft, once boasted that "there were men of eighteen different languages" on its streets.

My cousins and I are on our way to Peter Minuit Plaza. Once merely a wide place in the road, it was re-landscaped in 2009 as a monument to our Dutch heritage. The best addition is a bronze map of New Amsterdam. Sculpted by Simon Verity and based on a 1660 city survey, the map brings the old town into sharp relief. You can run your fingers across the cannons of Fort Amsterdam; see where the East River lapped against the bulwarks on Pearl Street; take stock of the palisade along the town's northern edge.

When Peter Minuit bought the island in 1626—and there is still dispute about whether the transaction was a sale, a lease, or something in between— a couple of hundred people lived on the island's southern tip. By 1660, there were fifteen hundred souls in the area depicted on the map, an area of less than fifty acres. I joke to my cousins that you could walk the city limits in twenty minutes.

"Really?" says one.

"Would you like to try it?" I respond.

They enthusiastically say yes, and we set off to see how fast we can trace the contours of Peter Stuyvesant's—and Johannes Nevius's—city. Little do they know just how few sites they are actually going to see.

Our first stop soon dampens their exuberance: a yellow brick rectangle laid out on the Pearl Street side of the ugly, brown skyscraper known as 85 Broad Street. These bricks are modern—put here in the 1980s—and are the only recognition that this was once the site of the first municipal government in New York.

In the twenty-one years between Peter Minuit's purchase of Manhattan and Peter Stuyvesant's arrival, the colony/company had three directors, none of them good. The worst was Willem Kieft, who served from 1638 to 1647. In 1639, Kieft and his councilors decided that the natives "whom we have until now protected from their enemies" should contribute to the Dutch coffers for their defense. If they refused, the Dutch would bring them around "by the most justified means."

Not surprisingly, the natives didn't like being hit up for protection money. Using the murder of a Dutch farmer as a pretext, Kieft launched bloody reprisals against the natives. Kieft's Wars, as they came to be known, threw the colony into disarray. As one of Kieft's advisers wrote to the company headquarters in the Netherlands in 1644, the director's "thoughtless bellicosity" had reduced the colony to "ashes."

In 1646, the Dutch West India Company announced that Kieft was being replaced with Peter Stuyvesant, a recently wounded war veteran. Two years earlier, as director of the Dutch holdings in the Caribbean, Stuyvesant had been ordered to capture the island of St. Maarten from the Spanish. On the first day of fighting, a Spanish cannonball crushed Stuyvesant's right leg. He returned to the island of Curacao, had the lower extremity removed, and sailed back to the Netherlands to be fitted for a proper wooden leg. Having survived the injury, the amputation, and the long voyage to Europe, Stuyvesant had proved his mettle; the Dutch West India Company rewarded him with the post in New Amsterdam. He and his new wife, Judith Bayard, embarked on a ship called the *Groote Gerrit* ("Great Crow"), arriving on May 11, 1647. As one observer later recalled, Stuyvesant strutted up and down the dock, promising to "be like a father over his children."

Did it actually happen that way? So much bad blood had passed between Stuyvesant and his citizenry by the time that recollection was committed to paper that it's hard to judge. But he was only thirty-five years old when he arrived, and he probably seemed like an ass.

Nevertheless, hopes were high for Stuyvesant; he couldn't possibly be worse than Kieft. Immediately, he took steps to improve the town. He banned wooden chimneys and thatched roofs to reduce fire hazards; he regulated the tavern industry, levying taxes on beer and spirits to help pay for civic improvements. One early project was building a dock to expedite shipping, the colony's primary economic activity. He also enacted harsh penalties for smuggling, which had been undercutting the Dutch West India Company's profit margin. But he also did things like institute a second Sunday service and forbid tapping beer on the Sabbath. The son of a minister and a stern Calvinist, Stuyvesant took his religion quite seriously.

Like Kieft before him, Stuyvesant appointed an advisory board of citizens—called the Nine Men—to help guide him. It was led by Adriaen van der Donck, the colony's only lawyer. Van der Donck, sensing an opportunity to effect change in the colony, hijacked the group, using it as a vehicle for trying to wrest control of New Netherland from the Dutch West India Company. Under Van der Donck, the board prepared a petition for the

Dutch parliament, outlining how the company was ruining the colony. Van der Donck personally sailed to The Hague to deliver it.

For a brief moment, it seemed like the government might side with Van der Donck, but ultimately they decided that New Amsterdam was better off remaining in the company's hands. As a consolation, parliament agreed to give the colony a small measure of self-rule. New Amsterdam would now have town magistrates, and to house this new government, the city tavern on Pearl Street—built during Kieft's administration—was handed over to them. On February 2, 1653, New Amsterdam became an official city and the city tavern became the Stadt Huis ("city hall").

That's a lot of story for a tiny rectangle of bricks to convey. Thousands of people walk over this spot every day, hustling to jobs in the financial sector, without any idea of what they are treading upon. There's a plaque nearby, but it has too many words on it for people to read. (Rule of thumb: Most people don't read historical signs with more than twelve words on them. Second rule of thumb: Historical signs with more than twelve words on them are generally wrong.)

I'm standing in the middle of this empty space telling this story to my cousins, and I don't blame them for growing restless. To appropriate Gertrude Stein, there's no *there* there. But I need them to hang on, because this story has a second act.

"In 1657, or maybe as late as 1658, Johannes Nevius was appointed the Secretary of the City of New Amsterdam. As part of that job, he moved into the Stadt Huis with his wife, Adriaentje, and their children. They lived here—on this spot—until after the city had fallen to the English and had been renamed New York."

"Right here?" one cousin says looking around. There's nothing to see, yet suddenly he *sees* it. His great-great-great-great-great-great-great-great-grandparents lived on the upper floors of the stout, brick building on this spot. As it is for me, this is the origin point for his family in America, our *patria*. I've stood on this spot hundreds of times, but it's enough to give me goosebumps too.

I show them a couple of pictures of the Stadt Huis, for the most part later renderings that may or may not be accurate. I save the best for last: a 1650 watercolor sketch of New Amsterdam, the earliest—and most vivid—depiction of the town. It was likely painted by Augustijn Heerman, one of the Nine Men, and was designed to show how terrible Manhattan had become under company rule. To the far left, a sad windmill stands with just two working arms; to the right is the building that would soon become the Stadt Huis and Johannes and Adriaentje's home.

"It looked like that?" the other cousin asks. I can't tell if he's disappointed or thrilled. Perhaps a bit of both.

"It's the biggest building in town," says the first cousin, proudly pointing at it.

I explain that when it was a tavern, it had transient accommodations in the upper floors, and it would likely have been those rooms that the Nevius family occupied. But my cousins have stopped listening.

It's the biggest building in town.

After the Stadt Huis we walk to nearby Wall Street. Often, in describing the nine-foot palisade erected to keep out the English during the First Anglo-Dutch War, I watch the *ah-ha!* moment in people's eyes. Yes—there was, indeed, a wall on Wall Street, though overgrown fence might be a more accurate description.

When Stuyvesant got word that war had broken out in Europe, he called the citizens together and demanded cash to pay for a northern defensive position. Johannes contributed one hundred guilders—or, using my beer rate of exchange, about $32,000.

Something doesn't seem right about this. Johannes was just one of dozens of people who contributed to the wall's construction and others gave more than he did. In the end, the citizens were assessed a total of 5,050 guilders for the wall; by my calculations, its modern equivalent would be $1.6 million. The wall was simply constructed of stone, earth, and wood. It was built, at least in part, by the company's enslaved Africans. There's just no way they spent $1.6 million on it.

I check my math. What else would a guilder have bought me in the seventeenth century? Well, in the 1630s, sixty guilders would have purchased forty gallons of French brandy. I ask in a wine shop, where I'm told they'll sell me 750ml of French brandy for thirteen dollars.

About five of these bottles equals a gallon, which would cost about sixty-five dollars. At that rate, 40 gallons = $2,600 = 60 guilders (the purchase price of Manhattan). At this new rate of exchange, my 2,400 tankards of beer would cost a mere $1.08 each. I can't think of a single happy hour where beer—even lousy beer—is still that cheap. But, of course, what I need to take into account is what economists call "relative price shift." In the same way that labor and materials for building the wall were cheap, so, too, were ingredients for beer. It may have cost even less than a dollar a tankard then.

Using these new calculations, which makes a guilder roughly equal to forty-three dollars, the defensive wall still cost a little over $217,000, a shockingly high sum considering how badly it worked.

The First Anglo-Dutch War never spilled over to the New World. Despite Stuyvesant's fears, troops never massed in the English-dominated towns in New Netherland, which included Flushing in Queens and Gravesend in Brooklyn. Indeed, the English colonists who lived within the Dutch borders got along with the Dutch West India Company most of the time. The Dutch lost the First Anglo-Dutch War, but they'd do better in upcoming conflicts with England; by 1688, a Dutchman would be seated on the English throne.

The wall *was* breached, however, in 1655, when native tribes decided to attack the city in a dispute over whether or not the Dutch should be using gunpowder as a unit of trade. Stuyvesant said no; the natives disagreed. So, while Stuyvesant and most of the male citizenry were down in Delaware fending off an incursion of Swedish settlers, the natives attacked. It was easy to get into the city. They just walked around the wall.

Nine years later, the English finally did show up, with four ships and a few hundred soldiers, to seize the city. The wall didn't keep them out either. They simply issued a list of demands and waited for Stuyvesant to capitulate. It took three days.

We set off again to walk south down Broadway. In Dutch, it was officially the Heere Straat ("Gentleman's Street") but most people called it the Broad Way. The English kept the unofficial designation until, through force of habit, it became official.

Before heading south, we pause at the old Irving Trust Company bank at One Wall Street. Johannes Nevius's first known home in the colony stood near this spot, a house he occupied until 1655. He and Adriaentje relocated to Pearl Street soon after the birth of their first child. The move came less than six weeks before the natives breached the wall.

The bank, named for New York author Washington Irving, opened in 1931, an impressive edifice in the face of the worsening Depression. Hoping to play up its ties to history, the bank invited Washington Irving's great-great-grandnephew and Avon M. Nevius, a Washington, DC–based banker, to the opening festivities, underlining the unspoken message of so many financial institutions during the Depression: We're not going anywhere. After all, our lineage goes all the way back to Johannes Nevius himself.

From the bank we walk quickly down Broadway, past Bowling Green and the old Custom House, which sits almost exactly on the spot of Fort Amsterdam. We skirt the edge of Battery Park and soon we are back at Peter Minuit Plaza. In what would have taken twenty minutes without stopping, we've walked around the entire town.

"So, there's really nothing left?" asks one cousin.

"Well—not down here. But if you're willing to travel further afield, there are places to see. In fact, the oldest house in New York dates back to 1652, the year Johannes Nevius arrived in America."

"Where is it?"

"The Flatlands section of Brooklyn."

Ah, the eyes say. *Brooklyn.*

Since I might have well said the moon, I let it drop.

———

In the seventeenth century, Brooklyn was ripe farm land, and in 1636, the first Dutch settlers moved to a village they dubbed New Amersfoort. The English later changed the name to Flatlands, an apt description.

In 1652, New Amersfoort welcomed two new residents: Pieter and Grietje Claesen. They were farmers who had recently moved south from Rensselaerswyck, a huge estate near Fort Orange, where Pieter had worked as an indentured servant starting in 1637. What brought the family downriver in 1652 is unknown, but that year they erected a one-room farmhouse on their new land in New Amersfoort. Today, it is not only the oldest building in New York City, but one of the oldest standing structures in the United States.

On a warm spring day, I head to Pieter and Grietje's house—first by subway, then bus, then on foot—and it seems like I'm heading to the very edge of the city. It's little wonder that few people ever take up my suggestion to visit; it seems nearly off the map. Actually, if you look at a New York City subway diagram, it *is* off the map. Trace the major subway lines out to Brooklyn and you'll see a hole in one section beyond the place where all the trains stop. That's Pieter Claesen's neighborhood. It's remote now; think how remote it would have been in 1652.

Today, the home—known as the Wyckoff House Museum—is set back from Clarendon Road in a small park. (Soon after the English takeover, legal surnames became mandatory; Pieter chose Wyckoff perhaps to honor family property back in his native Friesland.) The house sneaks up on you; you're practically on top of it when it reveals itself, almost cinematically.

On my most recent visit, this reminds me of the work of Frederick Law Olmsted in Central Park, or of Lancelot "Capability" Brown, the eighteenth-century landscape designer who built his reputation by dotting English country estates with fake Roman ruins and medieval hermitages. As I walk from the bus stop, past fast food restaurants and auto body shops, it's tempting to think that Pieter and Grietje's house is just an architectural folly, like one of Brown's hermitages or Central Park's Belvedere Castle.

However, once you enter the home, any thoughts of it being a fake are instantly dispelled. The house has been added to many times over the years, and the seams are visible. First, a new kitchen was added; then, around 1750, a major addition expanded the house to the east. By 1820, a hallway had been created and the ceilings raised. Still, the heart of the house is the kitchen, a fifteen-foot-square room dominated by a giant fireplace. When the house was built in 1652, this wasn't just the kitchen—it was the entire home.

Standing in the middle of the kitchen, the first thing that strikes me is how dark it is. Many people could not afford the glass for windows, so they were nothing more than rectangular holes with shutters. Once my eyes adjust to the gloom, they gravitate toward the fireplace. The expression "hearth and home" describes houses just like this one, where the fire was the center of daily life. Even so, I imagine it must have been difficult to keep warm during those frigid Brooklyn winters.

In another room is a Dutch *kas,* or cupboard; originally, this would have taken up a tremendous amount of floor space here in the kitchen. The *kas* served not just the practical purpose of storing everything from linens to porcelain to clothes, it was also an outward symbol of prosperity. An elegant *kas,* even if its contents weren't visible, spoke volumes about a family's station.

This is one aspect of Dutch life that I think is in every New Yorker's genetic blueprint. My Calvinist forebears had to appear outwardly egalitarian while at the same time making subtle-but-pointed statements about their wealth. Maybe it was an imported *kas* or fur-trimmed leather jacket. Perhaps it was Delft tile around the fireplace. Some, like Peter Stuyvesant, could afford to have a portrait painted. While the status symbols have changed with every generation, seeking that status certainly has not.

Above Pieter and Grietje's fireplace hang a few cooking utensils; to one side is a pair of water buckets yoked together, along with shelves of household implements. The Dutch were obsessed with cleanliness. Grietje no doubt spent an inordinate amount of her time keeping the small home clean—when she wasn't tending to the kitchen garden, cooking the family's meals, and raising the children. As the years passed, the family just kept growing. By 1665, Grietje had given birth to eleven children: Nicholas, Margrietje, Annetje, Mayken, Willemptje, Cornelius, Hendrick, Geertje, Garret, Marten, and Jan.

Today, the overwhelming feeling inside their home is one of eerie quiet. In the 1660s, there was probably never a moment not filled with sound, from the cock's first crow up until the last of the children, huddled in a straw bed on the floor, fell asleep by the light of the dwindling fire.

There are a few other homes from the Dutch era left in the city: the Lent (aka Riker) Homestead in East Elmhurst (ca. 1654); John Bowne's house in Flushing (ca. 1661); the Billiou house on Staten Island (1662). More importantly, when the English took over in 1664, the place didn't suddenly drop its Dutch heritage in favor of the new overlords. Homes built well into the eighteenth century are called Dutch, and it wasn't just the architecture that persisted. Martin Van Buren, the first president born after the Revolution, was himself a Knickerbocker—and he grew up speaking Dutch.

Inside the Brooklyn Museum, there's a marvelously intact Dutch home from 1675 that was built by Jan Martense Schenck. Schenck is my great-great-great-great-great-great-great-great-great uncle. Indeed, New Netherland was such a small place that I'm directly descended from many of the well-known early families: Polhemus, Voorhees, Van Couwenhoven, and many more. All these families mixed and intermarried; in one way or another, we're all related.

In 1691, one great-great-etc. aunt, Catherine—the youngest of Adriaentje and Johannes Nevius's children—married Garret Pieterse Wyckoff, the ninth of Pieter and Grietje's eleven children. There's a good chance they wed at the Flatlands Church, a half hour's walk up the King's Highway from the Wyckoff farmhouse, in a ceremony performed by my ancestor Johannes Polhemus. Perhaps the wedding feast took place under the cool shade of the trees like the ones that still surround the Wyckoff house in Clarendon Park.

The father of the bride wasn't there—Johannes Nevius passed away in 1672, the same year that Peter Stuyvesant died and was buried in the vault that now stands in the yard of St. Mark's-in-the-Bowery.

Adriaentje Nevius was likely deceased as well, but Pieter Claesen was still around, the patriarch of the family. I like to picture him, presiding over this gathering of all the Claesens and all the Nevii—a tankard of beer in one hand, a clay pipe in the other. Dutch wedding banquets were lavish affairs, usually open to the community. How many other of my relatives were there? Perhaps the Reverend Polhemus, along with his eldest daughter Margaret and her husband Willem Cornell. Maybe Koert Stevense van Voorhees, one of New Amersfoort's leading citizens, and his wife Marretje Gerretse van Couwenhoven. I imagine all these ancestors smiling and laughing and raising a glass to the health of the bride and groom.

It's nearly midnight and because all of these Dutch explorations have put me in a drinking mood, I'm headed to a recently opened tavern on Water Street called the Dead Rabbit. Water Street was once the edge of the island; all the streets at the southern tip of Manhattan reflect the city's insatiable desire for expansion over the centuries. The Pearl Street waterline was pushed out to Water, then Front, then South—each name marking the extent of the landfill. The tavern I'm seeking out was named for a gang that may or may not have existed in the middle of the nineteenth century—but I'm there to travel even further back in time.

Every drink on the menu is historically sourced. Three of them date back to the 1600s, one of them to 1648, during Peter Stuyvesant's tenure in New Amsterdam. That drink is called a Lamb's Wool. Served hot, it's a mixture of whiskey, apples, sugar, spices, and bitters. In Stuyvesant's time, the sugar would have come from Dutch possessions in the Caribbean; the nutmeg and other spices from the Dutch East India Company's vast holdings in Indonesia. The apples might have come from Stuyvesant's own farm up the Bowery road. It is the entire Dutch trading empire in one cup.

Did Stuyvesant drink something like this? Or Johannes Nevius? I imagine my ancestor in his home—a former tavern, after all—preparing a warm drink like this on a cold winter's night. Perhaps he went out on the *stoep*, the building's front porch, and watched the stars shine above the East River.

Warmed, I leave the Dead Rabbit and head to Peter Minuit Plaza. Minuit was a Walloon, and his last name was pronounced *min-wee*—it's French for midnight. In the plaza named for him, a small pavilion lights up each night as the clock strikes twelve in a remarkably understated tribute. For about five minutes, the lights subtly change from orange to blue to purple to green. Then, as suddenly as it started, it stops.

Around me, people rush by, as oblivious to this as they are to the nearby yellow-brick commemoration of the Stadt Huis or to the host of other impalpable Dutch symbols that reflect the city's history. There's a reserved character about my Dutch forebears reflected here. Do your job. Don't show off. Don't rock the boat.

But Minuit wasn't Dutch—and he wasn't reserved—so maybe this is the wrong tribute. After all he was the man who, in 1637, signed on as director-for-hire for a new Swedish colony on the Delaware River that he planted firmly in Dutch territory. Minuit was conniving, and maybe this is why I prefer the flagpole back in Battery Park. It may not be accurate, but I like the depiction of Minuit, eye-to-eye with a native, handing over the twenty-four-dollar string of beads.

This depiction gets to an essential element of New York: the hard bargain. Minuit's sixty guilders of trade goods—likely everything from wampum (not beads) to iron nails to gunpowder to alcohol—may seem like a small amount to us, but in a place where practically everything was imported, those materials were more dear than we're sometimes willing to give credit. And no matter how many ridiculous nineteenth-century drawings I see showing Minuit dazzling the natives with his European finery, I'm sure the natives bargained just as hard as Minuit. Even if, as many historians agree, the natives weren't selling the land outright to the Dutch, they were clearly ceding the use of Manhattan to outsiders. They would have wanted significant payment for this.

But there's an even deeper truth in this frozen moment in time. The native is on the verge of accepting that string of wampum from Minuit; when he does, he won't just alter the course of his own life, he'll change the story of New York and the trajectory of American history.

The Society of Friends Meetinghouse, Flushing, Queens.

CHAPTER 2

The Dissenters

I'M STANDING IN THE ATTIC OF THE QUAKER MEETING HOUSE in Flushing, Queens. Outside, I can see the traffic passing on Northern Boulevard through the gray of a rainy Sunday afternoon. Despite the fact that all that separates me from the blur of twenty-first-century New York is a thin sheet of glass, there's an ancient stillness.

In the center of the room is a long wooden table so simply made that it could be modern—or four hundred years old. In one window, three tin candle sconces—rusted relics of a bygone era—stand like sentinels. I've been in much older religious spaces in my life, from medieval mosques to Renaissance cathedrals, but none seemed as old as this space does.

The knotted and gnarled wide-plank floor beneath my feet was placed here in 1694, more for its strength than its beauty. The unadorned, hard benches in the meeting room downstairs were built by individual families; the benches all follow the same pattern, but some are deep and some are quite narrow. Perhaps this had to do with the amount of wood a family could afford; or maybe, as the volunteer showing me around that day believes, some benches had to be built to accommodate certain ample backsides.

This meeting house is the oldest house of worship in the city. The story of the people who built it stands in stark contrast to the conventional narrative of early New York. In the standard tale, New Amsterdam is apart from the other early colonies by its emphasis not on the Almighty but on the Almighty dollar (or guilder). If you paid your taxes and kept out of trouble, it didn't matter much if you chose to worship in a manner different from that prescribed by the Dutch West India Company—as long as it was in the privacy of your own home.

This narrative simply isn't true. The supposedly tolerant Dutch—at least under Peter Stuyvesant's watch—left little room for dissent. Yes, technically, if you worshiped in your home, *alone*, you were all right. But woe be to the person who expressed any public deviation from the Dutch Reformed Church.

It was simply a given that Catholics weren't tolerated. Not only had Protestantism been born out of a rift with Rome, the Netherlands owed its very existence to it. The nation had been created after the protracted Eighty Years War against Catholic Spain. Early America's anti-Catholic bias filtered down and infected America for most of its history. As recently as 1960, John Kennedy had to reassure Americans that if elected, he would take orders from Congress, not the pope.

America's anti-Catholic history can be difficult to bring up, even in a casual context. In Central Park, I often point out some ornate carvings on Bethesda Terrace and interpret them through the lens of the city's Civil War–era, intensely anti-Irish, anti-Catholic attitudes. Sometimes as I talk, I see the hackles raise. One person flat out told me: "You can't say that. That's not true." (As if the truth was contingent on whether or not it inflamed people.)

"Well," I replied. "That's how many old guard New Yorkers felt in the 1860s."

"But," she said, emphasizing that hers would be the last word, "it's not true."

I think that simple statement sums up how Peter Stuyvesant felt about so many things: If he didn't believe what you were saying was true, he'd simply forbid you to speak.

Yet every time Stuyvesant tried to stamp out one heresy another popped up in its place, despite the director-general's cruel punishments. In certain matters, he may have been more fair-minded than history gives him credit for. But when it came to religion, Stuyvesant was a tyrant, and the people who bore the brunt of his anger were not the Catholics—there just weren't enough of them to make trouble. The people Stuyvesant really hated were the Quakers.

The Religious Society of Friends was founded by English non-conformist George Fox in the 1640s. When Fox was hauled in front of English officials in 1650 on charges of blasphemy, he "bade them tremble at the word of the Lord." This admonishment led to the nickname Quaker, which took hold to describe Fox's adherents. The first Quakers came to the American continent in 1656; a year later, a handful of them came to New Netherland.

The ship that brought them, the *Woodhouse,* must have been a strange sight from the shore. It flew no identifying colors and it did not fire the usual welcoming salute. "We could not decide whether she was Dutch, French, or English," wrote New Amsterdam's pastor, Johannes Megapolensis. Things turned even stranger when the ship's master, Robert Fowler, met with Stuyvesant. Fowler insulted Stuyvesant by leaving his hat on ("like a goat") and by not giving him any real news from Europe, which was often the most precious commodity that vessels brought with them.

Stuyvesant did learn, certainly to his chagrin, that the boat was full of Quakers, so he must have been glad when they departed the next day up the East River, presumably to Rhode Island, "the receptacle of all sorts of riff-raff people," in the pastor's words. (Megapolensis also refers to Rhode Island as a "sewer" and a "latrine.")

Fowler had secretly left two young women behind, Mary Witherhead and Dorothy Waugh, who immediately began to preach in the streets. Here's Megapolensis's firsthand account:

> *As soon as the ship had fairly departed, these [women] began to quake and go into a frenzy, and cry out loudly in the middle of the street, that men should repent, for the day of judgment was at hand. Our people not knowing what was the matter, ran to and fro, while one cried "Fire," and another something else.*

Just to get this straight: One day, two strange women began preaching on the street, which was so alarming, it caused one upstanding New Amsterdammer to panic, and the only thing he could think to do was to scream "fire." I suppose that makes sense—for a strict Calvinist, it may have seemed like flames were leaping from the pits of hell itself.

The women were arrested, imprisoned for eight days, and put on the first ship to Rhode Island. If Stuyvesant thought this was the end of the matter, he was sorely mistaken. Some of the *Woodhouse*'s passengers had disembarked on Long Island, where the Quakers quickly established roots in the predominantly English towns of Flushing and Gravesend. When itinerant Quaker preacher Robert Hodgson reached Hempstead, the town sheriff had him arrested.

It's unclear if Hodgson was breaking the law. Certainly, a 1640 Charter of Freedoms and Exemptions, promulgated to draw feudal colonists to New Netherland, expressly forbade any religion that was not Dutch Reformed. On the other hand, the town charters of Gravesend and Flushing allowed for freedom of conscience; that wasn't exactly the same as freedom of religion, but it was among America's first protections from the government overtly telling its citizens what to think.

The twenty-three-year-old Hodgson was remanded to custody in Manhattan, where he was cast into a "dungeon full of vermin." (Was this located below the garrison in Fort Amsterdam—or was it the basement of the Stadt Huis? For Johannes Nevius's sake, I hope the former.) The next day, Hodgson was taken before Stuyvesant and the magistrates. He was given an interpreter—presumably so he'd understand the charges against him—but he was not allowed to defend himself. To the Calvinists, his crime was indefensible.

Had Hodgson been given a chance to speak, he might have said: "But what about the Jews? Are they not allowed their freedom? What about the Antinomian woman, Anne Hutchinson? Or the Anabaptist Deborah Moody out in Gravesend?"

Indeed, Hodgson, if he had any prior knowledge of life in New Netherland, might have been fooled into thinking that it was a tolerant place. He was about to be proven painfully wrong.

———❦———

For several years, I've been writing a New York City history blog, covering topics as diverse as the amusements out at Coney Island to the Embargo Act of 1807. If you'd asked me to wager what search term draws the most people to the blog, I'd have guessed it had something to do with the American Revolution or maybe the World Trade Center.

When I check, I'm surprised to discover the search term that garners the most traffic is "Anne Hutchinson." (She comes in just ahead of Robert Fulton, the Oreo cookie, and—of all people—Enrico Caruso.)

It's Hutchinson's significance as a pioneer in America's struggle for individual rights that makes people search for her; she's been singled out as a symbol of religious freedom. But I think that in New York—the place of her death—her significance is muted. Most New Yorkers know that a parkway and river in the Bronx are named for her, and may recall that she met a messy end, but her story, like so much from her era, has faded into the background.

Born in England in 1591, the daughter of an Anglican minister, Hutchinson and her husband, Will, were disciples of charismatic Puritan minister John Cotton. When Cotton's views got him kicked out of England in 1633, Will and Anne soon followed, packing up their eleven children and setting out for Boston, Massachusetts.

In Boston, Hutchinson began hosting weekly Bible studies—first for women only, then for men, including the colony's governor, Henry Vane—and found herself at the center of the brewing Antinomian controversy. The Antinomians (literally "against the law") believed that salvation came through grace alone, not through good works.

Hutchinson's chief antagonist, John Winthrop, called her an "American Jezebel"—a false prophet. When Winthrop replaced Henry Vane as governor in 1637, Hutchinson was put on trial for her heretical beliefs, convicted, and banished from the colony. The Hutchinson family and about sixty followers trooped down to Rhode Island—really, where else could they go?—and established the town of Portsmouth.

Will Hutchinson died in 1641, and two years later, Anne packed up the seven youngest children and her servants and headed south again, this time to the Eastchester section of what is today the Bronx. At the time, Massachusetts was making noises about absorbing Rhode Island, and Anne probably thought it wise to get beyond the reach of her Puritan antagonists in Boston.

Hutchinson could not have arrived at a worse time; Willem Kieft's persecution of the natives was in full swing. In February 1643, Dutch mercenaries massacred groups of Native American refugees in what is today the Lower East Side and Jersey City. In response, natives launched a full-fledged attack on New Amsterdam's outlying areas, including Hutchinson's sparsely populated section of the Bronx.

According to legend, the Siwanoy chief, Wampage, on the hunt for white settlers, led the attack against the Hutchinson settlement. He and his warriors scalped and killed the entire family except for daughter Susanna, who was found cowering in the crack of a huge boulder on the property. That rock—today known as Split Rock—is visible from cars speeding up the Hutchinson River Parkway at the spot where it crosses the New England Thruway and the Pelham Bay Golf Course. Susanna was taken by Wampage's men and lived with the tribe for a number of years before being ransomed back to relatives in Boston. Wampage, meanwhile, took the honorific "Anne Hutch" or "Anhook" after his most famous kill.

The immediate cause of Anne Hutchinson's death was not her religion—she was just in the wrong place at the wrong time. But religious persecution was such a part of her life that I'm curious if Hutchinson would have seen her life and brutal murder as groundbreaking steps on the road to American religious freedom. Would she consider herself a martyr? Or a victim of circumstance?

Around the same time that Hutchinson was moving to the Bronx, another "dangerous woman" was laying down roots in Brooklyn. Lady Deborah Moody's life followed a similar trajectory to Anne Hutchinson's. Born around 1586, she was the daughter of a Member of Parliament and granddaughter of an Anglican bishop. After her baronet husband's death, Lady Deborah chafed at her role as a landowner and became increasingly disillusioned with England's state religion. Spending more and more time in London, she attended underground Baptist and Quaker services, and eventually ran afoul of the Star Chamber, England's secretive court. In 1640, with gold sewn into the lining of her luggage, Moody and her thirteen-year-old son, Henry, left for Boston. She acquired a large estate near Salem and lived as one of the most prosperous residents in the colony.

However, as Governor John Winthrop would soon discover, while Moody was rich and "very wise," she also held "erroneous," Anabaptist views. The Anabaptists ("to baptize again") rejected infant baptism, arguing that a person needed to be old enough to comprehend what they were getting into. That meant that not only was Henry not yet baptized, but that Lady Deborah's daughter, who had died in infancy, had perished unbaptized. Winthrop and the Puritan orthodoxy were appalled.

Moody was quickly excommunicated, and in 1643 she and some of her followers left for—you guessed it—Rhode Island. It was a brief stay, and after an equally short sojourn in New Haven, Moody ended up in New Amsterdam, not long after Anne Hutchinson's murder in the Bronx.

Moody and her followers settled in Gravesend—probably named for her hometown in England—and in 1645 she secured a patent for the town from Director-General Kieft. Not only was the patent remarkable in that it was the first in the New World granted to a woman, it also guaranteed Moody and her followers freedom of religion "without magisterial or ministerial interference," one of the first such provisions in the New World.

Lady Deborah laid out the town of Gravesend in a perfect square. Two central roads—Gravesend Road running north/south (today called McDonald Avenue), and Gravesend Neck Road running east/west—bisected the community into quadrants and each quadrant was further subdivided into lots. Today, the streets of Lady Deborah's original town, with picturesque names such as Village Road North, still define Gravesend and are the oldest colonial roads in all of Brooklyn.

The neighborhood has almost none of this history intact. As I walk the streets that Moody laid out, Gravesend seems like any other Italian-American community in the borough. Old men sit on lawn chairs on the sidewalk taking the air. Under the shadow of the elevated F train, auto body shops have proliferated. Most houses, even older ones, are protected from the elements by a layer of siding.

But a few traces of an earlier era remain. On Gravesend Neck Road sits the village cemetery. Not only is Lady Moody probably buried there—in an authentically unmarked grave—so are a host of other old Brooklyn families: the Van Couvenhovens, the Wyckoffs, the Dyckmans, names that most New Yorkers now only know from street signs. There are so many Van Sicklens interred that they have their own section of the graveyard, now choked with weeds.

Across the street sits the so-called "Lady Moody House," though the lady herself never lived there. Perhaps, if the stories are true, she owned the land. Perhaps her son, Henry, built the home on the property in the 1690s. Or, maybe it is a century more recent. It, too, sits beneath layers of modern siding, reluctant to divulge its secrets.

Nearby, the Ryder house dates back to 1788 and its neighbor to 1840. In her 1945 book *Old Dutch Houses of Brooklyn*, Maud Esther Dilliard identified a home from 1750 just up McDonald Avenue. It turns out that was wishful thinking.

"Eighteen-thirties," the house's owner tells me as we chat in his front yard. He points to the taller addition. "Dilliard labeled that 1790s; I bought this house from the woman whose parents erected that addition in the 1920s." Still, the house maintains a significant Dutch feel, and I can tell how Dilliard, without the benefit of modern science—or bothering to talk to the owner—would have been fooled.

Lady Moody Triangle sits near the junction of Village Road North and Van Sicklen Street—at what would have been the northwest corner of the original town. Inside this small green space, a granite marker serves double duty as a monument to the neighborhood's World War II dead and to Moody and her followers. As I walk around the marker, I see that it has been vandalized. The words IN LOVING MEMORY OF are still visible, but the name below it has been hacked away—and, possibly, burned for good measure.

This not only seems crass, but pointless. Surely the name that was once emblazoned there can be found. Yet, when I go searching for it later, I can't easily locate it. A record must exist somewhere, but a quick Internet search yields nothing. It's yet another piece of New York that's been erased, perhaps never to be recovered.

It strikes me that this is one good reason to tell Anne Hutchinson and Deborah Moody's stories—not because their individual accomplishments were monumental, but because their names and stories are all that remain of the struggles of countless individuals whose lives helped shape the early city. So much of history is anonymous; it pays to hang on to those individuals whose lives we can know.

Lady Deborah died around 1659, meaning she was alive to hear Robert Hodgson preach in Gravesend. She'd admired the Quakers in London, and having been guaranteed religious liberty in Gravesend's charter, there's no reason to believe that she wouldn't have allowed him to spread the word. It also means she was alive to hear the tragic tale of his trial and punishment.

<hr />

The day after Robert Hodgson stood before the Dutch magistrates in Manhattan accused of heresy, he was sentenced to two years hard labor chained to a wheelbarrow "with a negro." To avoid this punishment, he was given the option of paying a 600 guilder fine. (My French brandy rate of exchange puts this at about $26,000 today.)

Hodgson had no means to pay, and when he refused to work, he was whipped by an African with a pitched rope until he fell to the ground. Hodgson's continued refusal to acquiesce to the Dutch demands—or even admit he committed a crime—led him to be confined without food or water; later, he was hung in a room with a heavy log tied to his feet.

What may have ultimately freed Hodgson was a personal appeal from Stuyvesant's sister, Anna Bayard. Stuyvesant released Hodgson in late October or early November 1657, on condition that he leave for Rhode Island immediately. Perhaps Stuyvesant was finally realizing that his abominable treatment of the Quakers was not having the desired effect of driving the Society of Friends out of New Netherland.

Not everyone shared Stuyvesant's opinion. I was glad to discover that my ancestor, the Reverend Johannes Polhemus, lamented that compelling the Quakers "to go before the court and be put under oath . . . [was] displeasing to God." On December 27, 1657, a handful of citizens in Flushing—none Quaker—drew up a petition asking Stuyvesant to calm down.

The document, today known as the Flushing Remonstrance, is seen by some as a direct forerunner to the First Amendment of the Constitution, ratified over 125 years later. The petition begins:

> *You have been pleased to send unto us a certain prohibition or command that we should not receive or entertain any of those people called Quakers because they are supposed to be, by some, seducers of the people. For our part we cannot condemn them in this case, neither can we stretch out our hands against them. . . .*

There was no threat against Stuyvesant, simply a note that if "persons come in love unto us, we cannot in conscience lay violent hands upon them . . . for we are bound by the law of God and man to do good unto all men and evil to no man." As the remonstrance pointed out, Flushing's charter, given to them in 1645 by Willem Kieft, supported their position. Moreover, in the Netherlands, even "Jews, Turks, and Egyptians" were given liberty of conscience. Why not in Flushing?

It should be noted that a few years earlier, a boat-load of Jewish refugees had arrived in New Amsterdam from Brazil. Stuyvesant wrote to the Dutch West India Company, railing against these "hateful enemies and blasphemers of the name of Christ," but his bosses pointed out that due to "the large amount of capital which they still have invested in the shares of this company" Stuyvesant should leave them alone. Though the director-general did not permit them the "free and public exercise of their abominable religion," he also knew he didn't need to worry about them proselytizing or quaking in the streets.

Stuyvesant had four of the Flushing Remonstrance petitioners arrested: Sheriff Tobias Feake, who delivered the remonstrance; Edward Hart, who drew it up; and Edward Farrington and William Noble, who were dispatched from Flushing to answer Stuyvesant's wrath.

Hart, Farrington, and Noble were all let off with a slap on the wrist. Stuyvesant toyed with the idea of meting out a stricter punishment on Tobias Feake, but in the end simply fired and banished him. To make sure nothing similar happened again, Flushing's new sheriff was to be well versed in both "the English and Dutch language, but also with Dutch practical law." Moreover, a new tax would be levied on the citizens of Flushing to pay for a Dutch Reformed minister. If the purpose of the Flushing Remonstrance was to expand religious liberty, all it did in the short term was allow orthodoxy to retrench.

Around the corner from the Flushing Meeting House is an even older building—the oldest in all of Queens, in fact—the 1661 home of John and Hannah Bowne. Where the Flushing Remonstrance had failed to gain any noticeable benefits for the area's Quakers, John Bowne's simple act of civil disobedience—opening his home for a Quaker meeting—put New York on the road to religious freedom.

The Bownes purchased land in Flushing in the 1650s, and had definitely built their home by 1661. Certainly, it was standing by 1662, when the Bownes invited the local Quaker community to worship there. When word reached Stuyvesant of John Bowne's crime, he had the Quaker arrested and brought to Manhattan, so that the tragic wheels of justice could once again be set in motion.

At first, however, Stuyvesant wouldn't even talk to Bowne. One thing that irritated the director-general about the Quakers since their first arrival—beyond their heresy—was their insistence on keeping their hats on. When John Bowne would not remove his hat in Stuyvesant's presence, the director-general stormed off. Eventually, when Stuyvesant decided to confront Bowne, he had the sheriff forcibly remove the Quaker's hat.

Bowne's case played out as expected: He was found guilty of harboring Quakers and fined. After refusing to pay, he was shackled in the dungeon. Stuyvesant told Bowne that if he'd simply agree to be banished from the colony, he'd let bygones be bygones. But Bowne refused this too.

Finally, Bowne was deported. In January 1663, he boarded a boat to the Netherlands, where he could plead his case directly to the directors of the Dutch West India Company. At first, the company tried to find a middle ground. Perhaps Bowne could summon his wife and children to live with him in the Netherlands? Bowne, obstinate that the Flushing charter granted him religious freedom, told them he wanted to go home. Ultimately, the company had no choice but to let him.

John Bowne returned to Flushing in 1664, not only a free man, but also a trailblazer, the man who had guaranteed the freedom of all religions in New Netherland. In a sternly worded rebuke to Stuyvesant, the company's directors wrote:

> *The consciences of men ought to be free and unshackled, so long as they continue moderate, peaceable, inoffensive, and not hostile to the government. Such have been the maxims of prudence and toleration by which the magistrates of this city have been governed; and the consequences have been, that the oppressed and persecuted from every country have found among us an asylum from distress. Follow in the same steps, and you will be blest.*

Stuyvesant likely didn't feel blessed. In August 1664, an English naval expedition arrived under the command of Richard Nicolls. Sent by James, Duke of York, they had come to capture the colony for the English crown. Nicolls came ashore in Gravesend, where a delegation of English townspeople greeted him as a liberator. Within a few days, Nicolls had forced Stuyvesant to surrender.

Suddenly, the shoe was on the other foot and Stuyvesant, the prosecutor, was in danger of becoming the prosecuted. The Quakers, the Puritans in Boston, the Anabaptists like Deborah Moody, Anne Hutchinson's Antinomians—all of them had been persecuted by Anglicanism, the official English state religion. So Stuyvesant negotiated twenty-three Articles of Capitulation, one of which read: "The Dutch here shall enjoy the liberty of their consciences in Divine Worship and church discipline."

It took generations, but the Anglican (later Episcopal) church slowly became the most important denomination in the city. By the time of the American Revolution, Stuyvesant's descendants had switched to the Episcopal Church, later donating the land over and around the director-general's grave for the building of St. Mark's-in-the-Bowery.

Behind the Flushing Quaker meeting house is a small, neatly tended graveyard. In 1676, John Bowne donated this land to the meeting for burials. Worship itself continued to happen at or outside Bowne's house; in 1672, George Fox, the founder of Quakerism, even came to Flushing to preach.

In 1692, Bowne arranged to buy the land neighboring the graveyard for a meeting house and the first recorded worship service took place in 1694. Meetings have continued here ever since, except when the building was occupied by the British during the Revolution.

The earliest graves are not marked. This colonial custom—early Dutch Reformed graveyards lacked stones, too, as did Lady Deborah Moody's—seems particularly fitting here. Anything ostentatious in the cemetery would seem out of place. According to tradition, John and Hannah Bowne are interred somewhere near the back wall, their graves marked only by turf and flowers. From the porch of the meeting house, I can see where they might be, but I keep a respectful distance.

In Manhattan, there are plenty of monuments to Peter Stuyvesant, including a sculpture of him by Gertrude Vanderbilt Whitney in Stuyvesant Square. There's no statue of Bowne in Flushing; in fact, there's no memorial to him anywhere. But the real spaces of his life—his home, his house of worship, his final resting place—are more significant than any plaque or marker. And the persistence of his dissent is what's most significant of all.

The rain has picked up. On the other side of the meeting house, I hear car horns blaring on Northern Boulevard, a jarring reminder of the twenty-first century; here, facing John Bowne's grave, it could be the 1690s again. I linger a moment in that past before opening my umbrella and setting off into the future.

Fraunces Tavern (the former Stephen DeLancey house).

CHAPTER 3

The DeLanceys and
New York's Lost Century

IN 1686, A YOUNG FRENCH MERCHANT NAMED Etienne DeLancey arrived in New York City. With the exception of 1673, when the Dutch retook Manhattan for one year, the city had been under English control for two decades. I'm curious if DeLancey was expecting to find a proper English town. Or did he realize that the city would be, in the words of his friend Charles Lodwick, "too great a mixture of nations . . . and English the least part"?

I try to keep Lodwick's comment in mind when I think about English rule in New York. By the time of the American Revolution, the city had acquired a British feel. But just as in the Dutch period, Manhattan remained the most ethnically varied spot in British North America, drawing residents from England, France, Scandinavia, Russia, the Caribbean—the list goes on. Not everyone was there by choice; by the time of the alleged slave revolt in 1741, nearly 20 percent of the city's population of ten thousand was enslaved Africans. After the Civil War, the topic of slavery was often minimized, so it became easy to forget that enslaving people hadn't been just a sideline in New York. It was absolutely central to the city's economy.

I'm thinking about all of this as I sit in a little landscaped plaza in Lower Manhattan called Hanover Square. The square is home to the Queen Elizabeth II Garden, which was dedicated to British citizens who died in the 9/11 attacks on the World Trade Center. Named for the Georgian monarchs, the square is a particularly appropriate place for this memorial—future King William IV even lived there briefly during the Revolution. However, only those who know the House of Hanover will even be aware that this is a British place.

That's not by happenstance. History is always an act of choice and compression; we shape our narratives as much by what we leave out as what we choose to include. In recounting the story of New York's first four centuries, most people have basically decided that an entire quarter of that period—the English-colonial era—isn't worth the telling. Partially, this is the result of simple patriotism: We won the war. But there's a darker force at work here too—a purposeful forgetting of the slave economy that drove British North America's success.

Often, history is written by the winners. That's too bad, because a lot can be learned from the losing side.

"You can't take a picture of that!"

Being admonished in museums and historic sites—as I unconsciously inch forward to take a closer look—is an occupational hazard, and I try to respect the No PHOTOGRAPHY signs. I just wasn't expecting it in Starbucks.

"Can I ask why not?"

"Corporate doesn't want anyone stealing our look and feel," the barista explains.

I look around. No Starbucks has much "look and feel" as far as I'm concerned, but this one does have something interesting: A print against the rear wall shows the Burns Coffee House, a meeting place of the Sons of Liberty, which once occupied this spot. I'm less interested in the site's Revolutionary history as I am in its earlier life; before it was the Burns Coffee House, it was the home of Etienne DeLancey—known then by his Anglicized name, Stephen DeLancey—and his son, James.

But the barista doesn't care. The DeLancey name means nothing to her except, perhaps, as a street on the Lower East Side. The fact that I'm searching out traces of the English colonial period impresses her even less.

In Lower Manhattan, few reminders of the English era remain. As I step outside the Starbucks, I see tiny Thames Street, named in honor of the river that flows through the heart of London. Walking east, I cross the island in a mere ten minutes to Hanover Square. Most of the other English names that once defined the city are gone.

From Hanover Square I walk south on Pearl Street toward the spot where the Dutch Stadt Huis once stood. To the English, this thoroughfare was known as Great Dock Street. The nearby Beaver Path—where pelts had once been carried to waiting ships—became Princess Street. During the eighteenth century, new roads were constructed north of Wall Street and given names like Crown, King, and Little Queen.

In a fit of patriotism in 1794, all these British names were swept away. Great Dock reverted to Pearl; in a sort of reverse fairytale move, the Princess was turned back into a Beaver. Pointedly, Crown Street became Liberty Street. In this case, history was written by the winners on the street signs.

I reach the Stadt Huis block and my destination: a pile of stones beneath a worn, Plexiglas shell. The stones are a building's foundations, and the oldest remnants of the English-colonial era in New York. On this spot once stood the Lovelace Tavern, built in 1670 by Francis Lovelace, New York's second English governor. But these poorly preserved foundations aren't much to look at, and I get a more rewarding view when I look across the street and face a row of mostly nineteenth-century commercial buildings.

One structure stands out: a three-story brick mansion with dormer windows and a tall chimney. No matter what the sign outside may say, the building I'm looking at isn't really a 1719 house—but that's a story for later. Nevertheless, the building is a remarkable point of entry into this all-but-forgotten era.

To tell the story of the British period, I've chosen the DeLanceys, the original residents of this house, whose lives not only span almost all the 112 years New York was a crown colony, but who were intimately connected to the events that shaped the era, including slavery. Stephen DeLancey, a merchant, was certainly involved in the slave trade, both as a businessman and as an owner of enslaved Africans. His eldest son, James, grew up in a world where slavery was the norm, and Africans could be passed on as property just like furniture or a house. By the time of the American Revolution, there had been slavery in New York for well over a century. Even when gradual emancipation began in 1801, it would still be generations before New York was rid of the terrible, "peculiar institution" for good.

Stephen DeLancey was born in Caen, France, around 1663—one year before Richard Nicolls took over New Amsterdam and renamed it New York in honor of the Duke of York. When DeLancey was twenty-two years old, Louis XIV revoked the Edict of Nantes, which had protected the Huguenot Protestants, and DeLancey fled to England.

After becoming a naturalized English citizen, he headed to New York, where he was naturalized again (for reasons that remain murky), changed his name from Etienne to Stephen, and swore an Oath of Allegiance to the Crown. Twenty years earlier, Richard Nicolls had forced the citizenry, from Peter Stuyvesant on down, to swear a similar oath. Now, Governor Thomas Dongan—perhaps sensing a test to his authority—was again insisting on a show of fealty.

The deeper I delve into this fractious period, the more I bump up against this constant sense of uncertainty. As the saying goes, "Just because you're paranoid doesn't mean they're not after you," and the English authorities had every reason to question the loyalty of New York's citizens. Stephen DeLancey was soon going to experience this firsthand.

On the death of King Charles II in 1685, his brother James, Duke of York, had been elevated to the throne. When it turned out James was a Catholic, his opponents staged the Glorious Revolution, deposing him in 1688, and replacing him on the English throne with his Protestant daughter, Mary, and her husband, the Dutch *stadtholder*, William.

When word of this regime change reached New York in 1689, a faction of citizens and militia led a coup. They installed Jacob Leisler, a German-born immigrant, as head of the militia, commander-in-chief of the colony, and head of the Committee of Safety.

William and Mary appointed Richard Ingoldesby to be lieutenant governor, and when he arrived in January 1691, he found the city sharply divided into pro- and anti-Leisler factions. Unable to convince Leisler to step down,

Ingoldesby waited through a series of tense, and sometimes bloody, standoffs. In March, when the new governor, Henry Sloughter, arrived, Leisler finally surrendered control of the city.

Immediately, Governor Sloughter had Leisler arrested and tried for treason. He was convicted and sentenced to be "hanged by the neck, to be cut down, drawn and quartered"—and then, for good measure, decapitated. Sloughter's rough justice cemented the crown's authority, but it also served to fan the flames of anti-royal sentiment in the city.

Early in this conflict, Stephen DeLancey sided with Leisler. DeLancey was quickly becoming a successful merchant, primarily in the fur, cotton, sugar, and slave trades, and probably thought an alliance with Leisler would protect his shipping interests. When it became clear that Leisler's side was losing, DeLancey switched his allegiance. The English status quo was going to be better for business, so DeLancey signed an anti-Leisler petition in May 1690; the document called Leisler out for being an "Insolent Alien."

DeLancey had already Anglicized his name. Now, he was beginning the process of Anglicizing his life.

In 1700, Stephen married Anne van Cortlandt, the daughter of the former mayor and granddaughter of Oloff Stevenson van Cortlandt, whose Stone Street brewery had made him one of the richest early colonists.

As a wedding present, Stephen and Anne received a lot at Broad and Pearl Streets, one of the newest and best pieces of property in the city. Fourteen years earlier—before the Leisler Rebellion—the shoreline on the east side of Pearl Street had been back-filled to create new lots. Anne's father, Stephanus van Cortlandt, was mayor at the time, and he'd purchased the corner property. Having never developed the land, he now presented it to Stephen and Anne, though they, too, would leave the lot undeveloped for almost two decades.

By marrying Anne, Stephen DeLancey was not only joining one of New York's oldest and wealthiest families, he was firmly becoming part of the anti-Leisler, pro-English establishment. In 1699, Anne's rich Uncle Jacobus had purchased the vast tract in the Bronx that is today Van Cortlandt Park. Just inside the park's borders sits the borough's oldest house, built in 1748 by Anne and Stephen's nephew, Frederick van Cortlandt. This house remains the best-preserved English-colonial home in the city—though, to be fair, there isn't much competition.

One morning, I set out to see if I can find any traces of the DeLanceys in what would then have been the countryside. Anne and Stephen DeLancey died before this home was completed, but their sons—Oliver, Peter, and James—would have known their cousins' property well.

Considering how easy the house is to reach—it sits less than a ten-minute walk from the northern terminus of the IRT No. 1 train, the city's oldest subway line—it's surprisingly empty. In fact, when I visit, the only other person there is a Dutch woman, who is very concerned with carefully examining every souvenir in the tiny gift shop. It is a recurring theme that the city's more off-the-beaten-path historic sites are either empty or, if they do have visitors, they are schoolchildren or foreigners. Where are the American tourists? Safely ensconced on Manhattan, I presume.

Soon, I discover that the Dutch woman and I won't have the place to ourselves. A costumed interpreter—I'll call his garb late-Colonial/early-Revolution—is leading a group of two-dozen fourth graders down the house's main staircase.

"Everybody likes to play!" he admonishes to no one in particular. "There's a time for play. But there's a time to be serious!" I will hear this advice reverberate through the house a few more times during my visit, though I will never see him or the children again.

As the children's footfalls fade, I am left staring into the house's formal parlor at a portrait of Frederick's son Augustus van Cortlandt. In the years leading up to the American Revolution, Augustus—a Patriot—was New York City Clerk; in 1775, he spirited the city's records out of Lower Manhattan to this farm, hiding them from the British in his father's burial chamber on nearby Vault Hill.

Tremendous care has gone into furnishing this home, from the seventeenth-century Dutch room on the second floor to the "best" bedchamber used by George Washington on his visits to the house. That room features a beautiful mahogany dressing table and an English chest of drawers from 1725, both of which descend from family members. They've draped a blue coat and a tri-cornered hat on one chair, as if General Washington has just stepped out for a moment.

But I'm dissatisfied. While I'm pleased that if any of the Van Cortlandts or DeLanceys were to come back today, they'd immediately recognize this place, I'm not getting any real sense of the history here; costumed interpreter aside, there's an emptiness that no amount of imagination can make up for.

At its peak, the Van Cortlandts would have operated a farm, timber mill, and brewery on the property, all of it primarily run by slave labor. But the noise of those industries has been silenced, and other than one mention in the self-guided tour of "enslaved servants" sleeping in the unfinished upstairs room, the voices of those workers have been silenced too.

I leave the Van Cortlandt House and ride the No. 1 train as far south as possible—back to Pearl Street and the property Stephen and Anne DeLancey had received as a wedding present. In 1719, Stephen applied for a strip of land on Pearl Street, three-and-a-half feet wide, to straighten his lot so that he might "build a large brick house, etc."

In the nineteen years since he and Anne had been given the property, Stephen's net worth had continued to rise. He owned numerous ships, and was on the verge of becoming New York's wealthiest merchant. He'd also been elected to the colonial assembly, and during the tenure of Governor Robert Hunter, he fought in vain against rising duties and taxes.

How large a part of DeLancey's fortune came from slavery is unknown. This period was also the peak of piracy in New York—the famous Captain Kidd called Lower Manhattan home—and merchants like DeLancey used pirate vessels to evade the government and their competitors. That's one reason why documentation is sketchy. We do know from import documents that during the 1680s and 1690s, merchant vessels owned by DeLancey came home from Africa with people who'd been enslaved in Madagascar as part of the cargo.

DeLancey made money not only trading in slaves as a commodity, but in profiting from their virtually free labor. And he was certainly not alone. As Ira Berlin and Leslie M. Harris have pointed out, many of New York's principal investors—including the deposed James II—"were also stockholders in the Royal African Company, which enjoyed the exclusive privilege of supplying slaves to Britain's New World colonies."

By 1720, the Pearl Street house was likely finished, and would have been the family seat until Stephen built their next home, ca. 1730, on Broadway near Thames Street (later the site of Burns Coffee House and, much later, the Starbucks where I was yelled at).

Of Anne and Stephen's ten children, only five survived into adulthood: James, Peter, Oliver, Susannah, and Anne. James, the eldest, would have been sixteen when the house on Pearl Street was built. It was a large house—a mansion, really, with fourteen fireplaces and a huge kitchen. I can picture the

DeLancey children running around inside the house—after all, everybody likes to play—so it's jarring that the first thing I encounter upon entering the Pearl Street building is a sign for whiskey.

But I shouldn't be surprised—no one comes here anymore because it was Stephen DeLancey's house; they come because this is Fraunces Tavern, George Washington's final headquarters during the Revolutionary War. It's this notoriety that has marked the building's place in history. In some form or another, it has served as a tavern ever since.

When the DeLancey heirs sold the property to tavern-keep Samuel "Black Sam" Fraunces in 1762 (who, despite later speculation, was probably white), he converted Anne and Stephen's second-floor parlor into the Long Room, where Washington had his farewell dinner for his officers on December 4, 1783. Because that room has been re-created to reflect Washington's time, it looks nothing like the room where the DeLanceys might have entertained.

Across the hall, the Clinton Parlor, named for Governor George Clinton (who also frequented Fraunces Tavern), seems more like what I've just seen at the Van Cortlandt house, but the kitschy wallpaper—which depicts Washington's victory at Yorktown somehow taking place along the banks of the Passaic River in New Jersey—jars in its incongruity. It may be period-appropriate, but it's weird.

I'm still dissatisfied. The museum does a fine job burnishing the legacy of the Father of Our Country, but any traces of the DeLanceys are long gone.

———

By 1731, the DeLanceys had reached the zenith of their influence and power. The family had moved to their new, three-story brick house on Broadway. Eldest son James had just been appointed to New York's Supreme Court. Soon, James would invest in three hundred acres of land on today's Lower East Side, including today's Delancey Street. What we think of as just another part of the city was the countryside then.

With James's elevation to the Supreme Court, the family's transformation from French Huguenot to English loyalist was complete. In 1721, James had been dispatched to England, first to attend Cambridge (where they called him "the handsome American"), and then to read law in London. James returned to New York, passed the bar in 1725, and immediately got involved in politics.

Soon after James's appointment to the Supreme Court, New York's new governor, William Cosby, sued the city for the back pay that had been collected by the interim acting governor, Rip Van Dam, before his arrival.

The court was split: James DeLancey voted in the governor's favor, as did his colleague Frederick Phillipse, but Chief Justice Lewis Morris questioned the court's legality to rule on such matters. In retaliation, Cosby had Morris removed from the bench and elevated James DeLancey to chief justice.

To counter the governor's growing power, Morris and his allies hired a printer named John Peter Zenger to publish an anti-Cosby newspaper, the *New York Weekly Journal*. The paper issued a slew of increasingly bitter—but anonymous—attacks on the governor. In retaliation, Zenger was arrested in November 1734, charged with seditious libel.

Cosby allowed Zenger to languish in jail for months, finally bringing him to trial in August 1735. After Chief Justice DeLancey twice dismissed Zenger's legal team, an attorney from Philadelphia, Andrew Hamilton, presented the defense.

Hamilton opened by acknowledging that the case against Zenger was factually accurate and that Zenger freely admitted to printing the attacks on Governor Cosby. That, Hamilton argued, was beside the point. *Because* what Zenger published was fact, it therefore couldn't be libel. When Chief Justice DeLancey pointed out that truth didn't come into play when considering seditious libel, Hamilton asked the jury to nullify the law by voting not guilty. He compared Cosby's unfettered power—and, by extension, the power of Chief Justice DeLancey—to "a great river which . . . brings destruction and desolation wherever it goes."

The chief justice instructed the jury to ignore Hamilton. Even so, they found Zenger not guilty, thus establishing the precedent of truth as a defense against libel, a fundamental anchor in American jurisprudence and First Amendment guarantees. The affair also laid bare the fault lines between New York's political factions. Lewis Morris's group came to be known as the Country Party and James DeLancey's as the Court Party. The factions would feud until the Revolution.

Today, it's easy to see the DeLanceys as being on the wrong side of history. They profited from piracy and slavery. They supported the monarchy in a colony that was growing restless under crown control. In the Zenger case, James stood firmly against liberties that Americans today take for granted. But in the 1730s, the narrative was not so clear-cut. New York was always in danger of slipping into rebellion and anarchy; as recently as 1712, there had been an abortive slave revolt. Two years later, Governor Robert Hunter wrote *Adroboros*—the first play published in America—which centered on a secret plot to take over the city. After Leisler, anything seemed possible; in that context, James DeLancey's law-and-order sensibilities probably seemed comforting to a great number of New Yorkers.

———

Stephen DeLancey died on November 18, 1741. He'd been in the colony for over fifty years, but the final months of his life would prove to be some of the most dramatic. Having survived one of the coldest winters on record—the Hudson River actually froze solid—the town was about to go up in flames.

On March 18, 1741, a fire broke out in Fort George at the foot of Broadway. The city was already on edge; not only was spring slow in coming, but the winter had been plagued by a petty crime wave, including the theft a few weeks before of some Spanish coins from a shop on Broad Street. The next day, a white sailor named Christopher Wilson (the likely culprit) pointed the finger at two enslaved Africans, Prince Auboyneau and Caesar Varick.

By this point, the British had imported roughly three thousand slaves into the colony in the first four decades of the eighteenth century. While some came from the plantations in the Caribbean, many individuals were captured in Africa and brought directly to New York. Though it cost more to transport them, custom duties were only half as much for people from Africa. (Today, we have a tendency to refer to these enslaved people simply as "Africans," but they all self-identified with their point of origin: Malagasay, Coromantee, Mandinga, and many more.)

New York had come to rely on enslaved labor for everything from unloading cargo to household servantry. The DeLanceys' Broadway house, for example, would have required a large number of household servants, and there's little doubt that the servants were enslaved. Though we don't know how many people ultimately worked for the family, it was certainly a show of status to have a large staff. As hard as it can be to wrap my mind around it today, for Stephen and James DeLancey, owning people was just another sign of success.

Because it was such a relatively small town, blacks and whites rubbed shoulders in every walk of life. It was an uneasy relationship, and the white population's greatest weapon in keeping blacks enslaved was the fear of bloody reprisal should anything go wrong.

So, when the fire started at the fort, some New Yorkers grew nervous, wondering if Africans were to blame. Other, more objective observers suggested it might have simply been a soldering iron left on during repairs to the roof.

Then on March 25, a house owned by Stephen DeLancey's son-in-law, Peter Warren, caught fire. Two more suspicious fires were sparked on April 4 and 5—then, over the next few days, four more.

One can only imagine how worried the DeLanceys must have been. Peter Warren's property had burned; some of the other fires were only a stone's throw from their Broadway house. Nevertheless, Chief Justice James DeLancey remained a picture of professional calm. He bid adieu to his family sometime around April 1, and departed on a scheduled trip to Rhode Island to help settle a border dispute.

DeLancey took with him his house slave, Othello. Was Othello glad to go with his master to get away from the swirl of recrimination that was overtaking the city? We have no documentation of their relationship, and no idea how DeLancey treated Othello. Works variously refer to him as DeLancey's butler or manservant, which implies a daily intimacy. I just can't imagine what it was like to have a relationship with another person knowing that at any time you could send him to the gallows with the stroke of a pen. And I certainly can't imagine being in Othello's shoes.

James DeLancey would not return to the city until July 1. During his absence, his fellow Supreme Court justice, Daniel Horsmanden, investigated what he believed was a wide-ranging conspiracy by enslaved Africans and their white, lower-class supporters to burn down New York. Much of the star testimony was given by Mary Burton, a sixteen-year-old Irish servant, who, seeking a reward proffered by the government, told the court anything it wanted to hear.

By the time DeLancey returned, nearly 150 slaves had been accused of being part of the conspiracy. In the end, eighteen enslaved Africans were hanged and thirteen burned at the stake. One of these was Othello; the chief justice had shipped him back in irons at the end of June upon hearing evidence from other slaves that Othello had been part of the conspiracy.

Othello denied knowing anything about the plot, but by the time DeLancey returned to Manhattan a week later, Othello had admitted to meeting with other Africans. Had these men discussed, at least hypothetically, the possibility of revolt? It's hard to say, but it was enough for Daniel Horsmanden. Othello was James DeLancey's highest-ranking servant; in the same way white society looked to DeLancey with respect, Horsmanden believed that Othello held a similar, parallel position of power within the enslaved community.

DeLancey's return signaled an end to Horsmanden's inquisition. Many convicted slaves were banished instead of executed—but not Othello. Certainly, the chief justice had the power to spare Othello's life, but he chose not to. Perhaps DeLancey thought it would be politically untoward to pardon his own slave; maybe he believed in Othello's guilt. Probably he wanted to make sure the balance of power stayed in his favor.

Whatever DeLancey's rationale, Othello was hanged—in part because he'd been enslaved by a very powerful man.

No one knows the exact spot where the executions of 1741 took place, but it would have been on the edge of what was known as the Little Collect Pond, an arm of the fresh water source that lay just north of the populated city, approximately where Foley Square sits today. The Collect (from the Dutch word for pond) was the city's best source of fresh drinking water, about a twenty-minute walk from the DeLancey house.

In 1697, Africans were banned from burying their dead within the city limits, so they began using the marshy area next to the Collect, a place known as the Cripplebush Swamp. Horsmanden must have found it very convenient to execute the alleged slave conspirators here—the spot was close enough to the city to draw crowds of spectators, while also being right next to the cemetery where the executed would be interred.

For centuries that cemetery remained hidden beneath layers of development. Every so often evidence of bodies would turn up, but in the nineteenth century that wasn't surprising. Potter's fields had been scattered around Manhattan since the first Europeans arrived; it would have been more surprising if they *didn't* stumble on graves now and then. Then, in May 1991, workers digging the foundations for a new federal office building found skeletal remains. By the time the archaeological excavations were through, 419 individuals in 424 graves had been unearthed, one of the largest African burial sites ever discovered in this country.

A portion of the excavated site is now the African Burial Ground National Memorial, the centerpiece of which is Rodney Leon's 2007 "Ancestral Libation Chamber." It's a moving site, and one of the few places I visit on tours that clients ask to come back to. New York's legacy of slavery has long been hidden; when I tell people that in 1801—the year gradual manumission of enslaved Africans began—New York was the second-largest slave-holding city in the country, people sometimes don't believe me. When I tell them that New York was the second-to-last northern state to emancipate its slaves, on July 4, 1827, they are flabbergasted. New York has always been about progress—how could we have been mired in this terrible practice for so long?

The small park in which the memorial stands is peaceful—too peaceful, in fact. Often, I'm the only one there. (Once, the only other people at the site were Rodney Leon and his family. His daughter sidled up to me and said, very matter-of-fact, "My dad made that," before hurrying away.)

Maybe I've been looking at this all wrong; maybe cost and convenience aren't the deterrents when it comes to visiting historic sites. Maybe it's simply the fact that in our 24/7 world, perhaps this type of history—be it a house or a significant cemetery—takes too much investment, too much time. Not just time to experience the place, but time to take in what it signifies, to wrap our minds around such giant concepts as enslavement and injustice.

Those who don't take that time at the African Burial Ground are missing out not only on the experience of Leon's tribute to the city's African past, but also on the knowledge that a place like this cemetery—which at its peak may have held fifteen thousand people—could be so thoroughly erased, only a handful of historians and experts even knew what it was when the first bodies were disinterred. A 1754 map of the city clearly shows the "Negroes Buriel Ground" marked near the Collect Pond; just twelve years later, the next map of the city has nothing marked. Put a plaque or marker in place, and people will trust its veracity. Remove one—erase a place from the maps—and its history simply vanishes.

Were any of those 419 bodies unearthed at the African Burial Ground victims of Daniel Horsmanden's zealous prosecution? Were any of them Othello DeLancey? Though the burials were studied extensively for a decade, no evidence linked the skeletons to the alleged conspirators. Indeed, there's a chance that as condemned criminals they would have been buried elsewhere, perhaps in secret. Who knows what future revelations lie in store when someone's shovel hits the earth in just the right place.

Stephen DeLancey died just as the final drama of the conspiracy trials was playing out. In the end, James DeLancey had guided the investigation down another path, and a white man named John Ury was accused of being the plot's ringleader and, worse, a secret Catholic priest; he was hanged that August. On November 11, 1741, Mary Burton, whose unreliable testimony had condemned so many, collected her government reward, effectively closing the books on the tragedy. A week later, Stephen DeLancey passed away, and the Broadway house was inherited by James.

By this point, the Pearl Street house had been rented out for a number of years. Starting in 1738, Henry Holt, a dance instructor, had advertised lessons there. In 1759, Stephen's youngest son, Oliver, took over the building for his mercantile business.

James, meanwhile, continued to consolidate his political power. He was named lieutenant governor (in addition to remaining chief justice) and served as acting governor for nearly two years starting in 1753. Around this time he rented out the Broadway house to Edward Willet, who opened a tavern in it called the Province Arms. DeLancey, perhaps affected by Othello's death and the 1741 fires, introduced a measure to tax the purchase of slaves, hoping to cut down on their importation. DeLancey argued that slaves would be replaced by "white servants, which will augment the strength of the country." The idea went nowhere.

James became acting governor again in 1758, when Governor Charles Hardy left to fight in the French and Indian War, and remained in the position until he died in 1760.

His brother Oliver sold the Pearl Street building in 1762 to Sam Fraunces. Though Oliver was initially sympathetic to the Sons of Liberty—who would sometimes meet at Fraunces Tavern—he ultimately joined the Loyalist side, fighting for the British and fleeing after the war to Great Britain. Indeed, by the time the fighting ended, Stephen DeLancey's children were all either dead or gone: second son, Peter, had died in 1770; daughter Susannah, who'd married Peter Warren, left for England a few years after the 1741 fires. The youngest daughter, Anne, and husband, John Watts, saw the writing on the wall and sailed for Wales in 1775.

In 1763, the Province Arms tavern was taken over by George Burns and became the Burns Coffee House. The Sons of Liberty met here as well, and it's funny to think how both of Stephen DeLancey's houses—built as symbols of English-colonial status and wealth—became hotbeds of American dissidence and insurrection.

The Broadway house is gone. During the Revolution, the Lower East Side property was seized, and later divided into lots and sold. Only Fraunces Tavern remains, but it is a historically convoluted re-creation. Having served after the war as everything from a Treasury Department building to a boardinghouse, the building by the turn of the twentieth century bore little resemblance to the house that Stephen and Anne DeLancey built.

In 1904, to save the structure from demolition, it was purchased by the Sons of the Revolution, who hired William Mersereau to restore the building back to what it would have been like when Washington had his farewell dinner. Despite Mersereau's best intentions, the restoration could at best only be conjectural. He had no pictures to work from and too much of the original building had been altered over time.

Even before the work was finished, critics began to pan Mersereau's job. One letter writer in the *New York Times* imagined the George Washington statue in Union Square crying out over the "scoundrelly piece of vandalism that they have perpetrated upon that hallowed building." In 1965, the *Times* architecture critic, Ada Louise Huxtable, was even less kind:

> *This "landmark" was built in 1907 virtually from scratch. It gives school-children a fair idea of what a Georgian building looked like and it gives local businessmen a fair lunch. But it is not old, it is not authentic, and under no circumstances is this kind of thing preservation.*

Fraunces Tavern was rebuilt at the dawn of an era where re-creating history began to take precedence. Its influence can be felt in Colonial Williamsburg, Henry Ford's Greenfield Village, Plimoth Plantation, and—closer to home—Historic Richmond Town on Staten Island, my final destination in my search for the remnants of the DeLanceys' New York.

I set off down Broadway to the island's southernmost tip and board the bright-orange Staten Island ferry. (Its orangeness—a tribute to the Netherlands—is an attempt to emphasize the city's Dutch roots.) At the other end, I board a bus and forty-five minutes later, I'm in the center of Historic Richmond Town, the best-preserved collection of colonial buildings in the city.

Like many Manhattanites, I go to California more frequently than to Staten Island, and I'm glad to be away from the hustle of the Financial District. I'm puzzled that some of the buildings—a food truck, a bed-and-breakfast—seem out of character, and I'm relieved when I find out that they are merely set dressing left over from the HBO series *Boardwalk Empire*.

Our avuncular tour guide takes us into three buildings: the 1695 school-house, the 1840 general store, and Joseph Guyon's 1740 home, moved to this site from New Dorp. There are contrasts between Guyon's house and the Van Cortlandt home in the Bronx, but what strikes me more is their similarities:

the Dutch vernacular style, the wide-plank floors, the hall clocks—even the staircases seem similar. Ada Louise Huxtable argued for preserving "the lively original" over the "dead copy," and standing in Joseph Guyon's home, you get a feel for what she meant.

The house was originally built just before the fires and great "conspiracy" overwhelmed Manhattan. Did that controversy affect them out here in the hinterlands? Or did life on Staten Island simply move forward, tied to the seasons and the sea, as it had—and would—for centuries?

At the end of the tour we stop briefly in the tinsmith's shop, where modern craftspeople use traditional techniques to make everything from bathtubs to candle stands. It's here that the true feeling of the DeLanceys' century takes hold. Historic houses often pride themselves on having authentically antique furnishings. But, of course, when the DeLanceys were equipping their homes in the 1700s, everything would have been fashionable, expensive, and new. The candle stands weren't tarnished—which would have rendered them ineffective—but instead were kept polished, reflecting light throughout the whole room.

It's a gorgeous day, and the late-afternoon sunlight catches on the tin stands in the window. I picture Anne van Cortlandt DeLancey shopping in a place like this, finding the finest wares, and taking them home to Pearl Street to show Stephen.

For the first time, I can picture her—or her enslaved servants—in that Long Room at Fraunces Tavern, lighting the candles as the sun begins to dip over the Hudson River. I still can't fathom this idea of people owning other people—it puts these characters at such a remove from my own experience that I have a hard time inhabiting their daily lives. But standing in this working shop, watching the shadows deepen across the old plank floor, I am finally satisfied I have recovered a small piece of the DeLanceys' lost century.

CHAPTER 4

Alexander Hamilton:
The Life and Death of a Patriot

STANDING ATOP THE PALISADES IN WEEHAWKEN, New Jersey, slightly out of breath, I should have been admiring the view. The Manhattan skyline spread before me, its majestic spires shining in the afternoon sun. But all I could think was: *After a climb like that? No wonder Hamilton missed.*

My pilgrimage to Weehawken was one of my last stops in an attempt to re-create the final days in the life of Alexander Hamilton, America's first treasury secretary and New York's greatest Founding Father. Though Hamilton's accomplishments are legion—we would not have our Constitution or the underpinning of our financial systems without him—his life is often overshadowed by his death: slain by Vice President Aaron Burr in a dispute of honor on the dueling grounds of Weehawken.

I've been a tour guide long enough to know that maps are unreliable. Often they reflect a landscape that has changed by the time the map is printed; sometimes, they are just wishful thinking. Still, on the ferry ride over from Midtown Manhattan to Port Imperial, my GPS—who for reasons best not explained is named Wanda Gladys—assured me it was an easy ten-minute walk to the Hamilton/Burr memorial. Well, Wanda Gladys didn't say it was easy; I assumed that part. Leaving the ferry terminal, I was immediately struck by the part a two-dimensional map had left out: the sheer cliff in front of me.

The little dot on my map winked at me. "Turn right," Wanda Gladys cooed.

Soon, I was walking over the light rail track, climbing 187 vertiginous steps ("Continue straight," said Wanda Gladys; she never said it was straight up), and huffing along Boulevard East to the monument marking the spot where Burr slew Hamilton.

Except, as the plaque set in place on the bicentennial of the duel in 2004 points out, this wasn't actually the place. Rather, the dueling grounds were "somewhere below this site."

I looked down the precipitous drop. *Below?*

Alexander Hamilton by John Trumbull.

Alexander Hamilton was born in 1757—or, maybe, 1755—out of wedlock ("the bastard brat of a Scotch pedlar," John Adams called him) on the island of Nevis in what was then the British West Indies. Hamilton was one of the few Founding Fathers not born in the American colonies. In some ways, this made him the ideal New Yorker, since one of the hallmarks of being a New Yorker is that you don't have to actually be from here. Becoming a New Yorker is really more like passing an audition; your birthplace matters little next to what you do once you're here.

After Hamilton's father, James, abandoned the family, his mother, Rachel, moved them to nearby St. Croix; Rachel died when Hamilton was twelve or thirteen. The Presbyterian pastor in St. Croix had the foresight to recognize that the smart, hard-working boy would be stymied on the small island. So the community raised the money to send him to school in America.

Hamilton enrolled in King's College—now Columbia University—which was then headquartered downtown on Park Place in the part of Manhattan known as "Holy Ground." The nickname was a joke—the area was land owned by Trinity Church, but it was also the city's red-light district (reportedly more than five hundred prostitutes plied their trade around King's College). Did the seventeen-year-old Hamilton partake? For a man whose well-known fondness for women later derailed his political career, one can only assume.

Young Hamilton arrived in New York City—probably in late 1773 or early 1774—to find it in the grip of revolutionary fervor. The city was fraught with tensions between Loyalists and patriots, and weighted down by a century of political backbiting: the English vs. the Dutch; the Court Party vs. the Country Party; and the Tory DeLanceys vs. the Patriot Morrises.

The first signs of revolt had come almost a decade earlier with the British Parliament's passage of the Stamp Act, a tax meant to defray the costs incurred during the French and Indian War. The day the act was to take effect, November 1, 1765, a group of angry New Yorkers headed down Broadway to Fort George, torches in hand, to demand justice. While acting governor Cadwallader Colden hid in the fort with the stamps, the mob hoisted an effigy of Colden on the gallows. Then they tore down the fence surrounding the Bowling Green, lit a bonfire, and burned Colden's valuable winter sleighs.

Six months later, the Stamp Act was repealed. While the Sons of Liberty continued to jeer at all signs of British authority, the Loyalist citizens of New

York, such as the DeLanceys, raised the cash to erect a gilded equestrian statue of George III to stand on the very spot in Bowling Green where the mob had rallied. In August 1770, the new gold statue of King George was unveiled by the Loyalists to great acclaim.

Soon after the Revolution began in 1775 in Lexington, Massachusetts, Hamilton volunteered as a member of the militia known as the Corsicans, or Hearts of Oak, composed mainly of other King's College students. Each morning before class, the militia would drill in the graveyard of St. Paul's Chapel a few blocks away.

Dedicated in 1766 as a chapel of Trinity Church, St. Paul's is the most significant pre-Revolutionary structure to have survived in Lower Manhattan. The graveyard is a cramped space. In good weather, it's overflowing with tourists who've come to explore the chapel's role hosting volunteers in the aftermath of the 9/11 terrorist attacks. It's always difficult for people to maneuver around each other and the graves. No one's ever quite sure where to step. Is it all right to walk over the graves—or is that sacrilege? Hamilton and his fellow soldiers had no such qualms. When I see visitors weaving amid the headstones, I try to imagine what this space must have been like as Hamilton dodged imaginary fire.

The Hearts of Oak had their first real taste of war on August 23, 1775, as the British were evacuating the garrison at Fort George onto the HMS *Asia*, which lay at anchor in New York harbor. American captain John Lamb ordered that the cannons defending the Battery be taken to the Commons (today's City Hall Park) to keep them from falling into British hands. Hamilton and his militia compatriots began the daunting task of hauling the guns up Broadway under the cover of darkness.

The British, fearing such a move, lay in wait on a patrol boat just off shore. When they spied the Hearts of Oak at work, the Redcoats opened fire, causing a quick artillery exchange with Hamilton's men. One British soldier aboard the patrol boat was killed.

As the militia redoubled their efforts to secure the guns, the *Asia* unleashed a volley of cannon fire. One cannonball pierced the roof of Fraunces Tavern. In the commotion, Hamilton passed off his musket to his friend Hercules Mulligan, a voluble tailor who would later become a key spy for the Americans. Mulligan was forced to abandon the musket at the Battery; when Hamilton later discovered this, Mulligan recalled that Hamilton immediately "went [back] for it, notwithstanding the firing."

In the end, Hamilton and the militia managed to capture twenty-one of the twenty-four cannons at the Battery. As I walk up Broadway, I try to imagine what it would have been like to move such a gun. Hamilton has been described as a slim five foot seven inches (John Adams, later Hamilton's greatest foe within the Federalist party, referred to him as "that little man"), and while the guns sat on wheeled carriages, they still each weighed about 220 pounds. Dragging a cannon three quarters of a mile up Broadway must have been an arduous task—and they were doing it on unimproved roads while drawing cannon fire from a British warship.

I'm standing on Centre Street just north of Grand at the end of a tour, in the no-man's land between Soho, Little Italy, and Chinatown. It's usually at this point that even the most interested person's attention begins to wander. I'm trying to finish strong with the gorgeous Beaux Arts former Police Headquarters, but one woman is looking at puppies in the window of the pet store across the street, while another couple makes fun of the vegan restaurant next door.

Topographically, this spot was very different during the Revolution. Not only was this the countryside, this place I'm standing was Bayard's Mount, a steep, rocky hill almost a mile north of the Commons.

Offhandedly, I say: "This is where Alexander Hamilton's artillery company defended the city from possible attack in 1776."

Suddenly the group is back with me, and the end of the tour evolves into a discussion of whether or not Hamilton's marital indiscretions unfairly hounded him from public service. The tour is over, but now it seems my group is just getting warmed up.

"What kept Hamilton from public service was a bullet," I say.

Nods all around. No matter what opinion you have of Alexander Hamilton, your opinion of Aaron Burr is probably worse.

In Hamilton's day, the Commons marked the basic limit of the populated city. To get to Bayard's Mount, he would have to skirt the edges of the Collect Pond on the Bowery, with the dense city of New York retreating behind him with every step. North from here, farms and forests spread out over Manhattan's increasingly rocky terrain. Eight miles due north stood the old Dutch village of New Haarlem (briefly renamed New Lancaster by the English and then, finally, Harlem), where Hamilton would ultimately spend the last years of his life.

Fresh from victories in Massachusetts, General Washington and the Continental troops arrived in New York in April 1776, prepared for an imminent British attack. It was then that Hamilton was put in charge of an artillery company at Bayard's Mount. New York was, in George Washington's words, "a post of infinite importance both to them and us," and plans were laid to defend Manhattan from every avenue of attack. I wonder if Hamilton and his crew had to drag the same cannons from the Commons all the way up here to shore up the northerly defenses.

We don't know if Hamilton and Washington knew each other at this point. While Hamilton would soon rise to become one of Washington's most trusted advisers, he and the general hadn't had much opportunity to cross paths. In fact, the person who was brought into Washington's inner circle first was Aaron Burr.

Aaron Burr and Alexander Hamilton were both about the same age, and like Hamilton, Burr joined the patriotic cause early. In 1775, he was a member of Benedict Arnold's campaign to Canada—part of the Continental Army's plan to turn the French to the American cause—and fought bravely at the ill-fated Battle of Quebec.

By the time Burr returned to New York, Washington had moved into a Greenwich Village mansion named Richmond Hill; Burr joined Washington's staff there for less than two weeks. Why Burr lasted such a short time in Washington's employ is unclear. Was Burr itching to get back to the battlefield? Or was there a falling out between him and the general? It is certain that from that point forward, Washington did little to advance Burr's career, and Burr left the army before the end of the war.

It is also clear that what Burr saw of Richmond Hill struck his fancy—he bought the mansion in 1794. It was from there he would depart on the morning of July 11, 1804, to head across the river to Weehawken to kill Hamilton.

On July 2, 1776, while Washington and his troops waited, the Continental Congress met in Philadelphia to vote on the Declaration of Independence. Twelve colonies voted in favor; New York's delegation—uncertain of just how much responsibility they'd been given—abstained. On July 4, while the New Yorkers headed to Manhattan to discuss the matter, copies of the Declaration were printed. Express riders left Philadelphia that night with broadside copies for each of the thirteen colonies.

The New York copy showed up sometime on the day of July 9, giving the New York delegation the opportunity to read it before becoming the thirteenth and final colony to ratify it. That evening, members of the Continental Army and Sons of Liberty gathered at the Commons to hear the Declaration read aloud.

What a remarkable moment that must have been—everyone had awoken that morning a British citizen in rebellion. Now they were truly Americans. The crowd lurched down Broadway with a single mind. In just minutes, they reached Bowling Green and its gilded statue of George III. It only took a few strong men with stout ropes to topple the king. As British citizens, that would have been treason. But they were British no more.

Once the statue of George III was down, the patriots chopped off the king's gilded head. Then, for good measure, they chopped off his nose to spite his face. It wasn't until I started thinking about poor King George that the gravity of this insult hit home. The patriots had already felled his statue. They had *decapitated* it. Still, it was an even graver insult to His Majesty to cut off his nose, disfiguring him forever.

Once down, the statue was dispatched by boat to Connecticut. The symbolic act of tearing down the statue had turned practical—underneath all that gilding, the statue was made of lead; the statue was melted down and molded into 42,088 bullets "to assimilate with the brains of our infatuated adversaries."

From a statue that large, there should have been more musket balls, but not every piece of the king and his horse made it to the foundry. Souvenir hunters pilfered sections, including the tail, which was later dug up by a farmer and is now housed in the lobby of the New-York Historical Society.

At Bowling Green, nothing remains from that night except the iron fence. Erected in 1771 to keep the park clean (and, presumably, to keep the king's statue from being preyed on by nose-chopping revolutionaries), the fence has a number of disfigured posts. These once sported royal finials, now missing. Every time I'm there, I run my fingers along the tops of them to remind myself of the violence with which they were removed. It isn't hard to imagine them being wrenched off by fervent patriots on the night of July 9.

As the Americans celebrated their new independence, the British amassed troops to attack New York. So many British naval vessels arrived that first week in July that one observer said it was like "all of London was afloat."

On July 12, to test the American defenses, the British sent HMS *Phoenix* and HMS *Rose* up the Hudson River. The American artillery companies sprang into action but to no effect. The ships were able to pass up the river out of the Americans' reach, anchoring north of Manhattan.

Hundreds of rounds were fired at the *Asia* and *Rose,* but when the smoke had cleared, almost no damage had been inflicted on the British. Meanwhile, New Yorkers had been terrorized, watching cannonballs—in the words of historian David McCullough—"slammed into houses" and "bounding down streets still swarming with people."

From here, the course of the war accelerated. The British landed troops in Brooklyn on August 22, and the subsequent Battle of Brooklyn was a major defeat for the Americans. Washington pulled off a daring escape across the East River to Manhattan on the night of August 29, but only managed to hold New York for another two weeks before retreating up to Harlem. Hamilton's company at Bayard's Mount barely made it out. It was only because Aaron Burr knew a way through enemy lines did they make it to safety.

After the retreat, Washington took up headquarters at the Morris-Jumel Mansion in Harlem. This 1765 mansion, built by Roger Morris, is Manhattan's oldest house. Did Burr visit Washington here? It would be interesting to think he did—almost fifty years later, in 1833, Burr moved into the house when he married the widow Eliza Jumel. Maybe it made Burr feel more patriotic to sleep in the places where Washington slept.

Sometimes, I jog by the Morris-Jumel Mansion on quiet Sunday mornings before the museum opens to pick up my friend, Spike, who lives nearby. Over the years, Spike and I have run thousands of miles and covered hundreds of years, exploring nearly every facet of the city's history. In Harlem, we'll run to the Morris-Jumel house; sitting on a bluff, it would have had a commanding view, but today as Spike and I pass by, it seems like a strange outlier, surrounded by twentieth-century apartment buildings and housing projects.

If I'm in a Revolutionary frame of mind, I'll sometimes guide our run up toward Fort Tryon Park, where Margaret Corbin became the first woman to fight in the Revolution and where Washington lost yet another crucial battle. We'll look out at the Palisades, where Washington's troops retreated when he finally gave up Manhattan for good.

By the end of 1776, New York was in British hands, and it would remain the center of British America until 1783. When Hamilton and Washington returned at the tail end of the war, they would find a radically different city.

Most people learn that the American Revolution ended in 1781, with the American victory at Yorktown. While that may have been the end of the fighting, it wasn't the end of the war. Scores of Loyalist civilians had fled to New York seeking a safe haven in the months following the American victory; they refused to depart until George Washington negotiated their safe passage.

On November 25, 1783, the last British troops finally pulled out. As their ship passed Staten Island, they unleashed a volley of fire, thus getting off the last shots of the war. As a final insult, they raised a Union Jack over the fort, cut the halyard, and greased the pole so that when Washington arrived in the city, he'd still see the British colors. A young sailor, John Van Arsdale, climbed the greased pole and replaced it with the stars and stripes just in time.

Hamilton, by then a colonel, served as General Washington's aide de camp and was instrumental in the victory at Yorktown. But as Washington triumphantly returned to the city on Evacuation Day, Hamilton probably wasn't at his side. He was busy moving his wife and family to Wall Street, where he would soon establish a law practice.

One week after the British evacuation, Washington hosted his farewell dinner for his officers at Fraunces Tavern. (Though evidence is muted, it seems likely that Hamilton was there this time.) The general bid his officers a fond farewell and began his journey back home to Mount Vernon. As far as Washington knew, he was never going to see New York again.

During the war, Hamilton had married Eliza Schuyler, the daughter of Philip Schuyler, a wealthy Albany landowner and politician. Schuyler would serve as senator from New York in the first Congress, only to be unseated by young Aaron Burr in 1791. After the victory at Yorktown, Hamilton retreated to the Schuylers' home in Albany to bone up on the law. He crammed about three years of study into a few months, and passed the New York bar. Burr had only recently begun to practice law himself; both men knew how desperately the new nation needed attorneys.

Hamilton had little time to establish his private law practice in New York City before being pulled into public life. During the period between the end of the war and the ratification of the Constitution, Hamilton advocated for the nation's capital to relocate to New York; once it was here, President Washington appointed him the nation's first treasury secretary.

From the time Washington was inaugurated, in April 1789, to the government's relocation to Philadelphia fifteen months later, Hamilton's influence was incalculable. He established the foundations of the federal banking system, which in turn gave rise to the New York Stock Exchange. He founded New York's only bank, the Bank of New York, and laid the groundwork for the United States Mint and the customs department.

Few traces of New York as America's capital remain. If Hamilton were roaming the streets of Lower Manhattan today, he'd find just three buildings he recognized: St. Paul's Chapel, and two homes—the Edward Mooney house (ca. 1785) on the Bowery, and the James Watson house (ca. 1792) on State Street. In a town as small as New York, there's a good chance Hamilton knew both Watson and Mooney.

Both buildings reveal the wealth of their occupants. Each was enlarged ca. 1807, but even before any additions, these were still big homes. Watson's stood on what would then have been the waterfront, allowing a perfect view of New York harbor. Every time I pass Watson's home, I'm reminded of the children's book *The Little House* by Virginia Lee Burton, where the poor country house is, season-by-season, encroached upon by the big bad city. The Watson house also went from being an elegant home on an elegant street, to a relic, a quaint reminder of a bygone era, sandwiched between hulking, glass skyscrapers.

As I stand by the Burr-Hamilton monument on the bluff at Weehawken, seven miles away, I can see where the James Watson house should be, but I can't see the house itself. I trace a line in the air from it to where Trinity Church stands, though I cannot see the church, either. A few days after his fateful trip to Weehawken in 1804, Hamilton would be laid to rest there.

To my surprise, I suddenly find I'm not alone. First, a group of Spanish tourists arrive, then an Irish family. Have they really traveled all this way to see not exactly the spot where Alexander Hamilton was slain?

Perhaps. But what they are concentrating on is the Manhattan skyline. I pull my camera out and capture a few snapshots too. Then, I look north toward Harlem Heights—today called Hamilton Heights—and wonder if I have enough time to get to Hamilton's magnificent country house before it closes for the day.

I hustle away from the tourists, down the 187 stairs, across the train tracks—only to find I've missed the ferry. Never mind. Though Hamilton's home is perhaps the most peripatetic building in New York, I'm sure it will still be there in the morning.

The two decades between the end of the Revolution and Hamilton's death have filled many volumes. But I want to answer one essential question: What chain of events put Hamilton at the receiving end of Aaron Burr's bullet on the morning of July 11, 1804?

In 1790, the seat of government left New York to appease Hamilton's cabinet rival, Secretary of State Thomas Jefferson, who wanted to build a federal district, Washington, DC, on the banks of the Potomac. While Jefferson's master-planned city was being laid out, the government took up temporary headquarters in Philadelphia. It was there that Hamilton committed political suicide.

For a couple of years, Hamilton carried on an affair with Maria Reynolds, a young blonde whose husband, James, had likely orchestrated the whole thing as a way of blackmailing the treasury secretary. In all, Hamilton gave James Reynolds over one thousand dollars from his own pocket. When Reynolds threatened to go further, and accuse Hamilton of using public money for speculation, Hamilton was forced to come clean. He told a Republican delegation, including Senator James Monroe, about the affair, but promised that no public funds were misappropriated.

That would have been the end of things—if Monroe hadn't later told Jefferson about it. Not long after, when Hamilton resigned from the treasury department in 1795, word of the Reynolds affair hit the press—there's a chance either Monroe or Jefferson leaked the story—and though Hamilton ably defended himself, it was the end of his career in public office.

Back in New York in private practice, Hamilton continued to be actively involved in Federalist politics. The city's small political and legal circles also meant he was forced to have more dealings with Aaron Burr. In 1799, he helped Burr establish the Manhattan Company, which was created to bring water from the Bronx River to Lower Manhattan. New York had long been plagued by disease, and the yellow fever outbreak of 1798 had been particularly virulent. Because the company needed state approval—and the state government was firmly in the hands of the Federalists—Burr recruited Hamilton to the cause. Hamilton took to the project with gusto, making suggestions and improvements for the water system.

The company, however, was a ruse. Due to a strategic last-minute change in the charter, Burr made it "lawful for the said company to employ all such surplus capital, as may belong or accrue to the said company . . . for the sole benefit of the said company."

Once established, the Manhattan Company used its "surplus capital" to open a Wall Street bank to rival Hamilton's Bank of New York. It expended very little effort bringing clean water to the city. (In fairness to Burr, the Manhattan Company *did* lay down the city's first water pipes; they just weren't very good.)

Hamilton was livid that he'd been tricked into backing Burr's banking scheme. However, any ill feelings were put aside in March 1800 when Hamilton and Burr joined future Supreme Court justice Brockholst Livingston to successfully defend carpenter Levi Weeks. The young man had been accused of drowning his fiancée, Gulielma Sands, in a Manhattan Company well on Spring Street.

On July 4, 1804, Hamilton and Burr dined together at an Independence Day party at Fraunces Tavern. Artist John Trumbull—whose portrait of Hamilton graces the ten-dollar bill—noted that:

> [T]he singularity of their manner was observed by all, but few had any suspicion of the cause. Burr, contrary to his wont, was silent, gloomy, sour; while Hamilton entered with glee into all the gaiety of a convivial party, and even sang an old military song.

It really shouldn't have surprised Trumbull that Burr and Hamilton weren't getting along. In 1800, Hamilton's animus toward his fellow Federalist, President John Adams, led him to publish a scathing pamphlet that helped cost Adams re-election.

As a result, there was a tie in the Electoral College between Thomas Jefferson and his vice presidential running mate, Aaron Burr. (In those days, electors cast ballots of equal weight for all candidates; the person with the most votes became president and the runner-up became vice president.) After thirty-six ballots, Hamilton intervened and negotiated a deal that broke the tie and secured Jefferson the presidency.

Knowing the animosity between Hamilton and Jefferson, it's surprising that the former treasury secretary would help his rival. However, while Hamilton had plenty of reasons not to like Jefferson, the prospect of a Burr presidency evidently frightened him more. It was just one more in a growing list of slights against Burr, and I'm certain that the newly elected vice president was carefully keeping track.

Burr, meanwhile, wasn't doing himself any political favors. During the electoral crisis, he alienated himself from Jefferson's inner circle by attempting to remain neutral. So, when Jefferson stood for reelection in 1804, he told Burr he was going to replace him on the ticket with New York's perennial governor, George Clinton.

Spurned by Jefferson, Burr decided to run on a fusion Republican-Federalist ticket in New York's gubernatorial race to replace George Clinton. But Hamilton would have none of it. Through his *New-York Evening Post*, which he had founded in 1801 as a Federalist mouthpiece, Hamilton railed against Burr, which certainly helped cost Burr the election.

That's when things started to get sticky.

In February or March 1804—in the midst of Burr's gubernatorial campaign—Hamilton attended a dinner party in Albany hosted by John Tayler. Hamilton and Tayler evidently spent most of the dinner tearing down Burr's reputation.

Tayler's son-in-law, Charles D. Cooper, was also at the dinner, and wrote a letter to a friend, outlining Hamilton's opinion of Burr. Cooper reported that Hamilton had called Burr "a dangerous man" who was "not to be trusted with the reins of government."

Cooper's letter soon fell into the hands of the newspapers, a relatively common occurrence in this era. Hamilton's *New-York Evening Post* published it, mostly to defend Hamilton. The paper included commentary from Hamilton's father-in-law, Philip Schuyler, who noted that Hamilton would not have bad-mouthed Burr in such a scandalous manner at the dinner table.

Cooper shot off a letter to Schuyler stating that not only *had* Hamilton said all those things, he also had a "still more despicable opinion"—likely unprintable—of Burr.

This letter also ended up in the newspapers, and Burr had finally had enough. He had lost the gubernatorial election to Morgan Lewis. He was about to lose the vice presidency to George Clinton. He was not also going to lose his honor.

Burr wrote to Hamilton demanding a retraction. Hamilton replied, noting:

> 'Tis evident that the phrase "still more despicable" admits of infinite shades from very light to very dark. How am I to judge of the degree intended?

Burr was not amused. The next day, he replied:

The common sense of mankind affixes to the epithet adopted by Dr. Cooper the idea of dishonor. It has been publicly applied to me under the sanction of your name.

Burr demanded a "definite reply." Hamilton demurred.

Five days later, on June 27, 1804, Burr's second, William P. Van Ness, delivered a request for a duel to Hamilton's second, Nathaniel Pendleton. At this point, there was nothing left for these two men to do but meet with pistols at dawn. Dueling, which dated back to the Middle Ages, had become popular in America after the Revolution as a "civilized" way for gentlemen to settle their differences, and in 1777, the *code duello* had been codified, outlining twenty-six rules for duelists to follow.

Most municipalities outlawed dueling, and since the penalties were stiffer in New York than in New Jersey, the dueling grounds at Weehawken, New Jersey, were selected, for the morning of July 11.

It's strange to think of John Trumbull seeing Burr and Hamilton at Fraunces Tavern on July 4, each aware that in less than a week they would be rowing across the Hudson to Weehawken to shoot at each other. The idea must have eaten at Hamilton. Just three years earlier, his eldest son Philip had challenged his rival, George Eacker, to a duel on the very same spot.

Philip, shot cleanly in the abdomen by Eacker, lingered painfully for a day before dying.

———

In the summer of 1802, Hamilton, his wife Eliza, and their children had moved from the crowded confines of Lower Manhattan to a new mansion in Harlem called the Grange. Situated on the highest point in the area, the Grange had a view of both the Hudson and Harlem Rivers. Building a stately mansion at age forty-five also showed that—while he might have been forced from electoral politics—Hamilton was successful enough to keep a country manor along with a city home near Wall Street.

Hamilton enjoyed spending time at the Grange; according to his son, John C. Hamilton, he took up gardening, often "mingling" with his "humble neighbors" to extract horticultural advice from them, which he repaid "with kind offices." He planted thirteen sweet gum trees to commemorate the original colonies that formed the United States. On Hamilton's final weekend alive, he relished spending time with his family at the house. John recalled:

Sunday, before the heat of the day, he walked with his wife over all the pleasant scenes of his retreat . . . and at the close of the day, gathering around him his children under a near tree, he laid with them upon the grass until the stars shone down from the heavens.

The next day, Monday, July 9, Hamilton rode down Broadway to his office. He prepared his last will and testament, but also made plans with a client to meet on Wednesday, July 11, a few hours after the scheduled duel. Then he waited for that fateful morning to come.

Riding back across the Hudson in the failing twilight, I can't help thinking about what was going through Hamilton's head that morning. Was he thinking of his son Philip, who was just nineteen when he made the exact same journey?

Did Hamilton have an inkling of how far Burr intended to take his revenge? According to the *code duello,* gentlemen only needed to meet on the field of honor and *delope,* or discharge their weapons. They could shoot into the ground and the debt would be satisfied.

Before the duel, Hamilton had resolved not to shoot Burr. In a letter discovered with his will after his death, Hamilton had written: "if our interview is conducted in the usual manner, and it pleases God to give me the opportunity, [I will] reserve and throw away my first fire, and I have thoughts even of reserving my second fire."

The two men arrived in Weehawken about a half an hour apart. Burr and his party got there first and began clearing the dueling grounds. Hamilton, Nathaniel Pendleton, and David Hosack, a physician, arrived around seven in the morning. By prearrangement, the seconds were to keep their backs turned away from Hamilton and Burr. Since dueling was illegal, this would give them the chance, if questioned, to say they hadn't seen anything.

Hamilton, as the challenged, had brought the pistols, and he was given the choice of his weapon. Hamilton took his time getting into position. He cleaned his glasses. He repeatedly tested his aim. Was this a show of nerves—or was he trying to provoke Burr? The pistols belonged to Hamilton's brother-in-law, and he may have had the opportunity to practice with them. Did that give him an unfair advantage? Even if it did, it turned out not to matter.

Hamilton fired first. His bullet flew above Burr's head, lodging in a cedar tree.

Then Burr fired. His aim was true, and his shot lodged in Hamilton's spine, having first lacerated his liver.

But Hamilton wasn't dead—not yet. He was ferried across the river to the home of his friend William Bayard on Jane Street. Bayard was from one of the oldest and richest families in the city—he was the great-great-great nephew of Judith Bayard, wife of Peter Stuyvesant—and owned vast property in what is now Greenwich Village. Hamilton was carried to a second-floor bedroom where Dr. Hosack attended to him. A rider was dispatched to the Grange to fetch Eliza, but only to tell her that Hamilton was suffering from "spasms." He had hidden the duel from her in advance—but he could hide it no longer.

Back in Manhattan, I step off the ferry and head toward Greenwich Village. It's just a few weeks after Hurricane Sandy has decimated much of the East Coast, but in this part of Manhattan, signs of the storm are few and far between. Still, when I reach the block of Jane Street that once housed William Bayard's country manor, I find myself squelching through mud. When Bayard owned this land, his house was practically at the water's edge. Hamilton would have been carried up a short dock to Bayard's front door.

I snap a few photos of the front of 80–82 Jane Street, but two men on the other side of the street scowl at me. They look like Mormon missionaries, or maybe insurance adjusters. Am I encroaching on their territory? Since I have had nothing but duels on the mind for days, I scurry away before they can ask me any questions.

The next morning, I head to the Grange so that I can be there when it opens. It's not that I'm anticipating a line—I've been there enough times to know that's never a problem. I just want to have the place to myself.

When Hamilton built the house, it stood near what today would be 143rd Street and Hamilton Place. But in 1889, with the area ripe for development, the house was lifted off its foundations and moved two-and-a-half blocks to Convent Avenue to allow 143rd Street to be built. Eventually taken over by the National Park Service as Hamilton Grange National Memorial, the plan was to move the house to a more bucolic spot, and in 2008, it was jacked off its foundations again and inched down the hill to St. Nicholas Park.

I open the door to the Grange and—as I'd expected—I'm the first one there. I peruse the bookshelf in the gift shop, certainly the most Hamilton-centric store in the city. "You look like a man on a mission!" a zealous park ranger says, and I explain that I'm visiting the spots that Hamilton would have been to on the final days of his life.

"Are most people who come here Hamilton fans?" I ask.

"Yes," the other ranger says, "though we sometimes get Burr supporters, too."

"There are Burr supporters?"

"You'd be surprised."

As we chat, I try to imagine the messenger, breathless, coming to the door to tell Eliza Hamilton that her husband was having "spasms." Did he actually use that cover story, or did he reveal the truth?

Eliza rushed to Hamilton—which, in 1804, probably meant a two-hour carriage ride. Word had spread quickly around the city of the duel and Hamilton's condition, and Eliza found William Bayard's house already packed with concerned friends and onlookers. Dr. Hosack noted Eliza's "frantic grief," but Hamilton—weak but alert—managed to calm her. Hoping to settle his accounts with the Almighty, Hamilton asked for Holy Communion from the Episcopal bishop of New York, Benjamin Moore. At first Moore balked; Hamilton was not exactly an avid supporter of the church. But with pressure from Hamilton's friends mounting, Moore relented.

The next morning, Hamilton was still alive, but the end was near. He received last rites from Bishop Moore. His children visited to say goodbye. And at two o'clock in the afternoon, he breathed his last.

"What do you do on the anniversary of the duel?" I ask at Hamilton Grange. "Act it out?"

The park ranger shakes his head. "In this neighborhood? We try to discourage gun violence."

That makes sense, I think. But I can't help but feel regret. The sitting vice president of the United States and the founding treasury secretary met each other on a field of honor, pistols drawn. To play down the duel is to sweep under the rug the fact that the blood and violence that birthed our Republic was still simmering in its earliest years.

"We read the letters," the ranger tells me.

I think of Burr's last letter to Hamilton:

Your letter has furnished me with new reasons for requiring a definite reply.

I have the honor to be
Your Obdt. St
A. Burr

And Hamilton's reply:

If by a "definite reply" you mean the direct avowal or disavowal required
in your first letter, I have no other answer to give than that which has
already been given. If you mean anything different admitting of greater
latitude, it is requisite you should explain.

I have the honor to be, Sir
Your Obdt. St
A. Hamilton

I have the honor to be, Sir, your obedient servant, A. Hamilton. That might
have been the last direct communication Hamilton had with Burr before
their duel. Did they speak at the Fourth of July dinner? Did they even speak
in Weehawken? Or did Burr merely shoot Hamilton and leave, shielded
under an umbrella so that he would not be seen—and wouldn't see what he
had done?

I thank the rangers and leave the Grange. It's a cool, late fall day and the
trees surrounding the house still hold onto their leaves. I hike to the IRT
subway, and venture downtown to the place where Hamilton's life in New
York both began and ended. I hop off the train at Wall Street, near the spot
where Hamilton's Bank of New York once stood.

The spire of Trinity Church looms in front of me. This is the third version
of the church on this spot. The church Hamilton would have known burned
down on September 21, 1776. As Washington pulled the American troops
out of the city, a conflagration began, destroying most of the populated area
west of Broadway. The British blamed the Americans; the Americans blamed
the British. It may merely have been an accident.

No matter the cause, it meant that the British took over a city, a chunk
of which was smoldering and in ruins. In the eight years they held the city
during the war, they never rebuilt; when Hamilton returned to the city in
1783, he would have found Trinity a burned-out shell.

I turn into the churchyard and wend a familiar path toward an obelisk by the south fence. Underneath the marble obelisk lies Alexander Hamilton, in the words of his epitaph:

The patriot of incorruptible integrity.
The soldier of approved valor.
The statesman of consummate wisdom.
Whose talents and virtues will be admired.

In front of Hamilton's oversized monument lies Eliza's more humble resting place. Eliza outlived her husband by a half a century, first at the Grange and ultimately in Washington, DC. It is amazing to think that she died in 1854—just six years before the election of Abraham Lincoln sparked the Civil War. People have a tendency to think of the Revolution and the Civil War as separated by a great gulf, but Eliza Hamilton shows just how close in time they really were.

As is almost always the case, I find Hamilton's monument covered in money. Admirers come from around the world and deposit coins here to honor the architect of America's financial system. Most are pennies and dimes, but I see a few quarters here and there. Clearing back a pile of wilted flowers, I see a crisp ten-dollar bill sporting John Trumbull's fine portrait of Hamilton. Soon, a custodian from the church will come and collect this money—as they do every day—for the parish's charitable work. I fish out a shiny new nickel and pause, Thomas Jefferson's face staring back at me. Would Hamilton mind his rival resting on his gravestone? I like to think he'd be more magnanimous than that.

Aaron Burr lived to age eighty, and had a wild life, including standing trial for treason for his alleged plans to invade Mexico with a private army. He was said to have remarked in his later years: "If I had read Sterne more, and Voltaire less, I should have known that the world was wide enough for Hamilton and me."

I put down the nickel next to the ten-dollar bill, replace the wilted flowers, and stroll back down Wall Street, listening as the church bells peal behind me.

DeWitt Clinton.

CHAPTER 5

DeWitt Clinton and the Making of the Modern City

WHEN YOU'RE A TOUR GUIDE, PEOPLE NATURALLY ask you a lot of questions—some more random than others:

"Is that the fountain from *Friends*?"

"Why do people still use window-box air conditioners at the Dakota?"

"What are the six flags of Six Flags?"

"Who's your favorite New Yorker?"

It's my answer to this last one that sometimes causes people to pause. I don't know what they're expecting to hear—Woody Allen? Robert Moses? Madonna?—but the two answers I often spit out surprise them: Boss Tweed and DeWitt Clinton. The Tweed answer makes people laugh; at least they've heard of him. He's a scoundrel, and an infamous one at that.

Clinton, by contrast, has been almost entirely forgotten, which is a shame. He was the most important politician of his generation—perhaps the most important politician New York has ever had—which, considering the company, is quite an achievement.

Clinton was New York's junior senator; then, he served ten one-year terms as the city's mayor between 1803 and 1815. Later, as governor, he oversaw the building of the Erie Canal, the biggest engineering project of its day, which radically transformed New York's economy. Had Clinton carried the state of Pennsylvania in the election of 1812—which he nearly did—he would have been president of the United States, and might have brought a quick resolution to the war with Great Britain.

Clinton's influence is incalculable. From expanding trade through the Erie Canal to overseeing the real estate revolution embodied in the city's rigid grid plan, the effects of Clinton's years in politics are still felt today by every New Yorker.

On November 4, 1825, in a ceremony for dignitaries and the press, Governor DeWitt Clinton poured a small cask of water into the Atlantic Ocean. An artist captured the moment: Clinton stands on the edge of a barge, the miniature cask grasped in his hands, as the water—collected ten days earlier in Lake Erie—gracefully cascades into the sea. Clinton looks almost like a lawn ornament, though as far as I can tell no one ever made replicas of this "Wedding of the Waters" (as it came to be known) for people to use as garden decor. They did, however, make a score of other souvenirs: commemorative plates, decorative wallpaper, even a medal box "made out of a piece of wood brought from Erie in the first Canal Boat."

Clinton's journey from Lake Erie had begun on October 28 on the packet boat *Seneca Chief*. A cannon in Buffalo fired a signal as the *Seneca Chief* passed by on the first day. Over the next ninety minutes, the report was passed, cannon-by-cannon, down the banks of the canal and the Hudson River to New York City, letting everyone know that Governor Clinton and his tiny cask were on the way.

I'm thinking about the Wedding of the Waters as I run around Governors Island one morning. This small island in New York Harbor, in addition to having its own connections to DeWitt Clinton, is the perfect place to consider packet boats, shipping, and the importance of the Erie Canal.

I'm participating in a 10K race on a hot Sunday morning; by the time the starting gun goes off at 8:30 a.m., the temperature is already climbing into the eighties. Surrounded as I am by water, I feel as if I should be cooler. As I complete the first of three two-mile loops of the historic section of the island, the waters of the harbor are quiet. A luxury yacht emerges from beneath the Verrazano-Narrows Bridge on its way toward the East River; the Staten Island ferry begins a trip from South Ferry, but other than that, the harbor is empty. By my third loop, commerce has picked up considerably. Tugboats guide barges through the Buttermilk Channel that separates Brooklyn from Governors Island; a cruise ship in New Jersey exhales a large puff of dark smoke, perhaps in preparation for an early-morning departure. But even at its busiest moments, New York Harbor today is only a pale shadow of what it would have been in DeWitt Clinton's era. When the governor died in office in 1828, just three years after the Erie Canal's completion, New York had become the undisputed capital of American commerce. The canal had made it so.

The Erie Canal may have been Clinton's crowning achievement, but as I pause to catch the breeze by Castle Williams, which sits facing Manhattan on the island's southern edge, I'm reminded that it was this fort—along with Castle Clinton on Manhattan, Fort Wood on Liberty Island, and many more defensive positions—that really set the stage for New York's eventual maritime and commercial dominance.

And while the abundance of ships may be gone, the vista in front of me is taken up by a different symbol: the new 1,776-foot-tall World Trade Center tower. Though you'll never hear his name mentioned when talking about it, the economic success enshrined in that tower is DeWitt Clinton's legacy too.

——◆——

DeWitt Clinton was born in 1769 in Little Britain (now New Windsor), New York, the grandson of Charles Clinton, the area's Anglo-Irish founder. Both his father, James, and uncle, George, were generals in the American Revolution. Uncle George was not only New York's governor, he also helped Washington negotiate the evacuation of New York City at the end of the war, and rode triumphantly into the city at Washington's side on November 25, 1783. DeWitt was named for his mother, Mary DeWitt, who descended from the Dutch settlers of Ulster County.

DeWitt Clinton began his political life in 1787 as secretary to Uncle George, who served as New York's governor for a record twenty-four years until becoming Thomas Jefferson's vice president. In an act of literal nepotism, George Clinton had first appointed DeWitt's older brother, Alexander, as his secretary. Following Alexander's untimely death, DeWitt was handed the job, an excellent stepping-stone to higher office.

After serving in both the New York State assembly and senate, DeWitt Clinton won a special election in 1802 to represent New York in the United States Senate. I was surprised to discover that even though our young republic had been electing senators for only thirteen years, Clinton was the tenth man to represent New York in the chamber. And, like every member of the senatorial class from New York before him, he would soon resign the office. Clinton barely lasted twenty months in Washington, DC. He packed his bags in November 1803, when the powerful New York State Council of Appointment—led by Uncle George—selected him to be mayor of New York City.

Much of the early American political landscape, particularly in New York, was shaped by appointment rather than elections. When DeWitt was elected to the United States Senate, it was by the legislature, not directly by the people. Similarly, the Council of Appointment had been created in the state's constitution to bypass the "anarchy which resulted from vesting too much power in the multitude," as one observer put it. In 1800, DeWitt had been placed on the council (thanks to Uncle George), which helped his friend, Edward Livingston, become New York City's mayor. Now, three years later, Clinton was reaping his reward.

Clinton took office just after Mayor Livingston laid the cornerstone for a new City Hall. When the building was finished nine years later, Clinton had served as mayor the entire time except for a brief period when the Council of Appointment fell into the hands of his political rivals. On July 4, 1811, Clinton welcomed the first official visitors to the city's new seat of government.

To some degree, all architecture is metaphor, and Clinton's new City Hall could not have been a better symbol to convey the complex political desires and stark realities of the young city. The building is a mix of democracy, imperialism, old-world tradition, new-world ideals, lofty ambition, and practical frugality. They were so frugal, in fact, that they didn't even originally put a marble facade on the back of the building—sitting at the northern edge of the city, they figured no one would care.

What first strikes me as I walk up the steps of City Hall—the nerve center of what would be the world's thirteenth largest economy if it were its own country—is how small it is. Actually, that's the second thing I think; the initial feeling that I get as I pass through the x-ray machines is that I'm trespassing.

In 1998, at the beginning of Rudy Giuliani's second term as mayor, the open plaza in front of the building was barricaded to dissuade the public from entering. It was impossible to keep the people out completely, but Giuliani was a man of secrets—his administration remains the most sued in the city's history—and whatever was going on inside City Hall was for his eyes only. In 2003, a city council member, James E. Davis, was gunned down on the floor of the council chamber by a political rival who'd entered the building with him. In the wake of that tragedy, security was beefed up yet again, with everyone—from the mayor on down—going through metal detectors and x-ray machines. However, when I take the guided tour offered by City Hall, none of this is mentioned; the security is offhandedly attributed to the 2001 attack on the World Trade Center. Our guide has a lot to show us in an hour, and when you rationalize a security decision by invoking "9/11," people stop asking questions.

It's also disappointing that I've come to City Hall to think about DeWitt Clinton's legacy and his name is never mentioned. Of New York's 108 mayors, only two are talked about at all: Mike Bloomberg, the incumbent, and Fiorello La Guardia, whose desk we see.

By far, the person we talk about the most is George Washington. We see his desk, preserved from the old Federal Hall on Wall Street; we admire a portrait of him by John Trumbull in the Governor's Room. (Uncle George Clinton is there too and gets a brief nod.) We talk about Jean-Antoine Houdon's Washington statue that stands beneath the rotunda, and the grand portrait of Washington's chum, the Marquis de Lafayette, which hangs in the council chambers. For a building that has seen over two hundred years of city history, it's interesting that it is mired in an even more distant past that it never experienced.

This over-emphasis on George Washington on the tour can partly be explained by the international character of my fellow visitors. Washington is an icon, while the name DeWitt Clinton isn't going to ring any bells. More to the point, our guide wouldn't be able to talk about Revolutionary-era art if the building wasn't filled with it. In many ways, the building celebrates our national character, not New York's. So there's no statue of mayor Seth Low, no portrait of Ed Koch. (To be fair, there *is* a portrait of DeWitt Clinton upstairs in an antechamber to the Governor's Room; the day I visit, the room is under renovation and the painting under wraps.)

In part, all the Revolutionary and early Federal art stands as a testament to this building's predecessor. When the English moved out of the Stadt Huis on Pearl Street, they built a new City Hall on Wall Street. That building was renovated by Pierre L'Enfant into Federal Hall where, on April 30, 1789, George Washington was sworn in as America's first president. Until August 1790, Federal Hall served as the United States Capitol. The Bill of Rights was drafted there, and Alexander Hamilton's banking measures were passed by a reluctant Congress in exchange for Hamilton's backing of Thomas Jefferson's relocation of the capital to Washington, DC.

When the federal government left, the building reverted to being merely City Hall, but it held on to its sense of importance. When the city's government moved to this new home in 1811, no one wanted to see New York's place in early American history taken away. DeWitt Clinton was fourteen years old when the Revolutionary War ended; it was his generation's task to keep the Revolutionary spirit alive.

At the end of our tour, one of my fellow visitors says he took a tour of Independence Hall where he was told that Philadelphia was America's first capital city.

"No!" says our guide. Up to this point, the guide has been such a soft-spoken individual that this takes everyone aback. "New York was first, Philadelphia was second, and Washington was third."

Well, yes—and no. New York was the first national capital after the ratification of the Constitution, but that narrative conveniently leaves out Philadelphia's role during the period when we were governed by the Articles of Confederation, not to mention the Continental Congress years. But who am I to argue with a New Yorker's obvious sense of pride?

— ⌒ ⌒ —

In 1812, DeWitt Clinton was nominated as the Federalist candidate for president. He was a Republican like the president, James Madison, but he was opposed to Madison's branch of the party, so he switched sides. Madison and his predecessor, Thomas Jefferson, were leading America to war with Great Britain. Clinton promised, if elected, to keep us out.

The simmering conflict, which eventually became the War of 1812, started as an offshoot of the Napoleonic Wars. American merchant vessels plying the waters between the United States and the Caribbean were routinely raided by the Royal Navy, which was looking for British deserters as well as attempting to disrupt American trade with France and its possessions.

In 1804, the British blockaded New York harbor to keep French vessels from making port. One of the blockaders, HMS *Leander*, fired a "casual shot" (as the captain called it) at an American vessel. The *Leander* hit the ship's boom and killed a sailor named John Pierce. Pierce's "mangled body, raised on a platform, was paraded through the streets to augment the vehement indignation, already at high pitch, against the British."

Press gangs, which could legally force British sailors into the Royal Navy, began also taking Americans. In June 1807, the USS *Chesapeake* was raided and American members of its crew impressed. Rather than go to war, President Thomas Jefferson decided to impose an embargo on all American trade with Britain, essentially crippling the economy of New York.

In response, Mayor Clinton urged the city to defend itself in case of war. By the fall of 1807, work had begun on new fortifications around New York harbor, including Castle Williams on Governors Island, and the Southwest Battery on Manhattan (renamed Castle Clinton some years later).

Clinton may have lost the presidential election, but he saved the city.

Of all the buildings in Lower Manhattan, Castle Clinton probably has the most intriguing—and convoluted—history. Another hazard of being a tour guide is sometimes having too much story to tell. With some sites, it can be hard to tease out enough details; at Castle Clinton, I have so much to say that sometimes visitors lose patience.

During the War of 1812, no shots were ever fired from Castle Clinton because the British never dared attack, validating Clinton's decision to over-build the city's defenses. Later, the fort was used as an official reception site; in 1824, it was here that then-Governor Clinton welcomed the Marquis de Lafayette, the French hero of the American Revolution. Soon thereafter, the structure became a theater; in the process, its name was changed to the more mellifluous Castle Garden. A second story was added, then a roof. After thirty years as a concert venue, the fort was handed back to the city to become the Castle Garden Immigrant Landing Depot, the busiest immigrant entry point in America before Ellis Island opened in 1890.

But we're not done yet.

The shift to Ellis Island for immigrant processing meant the demise of Castle Garden. In 1896, the fort was reborn as the New York Aquarium. In 1941, Robert Moses—in whose heavy footsteps we will tread in a later chapter—decided Castle Clinton stood in the way of his brand-new Brooklyn-Battery Bridge. That bridge was never built (instead, the Brooklyn-Battery tunnel runs beneath the fort), but the aquarium moved out anyway. Eventually, the fort was taken over by the National Park Service as a place to sell tickets to the Statue of Liberty.

As I rattle off these facts and figures, it often strikes me that what is unique about the space is how easily its history forges a connection with people. Some have fond memories of visiting the Statue of Liberty; others have researched family who passed through Castle Garden. In 1850, the building played host to famed soprano Jenny Lind, whose fame is linked to her promoter, P. T. Barnum, the greatest showman America has ever produced.

Ticket agency, aquarium, immigration center, theater—each of these lives has resonance, even in the twenty-first century. It's the building's original use as a fort that seems the most removed. That's because the conflict for which

Castle Clinton was built, the War of 1812, is so little remembered, and then only in bits of trivia: the Star Spangled Banner was written during the Battle of Fort McHenry; the White House was burned by the British; Andrew Jackson won the Battle of New Orleans. (Canadians know one additional fact: their country won—which it did, if *status quo ante bellum* is winning.)

Even though New York saw no action in the war, Castle Clinton's life as a fort is still its most important chapter. Had DeWitt Clinton never accomplished anything else, protecting New York from the British should still earn him a prime place in history.

Having seen Castle Williams and Castle Clinton—and Fort Wood, the star-shaped defense that sits underneath the Statue of Liberty—I want to see the city's other relic of the War of 1812. This one, off in the wilds of Central Park, doesn't get the honor of being named for someone. It is simply called Block House No. 1.

During and after the Revolution, there was essentially only one road out of the city; what was called the Bowery downtown ran up the island's east side (roughly today's Park Avenue) until it cut west and descended a steep gully known as McGown's Pass. This was the path by which Washington, Hamilton, Burr, et al., retreated on September 15, 1776, after the city had fallen to the British.

By 1815, little had changed in the area. Expecting British troops to attempt to take the city from the north, a string of fortifications were erected stretching from McGown's Pass through Morningside Park to Lower Harlem.

Of these, only Block House No. 1 remains, and finding it can be a challenge. Sometimes when Spike and I jog in the park, we can catch glimpses of it in fall and winter, after the trees have shed their foliage. At 102nd Street we enter McGown's Pass, still—as it was in Washington and Hamilton's era—a significant down slope. We run past Lasker Rink and just before we reach the bottom of the hill I point up to the left, trying to show Spike a hint of a rubble-stone wall.

"I know it's up there," Spike says. "I've climbed up there with Spike Junior."

Soon, the road begins ascending the Great Hill, and off to the left is a dirt pathway. We follow its twists and turns, and suddenly Block House No. 1 rises up in front of us in all its ruined glory. It isn't much, but in a case of the whole being greater than the sum of its parts, our journey here amplifies the destination.

Frederick Law Olmsted and Calvert Vaux, Central Park's designers, wisely allowed the thick forest to grow up around the block house, lending it an air of authenticity. (The irony is that this is inauthentic; when the fort was built, it would have had a commanding view of the surrounding area. It was, after all, a defensive position.) I can imagine American soldiers here—nervous, impatient—waiting for a British army that would never arrive.

As soon as the war ended, it was like nothing had ever happened. The Canadians retreated to the north ("We won!"); the Royal Navy set sail for home ("We won!") and New York merchants eagerly hung out their shingles, poised to reap the rewards for the war ("We won!"). Since the terms of the Treaty of Ghent returned everything to its pre-war status, Britain went from being our enemy to being our number one trading partner.

It was here that DeWitt Clinton's investments in the city's defenses paid off. While other places rebuilt, New York thrived commercially and the population of the city—which was already America's largest—began to grow hand in hand with the economy. Before the war, New York's population hovered around 98,000; by 1820, it would be nearly 125,000, and in the next decade it would leap by another 75,000.

What really molded New York's growth in this post-war era was the single greatest achievement of DeWitt's mayoralty, one that is so much a part of Manhattan life that we all take it for granted: the 1811 Commissioners' Plan. Today, most people know it simply as "The Grid."

In search of a remnant of the grid's creation, Spike and I keep jogging south in Central Park, past the reservoir, the lake, the 72nd Street transverse road, and around the bottom of the park. I swear Spike to secrecy, because there is an unspoken code among those of us "in the know" not to share this spot. I suppose this is prudent—I wouldn't want some vandal coming and ruining it for everyone else—but it also seems like this knowledge makes us part of an elite group. New Yorkers hoard information: out-of-the-way restaurants (like the original Shopsin's in Greenwich Village), that one coffee shop that always has available power outlets, a source for rent-stabilized apartments without a broker's fee.

This secret is a piece of metal driven into a hunk of bedrock; it has been there over two centuries, and it is, in all likelihood, the only remaining marker from the original survey for the Manhattan street grid. Next to Mason and

Dixon's line, the survey of Manhattan remains the most remarkable feat of surveying in American history.

In 1807, DeWitt Clinton appointed a commission to come up with a way for New York to regularize its northward growth. An earlier commission, led by Casimir Goerck and Joseph Francois Mangin (co-architect of City Hall), proposed a street grid covering much of what would later become the Lower East Side. Though their rectilinear plan was never formally accepted, a number of the streets were laid out south of Houston Street on what was James DeLancey's property. Goerck and Mangin named a pair of streets after themselves; Goerck Street was later erased by a housing project, but a tiny remnant of Mangin Street sits under the Williamsburg Bridge.

Clinton's three-man commission was made up of three eminent New Yorkers: Gouverneur Morris, who'd written the Preamble to the Constitution; Simeon DeWitt, Mayor Clinton's cousin and a noted surveyor and cartographer; and John Rutherfurd, who lacked experience, but was related by marriage to Gouverneur Morris, and was happy to rubber-stamp Morris's decisions.

The hardest work of the actual survey was managed by John Randel Jr., who mapped over two thousand blocks from Houston Street (which is essentially Zero Street on the grid) to 155th Street in Harlem. The commissioners knew that mapping such a great portion of the island would, to some people, seem like folly. As they later wrote: "It may be the subject of merriment that the Commissioners have provided space for a greater population than is collected at any spot on this side of China." But they were confident that at the rate the city was growing, soon a "considerable number [of people] may be collected at Harlem."

Their forward-thinking had limits, however. Randel's grid was to stop at 155th Street because "it is improbable (for centuries to come) the grounds north of Harlem . . . will be covered with houses." They feared if they mapped any farther north, it would only lead to the "pernicious spirit of speculation."

A rigid grid was picked, in part, to avoid the "circles, ovals, and stars" that defined some cities (read: Washington, DC). More to the point, since "strait-sided and right-angled houses are the most cheap to build and the most convenient to live in," why would anyone design a city with a plan that *wasn't* a grid?

Each of Randel's north-south blocks was exactly two hundred feet, bounded—except in a few cases—by streets sixty feet wide. This meant that it would be precisely twenty blocks to each mile. Randel's survey was so perfect that he was never off by more than a foot or two. Standard house lots on each block were to be twenty-five feet wide by one hundred feet deep. Since each lot would back up against an identical lot on the next street, also a hundred feet deep, it meant there would be no provision for stables or carriageways. The commissioners argued that eliminating alleys and public squares maximized the amount of land that could be developed. Many years later, Cass Gilbert would refer to the skyscraper as "a machine that makes the land pay." This neatly summed up the point of the grid too, and it was going to make some New Yorkers obscenely wealthy.

The other reason the grid lacked alleys and accommodation for adjacent carriage houses was simply practical: Very few people could afford a horse and carriage. As late as 1863, there were only five thousand private carriages in the city. That meant just 3 percent of the city's residents could afford to own, feed, and stable a horse. No wonder they didn't include alleys on the grid fifty years earlier—so few needed them.

One person who would profit handsomely from the new grid was Clement Clarke Moore. To his contemporaries, Moore was best known as a Greek language scholar at the Episcopal Church's General Seminary, and for his vast farm, Chelsea, which gave rise to the neighborhood of the same name. Today, people recognize him as the author of "A Visit from Saint Nicholas" (aka "Twas the Night Before Christmas"), the well-known poem that imbued the American Santa Claus with a healthy dose of his mother's family's Dutch traditions.

Moore complained that in the monotonous grid, "nothing is to be left unmolested which does not coincide with the street-commissioner's plummet and level. These are men, as has been well observed, who would have cut down the seven hills of Rome." Moore was somewhat right—there are plenty of places where you can find that the development of the city flattened out the island's natural contours—but he was mostly wrong.

Again, here's a place where running has proved a helpful research strategy; not only does it allow me to cover more ground, the exertion also helps bring the island's peaks and valleys into sharper relief. I still remember running in my first New York City Marathon and feeling the fatigue in my calves at mile twenty-three, which includes Fifth Avenue from approximately 103rd Street until the course enters the park at 90th Street.

This is some hill, I thought, as my fellow runners and I ascended a grade that, quite honestly, wouldn't have seemed that tough if it was mile three instead of mile twenty-three. As I reached the peak of this small gradient, I looked to the left and there was Andrew Carnegie's hulking mansion, the centerpiece of a neighborhood still called Carnegie Hill.

Carnegie Hill. I might have been so startled I said it out loud.

Nearby Lenox Hill is the same, as are all the heights on the west side—Morningside Heights, Hamilton Heights, Washington Heights—onward and upward. Yes, there's Randel's cartesian grid, with its X and Y axes that appear "rectilinear and rectangular," in the words of the commissioners. But there's a vertical Z axis, too, that runs from the flood plains of Battery Park to the peak of Bennett Park at 183rd Street, 265 feet above sea level.

Clinton's commissioners may have expressed their disdain for Pierre L'Enfant's Washington, DC, but it is those irregularities that have crept into the grid and give the city its character. The most well known of these, of course, is Broadway. In the original plan, the Bowery and Broadway, which diverged at City Hall Park, were brought back together at Fourteenth Street. The union of these two old thoroughfares was to signal the northern reach of the old city and the beginning of the new—and thus, Union Square. Everything north of the square was to be regular, planned, unerring.

But it is not as if the Bowery (aka the Post Road) or Broadway (known chiefly north of 14th Street as the Bloomingdale Road) simply disappeared. Most of the Post Road was subsumed into the course of Fourth Avenue, as Park Avenue used to be known. However, the Bloomingdale Road—cutting across the island at an angle—did not fit Randel's new plan. Randel and the commissioners simply assumed that as the population grew steadily northward, the demands of real estate would consign the old road to history.

As it turns out, roads are hard to get rid of. St. Nicholas Avenue, lower Broadway, Washington Mews, Brooklyn's Love Lane—centuries later, all of these and more still follow the course of Native American trails. Why build a new road when the old one is perfectly adequate? Such was the case with the Bloomingdale Road. It had always been there and no one wanted to get rid of a good thing.

When Spike and I run, we like to search out these remnants of the city before the grid. One day, we turn east at 125th Street—another road that, when you look at it on the map, doesn't adhere to Randel's grid—and then make a quick left onto Old Broadway, the last vestige of Broadway's original path in this area. The road exists for one block, stops at a city housing project, and then picks up for another short block to the north.

When we seek out these obscure byways, we always discover fringe benefits along the way. On the lower stretch of the street sits the Old Broadway Synagogue, a reminder that a century ago, Harlem was predominantly a Jewish neighborhood.

One day a few weeks later, the synagogue is open to the public for a special event, and I stop in. The congregation's president warmly welcomes me and gives me the full guided tour—from the boiler to the rafters. He's most amused at pointing out the inscription over the ark. In most congregations this would say (in Hebrew), "Know Before Whom You Stand." The inscription is written in Hebrew characters, but it's actually phonetically in English. And that's not the best part. The inscription dates from a mid-twentieth-century renovation and says: FROM THE LADIES AUXILIARY OF THE CHEVRA TALMUD TORAH ANSHEI MAROVI. The women in this Orthodox congregation, who attend segregated services in a male-dominated house of worship, uncharacteristically have their group's name—and influence—for all to see, front and center.

Later we run up Hamilton Place, the stretch of the Bloomingdale Road that would have skirted Alexander Hamilton's front door. Again, this street runs at an odd angle to Randel's plan, and climbs a rather precipitous incline. It serves as just another reminder that Clement Clarke Moore was wrong.

Moore realized he was wrong too, but not before publishing a pamphlet where he railed against the "injustice, cruelty and oppression" of the street grid. (This is also where he complained about cutting down all the hills.) Moore soon figured out, however, just how much money was to be had from subdividing his Chelsea farm along the lines of the Commissioners' Plan. John Jacob Astor, America's richest man at the time, was already making a fortune on real estate speculation. (Astor's dying words, supposedly, were: "Could I begin life again, knowing what I now know, and had money to invest, I would buy every foot of land on the Island of Manhattan.")

By 1835, Moore had allowed his property to be subdivided, keeping only one parcel—the former orchard—for the General Seminary. In order to lure only the best people to the neighborhood, Moore attached covenants to the deeds specifying what building materials could be used, what structures would be prohibited—including stables—and how long you could keep your property vacant before building on it. In 1820, Moore's farm had been valued at $17,000; thirty-five years later he had a personal net worth of over half a million dollars. Presumably all of the newfound wealth was thanks to the grid.

Today, Chelsea is one of the hottest neighborhoods in the city, a fact largely attributable to the High Line, a park built on the old freight rail beds that ran over Tenth Avenue. Running isn't allowed on the High Line, but early one Sunday morning Spike and I are there in the midst of a colossal downpour. We climb the steps at Fourteenth Street to find the park empty, so we run north, Clement Clarke Moore's property spreading out around us on all sides.

The grid has had famous proponents, such as urban thinker Jane Jacobs, but it has also had many detractors. Chiefly, people complain that it inspires uniformity, and that it values commerce over community. Frederick Law Olmsted, half of the duo that created Central Park, lamented that it provided no open space—not so much for parkland, but for grand architectural monuments. "There is no place under the system in New York where a stately building can be looked up to from base to turret." The grid, with its narrow streets, offended his artist's eye.

As Spike and I continue north on the High Line, we look out at the buildings in front of us—the frosted glass sails of Frank Gehry's IAC building on one side, the brownstones of Tenth Avenue on the other—and we can see how wrong Olmsted was. From 1811 onward, New York City has been painted on DeWitt Clinton's grid. When Clinton died in 1828, real estate developers were taking their first tentative steps to develop the new city, but as the population spiked in the 1840s and 1850s, the city blossomed, buildings filling the empty rectangles between streets with an almost mathematical precision. By the time of the skyscraper era, Clinton seemed prescient, having created a city where mighty steel structures could stretch ever higher. Around the world, New York's skyline evokes the romance and thrill of the city, but to me, it will always serve as a monument to DeWitt Clinton, the city's greatest mayor.

CHAPTER 6

Gertrude Tredwell:
At Home in Greenwich Village

IN 1950, OLIVIA DE HAVILLAND WON AN ACADEMY AWARD for her ability to navigate a staircase. The movie was *The Heiress,* and at various points in the film she eagerly runs down the stairs, tearfully ascends them, and—in the climax—climbs slowly and deliberately away from the man banging on her front door.

I'm not being sardonic. De Havilland is a superb actress throughout the film, but in these silent moments—where she communicates with nothing more than a look—she embodies the emotional life and transformation of her character, Catherine Sloper.

The story, based on Henry James's novella *Washington Square,* follows Catherine's doomed love for Morris Townsend (played by Montgomery Clift). Catherine is the only child of the widowed Doctor Austin Sloper, who doesn't think she'll ever amount to much or live up to his idealized remembrances of her departed mother. When Townsend comes calling with amorous intentions, Doctor Sloper assures Catherine that Townsend is just after her money—a $10,000 a year inheritance from her mother, and the promise of $20,000 more when her father dies. I won't detail how it all plays out, but no one is happy in the end.

In the film and the novel, both set in the 1840s, the Slopers' house is located at 16 Washington Square; at the time, this would have been one of the finest addresses in New York. Still, I can't help but think as I watch de Havilland ascending that staircase that I've seen it somewhere before, and not on Washington Square. In fact, while the Hollywood sets for *The Heiress* are a hybrid of various mid-century New York townhouses, that staircase is a replica of one in a home only a few blocks away at 29 East Fourth Street. Today known as the Merchant's House Museum, it is the best preserved early-nineteenth-century townhouse in the city, and its preservation owes much to the fact that from 1835 until 1933, it was occupied by just one family: that of hardware merchant Seabury Tredwell.

The front entry to Gertrude Tredwell's home at 29 East Fourth Street.

Seabury Tredwell's youngest daughter, Gertrude, was born in the house in 1840, and died there in 1933. In those ninety-three years, amazingly, very little had changed. She'd kept the furnishings her father had brought with them when they first moved in. Even the chandeliers were still gas. As the city grew and changed around Gertrude, she was holding onto the past. Without intending to, she had maintained much more than a house; she'd preserved an entire way of life.

Gertrude had never married. According to some, she had just one suitor, whom her father rebuffed, and Gertrude had never wanted to settle for another man. As I watch Olivia de Havilland climb those stairs, I realize it's not just that banister that *The Heiress* lifted from the Merchant's House. Though Catherine Sloper isn't Gertrude Tredwell, the parallels of women choosing their destiny in a man's world are striking.

When Henry James wrote *Washington Square* in 1881, he placed Catherine Sloper's house on the north side of the park, just west of Fifth Avenue. His readers would have known exactly what this meant about the Slopers' social and economic status; by the 1880s, the north side of the square had become synonymous with an entrenched, conservative upper middle class for which Dr. Sloper was the perfect symbol. The houses on the east side of Fifth Avenue, a terrace of nearly identical Greek Revival homes built in 1831, were so famous that one didn't even need to refer to them by their address. They were simply "the Row."

I often start our tours of Greenwich Village steps away from where Catherine Sloper would have lived. We begin under the shadow of Stanford White's monumental Washington Square Arch, a relic of the area's brief flirtation with Gilded Age architecture. It's the perfect place to absorb the sights and sounds of modern Washington Square: children frolic on playground equipment; a doo-wop group practices under the arch; a reedy busker channels Bob Dylan.

Not only does this version of the square bear little relation to the place dedicated as the Washington Memorial Parade-Ground on July 4, 1826, it completely masks an even older history. Underneath the park's asphalt and grass are the bodies of countless New Yorkers buried between 1797 and 1825.

When I begin the tour telling people they are standing on top of thousands of dead bodies, I'm not sure what disturbs them more: the fact that they're treading on corpses, or the fact that the city had so little regard for these bodies that no one bothered to re-inter them elsewhere when the square was built. In those days, few New Yorkers cared.

In the late eighteenth century, most of the land north of what would become Washington Square was owned by Stephen DeLancey's son-in-law, Peter Warren (who, though later an admiral, was a pirate), and Captain Thomas Randall (also a pirate).

In 1797, the city opened the graveyard just south of the Warren and Randall farms to inter its poorest citizens. At the time, the worst seasonal killer was yellow fever, and each summer, wealthier New Yorkers fled the confines of the city—most coming to the Village. Unfortunately, those who could not afford to relocate were more likely to succumb to the disease. The future home of Washington Square was where the city dumped the bodies.

Local landowners were livid when the graveyard opened. Alexander Hamilton, a Randall family friend, fired off a letter complaining on behalf of those who had "at great expense erected dwellings . . . for the health and accommodation of their families during the Summer season." Not only would a cemetery drive down property values, it might import the very sickness from which they were trying to escape. It was a commonly held belief that the miasma (the noxious vapors emanating from the graves) would be harmful if inhaled.

That same year, Thomas Randall died—probably not from the miasma—and his eldest son Robert inherited the farm. Just four years later, Robert grew ill, and days before he died, he drew up a will designating that the land be used for a home for the "aged, worn-out, and decrepit sailors" that had crewed alongside his father. This new organization was to be called Sailors' Snug Harbor.

In creating Snug Harbor, Robert disinherited his entire family. At the time, in what was called an "old New York will," every relative, even distant cousins, expected to inherit; as Edith Wharton later explained, a person's "kin benefited in proportion to their consanguinity," all the way down to cousins many times removed.

Not surprisingly, Robert's family sued, sparking a protracted legal battle that would take decades to resolve. His brother Paul, who'd fled to France to escape debtor's prison, died there in 1820, broke, waiting for the dispute to be settled.

In 1822, Greenwich Village changed radically. That summer, the city saw the worst yellow fever outbreak in its history, forcing city leaders to impose a quarantine. So many people fled the city that one observer reported that in the West Village "a hotel of rough boards, capable of holding 500 guests, had gone up between Saturday and Monday in a field where the ripe wheat was waving Saturday." That may be an exaggeration, but it gives a sense of just how quickly people were leaving the city for healthier climes. Almost overnight, the Village changed from country to city.

Today, the best place to see the neighborhood's moment of transition is to walk down Grove Street, one of the oldest streets in the Village. From Waverly Place, it runs west, dead-ending at Hudson Street, which was once the last street before the island sloped down to the water's edge.

At Grove and Hudson, Clement Clarke Moore erected the area's first Episcopal Church, St. Luke in the Fields in 1821. It still stands, a rare example of a plain, Federal-style brick country church. Moore, whose Chelsea farmhouse was about a half-hour's walk to the north, had acquired the property so that churchgoers in the Village and outlying areas wouldn't have to commute all the way to Lower Manhattan on a Sunday morning.

Soon after the church was dedicated, the 1822 quarantine was imposed and the population of the Village soared. That year, one block east of the church, a window-sash maker named William Hyde erected a two-story clapboard house, along with a small workshop in the back. The house is not only one of the area's most charming buildings, but is also a wonderful reminder that as people raced to move to the Village that summer, they would have needed skilled craftsmen to build their homes. The work here—from the shutters to the six-over-six double-hung windows— speaks to Hyde's skill. I can picture people getting off boats from the city at the Christopher Street pier, spying this house, and saying, "Yes—that's what I want."

On tours, after I bring people to St. Luke's, I will come to this corner to talk about William Hyde, but I often find myself competing with the hordes of tourists, cameras in hand, taking photos of the nondescript apartment building that faces the Hyde house. Eventually, I'll stop talking about window sashes and yellow fever and point to the apartment building, "They used that for the exterior shots on the TV show *Friends*."

Suddenly, the cameras in my group are out too, and people are posing in front of the restaurant (today called the Little Owl) that was supposed to be Central Perk. It's the only place in the entire city where I can be guaranteed to have people stop for pictures. It's strange that what resonates most as a "real" New York place is from a 1990s television show where 99 percent of the scenes (including the famous fountain in the credits) were shot on a Hollywood soundstage.

I've never had the chance to go inside the Hyde house, which remains a private residence, but when you're a tour guide and hang out enough outside the same buildings, locals will strike up conversations with you. I've talked to house employees, watching their eyes widen as they describe the 1822 wide-plank floors. I've been stopped by long-term West Village residents who will point out that James Baldwin liked to hang out at the house, or that the woman who inspired the Barbie doll once lived there. Like a lot of Village stories, these may be lore, but even myths enrich the experience. One day, Joey Campanaro, the chef/owner of the Little Owl, came out and gestured at the roof of the Hyde house. On the cornice is a ceramic owl to scare away pigeons. He saw it and decided it would be the perfect name for his new venture.

When I come across an old episode of *Friends* on television, what always makes me pause is when the camera pans across the street and shows the Hyde house, in all its wood-frame glory. Some local residents were peeved whenever the *Friends* crew would show up, trampling flower beds and generally acting annoying. But I like the fact that every day, in countries around the world, this little pocket of the old Village gets beamed into people lives.

❧

Following the 1822 quarantine, the population of the Village grew rapidly. In 1825 or 1826, Lafayette Place, a five-minute walk east of Washington Square, was cut south from Astor Place to Great Jones Street. The lots on the west side of Lafayette, owned by the Astor family, were put on the market, and in 1830, developer Seth Geer began constructing La Grange Terrace, a row of nine gleaming, marble townhouses.

Removed from the hubbub of Broadway and the Bowery, La Grange Terrace appealed to the city's wealthiest citizens. The houses were gigantic by any standard—most had twenty-six rooms. Even though New York would not get running water until 1842, La Grange Terrace somehow had indoor plumbing, as well as central heat. John Jacob Astor purchased No. 37; Warren Delano, grandfather of Franklin Delano Roosevelt, resided at No. 39. Other residents included other Astor family members, a future two-term governor, and Julia Gardiner, who would soon marry President John Tyler.

Today, only four of the original nine buildings remain, and they are in a sad state. The marble is crumbling and badly discolored. A hodgepodge of penthouse additions mar the roof line. Even standing across the street to take in all four buildings at once, I'm hard-pressed to see the elegance that was once there.

But one day when I'm uptown at the Metropolitan Museum, I stumble upon some fragments of La Grange Terrace. In the Charles Engelhard Court in the American wing, off to one side, is a fragment of a giant column. This, it turns out, once adorned the front of one of the demolished houses on Lafayette Place. I'm impressed not only by its size, but by how much it looks like it could have just been carved. These columns spread across the terrace in the 1830s must have dazzled, both with their beauty and their expense.

Then, I discover a period room with furnishings inspired by La Grange Terrace. There's even a mantelpiece set into the wall that may have come from one of the demolished homes. It's not much, but I'm beginning to understand that these houses weren't just neoclassical on the outside. During this first wave of Greek Revival architecture, everything from sofas to mirrors to hall clocks reflected America's growing obsession with antiquity.

Part of this stemmed from America's desire, in the age of Andrew Jackson, to stress the ancient roots of democracy and a certain level of erudition. Scholar Talbot Hamlin pointed out that our embrace of Greek styles (more of a catch-all neoclassicism) also showed our support for Greek independence. The Greeks themselves, who were fighting the Ottoman Empire at the time, probably would have preferred if we'd just sent guns. Instead, what they got was an America filled with miniature temples, scroll-foot chairs, and Greek-key crown molding.

The refined air of Lafayette Place spread to the surrounding streets. Bond Street, Great Jones Street, and East 4th Street all began to lure wealthier New Yorkers to live "above Bleecker." In 1832, a hatter named Joseph Brewster built a house at 29 East 4th Street; three years later, Seabury Tredwell would purchase this house and move in with his wife and seven children.

Little is known about the background of the Tredwell house. The report accompanying its nomination for the National Register of Historic Places attributes it to architect Minard Lafever, but that attribution is far from secure. In most cases, architects and builders were one and the same, and builders relied on pattern books, such as Asher Benjamin's *Practical House Carpenter* or Lafever's *The Modern Builder's Guide*. There's a chance that Brewster designed the building himself following Lafever's guidelines.

We do know that the Tredwells began occupying the house in 1835, moving from Dey Street in Lower Manhattan, a block from St. Paul's Chapel. The

Tredwells sold the Dey Street house in November and probably moved that month, just weeks before the devastating Great Fire of 1835 destroyed the final vestiges of the old Dutch- and English-colonial city. Over the course of three freezing days, hundreds of buildings burned down; the city's volunteer firefighters, unable to find any water that wasn't frozen, were helpless to do anything. The Tredwells' Dey Street house was outside the path of the fire, but it was just one more sign to New York's richest citizens that living above Bleecker Street was the right thing to do.

To step inside the Tredwell house today is to almost see it as the Tredwells did that first day in 1835. Though some furnishings were acquired later, many pieces came with them, including a dining room set by master American craftsman Duncan Phyfe that had been purchased in 1815.

Like any guest, you must enter the house by climbing the seven steps of the entry stoop to reach the door. The stoop was one of the essential elements of a New York home. First and foremost, it was about household traffic. In a city that had almost no back alleys, servants and tradesmen were forced to enter houses from the street. To separate those who lived in the house from those who worked there, two entrances were always built at the front: one at the top of the stoop for the owners; one hidden beneath the stoop for the servants.

Over time, stoops came to serve as shorthand for the wealth of the residents. A house set back from the pavement allowed for a grander stoop. As front doors became wider (the one in *The Heiress* is immense compared to the actual ones on Washington Square or the one here at Gertrude Tredwell's home), stoops had to grow wider as well. Big doors meant big furniture, and the width of an entry staircase became a proxy for knowing how lavish the furnishing inside must be. It was the three-car garage of its day.

Once inside, a servant would take your calling card and show you into the front parlor. All New York houses were built on the same basic layout: kitchen and informal dining room downstairs, a front and back parlor on the main floor—separated, as need be, by sliding pocket doors—and bedrooms above.

When I visit the house, there's no servant to greet me, take my gloves and hat, or show me to the parlor. Instead, I make my way to the back of the building, where a small sunroom has been converted into the ticket office and gift shop.

Whenever I go to the house and confess my interest in Gertrude Tredwell, no one ever says, "Because of *The Heiress*?" Instead, they nod sagely and begin to talk about her ghost. I shouldn't be surprised: Gertrude the spectral figure seems to intrigue more people than Gertrude the historical person. Her ghost has been featured in countless television programs and books of ghost stories. But I'm more interested in her life than her afterlife.

Tours of the Tredwell house examine every facet of a nineteenth-century life. The household would have been managed by Seabury's wife, Eliza, along with her five daughters. Though many women had little agency in the nineteenth century outside the home, they ruled the domestic sphere. In part, this meant hiring servants, budgeting household expenses, and shopping for food and essentials. But it also meant playing an integral social function in their husbands' businesses. As Mary L. Knapp points out in *An Old Merchant's House,* the New York custom of paying social calls—where women would drop in on each other for ten to fifteen minutes at a time—served to grease the wheels of commerce. "A woman carried not only her cards, but her husband's as well. She would leave two of her husband's cards—one for the lady of the house, and one for the husband." Knapp notes that when a woman married, she was signing up for decades of social calls. No wonder an anonymously authored treatise from 1852 extolled the virtues of "single blessedness."

Much of the daily routine in the Tredwell house revolved around the basement kitchen. The Tredwells employed servants—in 1855, four Irish women lived in the house with the family—who would have taken care of cooking, cleaning, and other household chores. Against the far wall, a beehive stove was kept busy with breads and pies, which were eaten with most meals. By another wall, a perforated pie safe stands as reminder that foods had to be kept as fresh as possible without refrigeration. (The Tredwells would have had an icebox, but it was for keeping items like butter and milk from going rancid.)

When the family was alone, they would have dined in the basement, in a small room at the front of the house, where they could admire the feet of passersby. Upstairs, the back parlor could also be used as a dining room, but this was reserved for more formal entertaining.

On the upper floors, the bedrooms are comfortably sized, but not huge; it's hard to imagine all of the Tredwells living there at once. At one point, after daughters Mary Adelaide and Elizabeth had married—but had not moved out—eighteen people lived in the house, including four servants and three small children.

There's something especially compelling about the servants' quarters in the attic. From census figures we know the names of some of the Tredwells' servants, but even so, they remain elusive. They would have trudged up and down these stairs countless times a day as they made the beds, served the food, and tended to every household need. By the end of the day, lying underneath these huge dormer windows, they must have been exhausted.

It's staring out these dormers that I really get a sense of the scale of the house. The rooms are small and plain, but the dormers are huge, and they put the entire building into scale. As I walk back down the staircase to the parlor floor—imagining, perhaps, that I'm Catherine Sloper, still flushed with the excitement of having a gentleman caller, or that I'm one of the Tredwells' maids making this trip for the umpteenth time that day—the overwhelming space of the house unfolds before me.

In 1826, businessman Philip Hone was appointed to a two-year term as mayor, which would be a catalyst for the development of the neighborhood.

On taking office, Mayor Hone faced the first major challenge to the 1811 Commissioners' Plan: a proposal to do away with the military parade ground at Madison Square that had appeared on John Randel Jr.'s original survey. With the city poised for expansion, the Common Council was regretting having kept such good real estate from development. Parade grounds served a civic vital function—but did militia companies *really* need so much space to drill?

Another item on Hone's agenda was America's fiftieth birthday—the semi-centennial of the ratification of the Declaration of Independence— which was just six months away. The mayor thought New York, as America's largest city and first capital, should host the national jubilee. The obvious location for such a celebration would be the military parade ground, but now the Common Council wanted to get rid of that.

In a stroke of genius, the mayor found a solution. He asked the Common Council to annex the Greenwich Village potter's field as a new military parade ground, which he would also use as the site for his party. The graveyard, which had closed the year before, had outlived its usefulness. And this wasn't just a short-term fix. Hone was playing a long game, and this new "Washington Parade-Ground" was just the opening gambit.

On July 4, 1826, the celebration began with the Seventh Regiment militia— of which Hone was a member—parading from Fulton Street to Castle Clinton to receive the regimental colors from Governor DeWitt Clinton.

Following the ceremony, Mayor Hone, Governor Clinton, and the senior officers rode to the brand-new Washington Parade-Ground.

The *New-York Evening Post* estimated fifty thousand people passed through the parade ground that day—almost one-third of the city's population. When the party had been cleaned up, New York had its militia training ground—at least on paper.

Mayor Hone knew better—he knew it was a park. Soon, the city purchased the land east and west of the former graveyard and began landscaping. By 1828, the pretense that Washington Square was a place for militia companies to drill had been almost entirely dropped.

Then, in 1830, the case of Inglis vs. the Trustees of Sailors' Snug Harbor (Inglis was one of Robert Randall's cousins) reached the United States Supreme Court, which ruled decisively in favor of the foundation. All claimants were denied. Since the newly landscaped Washington Square was already a springboard for rising real estate values, Snug Harbor (which, not coincidentally, counted Philip Hone among its trustees) could now lease the land on the old Randall farm at a premium rate. Instead of housing the old sailors in this newly affluent neighborhood, they could instead use the proceeds of the land leases to put the sailors somewhere cheaper.

Within a year the foundation was soliciting proposals for a campus on rural Staten Island (ultimately built by Minard Lafever), and in 1830, the first Randall farm leases were drawn up for what was to become the Row. (In all likelihood, the fictional Slopers would have moved to No. 16 Washington Square around the same time.)

The Randall farm lots were huge—on average twenty-seven feet wide—and deep enough to accommodate stables along a carriage mews in the back. To ensure high-caliber residents, a number of "covenants and conditions" were attached to the leases. These included forbidding the establishment of any "manufactory, trade, business or calling whatsoever, which may be in anywise noxious or offensive to the neighboring inhabitants."

These provisions were designed to attract some of New York's first commuters. Soon horse-drawn omnibuses were hauling businessmen downtown to the Financial District; for the first time, there was a complete separation of work life from the domestic sphere. Today, most people think nothing of the fact that every morning they will have to travel to another neighborhood—or a completely different city—for work; in the Tredwells' generation, it was a novelty and another marker of status. For many working-class New Yorkers, whose only transportation was their own two feet, work and home remained close together until the dawn of the twentieth century.

The lessees on the Row also agreed to "erect and build a good and substantial dwelling house, of the width of said lot, three or more stories high, in brick or stone," to be built "12 feet back of and parallel" with Washington Square North. These mandates about height and building materials spoke to the economic status of the people the foundation hoped to attract. Cheaper houses were still made out of wood, which was the least expensive—and least desirable—building material. By contrast, bricks were still handmade, thus adding to their cost. People find the William Hyde house charming today, but many in the 1820s would have considered it down-market; after the Great Fire, wood houses only appeared in the city's poorer quarters.

The Row was finished by 1832; by this time—just six years after Philip Hone had created the parade ground—the square had firmly established itself as the center of Greenwich Village and of the Fifteenth Ward, its new common council district. Today, names of streets like Great Jones, East Fourth, and Lafayette don't conjure up ideas of refinement, but for the Astors, Tredwells, and Philip Hone, these were the hallmarks of status. The only name that still lingers in our collective memory—thanks, certainly in part, to Henry James—is Washington Square, and these elite houses on the Row.

❧

There's no evidence that Henry James crossed paths with Gertrude Tredwell, but even though New York was a huge city by 1881 when he wrote *Washington Square*, he probably knew who she was. James had been born just three years after Gertrude in a house on Washington Place, a short walk from the Tredwells. The families of the Fifteenth Ward might not have all traveled in the same circles, but they certainly occupied similar spaces. The world James knew growing up was so similar to Gertrude's as to be almost identical.

Is Gertrude Tredwell the model for Catherine Sloper? James wrote in his journal that the anecdote had come from his friend, actress Fanny Kemble, who regaled James one evening with the story of her brother Henry's unsuccessful attempt to woo a young woman named Mary Ann Thackeray for her money.

Still, Gertrude Tredwell's story shows clear similarities. According to Mary L. Knapp, Tredwell family lore always maintained that Gertrude had a suitor, Louis Walton, whom her father rejected out of hand because he was

Catholic. When Gertrude couldn't marry him, she—like Catherine Sloper—chose to marry no one rather than give up on her soul mate.

I wish we could know directly from her, but she kept no diary; or, perhaps she did and it was discarded when the home was being converted into a museum in the 1930s. Her cousin, George Chapman, who founded the museum, was much more interested in celebrating Seabury Tredwell's business accomplishments (it's called the Merchant's House Museum, after all) than the life of Gertrude, the only person who saw almost a century go by in the house. Perhaps Gertrude kept letters from Louis Walton all her life; we'll never know.

The ideal of romantic love above all else, popularized by authors such as Sir Walter Scott—the best-selling writer in America in his lifetime—had real currency in Gertrude's generation. There's a great moment in *The Heiress* when Dr. Sloper, played by Ralph Richardson, sneers at his daughter in disgust, "She's been taken in. She's in love."

Later, when Catherine Sloper's world has collapsed around her, she accuses her father of trying to ensure she remained, as Henry James called her, an old maid. "You'd like to think of me sitting in dignity in this handsome house, rich, respected, and unloved," she says.

This isn't how I think of Gertrude. Perhaps she did spend her life mourning the loss of Louis Walton, but she was at least a woman with choices, and she made them wisely. First, as Knapp suggests, she may have seen how much work was required in marriage and child-rearing—two older sisters continued to live with the family after their weddings—and said, "No, thank you." Marriage in the middle of the nineteenth century also meant a loss of autonomy, the subsuming of a woman's life into her husband's. For a woman with no money and few educational opportunities, marriage was often the only way to secure a roof over one's head. But that wasn't the case with Gertrude, who along with her sisters, inherited cash and property from her parents, which gave her a path to independence.

James paints Catherine Sloper as a lonely old spinster; Gertrude was not, though her decision to stay on East Fourth Street—as the neighborhood gave way to immigrants and manufacturing—did brand her an eccentric. Even as early as the 1860s, the area was changing; the *New York Times* noted that nearby Bond Street—only a few years earlier among the most fashionable addresses in the city—was "yielding to the irresistible tide of business."

Three other Tredwell sisters, Sarah, Phebe, and Julia, also never wed. Sarah moved to a hotel, but Phebe, Julia, and Gertrude lived together at 29

East Fourth until the years took them—Phebe in 1907, Julia in 1909. After Julia's death, a nephew moved in to help take care of Gertrude, but he died in 1930. Still, Gertrude was never alone. She had servants and paid caretakers all the way up to her death in 1933. In her final years, money was tight, but she owned the house outright and lived a frugal life within her limited means.

I admire the fact that Gertrude's life is the antithesis of our consumer culture. The house is such a perfect time capsule not because she was eccentric, but because she didn't feel the need to waste money on new furniture when she already owned magnificent pieces, like the Duncan Phyfe chairs. She didn't bother to have her house wired top-to-bottom for electricity when candles and oil-lamps would do. One way to think about Gertrude is to see her mired in the past, but I think that misses an essential element of her personality. Our faster-farther-better-newer culture tends to preserve things because they have educational or artistic merit. We view them as objects that can impart lessons from the past. Gertrude simply lived in that past because it was the place she wanted to be. Every item in the house was a touchstone; any one of them could have pulled her back to the raucous days when all eighteen of them—her father in his study, her mother in the parlor, the children in the garden—had made the house their home.

It's this spirit that I like to think of as haunting 29 East Fourth Street—a spirit of the past, to be sure, but also the spirit of an independent woman doing exactly as she pleased.

Washington Irving and His Friends at Sunnyside by Christian Schussele.

CHAPTER 7

"A Ghastly Poverty":
Edgar Allan Poe

In 1864, Christian Schussele completed an oil painting, *Washington Irving and His Friends at Sunnyside*. The portrait—widely distributed as a print—was designed to venerate Irving, who had died five years earlier, surrounding him with fourteen literary peers and acolytes. Together, these men represented the zenith of American letters. Upon its completion, the *New York Times* dubbed it "the best national picture ever painted in America."

Today, some of the names of Irving's friends are commonplace: James Fenimore Cooper, Nathaniel Hawthorne, Henry Wadsworth Longfellow,

Ralph Waldo Emerson. Irving himself has dropped a few notches in the public's memory, but people still remember he wrote "The Legend of Sleepy Hollow." The remaining ten men have suffered less charitable fates. William Hickling Prescott and Nathaniel Parker Willis aren't on very many "must-read" lists. William Cullen Bryant is better remembered as a newspaper editor (and early champion of Central Park) than for his poetry. Once-popular poet Fitz-Greene Halleck was drinking away his legacy by the time he sat for the portrait. He died three years later, and while his friends put up a statue to him on the Mall in Central Park, it didn't salvage his reputation.

What intrigues me, however, is who's left out of the painting. Where's Hawthorne's friend Herman Melville? And where's the man who is today the best-selling and best-known American of this period, Edgar Allan Poe?

Poe's absence from this painting reflects his long banishment from America's literary canon. When he died in Baltimore in 1849—suggestions of what killed him range from murder to rabies to alcohol poisoning to a brain tumor—he had achieved a small measure of celebrity with stories such as "The Gold Bug," "The Pit and the Pendulum," and "The Mystery of Marie Rogêt." His best-known work was "The Raven," a poem which netted him nine dollars when it was first published. Beyond that, fame—and certainly fortune—were elusive. Soon after Poe's death, his literary executor, Rufus Griswold, set out to sully Poe's name and denigrate his writings. (Note to future writers: Don't appoint someone with whom you've had a longstanding feud as your literary executor.) By the time Schussele painted *Washington Irving and His Friends,* Poe was known to the world as a degenerate drunk.

Only some of this can be blamed on Griswold. During his life, Poe did plenty on his own to sully his legacy. For a start, Poe suffered from what he called the "ghastly poverty" of being an occasional magazine editor and contributor. While financial success wasn't the same as critical success, a few bestsellers might have gone a long way toward securing Poe some fame.

More to the point, in 1846, he'd published a series of gossipy sketches under the title "The Literati of New York City," critiquing the literary scene. Though some writers were singled out for praise, most were excoriated. The talents of Nathaniel Parker Willis—the most successful magazine writer of his day—were put down to one-third "mental ability" and two-thirds "physical temperament" (i.e., good looks). Poe damned Fitz-Greene Halleck with faint praise, ranking him a few steps below Longfellow, whom he thought a hack and a plagiarist.

Poe spurned the literary world he wished to join. If Schussele had chosen to include him in the portrait, he probably would have placed him to the far right of the canvas, his nose forlornly pressed against the glass.

On West Third Street, just south of Washington Square Park, there's a three-story brick townhouse facade that's almost completely swallowed by Furman Hall, a New York University law school building, which surrounds it left, right, and above.

I've been loitering down the block since 8:50 in the morning waiting for signs of life. At nine o'clock a tourist couple standing at the house's front door try the handle. At 9:01 they peer in the window. At 9:02, they shrug and walk away.

I go up to the door and try it myself, unsurprised to find it locked. I peer through the louvered blinds. For a moment, expecting to see something akin to a nineteenth-century front parlor, I'm taken aback by the twenty-first-century vestibule behind this wall. This shouldn't have come as a shock—I've known for years that no matter its claims, this isn't really Poe's house.

Poe did live on this block, farther down the street at 85 Amity Street (as West Third was known in Poe's day). In the fall of 1845, he moved into a Greek Revival townhouse-turned-boardinghouse, where he shared rooms with his wife, Virginia, and his mother-in-law, Maria Clemm. This brick facade in front of me, however, has no connection to that building except in name. It's not even a reasonable facsimile.

Through the window, I can see a small display of artifacts in a glass case; I'm guessing they relate to Poe, but from the outside I can't know for sure. I go around the corner to Furman Hall's main entrance, where the guard confirms that he's "heard of" the Poe Study Center. He also tells me that there's no one there who can assist me, but that he's happy to have me wait.

I decline—I've seen plenty.

The story of the Poe Study Center is one chapter in a larger battle between NYU and the community, and between preservationists and the city's Landmarks Preservation Commission. I don't envy New York City's landmarks commissioners; most of the time, their job seems to entail making people angry. Developers complain that they stymie creativity and urban renewal.

Preservationists gnash their teeth every time a significant building is torn down. This triggers the essential question: What makes a building significant?

Edgar Allan Poe lived in New York three times: for a few weeks in 1831, after he'd purposefully gotten himself court-martialed from West Point; from 1837 to 1838, arriving during a disastrous, nationwide economic slump; and again from 1844 until his death five years later.

Other cities have stronger associations with him: Richmond, where he was raised, worked, and married Virginia (his thirteen-year-old first cousin); Philadelphia, where he wrote some of his best-known mystery and horror stories; and Baltimore, where he died and later had a football team named for his most famous poem. But it was in New York—which by the 1830s was becoming the center of America's literary scene—where Poe hoped to make his mark.

The Poes lived nine places in the city, seven of them in just a two-year period, a striking contrast to Gertrude Tredwell, who lived all of her ninety-three years in the same spot. The Poes moved as their finances and Virginia's health required. She had contracted tuberculosis in 1842 in Philadelphia, coughing up blood one day as she played the piano. Poe spent much of the rest of her short life tending to her.

Having published "The Raven" in the *New York Evening Mirror* in January 1845, Poe set to work at 85 Amity Street revising the poem for *The Raven and Other Poems,* published that November. He also began his series "Literati of New York City" while residing at 85 Amity, and may have written the bulk of "The Cask of Amontillado" at the boardinghouse too.

By the dawn of the twenty-first century this was the only Poe home in Manhattan still standing. With that in mind, it's logical to assume it would have merited at least some consideration by the Landmarks Preservation Commission. But in 2000, the commission declined to even hold a hearing. On one hand, this seemed ironic—back in 1969, when creating the Greenwich Village Historic District, the commissioners cited Poe as one of the literary figures whose residence made the neighborhood historically important. Yet, at that time, they had not extended the landmark district's boundaries the one block necessary to include the Poe house. Three decades later, the commission was not going to raise NYU's considerably powerful ire by revisiting that decision.

Not everyone agreed that the house was worth saving. Kenneth Silverman, a Poe scholar employed by NYU, pointed out that the building had been so significantly altered since 1845 that Poe wouldn't even recognize it as his own home. He had a point: The stoop had been removed, and the lower floors turned into commercial space. Arched window frames replaced the Greek Revival originals; an incongruous tiled awning jutted out between the second and third stories.

What's more maddening than the Landmarks Preservation Commission's decision—or, more accurately, their abdication from making a decision—is what NYU did next. In an eleventh-hour move to placate the community, they agreed to rebuild the facade of Poe's house as part of the new building, install the home's staircase inside, and provide a room for Poe readings and events. No one was ecstatic about this, but it was better than nothing.

Instead, what people got was worse than nothing. The scaffolding came down from Furman Hall in October 2003 to reveal an ersatz Poe home. Nothing had been preserved; nothing had been rebuilt. It wasn't even in the right spot.

"Unfortunately, there was not enough of the original bricks to use on the full facade," an NYU associate dean told the *New York Times*. "What we did instead was save a portion of them, and put a panel inside the room of the original bricks."

I don't dispute this account. I imagine that the building was probably held together by little more than inertia. But I've always suspected NYU knew there wouldn't be anything they could save. The agreement they'd brokered called on them merely to make a "good faith effort" to save Poe's house. I wonder how much effort was actually expended.

I have a little time to kill when I leave NYU—time I would have used to examine the panel of bricks inside the study center—and I walk toward Waverly Place to grab a coffee at my favorite cafe. The cafe sits a few doors west of Sixth Avenue, near the spot where another of the Poes' boardinghouses once stood.

At the time, Sixth Avenue would have acted as a dividing line between two very different sections of Greenwich Village. There was the Fifteenth Ward to the east, with its genteel houses of the Row on Washington Square, and the homes of people like Seabury Tredwell, John Jacob Astor, and Philip Hone. Then, there was the area west of Sixth Avenue, which was becoming more crowded with tradesmen and servants every year.

It hadn't always been this way. Before the yellow fever outbreak of 1822, most of the western section of Greenwich Village had been dotted with country estates. The most famous of these was Richmond Hill, Aaron Burr's home. Today, only one mansion remains: the 1830 Samuel Whittemore home on Grove Street.

I detour to take a look at the Whittemore house; despite much alteration—including the addition of two stories in 1871—the building has maintained much of its late-Federal style. Poe would certainly recognize this building.

By the time the Poes moved to the neighborhood, Richmond Hill had been converted into a theater (it would be demolished in 1849, the year of Poe's death). The Whittemores still owned their mansion, but in 1851, they would finally accept that the neighborhood had inexorably changed and sell. The new owners converted the building into a boardinghouse. While newly arrived immigrants generally clustered in ethnic enclaves such as Five Points and Little Germany, struggling Americans, like Poe, flocked to boarding-houses. By some estimates, as much as 30 percent of New York's population lived in boardinghouses, where cheap rent bought you an eight-by-six room and three meals a day. Even John Jacob Astor and Seabury Tredwell had lived in boardinghouses before getting married. (In fact, both men had married their landladies' daughters.)

I circle back on Grove Street until it dead-ends on Waverly Place; here, a block from the Poes' boardinghouse, is one of the most famous buildings in the Village, the Northern Dispensary. Noteworthy for its triangular design, this Greek Revival building dates from 1831. It was a low-cost clinic, staffed by paid and volunteer doctors, established to do philanthropic work in the neighborhood. Samuel Whittemore himself was a trustee here.

Many Poe biographers take it as gospel that the author was treated here in 1837 for "a head cold." If he'd fallen ill while living down the block, it makes sense that this was the place he'd go. Other historians are more skeptical. Stories abound in Greenwich Village that have no basis in fact—more here, I think, than in any other neighborhood. I've passed more than one tour guide standing in front of the Whittemore mansion talking about how John Wilkes Booth planned the Lincoln assassination there. (Booth confided his plans to a boarder at the house in 1865, but that's all.) Nearby, a plaque at one end of Commerce Street details the cherry trees that once grew there (they didn't); at the other end of the street sit two homes that were not built by a ship captain for his feuding daughters—as the oft-repeated legend would have it—but by a milkman looking to make some rental income. I could conduct an entire tour of lies, rumors, and innuendo in Greenwich Village. Perhaps the area's literary history has simply made everyone a storyteller. I'm sure Poe, who loved hoaxes, would approve.

There's another unproven story attached to Poe in Greenwich Village, which concerns the profusion of churches in the area. No matter where Poe lived, he was always bugged by noise. In 1844 he wrote, "the amount of general annoyances wrought by street-noises is incalculable; and this matter is worthy our very serious attention." And it wasn't just workdays; on Sunday mornings he would be rudely awakened by what he later put down in poetry as "the tintinnabulation of the bells."

Maybe he and Virginia moved around so much because they were trying to escape those pesky bells.

———— ❦ ————

On a chilly spring morning, Spike and I are running in Riverside Park on the Upper West Side. As usual, I'm searching for something and he's just along for the ride. We jog down the Robert Moses–era promenade, past the World War II memorial to the Jewish victims from the Warsaw ghetto, and stop at a large outcropping of Manhattan schist. Embedded in the stone is a bronze plaque dedicated to Cyrus Clark.

"Who's Cyrus Clark?" Spike asks.

(Admittedly, I have no idea; I look him up later and discover he founded the West Side Association and fought to preserve and expand the park.)

As I'm taking pictures of the plaque, a woman walking her dogs looks at us strangely. People take photos of all sorts of odd things in New York, but no tourist would ever bother with something this esoteric, and locals are so used to the plaque that it blends into the scenery. She assumes we're up to no good and gives us a wide berth. Honestly, I'm used to it; I've taken photos of stranger things in the name of research.

In fact, it isn't even this piece of schist that I've come to see. Spike and I climb the nearby hill and I begin taking pictures of an equally unimpressive pile of stone. This is Mount Tom. It may seem like dozens of other rocky promontories that litter New York City parks, but this one is special—this is where Poe composed "The Raven."

Even Spike is impressed.

Poe's literary importance is so vast that it's hard to believe that he accomplished so much in such an abbreviated lifetime. With "The Murders in the Rue Morgue," he invented detective fiction and became master of the form. He remains the undisputed king of gothic horror. His poetry appealed to the masses and critics alike. His own criticism, while often stinging, peeled back the veneer on the old boy's club that was American letters. He argued passionately for greater copyright and royalty protections for authors. He had a wicked sense of humor, and in 1844 perpetrated the "Great Balloon

Hoax," convincing unsuspecting readers of the *New York Sun* that the Atlantic had been crossed in three days by hot air balloon.

Yet, it's "The Raven" that holds a special place in the public's imagination. It's always been this way. The artist Edward Valentine recollected as a child going out on the street to see the famous Edgar Allan Poe walk by. Other children ran behind him, croaking "Nevermore!"

After leaving New York in 1838, the Poes returned to the city in 1844 without Maria Clemm, first living in a boardinghouse at 130 Greenwich Street, a stone's throw from Trinity Church and near all of the newspaper and magazine publishing houses. As Virginia's tuberculosis worsened in 1844, the Poes took the only advice most doctors could give: move out of the city and get her into cleaner air.

By this point, Virginia's mother was back with them; they rented rooms from Patrick and Mary Brennan in "an old-fashioned, double-framed" farmhouse on the west side on what would eventually be 84th Street. The house was surrounded by 216 acres of woods. According to one of Poe's earliest biographers, the family "received no visitors, and took their meals in their room by themselves." Mrs. Brennan recalled Poe as a "shy, solitary, taciturn person, fond of rambling alone through the woods or of sitting on a favorite stump of a tree near the banks of the Hudson River." In Poe's era, Riverside Park had not been created, and the waterfront was not yet developed this far north. This meant Poe probably didn't actually scramble all the way down the Hudson's banks for his reveries; he watched the river drift by from the top of Mount Tom.

The Poes' room—unaltered until the house was torn down in 1888—was small but filled with light, having windows that faced the river on one side and the Brennans' forest on the other. Years later, people who knew the house recollected that the Poes' room was exactly like the chamber in "The Raven," complete with the "pallid bust of Pallas" above the door. This may have been wishful thinking, but the house does seem, from photos and drawings, to have been a pleasant place. Pleasant enough, in retrospect, to make one almost forget the Poes' straitened circumstances. Poe had difficulty making the rent. For much of his marriage, he had trouble putting food on the table. When Poe won a $225 judgment in a libel lawsuit, he used the money to buy some furnishings and a new suit; he could never afford to own more than one suit at a time, and the previous one was probably beyond repair.

Most inconveniently, the Brennan house's distance from the city may have provided fresh air, but it also meant that any time Poe needed to meet with a publisher, he either had to take a stagecoach down the Bloomingdale Road—a costly inconvenience—or walk the ten miles round-trip.

Ultimately, it was this distance that drove them back to the city, probably to 15 Amity Street (creating a coherent Poe chronology is a maddening task), then to 195 East Broadway on the Lower East Side, before heading to 85 Amity Street sometime in the fall of 1845. Along the way, he started working for Nathaniel Parker Willis at the *New York Mirror* as a "mechanical paragraphist"—a catchall job that entailed copywriting and editing—after Maria Clemm begged Willis to give her son-in-law a job. Poe, who was never quite sure when to thank his friends or attack his enemies, later skewered Willis in "The Literati of New York City."

When the Brennan house was demolished in 1888, one item from the "Raven Room" was saved: a black mantel into which—the story goes—Poe absentmindedly scratched his name. The mantel was salvaged by William Hemstreet of Brooklyn, who installed it in his house. "I insisted on paying $5 for the relic of Poe and the greatest poem he ever wrote," Hemstreet said.

Twenty years later, Hemstreet offered the mantelpiece to "any public institution that will completely preserve it." In 1908, Columbia University's president, Nicholas Murray Butler, accepted the gift and appointed a committee to "select a suitable location" for the Poe mantel. Journalist Benjamin Waldman has traced the mantelpiece's journeys around Columbia, from Low Library to Philosophy Hall to the Rare Book and Manuscript library, where it remains to this day, almost—but not quite—on public view. It seems that after accepting the gift, the university didn't ever know what to do with it. (Frankly, when a friend snuck me in to visit the mantelpiece, I was more impressed by the case nearby where Columbia has Alexander Hamilton's wedding handkerchief and Eliza Hamilton's wedding ring.)

After the Poes left Amity Street—and, again, sources are contradictory—they moved to rural East 47th Street (near today's United Nations) for a few months in early 1846. By May, they'd left Manhattan completely for a farmhouse in the Fordham section of the Bronx, which they rented for one hundred dollars a year. This small cottage would be both Edgar and Virginia's final home.

When I visit the house, it's actually by happenstance; I've exited the subway a stop too early and find myself just north of what is known as Poe Cottage. A quick look at the sign informs me it's open for visitors.

Still, when I ring the bell, no one answers. This is becoming a habit with Poe places.

Actually, this isn't my first encounter with Poe's Bronx home. Years ago, when I was researching a possible tour of the environs of Fordham University and the Grand Concourse, I found myself in Poe Park. The park was shabby and the house was locked up tight—I later discovered it's only open weekends—but the whole place gave off the air of something forbidding, maybe even ominous. It was a sunny morning, but I was spooked. (It doesn't surprise me that this is where Bob Kane and Bill Finger hung out when they were inventing Batman.)

I ring the bell again, and just as I'm about to give up, the docent swings open the door.

"Can you wait here?" he asks. "I'm finishing up another tour."

I cool my heels in the cramped vestibule/gift shop, looking at reproductions of "The Raven" and Poe dolls. When the docent is finished with the previous visitors, he comes back to begin the tour. He explains that the house, built in 1812, is owned by the city, and as he rightfully points out, it's usually rich people's homes that are thrown open to the public—like Seabury Tredwell's—where you can see the trappings of wealth and power. This is the only house where you can picture what it's like to be dirt poor.

In the small parlor, the guide explains the dearth of furniture. Not only were the Poes poor, but after both Virginia and Edgar died, Maria Clemm was forced to sell off what few household furnishings they did have. All that remains that was definitely owned by the Poes are a plain, wicker rocking chair and Virginia's bed in the next room.

The bed is just heartbreaking. It was here that Virginia finally succumbed to tuberculosis on January 30, 1847. To keep her warm, Edgar and Maria covered her in every article of clothing they could find. The docent is telling another story, but I keep looking at the small rope bed, neatly covered now in a blanket. The sense of loss in the space is palpable.

Poe mourned the death of Virginia (he called her "Sis," and many scholars believe the marriage was never consummated), but her passing was in some ways liberating. He channeled his grief into his work, including his famous final poem, "Annabel Lee." When I read the lines of the final stanza ("And so, all the night-tide, I lie down by the side/Of my darling—my darling—my life and my bride"), I can picture Poe in this tiny room, holding the hand of his darling wife, as the life ebbs from her.

A year later, Poe wrote to his friend George W. Eveleth about the perpetual anxiety caused by Virginia's illness:

Six years ago, a wife, whom I loved as no man ever loved before, ruptured a blood-vessel in singing. Her life was despaired of. I took leave of her forever & underwent all the agonies of her death. She recovered partially and I again hoped. At the end of a year the vessel broke again—I went through precisely the same scene. . . . I became insane, with long intervals of horrible sanity.

But Poe concludes: "I had indeed, nearly abandoned all hope of a permanent cure when I found one in the *death* of my wife. . . . In the death of what was my life, then, I receive a new but—oh God! how melancholy an existence."

That melancholy existence must have been exacerbated out in the countryside, with no one in the house but Poe, his mother-in-law, and the cat. At least at the Upper West Side farmhouse, they'd had the Brennans and their children for company. In the Bronx, neighbors were remote. Poe would sometimes walk over to St. John's College (today Fordham University) to play cards with the Jesuits. He continued to write and publish—most notably the philosophical essay "Eureka" in 1848.

In the summer of 1849, Poe decided to find a new wife. He traveled to Richmond, where he proposed to Sarah Elmira Royster, to whom he had been secretly engaged in 1825 when he was very briefly a student at the University of Virginia. Royster's response is a mystery. Poe left her in Richmond on September 27, en route to New York via Baltimore. On October 3, he was found in Baltimore "in great distress" and apparently wearing another man's clothes. He was taken to the hospital where he slipped in and out of consciousness. On the morning of October 7, Poe died.

Two days later, Rufus Griswold—writing under the pseudonym "Ludwig"—published an obituary of Poe in the *New York Tribune*. Griswold opened by noting that "few will be grieved" by the poet's passing. He scolded Poe for being "irascible, envious . . . varnished over with a cold, repellant cynicism." While he praised the "masterly ingenuity of versification" in "The Raven," he had little else good to say. In life, Poe had been highly critical of Griswold's work as an editor; now, in death, it was time for Griswold to settle the score.

First, Griswold—a powerful figure in the publishing world—convinced Maria Clemm that Poe had appointed him his literary executor. Then, Griswold took it upon himself to seal Poe's legacy. While it's true that some of Poe's most famous poems, such as "The Bells" and "Annabel Lee," were published posthumously under Griswold's direction, Griswold did this for his own profit. In 1850, he oversaw a release of Poe's complete works—no money went to Poe's family—that included a libelous "memoir" which painted Poe as a drunkard and a madman.

Over a century and a half later it's this view of Poe—which was, to be certain, popularized by the films and recordings of Vincent Price—that remains. Dark, mysterious, creepy, dissipated, a loner, a social outcast . . . it's little wonder Christian Schussele didn't want Poe in his portrait, standing shoulder to shoulder with titans like James Fenimore Cooper and Washington Irving. It's hard to imagine those three sitting down for tea.

For ghost hunters, Poe is easy prey. According to *Ghosts of New York City*, his "psychic energy" ripples throughout Poe Cottage. *New York City Ghost Stories*, published in 1996, invites the curious to look for "Eddy" on the third floor of the now-defunct 85 Amity Street. (Maybe he now haunts NYU—it would serve them right.) Sometimes, he's seen in the company of Mary Rogers, the "beautiful cigar girl" who was murdered in 1841, and whose death became the basis for Poe's story, "The Mystery of Marie Rogêt."

Rogers, like Poe, arrived in New York in 1837, and began working as a clerk at Anderson's Tobacco Emporium at 319 Broadway in Lower Manhattan. On October 5, 1838, Mary disappeared, leaving behind an apparent suicide note. Her distraught mother, Phoebe, went to the police and the newspapers quickly reported the story. How many days Mary was missing is unclear—perhaps as much as two weeks—but she did return, unharmed, and claimed to have just been visiting friends. Some newspapers hinted that she'd been in the company of a "Lothario" or a naval officer; others put the whole affair down to a hoax perpetrated by Anderson's Tobacco Emporium to boost sales.

Mary, however, soon quit the cigar store to help her mother run a boardinghouse at 126 Nassau Street, near City Hall Park. Here she met a boarder named Daniel Payne; by the summer of 1841, despite her mother's objections, Payne and Rogers were engaged.

On July 25, Mary left the boardinghouse for a visit with her aunt on Jane Street, and asked Payne to meet her that evening when she returned. When the time came for Payne to meet her, it was pouring rain. Guessing that Mary wouldn't venture out in such weather, Payne figured she'd return in the morning.

Three days later, Mary's savagely beaten body was found floating in the Hudson River near Hoboken, a popular spot for New Yorkers on their days off.

Most people came to stroll along the River Walk and see the sporting teams at the Elysian Fields (the birthplace of modern baseball). One popular watering hole on that side of the river was Nick Moore's Tavern, run by Frederica Loss.

The newspapers jumped on the Mary Rogers story—it was, at that time, the most sensationalized murder investigation in American history—and Poe would have followed it in the Philadelphia and New York papers. Like the rest of the country, Poe would have been gripped by the salacious details of the case, but he might have had a more personal interest as well—he might have known Mary. Evidence for their connection is shaky, but years later, New York's police chief, George Walling, recalled in his memoir that numerous "prominent New Yorkers" knew Rogers at the cigar store. Among those on Walling's list were "[James] Fenimore Cooper, Washington Irving, N. P. Willis, and Edgar Allan Poe."

Though the newspapers came up with competing theories about Mary's death—ranging from gang rape at one extreme to her actually still being alive at the other—the police investigation ground to a halt. To complicate matters, Daniel Payne, who'd never seriously been considered a suspect, committed suicide. Was it remorse over killing Mary? Or simply grief over losing his betrothed?

At this point, Poe stepped into the mix. In order to bring back the private investigator who'd solved "The Murders in the Rue Morgue," C. Auguste Dupin, Poe moved the Rogers case to Paris, changed the river to the Seine, and Mary became Marie Rogêt.

In the story, Dupin is a stand-in for Poe. Reading only what the newspapers reported, the detective attempts to solve the case, ruling out, one-by-one, the more outrageous or untenable theories. Though Poe gave the newspapers French names, he didn't bother to rewrite the reports themselves, lifting whole passages from the *New York Herald* and the *Tattler*.

Poe arranged to have the new story serialized in *Ladies' Companion* in three monthly installments beginning in November 1842. The first installment sold so well that it was reprinted to accompany the second installment in early December. But as the magazine was preparing its end-of-year issue—and Poe's final installment—there was a development in the Mary Rogers case. Frederica Loss, the proprietor of Nick Moore's Tavern in Hoboken, lay dying from an accidental shotgun blast. On her deathbed, Loss admitted that she and her sons had "kept one of the most depraved and debauched houses in New Jersey" and they had all been "participators in the murder of said Mary C. Rogers, and the concealment of her body."

Rumors soon spread that Mary had gone to the tavern to see an abortionist and had died from complications from the abortion. Then, her body had been mutilated and dumped to hide the evidence.

On its face, this theory makes a lot of sense. Abortions were mostly unregulated; while there were eminent practitioners (New York's Madame Restell boasted of only losing one patient in forty years), those abortionists charged three hundred dollars for a week's stay—a much greater sum than Mary Rogers could have ever come by. To put this sum in context, it was the total amount Poe would earn from his published books in his entire lifetime.

A back-room abortion at Nick Moore's Tavern had a much greater chance of taking a bad turn. An earlier abortion would also explain Mary's disappearance in 1838. Poe halted production on the third installment of "Marie Rogêt," making alterations to the story hinting at, but not endorsing, the abortionist theory. Indeed, Poe's detective, Dupin, doesn't solve the crime at all—he merely suggests that it has a solution, pointing his finger at the Lothario naval officer that the newspapers had talked about during Mary's first disappearance. Such a person must exist, Dupin reasons; find him, and you've found your murderer.

I don't believe in ghosts, but here's a strange occurrence. Some years ago, Spike and I were in Hoboken to run a charity 5K. We started near the PATH station and headed north, along Frank Sinatra Drive and up toward Elysian Park, which commemorates the one-time home of the Elysian Fields. Then we looped back to where we'd started from. I'm constantly boring Spike with stories when we run, pointing out arcane bits of architectural trivia, or places where long-forgotten New Yorkers did things that no longer matter very much.

As we ran our five kilometers in Hoboken, I told Spike the story of Mary Rogers's body being found just off the shore where we were running. But here's the thing: I didn't know that story back then, or rather, I didn't know that I had known it. I'd read "Marie Rogêt" at some distant point in the past, but the Mary Rogers murder was a topic I'd never really thought much about. And yet, I *knew* that this was where her lifeless body had been dredged from the Hudson. I realize now that I probably *had* read the story somewhere, but it still strikes me as odd—and exceptionally Poe-esque.

Who knows—maybe we'll be running some early morning past Mount Tom and we'll hear a faint rustling in the leaves that stops us. Will it be the spirit of Edgar Allan Poe?

"Dude, that's a rat," Spike will say, and we'll run on.

Central Park, Winter: The Skating Pond by Currier & Ives, 1862.

CHAPTER 8

The Birth of Central Park

WHEN I'M ASKED TO SUGGEST AN AREA TO TOUR IN THE CITY, my recommendation of Central Park is often met with skepticism.

"A tour in Central Park? What would there be to see?"

You would think that response would come from out-of-towners, but I actually get it mostly from New Yorkers, who simply think that the park is just, sort of, *there*. So, they're surprised when I tell them that Central Park is the greatest piece of landscape design in America—perhaps in the world. It ranks among the finest architectural achievements of our species, up there with the Parthenon, the pyramids, the Eiffel Tower, and the Taj Mahal. Yet, you'll rarely hear it discussed with those other structures because . . . well, it's not a *structure*. It's just a park.

It's so cleverly constructed that it's been fooling people into thinking it is "just a park" since it first opened in 1858. To this day, many people assume that the park's designers, Calvert Vaux and Frederick Law Olmsted, simply erected a wall around primeval New York. Vaux took delight in pointing out that when *New York Tribune* editor Horace Greeley first visited, he said, "Well, they have let it alone a good deal more than I thought they would."

They hadn't let anything alone. Every tree, flower, and blade of grass is planted; every body of water is carefully honed for maximum effect. Even the bedrock that juts above the surface was worked and shaped to fit Vaux and Olmsted's plans.

"It's not nature," I tell people. "It's *better* than nature."

I get a lot of flack for this statement, but I think it's true.

In the park's earliest days, plenty of people were dubious: it was going to be too big, too costly, too elite (or, conversely, not elite enough). Then, as the park quickly became an integral part of the city, there was a rush to take credit for it. A web search for "Father of Central Park" usually brings up three men: Andrew Haswell Green, the park commissioner who was a key early champion and, later, the guiding hand behind five-borough consolidation; co-architect Frederick Law Olmsted, who often promoted himself at the expense of his partner, Calvert Vaux; and landscape architect Andrew Jackson Downing, who would have designed the park if he hadn't died in an accident just as the park was getting off the ground.

There's a name conspicuously absent from that list: William Cullen Bryant. Bryant was a poet, lawyer, and for fifty years the editor of Alexander Hamilton's *New-York Evening Post*. Though Olmsted, Vaux, Green, and Downing all played crucial roles in creating the park, it was Bryant who planted the seed.

On July 3, 1844, the *Post* published his editorial, "A New Public Park," which began:

> *The heats of summer are upon us, and while some are leaving the town for shady retreats in the country, others refresh themselves with short excursions to Hoboken or New Brighton, or other places among the beautiful environs of our city. If the public authorities, who expend so much of our*

money in laying out the city, would do what is in their power, they might give our vast population an extensive pleasure ground for shade and recreation in these sultry afternoons, which we might reach without going out of town.

Bryant's timing was not a coincidence; the next day, Independence Day, was the biggest holiday of the year. In fact, for most working-class New Yorkers (which is what Bryant meant by "vast population"), it was to be the *only* weekday they'd be guaranteed to get off work the entire year. Why force them to spend their hard-earned money going to Hoboken, a trip that cost three or four cents? (That extra penny allowed passengers to depart for Hoboken's Elysian Fields directly from West 19th Street, and skip the "more disagreeable portions of the city.")

Bryant's editorial was written just three years after Mary Rogers's sensational murder across the river, which had done nothing to dampen the crowds. As many as twenty thousand traveled to Hoboken on a summer Sunday. Bryant wondered if those twenty thousand might not be better served with open space on Manhattan.

Bryant had already picked out the perfect spot: Jones Wood on the Upper East Side, controlled by the Schermerhorn family. Bryant described it as "beautiful woodland. . . . The surface is varied in a very striking and picturesque manner, with craggy eminences, and hollows, and a little stream runs through the midst. . . ."

There was only one catch: the "difficulty of persuading the owners of the soil to part with it." Though some advocates of a new park would continue to press for the Jones Wood site for the next decade, it was soon apparent the new park would require a lot more space.

Progressive New Yorkers jumped on the park bandwagon, from the mayor to the *Tribune*'s Horace Greeley to landscape architect Andrew Jackson Downing, who championed a larger "people's park" (which, he had to assume, he would be asked to construct). At the center of all these plans was Bryant's modest editorial. In fact, he was so modest—"we are ready to resign . . . any claim to the credit of originally suggesting it"—that his pivotal role in the park's creation would soon be all but forgotten.

Central Park is home to fifty-two statues, fountains, and other monuments, but if you go looking for a commemoration of William Cullen Bryant, you'll be out of luck. Of all the men who shaped the park's early life, only park commissioner Andrew Haswell Green receives a monument, a forlorn bench near McGown's Pass (and that's really there to mark Green's work unifying Greater New York City). All Vaux and Olmsted get is a street sign.

For Bryant, his absence isn't for lack of trying. In 1864, on his seventieth birthday, the Century Association—a club Bryant had founded to promote interest in the arts—presented a bronze bust of their founder to Central Park. The park's commissioners accepted the gift, but declined to display it, citing the park rule that you had to be dead for at least five years before they'd erect a statue.

Ten years later, the Century Association tried again, asking the commissioners to place the bust, an "admirable work of art [that] has been lost to the sight of the public," inside the brand-new Metropolitan Museum of Art. The park agreed, and moved the bronze to the museum (then, located outside the park). It's still there, though, alas, no longer on public view.

Bryant died in 1878, ironically because he'd become the park's go-to guy for dedications and ribbon cuttings. Bryant always showed up, speech in hand. At the unveiling of a bust of Italian patriot Giuseppe Mazzini on the park's west side near the sheepfold, the sun was blazing hot; as Bryant sat on the dais, he began to feel weak. He gave his prepared remarks, then walked across the park to rest at his friend James Grant Wilson's house. As he mounted the front stoop of Wilson's home, he collapsed, fell backward, and struck his head. Bryant lingered a few days before dying from his injuries.

The Century Association, perhaps thinking the park now owed Bryant something, asked for the portrait bust to be moved from the Metropolitan Museum into the park. The commissioners gently reminded them of the five-year rule. Eventually, sensing that Central Park was never going to honor their friend, Bryant's supporters turned their attention elsewhere.

To find Bryant's memorial, I exit the park at Sixth Avenue and 59th Street and walk south through the crowded streets of midtown. I'm always dispirited on these blocks; somehow, this stretch of post-war office towers always strikes me as the most generic in New York, even with the playful architectural details of Rockefeller Center wedged in along the way. One set of towers is so interchangeably bland they're even called the "X-Y-Z" buildings.

What a change from Bryant's day; in the 1840s, when he was first proposing Central Park, this was the hinterlands. The majority of the city's half million people lived south of 23rd Street. If you lived as far north as 34th Street, as Caroline and William Astor did, you were considered a pioneer.

My walk brings me to 42nd Street and the back facade of the massive New York Public Library. Just two years before Bryant proposed Central Park, he had witnessed the construction of a huge reservoir for the city's new Croton water system on this spot. Facing the Sixth Avenue side of the reservoir was ten acres of open space known as Reservoir Square; in 1884, that square was renamed Bryant Park. In 1911, the same year the library replaced the reservoir, a dour statue of Bryant was installed beneath a domed canopy.

The statue, by Henry Adams, is a good likeness—Bryant always looked self-serious—but it seems to me that some of his unhappiness stems from his being brushed aside by history. Every time I bring visitors to this spot, I have to explain who Bryant was; even those who recognize the name have a hard time remembering why he's important. Sometimes, I read a few lines from "Thanatopsis," the poem that launched his literary career when he was just seventeen years old:

> *The hills*
> *Rock-ribb'd and ancient as the sun,—the vales*
> *Stretching in pensive quietness between;*
> *The vernal woods—rivers that move*
> *In majesty, and the complaining brooks*
> *That make the meadows green. . . .*

It almost sounds like he's describing Central Park—or Asher Durand's painting *Kindred Spirits*, even though it was painted thirty-eight years after the poem.

I used to be able to pop into the library and take people to see the marvelous landscape painting, which shows Bryant and his friend, the artist Thomas Cole, standing on a rocky outcropping in the Adirondacks. However, in a hurriedly arranged auction in 2005, the library sold the painting to Alice Walton, heir to the Walmart fortune, for $35 million. Many New Yorkers were dismayed at the sale. Though couched in critical language about the painting being "integral to the city's heritage" (as Michael Kimmelman wrote in the *New York Times*), it was clear that people were annoyed that déclassé Wal-Mart was triumphing over a great city institution like the New York Public Library—even if it meant the library now had $35 million to buy books.

The fact that the painting was being spirited away to Bentonville, Arkansas (pop. 20,000), also rubbed New Yorkers the wrong way. I can't help but think of that famous Saul Steinberg cartoon where everything beyond the Hudson River is a vague blur until the Pacific Ocean. Arkansas is where, exactly?

No matter where the painting lives, it is incredible. Painted by Durand as a gift to Bryant and a tribute to the recently deceased Cole, it is a sterling example of the Hudson River School, with, as travel writer Bill Bryson notes in *A Walk in the Woods*, "a long view of gorgeously forbidding blue mountains" and "disorderly ranks of trees, which immediately vanish into consuming darkness." Bryson, writing of the power of this pre-industrial wildness, longs to "step into that view."

Bryson isn't alone. The Hudson River School artists created landscapes of such compelling detail that viewers can't help but be drawn into their worlds. Here's the thing—you *can* actually step into Durand's canvas. Frederick Law Olmsted and Calvert Vaux brought it to life in Central Park.

On July 21, 1853, the New York State legislature approved a measure to seize "759¾ acres for park purposes." This was a 575 percent increase from the 132 acres of the Jones Wood site that William Cullen Bryant first proposed, though the Jones Wood backers weren't going down without a fight. Earlier that year, proponents chartered a boat to take politicians—including the newly elected president, Franklin Pierce—on a sojourn up the East River so that they could extol the virtues of the Jones Wood plan. But even with the backing of such high-powered figures, their scheme was losing steam. The area was too small, and too far removed from the bulk of the population downtown.

Instead, the park would span a half mile between Fifth Avenue and Eighth Avenue and run north from 59th Street to 106th Street, nearly two-and-a-half miles. It's important to remember that even though these streets had been surveyed by John Randel Jr. as part of the grid plan, most existed only on paper. Some major thoroughfares like Fifth Avenue had been graded (though they were still dirt roads), but most had not.

One large chunk of the park's future home was already owned by the state: the Croton receiving reservoir north of 81st Street. The park would have to acquire the rest using eminent domain, displacing a religious community known as Mount Saint Vincent near McGown's Pass, a group of Irish pig farmers near Fifth Avenue in what was known as "Pigtown," and the well-established Seneca Village, populated mainly by African Americans, the bulk of whom had moved there after New York State's emancipation day on July 4, 1827.

Today only four man-made traces remain of life in the area before the park was built: Randel's survey pin; Block House No. 1 from the War of 1812; a munitions arsenal from 1848; and what is believed to be a lone foundation stone from a building in Seneca Village.

Finding that stone can be tough. I've seen it a number of times, but when visitors ask me to point it out to them, it inevitably turns into detective work. We enter the park on West 85th Street and troll the lawn. We look like we're on a bizarre Easter hunt for invisible eggs. Ultimately, when I do find the stone, it's anticlimactic—after all, it's just a stone in the grass. But it's an apt symbol of how thoroughly the park destroyed what was here before. Hundreds of families were forced to relocate; churches, houses, and shops were torn down so that Olmsted and Vaux could turn back the clock, allowing "nature" to triumph over civilization.

With this in mind, it's ironic that one of their motivations in dislodging those residents was, in fact, to civilize people. As Vaux's mentor, Andrew Jackson Downing, had written shortly before his death: "Every laborer is a possible gentleman, not by the possession of money or fine clothes—but through the refining influence of intellectual and moral culture."

Olmsted and Vaux were about to embark on a grand experiment. Could a place like Central Park turn laborers into gentlemen?

Vaux and Olmsted weren't the park commissioners' first choice to design the park. Had fate not intervened, the commissioners surely would have picked Downing. However, on July 28, 1852, the steamboat on which Downing was riding, the *Henry Clay*, burst into flames on the Hudson River, killing the architect and eighty others.

Eighteen months earlier, Calvert Vaux, a young London-born architect, had joined Downing's landscape design firm. Downing had taken Vaux under his wing and soon elevated him to partner. In 1851, Downing introduced Vaux to Frederick Law Olmsted, a sometime farmer and citizen journalist who was at work on a book called *Walks and Talks of an American Farmer in England*. Though they didn't see each other again for years, the visit clearly left an impression on Vaux.

After New York State acquired the land for Central Park (it would remain a joint city/state park until a new city charter in 1870), the job of surveying the landscape fell to Egbert Viele, an engineer whose name has mostly been forgotten. Not only did Viele prepare the detailed topographical survey of the park, his 1865 map of Manhattan's water courses and bedrock deposits is still being used by architects today.

Calvert Vaux apparently couldn't stand him. In 1856, Viele submitted a plan for the park, which the city's new mayor, Fernando Wood, hastily approved. Vaux was appalled and, "being thoroughly disgusted with the manifest defects of Viele's plan . . . [argued] it would be a disgrace to the City and the memory of Mr. Downing to have this plan carried out."

Vaux began a whispering campaign with the park's commissioners that they should, instead, advertise a contest for the park's design. Make the choice democratic, Vaux reasoned, and the best man will win. The commissioners agreed and set aside Viele's plan. Now, all Vaux had to do was come up with a winning proposal.

In late 1857, Frederick Law Olmsted, short on cash and desperate for a job, had campaigned to be appointed park superintendent, a position that reported to Viele. Calvert Vaux, remembering Olmsted's *Walks and Talks of an American Farmer* and his keen interest in the principles of park design, approached him to form a partnership. Vaux, the trained architect, brought to the table his drafting skills, his knowledge of construction, and a sense of how to sell a project. Olmsted would be responsible for the overall vision and serve as construction supervisor.

The commissioners received thirty-three proposals; Vaux and Olmsted's—entry no. 33—arrived on March 31, 1858, one day before the deadline. That deadline had already been pushed back a month, ostensibly to accommodate new specifications that had been added to the contest, but perhaps because Vaux and Olmsted weren't ready. There's no evidence the contest was rigged, but the second-, third-, and fourth-place winners also already worked at the park. It makes one wonder.

Still, their winning design, the "Greensward Plan," was not only the most far-reaching proposal, but the best presented. On a series of boards, Vaux mounted black-and-white pictures they'd been provided by the studio of famed photographer Mathew Brady, which documented just how desolate the area under development was. Each photo was matched to a watercolor or oil painting by Vaux, his brother-in-law Jervis McEntee (a noted Hudson River School painter), or Vaux's friend Jacob Wrey Mould, who would soon become an integral figure in the park's development. They provided classic before-and-after views: before—dismal and gray; after—verdant and in full color. It was like Dorothy arriving in Oz.

On April 28, with Commissioner Andrew Haswell Green casting the deciding vote, Vaux and Olmsted were declared the winners. Egbert Viele, who had resubmitted his original plan to the contest, was fired six weeks later, with Olmsted assuming all of Viele's duties. Stung by the rejection, Viele sued just about everyone he could, and bitterly complained that Vaux and Olmsted had stolen his ideas. Comparing Viele's 1856 proposal to Vaux and Olmsted's winning Greensward Plan from two years later, it's tough not to see the similarities. Did they plagiarize Viele? Probably. But like Shakespeare stealing from *Holinshed's Chronicles*, Olmsted and Vaux's vision was far beyond anything Viele had imagined.

For such a big place—ultimately 843 acres after the park's northern border was moved to 110th Street in 1859—the genius of Vaux and Olmsted's plan for Central Park reveals itself in the details.

First, the designers solved two major problems with traffic flow. The city, worried that this huge park would hinder river-to-river traffic, mandated that four roads be cut through the park. Olmsted and Vaux came up with the idea of creating sunken transverse roads—essentially open-cut tunnels through the park—that would allow crosstown traffic to move below the level of park users. These roads are so well disguised that I can be walking right next to one with visitors and they won't notice it until I point it out.

The other traffic issue concerned the park's users. Vaux and Olmsted came up with three categories of roadway that they simply called the "Walk" (for pedestrians), the "Ride" (for horseback riding), and the "Drive" (for carriages). All together, there are today about seventy miles of Walk, Ride, and Drive wending through the park. In the master plan, none of these paths ever touched. If the Drive crossed the Walk, a bridge was constructed to pass pedestrian traffic below the carriages. Similarly, the Ride was kept separate from the other paths so that horseback riders would never have to rear up suddenly when confronted with an obstacle.

Though a handful of the original bridges in the park have been torn down, when I lead tours in the park or go running there, I try my best to keep to Olmsted and Vaux's original scheme. This isn't to be historically appropriate—it's because crossing the Drive (now known as the East and West drives or "ring road") can be such a pain. Bicyclists, runners, and cars—all phenomena that Vaux and Olmsted didn't imagine—speed around the ring road seven days a week. Sometimes, Spike and I will enter the park for a run at Columbus Circle. We'll head north to the Great Lawn (which sits where the original Croton receiving reservoir once stood) and cover nearly half of the park without being forced to cross traffic on the Drive even once.

On its face, Vaux and Olmsted's traffic plan seems eminently practical, but there was more than simple engineering afoot. Since only the wealthiest New Yorkers could afford a carriage or the luxury of horseback riding, the Drive and the Ride were de facto upper-class thoroughfares. In most places, they were kept at a safe remove from the working-class Walk, though sometimes the Drive was paralleled by walking paths, presumably so that poorer New Yorkers could see what they were missing—and so that the rich could set a good example.

This isn't to say the rich didn't walk in the park. In fact, the Mall was one of the park's most popular spots, and the only place in the city where unmarried couples could amble unchaperoned. To ensure the Mall remained chaste, however, the richest New Yorkers had to work to keep their working-class brethren at bay. William Cullen Bryant and Andrew Jackson Downing may have advocated a people's park, but in its first decades, Central Park was in danger of turning into a rich person's playground.

Work schedules favored the upper class. Laborers who toiled six days a week could only really come to the park on Sundays and holidays, so the more flexible upper class had the place pretty much to themselves 85 percent of the time. To better observe the Sabbath, blue laws were enacted limiting Sunday activities: no beer, no music, no sports, no recreational activities. The rules had the desired effect—working-class New Yorkers, who were already hard pressed to pay the streetcar fares to bring them from Lower Manhattan (it was cheaper to go to Hoboken), stayed away.

Recreation in Central Park favored the city's elites as well. The number one sport in the park was winter skating, when the depth of the Pond or the Lake—both artificial bodies of water—would be lowered to encourage freezing. Skating was expensive; in the Currier & Ives print of *Central Park, Winter: The Skating Pond* (reproduced at the beginning of this chapter), women glide by in fur-trimmed jackets, muffs, and hats, or are pushed in skating chairs by their gentlemen friends. These outfits and accoutrements could cost hundreds of dollars, while most working-class New Yorkers earned between $1.25 and $3.00 a day.

It's hard to know how much this bothered Vaux and Olmsted. Vaux viewed the entire park as a "translation of the republican art idea," open and welcoming to all. Olmsted, like Downing, also firmly believed that the park could have a "harmonizing and refining influence upon the most unfortunate and lawless classes of the city." Still, Olmsted was also a "keep off the grass" kind of guy—if his park was to be a living Hudson River School painting, hordes of people would just ruin the effect.

This presented a conundrum. If the working class were kept from the park, how could they be harmonized and refined? After all, wasn't that the main purpose of the park?

◆

Standing by the balustrade overlooking Bethesda Terrace is one of my favorite views in the park. Vaux and Olmsted planned it that way, so I'm not unique, but it still feels special and personal. I love being there just after the park has opened at dawn; I'm in the middle of the living heart of a city of 8.3 million people, but it will just be me and the birds. And Spike, but he's run to find an open restroom—so for a moment I'm alone with my thoughts.

It's a testament to Vaux and Olmsted's vision that if I were standing on this same spot in 1873, my view would be almost the same as it is now. In the foreground, I'd see the same intricate carvings on the terrace designed by Jacob Wrey Mould. Next, my eye would travel to the newly unveiled *Angel of the Waters,* by Emma Stebbins, the first major public sculpture by a female artist in the United States. Beyond that, I'd see the serene lake, and then the heavily wooded Ramble, so cleverly designed that people assume it's unadulterated nature.

But there's one major difference. Today, the treetops brush the orange-blue morning sky. In 1873, I would have seen the American flag flying from atop a castle off in the distance.

Spike comes back from the bathroom, and we jog down the stairs, cross the Lake on Vaux's gorgeous Bow Bridge, and wend our way up a circuitous, wooded pathway through the Ramble. At the top of the hill, we emerge next to the castle, which is actually quite small. This is Belvedere Castle, an architectural folly built by Vaux and Mould in 1867. It was designed to do nothing more than provide the optical illusion for viewers at Bethesda Terrace that somewhere deep in the park was a giant castle. It was the pinnacle—excuse the pun—of Olmsted's picturesque vision for the park.

When the Central Park commissioners first saw the map of the Greensward Plan, I'm sure many of them didn't realize how far-reaching Vaux and Olmsted's design would be. The designers understood that in contrast to the monotony of the city, defined as it is by DeWitt Clinton's grid, the park would embrace the natural topography. This would immediately mean that no two places in the park would be the same. On top of that, the tens of thousands of trees they would plant would provide "the broadest effects of light and shade . . . [producing] the impression of great space and freedom." What an "exhilarating contrast" this would be, the designers wrote, from "the walled-in floor or pavements to which they are ordinarily confined by their business."

The greatest amounts of the park were to balance the principles of the picturesque—thick woods, painterly contrasts of light and shadow, and the occasional castle—with the pastoral: sweeping vistas, sloping greensward, open meadows, and an actual pasture.

From 1864 to 1934, sheep occupied the sixteen-acre green (called Sheep Meadow by everyone to this day) that had been designated on the original plan as the military parade ground. As with the creation of Washington Square thirty years earlier, a parade ground had been stipulated in keeping with longstanding ideas about the use of public space for militia companies. However, few of the park's commissioners favored its inclusion, and when Vaux and Olmsted moved sheep onto the lawn instead, nobody seemed to care.

To contrast with these open green spaces, Vaux and Olmsted and their chief gardener, Ignaz Pilat, planted wooded areas such as the Ramble and the North Woods, forty acres in the northwestern corner of the park that were landscaped to mimic an Adirondack forest, complete with ravines, rustic wooden bridges, and a "loch," all straight out of an Asher Durand painting.

Lastly, Olmsted and Vaux realized the importance of also including a formal centerpiece to the park. The Mall, one of the first areas of the park to open to the public, is not just a straight path, it runs exactly north-south and is lined with four rows of American elms. Pedestrians, led due north along the promenade, come to Bethesda Terrace, the artistic jewel of the park.

The shock of this overt formality reminds viewers just how informal the rest of the park seems. Similarly, the picturesque touches—a wooden gazebo here, a fake castle there—create views that are almost *too* much like postcards. And so the mind says: *Ah, well if these views are fake, everything else must be real.*

It is amazing how quickly—and seamlessly—park users can slip from one landscape to the next. I can run from the Sheep Meadow to the statue-lined Mall to the deep woods of the Ramble in less than ten minutes. It's awesome—in the literal sense of the word.

Spike and I run from Belvedere Castle past the Turtle Pond to a statue of King Jagiello with the word POLAND inscribed in huge letters on its base. Somewhere, I hear the sound of Olmsted turning in his grave. He was strenuously opposed to these "incidents," as he called them, in part because they weren't in the Greensward Plan, but also because he feared New Yorkers would honor every dead politician they could. To that end, the five-year rule was implemented, stating that "a statue, commemorative of any person, shall not be placed in the Central Park . . . until after a period of at least five years from the death of the person represented."

Mostly, this rebuffed politicos and celebrities, though a few snuck in. Instead, civic groups raised money to honor their heroes. The German-Americans placed Beethoven and Schiller on the Mall; the Italian-Americans honored Mazzini; the old-guard Protestants erected a politically charged "Spanish Columbus" on the Mall in 1892 as a rebuke to the Italian-Americans; lovers of poetry (including future assassin John Wilkes Booth) honored Shakespeare—the list goes on and on. After Hitler invaded Poland, the statue of Jagiello, which stood proudly in front of the Poland pavilion at the 1939 World's Fair, was orphaned. Eventually, it wended its way to the park too, to serve as a symbol of Polish resistance to Nazism.

Spike and I run north, past the ancient Egyptian obelisk—the picturesque nature of which Olmsted would have liked, I think—and around the reservoir. At 90th Street is a gilded bust of one of the only politicians—and the only New York City mayor—honored in the park, John Purroy Mitchel. He volunteered to serve his country in World War I, but never made it to the front; Mitchel fell to his death from an airplane during a training exercise.

Farther north, we detour past the Andrew Haswell Green bench. Green, who broke party ranks to champion Vaux and Olmsted, turned into one of their greatest antagonists, mostly over matters of money. Sometimes, Vaux and Olmsted would just get fed up and leave the project. During the Civil War, Olmsted resigned to help in the war effort; when the commissioners decided to bring on other architects to help Vaux, he stormed off. In my collection of antiquarian books, I have an 1863 city directory where the original owner has carefully gone through and crossed out in pencil Vaux and Olmsted's names wherever they appear. By the end of the war, they were back, but my book's owner never bothered to erase the strikethrough. Perhaps that was just as well; in 1870, they'd quit again, before being enticed back two years later.

A side effect of the constant conflict between Olmsted and Vaux's desire to spend money and Andrew Haswell Green's fiscal prudence was that some portions of the Greensward Plan went unfinished. At 72nd Street on the East Side is a lovely model boat pond. It's supposed to be the centerpiece of a flower conservatory—maps still label it the "Conservatory Water"—but the garden was never built. It wasn't until Robert Moses took over running the park in the 1930s that a formal flower garden was constructed—much farther north at 105th Street.

Now, Spike and I have reached the less-populated northern section of the park. We dip down a narrow path into the North Woods, pausing when we hear a woodpecker knocking into a hollow tree. Other than that and the sound of a waterfall rushing behind us, the area is silent and we are alone. Ahead, a piece of bedrock juts precipitously from the ground near a stand of sycamores. A starling lands on the path; like every starling in America, it descends from a crate of birds released in Central Park in 1880 by a Shakespeare enthusiast who wanted to introduce Americans to all the birds in the Bard's plays. In a way, this stunt wasn't that far off from the park's mission. Wouldn't seeing a bird from Shakespeare make the park's patrons better people?

Our reverie is broken when two neighborhood kids whip by on their skateboards. An early morning ride? It's more likely their late night has morphed into morning.

It took more than a century, but Central Park has truly become the people's park—old, young, rich, poor. The park radiates a living energy, drawing in people like a magnet. I can already tell that the day is going to be beautiful. By noon, when I come back to the park to lead a tour, the place will be teeming with people: runners and bikers sweating it out on the Drive; families picnicking on Sheep Meadow; old men dressed all in white tossing a *bocce* ball as Mazzini looks on, approvingly.

Spike and I are only a block from the hard edges of the city. I'm tired, and part of my mind is eager for the bagel and coffee that I know awaits me outside the park's confines. Yet, we linger a moment in this living landscape painting, the worlds of Vaux, Olmsted, Bryant, and Durand swirling around us. We know it's not authentic. It was put here by the hands of thousands of laborers, most of whom will always be anonymous. And yet, it really is better than nature, a testament not only to human ingenuity, but to the power of using trees and flowers and rocks and rivers to create a place that feels truly sublime.

Abraham Lincoln, photographed by Mathew Brady on February 27, 1860.

CHAPTER 9

Abraham Lincoln and the Civil War

JULY 1863 WAS HOT—SO HOT THAT THE *NEW YORK TIMES* warned of the "close and uncomfortable weather." Still, the rising temperatures did not stop a crowd of at least 150 people assembling inside the Ninth District draft office on Third Avenue and 46th Street on the morning of Saturday, July 11, 1863. Some were merely spectators, there to watch the show. Others had a personal stake in what was about to happen: the first large-scale military draft in America's history.

On stage, a two-foot-high wooden drum stood front and center. To ensure impartiality, the clerk charged with selecting the names was blindfolded. After the names were mixed, the clerk put in his hand and extracted the first cylinder of paper. He handed it to Provost Marshal Charles Jenkins, who read out: "William Jones, Forty-Sixth Street corner of Tenth Avenue."

The crowd broke out into nervous chattering and bad jokes.

"Poor Jones!" someone cried.

"Good for Jones!" said someone else.

As the day wore on, the process turned monotonous, though observers tried to remain "jocular" (in the words of the *New York Herald*). By four o'clock in the afternoon, about twelve hundred names had been pulled—nearly half of the district's quota. The office would be closed on Sunday, but the draft was set to resume on Monday morning at 9:00 a.m.

I wonder when word finally reached William Jones that he had the dubious honor of being the first name picked. Was he with the crowd that showed up that Monday morning—their jocularity long since replaced with fury?

As soon as the draft resumed Monday, it was chaos. First, the crowd shattered the windows; then they torched the Ninth District draft office. The insurrection that began that morning, known now as the New York City Draft Riots, lasted four days—still, a century-and-a-half later, the deadliest civil disturbance in American history. Hundreds were killed and perhaps as many as ten thousand injured. The fact that this is nothing compared to the

carnage of the war itself—almost eight thousand people had been slaugh-
tered over two days at Gettysburg just ten days earlier—does not diminish
the size of these riots. If anything, it shows how bloody and awful the Civil
War had become. It was a conflict, from the beginning, in which New York
didn't even want to take part.

———

The spark that ignited the Civil War came on April 12, 1861, when Confederate soldiers began bombarding Fort Sumter in Charleston, South Carolina. However, the war's kindling had been smoldering for months, at least
since December 20, 1860, when South Carolina seceded from the Union,
and really since November 6, 1860, when Abraham Lincoln just barely won
the presidency.

It's easy to forget that Lincoln wasn't the preordained choice for the
Republican nomination. At the May nominating convention, it seemed the
nod would go to William Seward, New York's governor; Seward, however,
was ultimately deemed too much the radical abolitionist, so the nomination
went to the more moderate Lincoln. Seward would later agree to serve as
secretary of state.

Only three months earlier, Lincoln had come to New York for a crucial
campaign stop. As part of that trip, on Sunday, February 26, he attended services at the Plymouth Church in Brooklyn. At the pulpit was Henry Ward
Beecher, at the time perhaps the most famous abolitionist in the nation.
Lincoln sat in the fourth row of the church, listening in rapt attention to the
sermon. Afterward, he met with Beecher and shook the hands of hundreds
of parishioners.

Later recollections portray Lincoln's visit to be almost by happenstance,
which seems unlikely. Beneath his homespun exterior, Lincoln was a shrewd
politician, and by appearing in Beecher's congregation, he was garnering a
crucial—if unspoken—abolitionist endorsement. It may not be a straight line,
but there's a real connection between the candidate in Pew 89 at Plymouth
Church—four rows back, left of center—and William Jones's name being
pulled from the drum at the Ninth District draft office forty months later.

Like many houses of worship around New York, the Plymouth Church is usu-
ally closed to the public except for services, so I'm delighted to discover one
Friday night that it will be open the next day as part of a "Sacred Sites Open
House Weekend" sponsored by the New York Landmarks Conservancy.

I take the subway to Brooklyn Heights—Lincoln would have taken the Fulton Ferry and walked uphill from the river—which deposits me two blocks from the church. I'm immediately ushered to the front to see Lincoln's pew and hear the story of the church.

From the pulpit, Beecher would rail against the evils of slavery, but he also backed up his words with action. For obvious reasons there are scant records, but it's generally recognized that the church basement became a stop for fugitives on the run from enslavement. So many stopped there en route to Canada that it was later nicknamed the "Grand Central Station of the Underground Railroad." Beecher secretly armed combatants in "bleeding" Kansas by shipping rifles in boxes marked "Bibles, Plymouth Church, Brooklyn, New York."

Just three weeks prior to Lincoln's visit, Beecher had organized a slave auction at the church so that congregants could see firsthand how their fellow humans were being bought and sold. The young girl Beecher had brought to auction off was called "Pinky," an acknowledgment of her light skin and the unspoken miscegenation behind it. At these mock slave auctions, Beecher would challenge the congregation—as many as three thousand people—to buy an enslaved African's freedom. For Pinky, the assemblage emptied their pockets, raising much more than needed.

As we tour the sanctuary, I pepper the guide with questions, and sparked by one of my queries, we head to the parish hall to see the Tiffany stained-glass windows procured in the 1930s from the Church of the Pilgrims—a nearby Congregational Church that merged with Plymouth Church—then into a different room (a hallway, really) to see Pinky's "freedom ring."

When the collection plate wended its way around the church at Pinky's auction, actress Rose Terry suddenly realized she wasn't carrying any money. Rather than not contribute, she pulled the ring off her finger and donated it. When the collection plate made it back to Beecher, he spied the ring, placed it on Pinky's finger, and said, "Now remember—this is your freedom ring." Eighty years later, Pinky, who called herself Rose Ward in honor of her benefactors, returned to the church and donated the ring to the congregation.

Our guide whisks us back into the sanctuary. Propped on an easel next to the pulpit is a reproduction of a portrait of Pinky by Eastman Johnson. She sits on a rug in Johnson's studio, lost in thought as she admires the ring. The guide explains that the picture is now in the corporate collection of Hallmark, which allows the church to use the image on cards.

That the painting ended up in the hands of a greeting-card company seems somehow appropriate. Beecher was the ultimate showman—his endorsement deals included everything from throat lozenges to soap (cleanliness *is* next to godliness, after all). The day after his theatrical slave auction, Beecher took Pinky to Johnson's studio so that the painter could create an image to capture the public's imagination and "sell" the idea of freeing the slaves. Johnson was already well known for his depiction of plantation life (his *Negro Life in the South* had recently garnered a large, enthusiastic audience), but this would be his first painting of an actual freed slave.

It didn't hurt that Pinky was so light-skinned as to appear white; two of the most compelling black stereotypes for Northern progressives were the martyred Uncle Tom—created by Beecher's sister, Harriet Beecher Stowe, in the novel *Uncle Tom's Cabin*—and the "tragic mulatto," whose fate, when her African heritage was discovered, would be worse than death. Johnson's painting tapped into Northerners' mixed emotions: they could congratulate themselves about Pinky's freedom, while at the same time feeling tremendous guilt about all the other "Pinkys" still trapped in servitude.

My guide then points to the rear of the church to talk about some of my favorite stained-glass windows in New York. In Beecher's day, the church would have had modest, clear glass in keeping with its Calvinist roots. By 1907, tastes had changed, and the church spent two years installing a series of windows by Frederick Lamb depicting scenes from the history of the Puritans in America.

On the back wall, a large figure looms over the second story. In a cathedral, this spot would be reserved for the rose window, at the center of which would be Jesus. Here, the Christ position is filled instead by Abraham Lincoln. In the two adjoining windows, instead of saints or apostles, Henry Ward Beecher, his sister Harriet, and their father, the Reverend Lyman Beecher, stand like acolytes. After his assassination, Lincoln's detractors feared that the Republicans would deify him. Little did they know how accurate this fear would turn out to be.

After the service on February 26, 1860, Lincoln walked over to 90 Willow Street with his host, Henry Bowen, the publisher of the *Independent*, a leading Congregational newspaper. Bowen's house is gone, alas, but walking today between the Plymouth Church and Willow Street, I pass many of the same townhouses that Lincoln would have seen on his short walk, including one of my favorites in the neighborhood, the handsome Greek Revival house on Willow Street that almost a century later would be home to Truman Capote as he wrote *Breakfast at Tiffany's*. (History makes for strange bedfellows—it now houses the man behind the *Grand Theft Auto* video games.)

Though he'd been invited in for lunch, Lincoln stopped at the gate. "I am not going to make a failure at the Cooper Institute to-morrow night," Lincoln said. "Please excuse me and let me go to my room at the hotel, lock the door, and there think about my lecture."

The speech was the real reason for Lincoln's visit to New York. The previous fall, he'd been invited to speak at the Plymouth Church for two hundred dollars. By the time of the speech, the location had been transferred to the brand-new Cooper Union on Astor Place; however, the fact that the original invitation was to go to Beecher's church makes it unlikely that Lincoln ended up there on Sunday, February 26, merely by chance.

On Monday, February 27, Lincoln woke to find the Republican-controlled newspapers stirring up anticipation for his speech. Some of his hosts, members of the Young Men's Central Republic Union, called on Lincoln at the Astor Hotel, where they were embarrassed to find him disheveled, dressed in "a suit of black [that was] much wrinkled. . . . His form and manner were indeed very odd, and we thought him the most unprepossessing public man we had ever met."

Later that day, Lincoln headed up Broadway to Mathew Brady's photography studio. Today, people seeking out remnants of Civil War–era New York are often stymied, almost as if the period has been purposefully hidden from view. But when I retrace Lincoln's steps from the Astor Hotel to Cooper Union, the streetscape the future president would have known comes into sharp focus.

Though the Astor Hotel is now gone, Lincoln's walk would have first taken him past City Hall, and then A. T. Stewart's famed "marble palace" department store. This building, later the home of the *New York Sun* and now owned by the city, still stands, as stately as ever, at the corner of Chambers Street. Farther up Broadway, just south of Franklin Street, Lincoln would have seen a sign on the side of 369 Broadway advertising Mathew Brady's studio; the photographer had only just moved out of the top three stories of this building to temporary headquarters up on Bleecker Street. Brady's later studios have been torn down, but 369 Broadway, an Italianate building from 1852, still stands. It's in a strange no-man's land between Chinatown, Tribeca, and the Financial District; maybe that's why these old buildings have never fallen prey to development.

As Lincoln continued north, his path would have taken him through the finest shopping district in the city, passing by E. V. Haughwout's massive cast-iron china store on the corner of Broome Street. The shop had opened three years earlier with a clever marketing gimmick: it had the world's first passenger elevator, installed by Elisha Otis himself. Somewhere along the way, Lincoln stopped and bought a new hat.

At the studio, Brady and his assistants posed Lincoln standing, his right hand resting on a stack of books to show his erudition; behind him sits a classical pillar, a similar trope found in many formal portraits and statuary.

After the photo was taken, Brady retouched it in the darkroom, including fixing Lincoln's wandering left eye. He couldn't, however, do anything to make his jacket fit any better—Lincoln's right shirt cuff sticks out far beyond his sleeve—nor could he do anything to smooth out the future president's wrinkled suit.

That evening, Lincoln addressed a huge audience at Cooper Union. Industrialist and inventor Peter Cooper had built the school just a year earlier as a free institution of higher learning. The Great Hall remains one of the largest lecture halls in New York, and, as anticipated, Lincoln drew a standing-room crowd.

The speech, today most commonly known as the Cooper Union Address, was divided into three sections. In the first, Lincoln laid out a lawyerly argument that the thirty-nine signers of the Constitution—"our fathers who framed the Government under which we live," he called them (quoting his antagonist, Senator Stephen Douglas)—were against the expansion of slavery. In the second section, Lincoln addressed Southerners directly, admonishing them for being the ones stirring up dissent:

> *Your purpose, then, plainly stated, is that you will destroy the Government, unless you be allowed to construe and enforce the Constitution as you please. . . . You will rule or ruin in all events.*

Lastly, speaking to the Republicans in the hall, Lincoln tried to hold to a moderate line. He was against slavery, but argued that "wrong as we think slavery is, we can yet afford to let it alone where it is" without allowing it to spread to the territories.

Lincoln closed with the stirring lines that would soon be repeated in newspapers across the country—in all capital letters, as if he were shouting:

LET US HAVE FAITH THAT RIGHT MAKES MIGHT, AND IN THAT FAITH, LET US, TO THE END, DARE TO DO OUR DUTY AS WE UNDERSTAND IT.

Then, he went for a drink. At least that's how the story goes. It has been a part of Lincoln lore for years that after the speech, he was escorted to McSorley's Old Ale House around the corner on Seventh Street, perhaps by Horace Greeley (editor of the *New York Tribune*) and Peter Cooper himself. There are problems with this story: for one, Lincoln was a teetotaler (as was Greeley); second, a firsthand account of that evening makes no mention of McSorley's, noting simply that "from the Institute a few friends accompanied Mr. Lincoln to the rooms of the Athanaeum Club."

McSorley's, founded in 1854, is the oldest bar in New York. (The Bridge Cafe, on Water Street, is older, but has been many different eating and drinking establishments since 1794; McSorley's has just been McSorley's.)

My most recent trip to the bar is on a bitterly cold afternoon. The couple I'm touring with in the East Village are Canadian; we're only halfway into the tour, but they're ready to give up. As we stand on Astor Place talking about Peter Cooper—who, in addition to founding Cooper Union also patented edible gelatin—they decide we need to find someplace warm. *Right now.*

"With a fireplace," the wife says.

"I know just the place," I say, crossing my fingers that my recollection is correct and McSorley's still has a pot-bellied stove.

We skirt the edge of Cooper Union and nip into McSorley's. Immediately we are met by a blast of warm air; as my guests peel off their layers, I tell them that I hope they like beer.

"McSorley's only serves their own beer," I explain. "And you have to order a round."

The husband looks at me quizzically.

"It's really just two small mugs of beer. I order a 'one and one': light and dark."

After we've ordered our rounds, I pick up the story I was telling outside Cooper Union. I show them the Mathew Brady photograph of Lincoln and tell them about the speech.

"I've heard of that speech," the wife says. "You'd be surprised how little US history makes it north of the border, but we know about Abraham Lincoln."

I draw their attention to a poster on the wall, one of only a handful of WANTED posters printed in the days following Lincoln's assassination in 1865. In the upper center is a photograph of John Wilkes Booth. An actor by trade, he originally used this same picture as a souvenir for his fans. In it, he stares off to the side, pensive, brooding.

We sip our beers in silence for a moment. "He was bad news," the wife finally says, a classic Canadian understatement. Then again, why say more? That pretty much sums it up.

———

Lincoln was elected November 6, 1860; he won seventeen Northern states, including New York, but he wasn't able to capture the city itself, a staunch bastion of the Democratic political club, Tammany Hall, and the anti-war faction of the party known as copperheads. Had Lincoln lost in just one other metropolitan area in the state, he would not have carried New York— and thus would not have the requisite number of electoral votes for victory. In that case, the election would have been thrown into the House of Representatives. Anyone who's a fan of the movie *Lincoln*, which depicts the tortuous process of passing the Thirteenth Amendment to the United States Constitution, can guess how difficult that would have been.

During Lincoln's first term, he was usually stuck in Washington, DC, but Mary Todd Lincoln came to New York frequently. Mrs. Lincoln's first trip after her husband's inauguration was in May 1861, just one month after the attack on Fort Sumter, and seems typical of her city sojourns. Mrs. Lincoln checked into the posh, new Metropolitan Hotel at Broadway and Prince Street, in the heart of the shopping quarter. This section of Broadway south of Bleecker Street had almost everything an out-of-towner could hope for: hotels, theaters, shops, restaurants. It was the Times Square of its day, and like its modern counterpoint, there were probably visitors who checked into the Metropolitan Hotel and never left the environs of Broadway and Prince Street.

Mrs. Lincoln arrived on a Saturday; the next day, she attended services at the Plymouth Church. On Monday, she shopped at A. T. Stewart's marble palace; on Tuesday, Lord & Taylor's was on the agenda, as well as a trip to Laura Keene's theater, which stood on Broadway near Bleecker, just a five-minute walk from the hotel. On Wednesday, Mrs. Lincoln made what was probably her most lasting purchase: new White House china from E. V. Haughwout's emporium at Broadway and Broome.

The next day, Mrs. Lincoln toured the Brooklyn Navy Yard; the following morning, Mrs. Lincoln inspected the "Park Barracks"—perhaps those in City Hall Park outside the Astor Hotel. Amazingly, the barracks were just about the only sign that America was at war.

Mrs. Lincoln would return to New York many times, ostensibly as shopping excursions, but also, certainly, to get away from the mounting war pressures in Washington. In the summer of 1863, Mrs. Lincoln spent four days in New York, seeing friends, and being entertained on the French frigate *Guerriere*. It had been less than a month since the draft riots, but Haughwout's and Stewart's were open for business, and the theaters on Broadway were full. It was almost as if nothing had happened.

———

A hundred and fifty years later, the Civil War draft riots remain an enigma. In part, this is because they don't fit neatly into the narrative of the war. In 1863, many Americans took the riots as an example of how foreign New York City was, cut off from the realities of the rest of the country, almost a nation unto itself. Honestly, it still feels that way to some people.

Soon after South Carolina's break from the Union, New York's mayor, Fernando Wood, actually proposed that the city too secede and become an independent city-state. Wood's proposal pointed to the city's status as an outlier. Democrats like Wood were more sympathetic to "our aggrieved brethren of the Slave States" than with those "imbued with the fanatical spirit which actuates a portion of the people of New England."

Those New England fanatics Wood was talking about weren't just up in Boston. Many people in Henry Ward Beecher's Brooklyn thought of themselves as living in the southernmost point of New England. With no bridges yet spanning the East River, the waterway served as a genuine dividing line: on the Brooklyn side of the river were Puritans, abolitionists, and Republicans; on the Manhattan side were Episcopalians, copperheads, and Democrats.

In March 1863, Congress passed the Enrollment Act, calling for the conscription of new Union troops from every congressional district. Just two months after the Emancipation Proclamation, Lincoln was hoping a draft would turn the tide of the war in the Union's favor. One particularly controversial aspect of the draft law was the provision for commutation: Anyone who was drafted and didn't want to serve could either pay for a substitute or pay a $300 commutation fee to get out of service.

For poorer New Yorkers, many of them Irish immigrants, this was the last straw. Some worried that the Emancipation Proclamation meant that once the war was over, freed blacks could come take their jobs. This draft would force them to fight in a war that would cost them their livelihoods. The rich, who had no such fears, could afford to stay home.

Saturday, the first day of the draft, went off without incident, but tensions rose on Sunday. Joel Tyler Headley, who wrote a firsthand account of the riots, noted that as Sunday wore on, the list of draftees was "commented on all day by men who enlivened their discussion with copious draughts of bad whiskey."

Monday morning, the throng approached the Ninth District draft office, waving placards that read No Draft. A local fire company, the Black Jokers, led the charge. (Traditionally, firemen were exempt from military service, but not in this draft.) Amid shouts of "down with the rich men!" the crowd attacked, smashing the windows before setting the building on fire.

Mobs spread through the city. Lawyer George Templeton Strong, hearing rumors the city was on the verge of a full-scale riot, took a streetcar uptown to see the action firsthand. He noted in his diary:

> They turned off west into Forty-fifth Street and gradually collected in front of two three-story dwelling houses on Lexington Avenue, just below that street, that stand alone together on a nearly vacant block. . . . The mob was in no hurry; they had no need to be; there was no one to molest them or make them afraid. The beastly ruffians were masters of the situation and of the city. After a while sporadic paving-stones began to fly at the windows, ladies and children emerged from the rear and had a rather hard scramble over a high board fence, and then scudded off across the open, Heaven knows whither.

As the day progressed, the mob grew more violent. The Colored Orphans Asylum on Fifth Avenue was burned to the ground. A black man named William Jones—no relation to the initial draftee from Saturday—was on his way home with a loaf of bread when he was attacked, lynched, and burned.

Of the hundreds of people killed or injured during the four days of rioting, eleven blacks were lynched, and the African-American population began to flee the city. Some took refuge in the village of Weeksville in Brooklyn, one of the oldest free-black communities in New York. They could only hope that the riots, then spreading like wildfire, would burn out before reaching that far into Brooklyn.

Today, all that remains of Weeksville, which at its peak encompassed hundreds of people, is a small string of wood-frame houses tucked into an alley off Bergen Street in what is now the Bedford Stuyvesant section of Brooklyn. The houses were so well hidden that for years no one remembered they were there. Weeksville had been mostly lost to time.

In 1968, historian James Hurley and pilot Joseph Haynes did an aerial survey of the Bedford Stuyvesant area searching for any remnants of Weeksville's past. Flying over Bergen Street, they hit paydirt: a road running at an angle from Bergen had four houses fronting it. Hurley reasoned these must be important and consultations with old maps confirmed that the dirt road was one of the only remnants of Hunterfly Road.

Upon initial inspection, these Hunterfly Houses (as they came to be known) were deemed to date from the late nineteenth century, around Weeksville's peak. Subsequent archaeological work has pushed the date of the oldest house back to the 1840s, making it one of the original homes in the settlement.

Landmarked in 1970, the Hunterfly Houses are the centerpiece of the Weeksville Heritage Center. When I visit the center in the summer of 2013, it is on the cusp of change. Across a wide lawn from the historic homes sits the center's brand-new, but not-yet-operational visitor center. My guide talks about all the things that will happen there: education programs, exhibits, community outreach. The building is beautiful and large and calls to mind architect Daniel Burnham's famous exhortation to "make no little plans." Still, I'm concerned—while plenty of schoolchildren flock to the site on field trips, it's a pleasant Friday afternoon and there are only three of us on the only public tour of the day.

The three Hunterfly Houses (a fourth burned down in the 1990s) have each been "interpreted" (to use museum-speak) as a different time period: 1860s, 1880s, and 1930s. We enter the 1860s house, furnished and decorated to look as it might have at the end of the Civil War, and I'm immediately struck by two things. First, we are allowed to roam around freely, looking into every room, examining the objects on the shelves, asking questions. It's such a stark change from so many historic sites where the interesting parts are all beyond the reach of a velvet rope. Suddenly, I'm glad there are only three of us—this intimacy would be impossible with a group of thirty.

What also piques my interest is that the 1860s houses (actually it's one house, built as a duplex) are spartan, but don't have the melancholy cast that I've encountered at the Poe Cottage or I will see at the Lower East Side

Tenement Museum. These are the homes of people who weren't prosperous, but weren't poor; as I scour journals and books for mentions of Weeksville, the words that come up, time and again, are "middle class." New York didn't have anywhere near as large a middle class in the Civil War era as it does today. Most people were poor, and a small number were obscenely rich. There wasn't that much room in between, but somehow the residents of Weeksville managed it.

African-American upward mobility was a longstanding cause of friction with the white community, and Weeksville was no different. Papers such as the *Brooklyn Daily Eagle* went out of their way to convince people that beneath its facade, Weeksville was really a slum.

In one room, I'm captivated by a Currier & Ives print, *Death of President Lincoln*. It shows the president in repose at the lodging house across the street from Ford's Theatre. The Lincolns and their friends, Henry Rathbone and Clara Harris, had gone to the theater on the night of his assassination to see Laura Keene—who Mary Todd Lincoln had enjoyed seeing in New York—in *Our American Cousin*.

In the print, Robert and Mary Todd Lincoln bury their faces in handkerchiefs; young Tad Lincoln clings to his mother's skirts. To one side, many members of Lincoln's Cabinet look on. The demand for these prints—as well as scenes of Booth's attack in the Lincolns' box at Ford's Theatre—was massive, and Currier & Ives went into overtime production. The image I'm looking at was available for purchase a mere nine days after Lincoln's death, an unheard of production schedule in 1865.

I wonder if this room housed refugees from the draft riots. As Harry Bradshaw Matthews noted, just six months earlier—in response to the Emancipation Proclamation—the *Weeksville Free Press* had written, "Let all the people rejoice! Let them praise God . . . that he has given us ABRAHAM LINCOLN for President. . . . THE DAY OF JUBILEE HAS COME." With their brethren in Manhattan now beaten, bullied, burned, hanged, and terrorized over those four terrible days in July, it certainly seemed as if the Jubilee had come to a crashing halt.

While Lincoln's popularity ebbed in New York following the riots, he was still able to carry the state in the 1864 elections—but, once again, he lost badly in New York City. The draft riots had only lasted four days, but the embers of class and racial enmity continued to burn for years to come.

Still, whatever disdain New Yorkers felt for Lincoln would evaporate on April 14, 1865, when John Wilkes Booth's bullet tore through him; it was a mere five years since he'd sat in Pew 89 at the Plymouth Church, but in that time, it seemed as if America had been turned upside-down. The war had ended just a few days earlier, but the country would never be the same.

—⁃—

On the evening of November 25, 1864—less than three weeks after Abraham Linclon's re-election—John Wilkes Booth stepped out on stage of the Winter Garden Theater on Broadway near Houston Street. He was in New York City for a one-night-only performance of Shakespeare's *Julius Caesar* co-starring his two older brothers, Edwin and Junius. It was the first and only time the three men would perform together.

John Wilkes Booth is now so infamous that it's easy to forget that before he shot Lincoln, he was merely famous. Edwin was the bigger star in the family, considered by some to be the greatest tragedian of his age (his statue, showing him dressed as Hamlet, stands in the center of Gramercy Park). But John Wilkes was well known in his own right; when he jumped down from the president's box at Ford's Theatre and called out *"Sic semper tyrannis!"* most people in the audience would have recognized him.

The Booths were from Maryland and embodied the divide in that state at the time. John Wilkes considered himself a Southerner; Maryland may not have seceded, but he certainly owed no allegiance to the Union. Edwin, meanwhile, had already established himself in New York and was sympathetic to the Union cause. This political disagreement, however, did not stop them from joining their eldest brother, Junius, for this benefit performance to raise money for a new statue of Shakespeare by JQA Ward to be erected on the Mall in Central Park.

When the curtain rose on the second act, theatergoers could tell something was wrong. As John Wilkes took the stage, people began to smell smoke. Edwin came out to halt the production and calm the audience. The back doors of the theater flew open and the fire company burst in, trailing their hoses behind them.

It turned out the Winter Garden was not on fire; it was the LaFarge Hotel next door. A small blaze had been set in a stairwell and was easily contained. After the excitement had worn off, the Booth brothers returned to the stage and finished the show, earning a handsome $3,500 toward the Shakespeare statue fund.

People awoke the next morning to find that the LaFarge fire wasn't an isolated incident. Nineteen hotels—including the Astor, where the president had stayed in 1860, and the Metropolitan—two theaters, and P. T. Barnum's American Museum had all been attacked by arsonists the night before. As the details emerged, it became clear that there had been a Confederate plan to burn New York. Luckily for New Yorkers, the plan was ill conceived and poorly carried out—many of the fires were set in rooms with little oxygen, so they didn't spread.

John Wilkes Booth, Confederate sympathizer, left the city under no suspicion—and, indeed, there was no link between Booth and this plot, which was carried out with the tacit approval of the Confederate government.

A month later, Booth was back in New York, and this time he had a rogue plan of his own to help the Confederate cause: kidnapping the president. He visited his friend Sam Chester at his boardinghouse on Grove Street in the West Village to tell him about a "speculation." They walked down to Houston Street, where they dined at a pub called the House of Lords, then walked up Broadway. At Bleecker Street, Booth decided that it was too crowded to tell Chester anything in confidence; they continued up to West Fourth Street.

Finally Booth told Chester his plan: kidnap Lincoln and other top officials at Ford's Theatre—which Lincoln was known to frequent—and spirit them away to the Confederate capital at Richmond. They'd ransom them back in exchange for the cessation of hostilities. Chester, who had worked with Booth at the theater in the past, was offered the job of holding open the back door so that Booth could make his getaway. Chester turned Booth down.

Booth went away, disappointed but not dissuaded. By April the kidnapping plan had changed to assassination. (Some argue that the kidnapping story had always been a ruse to get Sam Chester involved.) Booth ensured that Lincoln would return to New York City one final time: as the centerpiece of an elaborate funeral procession.

On April 25, 1865, the president lay in state at City Hall, as mourners trailed into the rotunda to pay their respects. One enterprising photographer climbed the spiral staircase and captured the only known photo of Lincoln in his casket before being chastised and chased away. Another photographer, documenting the procession as it made its way through Union Square, inadvertently shot a photo of a little boy sitting in an open window watching the parade. The little boy was Theodore Roosevelt, New York City's only native-born president.

Monuments to the Civil War are strewn all around New York. After his presidency, war hero Ulysses Grant moved to the city to write his memoirs.

When he died shortly after their completion, many cities vied for the honor of burying the great general, but New York ultimately prevailed, building the country's largest presidential mausoleum on a high point in Riverside Park. Today, the tomb is rarely visited, but upon its completion in the 1890s, it was New York's top attraction. After General William Tecumseh Sherman died a few years later, a plan was drawn up to place a grand equestrian monument to him near Grant's Tomb. When Sherman's family objected to the location, the gilded statue by Augustus Saint-Gaudens was moved to the Fifth Avenue entrance to Central Park.

Meanwhile, the Civil War draft riots faded from memory. There are no monuments to the burned-out Colored Orphans Asylum or to William Jones, hanged merely for being an African American on his way to buy a loaf of bread. Many African-American families that fled—to Weeksville and other places—never returned and, as Iver Bernstein points out in *Slavery in New York,* "by war's end, as many as 20 percent of New York's blacks had disappeared." Though there was no way to make up for the damage that had been done, merchants and churches stepped forward to help black families and thousands of dollars was raised in the relief efforts.

In the garden outside the Plymouth Church is a statue of Henry Ward Beecher by Gutzon Borglum, who later went on to carve Mount Rushmore. The statue isn't Borglum's best work—and is nowhere near as good as JQA Ward's masterful Beecher statue in nearby Cadman Plaza. However, set into the wall next to Beecher is another piece by Borglum that is much more compelling: a bas-relief bronze of Abraham Lincoln, commemorating his visit to the church.

One day, when I'm pointing out these statues to a family of tourists, I take pains to explain Beecher's role in history, but don't bother to give Lincoln's. This, it turns out, is a mistake.

The thirteen-year-old interrupts. "Which one is Lincoln again?"

I point to the bronze portrait of Lincoln in the wall. Borglum has made an interesting artistic decision here; rather than show Lincoln as the beardless, younger candidate who visited in February 1860, he depicts the bearded president, weighed down by years of civil conflict, the burdens of his office clear on his face.

I explain all this, but the thirteen-year-old interjects again. "Lincoln was the president?"

Even his parents are shocked.

"Yes," I say. "He was president of the United States from 1861 'til his murder in 1865."

The boy nods. He's heard the name before, but isn't clear who we're talking about.

His father pulls out a five-dollar bill and hands it to him to look at the portrait.

"You don't need to know all the presidents," I say. "No one's going to care if you can't remember what Millard Fillmore did. But it's a good idea to know the ones whose faces are on the money."

The boy seems brightened by this project.

We move a few paces down the street so that we can see—just barely—the Lincoln window above the narthex in the Plymouth Church. It's such a startling contrast: the Lincoln here, practically deified, and the Lincoln the boy doesn't quite know from the five-dollar bill he's still clutching in his hands.

CHAPTER 10

Boss Tweed

ON THE MORNING OF APRIL 12, 1878, New York was filled with the cacophony of construction. On the East River, teams of laborers strung steel cabling across the nearly completed Brooklyn Bridge. Nearby, on Third Avenue, the finishing touches were being added to the new elevated train line, which promised to revolutionize public transportation, sweeping passengers from South Ferry to Grand Central Station in twenty-five minutes. Calvert Vaux and Jacob Wrey Mould's Metropolitan Museum of Art was also fast approaching completion; it would be Vaux's final contribution to Central Park, the end of a twenty-five-year association with the project.

The bulk of the stone cutters, carpenters, teamsters, and day laborers employed in these projects were Irish and German immigrants from the downtown neighborhoods of Five Points and Little Germany. Many were Democrats loyal to Tammany Hall, the city's most powerful political organization.

For much of the last two decades, Tammany Hall had been synonymous with one man, a towering figure who'd controlled the city from the mayor's office down to the file clerks and bookkeepers: William M. "Boss" Tweed. Every one of these building projects owed its existence to him, and many working-class New Yorkers owed him their livelihoods.

That morning, Tweed was dying.

As workers hustled at their jobs, Tweed flickered in and out of consciousness. Word had spread that the Boss was on his deathbed, and a crowd of onlookers and newspapermen had gathered outside the Ludlow Street Jail where Tweed had been incarcerated—except during the period of his audacious escape—since 1875. Tweed confided in his last breath that he blamed his death on Governor Samuel J. Tilden, and District Attorney Charles Fairchild, the men who had—in his opinion—unfairly imprisoned him. Around noon, he breathed his last.

Tweed-le-dee and Tilden-dum by Thomas Nast; *Harper's Weekly,* July 1875.

Quickly, word spread that the Boss was dead. Did the laborers at the Brooklyn Bridge remove their hats for a moment of remembrance? Probably not—there was too much work to do.

William Tweed's influence on New York was—and remains—immense. Quickly climbing through the ranks of Tammany Hall politics, he established himself by the end of the Civil War as the city's Democratic power broker. In terms of infrastructure, Tweed left an indelible stamp on the city—not just through big projects like the Brooklyn Bridge or the Metropolitan Museum, but in countless public works, from sewers and paved roads to charming decorative delights such as Jacob Wrey Mould's fountain in City Hall Park and the restaurant Tavern on the Green.

Tweed did all of this for a complex mix of reasons. Not only did he keep his constituents working (securing their fealty at the ballot box), he also genuinely loved New York and wanted to see it grow and prosper into a world-class city. But most importantly, he was stealing a phenomenal amount of money from the city as he went. As far as Tweed was concerned, his position allowed him to do good and do well at the same time. And, if it was illegal—well, what was anyone going to do about it?

Tweed was born on Cherry Street in 1823—near where the Brooklyn Bridge's Manhattan pier would later rise—on the same block where George Washington had lived as president thirty-four years earlier. The neighborhood had radically changed in that time and, as more immigrants poured into the city, the streets near the East River would be subsumed into the greater Five Points area. In Washington's era, the neighborhood was on the edge of the countryside. In Tweed's youth, it was urban and tough, and he became good with his fists and an ax. A born leader, he soon led a small street gang.

As a teenager, Tweed joined his local volunteer fire brigade, the Americus Company or "Big Six." It wasn't long before Tweed had ingratiated himself with the company and they'd voted him foreman. It was Tweed's first taste of politics, and he took to it like a natural.

The Big Six fire company, like all of New York's volunteers, was eventually replaced by a professional company, but reminders of the Tweed era remain. One is a former Big Six firehouse at 269 Henry Street. Leading tours, I often walk to this spot from Chinatown and point out the generations of New Yorkers who've left overlapping traces of their heritage: the imposing Beaux-Arts East River Savings Bank on the Bowery stares down at the Buddhist

Mahayana Temple. We pass the triumphal arch of the Manhattan Bridge, under which Fujianese fruit and vegetable sellers vend from pushcarts in the shadow of an old synagogue that's now a Greek Orthodox Church.

As we push east, more buildings with Jewish history appear— Jarmulowsky's Bank, the *Forward* building, the Educational Alliance—and then rows of tenements and stout townhouses, relics from an earlier time.

People disappear from the streets; in fifteen minutes we've gone from elbow-to-elbow traffic on Canal Street to being the only people out and about. That's certainly not what Tweed would have experienced. When the Big Six Company moved to Henry Street in 1854, New York's population had just exploded. In 1845, as William Cullen Bryant's proposal for Central Park was gathering steam, approximately 320,000 people lived in the city; by 1855, the population was 630,000—this huge influx thanks to the Irish potato famine and the failed 1848 revolutions across Europe. By some accounts, 200,000 people came to the city in 1847 alone, the worst year of the Irish famine; most of these new immigrants settled in the area known as the Five Points.

After the old Collect Pond had been drained and filled in the first decades of the nineteenth century, a neighborhood grew up centered around the intersection of Anthony, Orange, and Cross Streets. That five-cornered intersection came to be called "Five Points," and soon the name was synonymous with Irish immigrants and—to some New Yorkers—everything that was wrong in the city.

Tweed didn't agree. He was American by birth, Scotch-Irish by ancestry, and an Episcopalian by choice, but he held a great affinity for the Irish immigrants. As his power grew, this was certainly in part a *quid pro quo,* jobs for votes. But I don't think that was Tweed's motivation. I think he was just adamantly opposed to the bigoted forces at work in the city.

Take, for example, Tweed's greatest antagonist in the press, cartoonist Thomas Nast. Some people have fond feelings for Nast because he helped bring down Tweed—and because he invented the modern image of Santa Claus, jolly and red-cheeked. But Nast was a truly awful person. He consistently drew the Irish as brooding apes. He depicted the Catholic Church as a network of shadowy, sinister forces. In one typically horrifying cartoon, he showed Catholic bishops in a river, their miters turned into sharp-toothed alligator snouts, ready to devour innocent Protestant children.

There's an urban myth that the word "nasty" comes from Nast. That's not true, but the fact that the myth exists says a lot. Nast is just one example of what the Irish and Tweed were up against. Fire companies, like the Big Six, were stepping-stones for new immigrants. As historian Robert Ernst has pointed out, "as fire laddies, immigrants acquired a social prestige which lifted them out of their humdrum existence. . . . The Irish eagerly joined the social organizations of the firemen . . . [and] some fire companies were completely dominated by persons with Irish names."

The fire station on Henry Street is now empty—a victim of FDNY consolidation after the World Trade Center attacks—and the handsome four-story brick building by Napoleon LeBrun dates to five years after Tweed's death. But a half-hour's walk to the southwest—passing the spot where Tweed's Cherry Street house would have stood—brings me to the current Big Six company on Beekman Street. Since the days of Tweed, a Bengal tiger has been the company's symbol and a fierce example is painted on the bright red door here. Like every fire station, it is touched by melancholy; this company, one of the closest to the World Trade Center, lost four men in the collapse of the North Tower. I read the names of the dead: O'Hagan, Beyer, Johnston, Holohan. The ranks of Tweed's fire company are still filled with the Irish, all these years later.

———

By the late 1840s, Tweed was married and had entered the family chair-making business. In 1851, he was picked by Tammany Hall to run for alderman and took his first elected seat. Since the days of mayors DeWitt Clinton and Philip Hone, the makeup of city government had changed. Starting in 1834, mayors were elected, not appointed, making the job more democratic, but also more firmly in the hands of political machines. As organizations like Tammany Hall thrived, fewer wealthy merchants sought out political jobs, and the ranks of the city's legislature were filled with saloon-keepers, grocers, and chair-makers, like Tweed.

Tweed served one uneventful term in the US Congress, 1853 to 1855, then returned to the city and was soon appointed to New York City's newly expanded Board of Supervisors. In 1857, a revised city charter had created the bipartisan board to give the city some financial oversight, and serve as a state (read: Republican) check against the power of the city's traditionally Democratic mayor and aldermen. Tweed discovered it was standard operating procedure that any contract approved by the board had to include what was essentially a 15 percent fee for doing business. Of course, that fee went straight to the supervisors. It was the beginning of Tweed's understanding of how much money there was to be made in New York—there was just so much to build.

Though Tweed's power was growing in the 1850s, he didn't really make a name for himself until 1863. That year he was named the head, or Grand Sachem, of Tammany Hall; more importantly, following the riots that summer, he negotiated a way for the Union draft to continue.

When the draft riots ended, President Lincoln was still faced with the dilemma of needing troops. New York City's Board of Aldermen, dominated by anti-war Democrats, proposed that the city simply pay the $300 commutation fee for each person drafted, a move that would have ruined the city's already precipitous finances.

Tweed had a better idea: First, those traditionally exempted from service, such as policemen and firemen, would be removed from the draft. Second, if you were conscripted but couldn't afford the $300 commutation fee, the city would find—and pay for—your substitute, using a new municipal bond. Third, if your name was drawn and you *did* decide to join the army, you'd get the $300 for yourself as a bonus. Tweed and his Republican partner, Orion Blunt, went to Washington to sell Edward Stanton, Lincoln's Secretary of War, on the idea. When Stanton agreed, Tweed and Tammany Hall took over the administration of the draft.

It went off without a hitch.

In 1863, Tweed was also appointed deputy street commissioner, a role that allowed him to create patronage jobs (there were a dozen "manure inspectors," for example) as well as to push the city northward. He more than doubled the department's budget, quadrupled the workforce, and began paving streets in Midtown that had been dirt tracks since the layout of DeWitt Clinton's grid five decades earlier.

Though the pace of construction flagged during the Civil War, the city had already embarked on at least one ambitious project—a new county courthouse on Chambers Street. The initial budget was set at $250,000, but in 1859, the commission asked for the budget to be upped to $1 million. The city refused, but that didn't stop architect John Kellum from beginning construction on September 16, 1861. As everyone was ultimately going to find out, both the $250,000 and $1 million figures were complete fictions anyway.

When I stand beneath the rotunda of the Tweed Courthouse, as it is now officially known, I'm always in awe of the size of the place, especially when compared to nearby City Hall. Yes, the Tweed Courthouse was designed to hold a tremendous number of legal entities all under one roof, but the size here doesn't immediately suggest practicality. Maybe it's because I know the story, but all I can think about is graft. It is called the Tweed Courthouse, after all.

This is one of the most opulent interiors in the city. Polychromatic brick arches run in courses around the rotunda, held aloft by intricate cast-iron columns. Light beams down from the octagonal skylight, giving the place an airy openness. As I stand there, I think about the frauds committed in the name of this building. Andrew Garvey, the plasterer, received $133,187—more than half the building's original budget—for two days work. Garvey, quite coincidentally, was Gertrude Tredwell's next-door neighbor on East Fourth Street. I wonder if he bought his house with his ill-gotten gains.

Garvey's plasterwork became a metaphor for the building itself. A satirical poem from 1871, "The House That Tweed Built," singles out Garvey, "who made it his little game / To lay on the plaster, and lay it on thick, / On the roof and the walls / And the wood and the brick" until the only thing holding the building up was the plaster.

Here in the rotunda, I suddenly realize that's not true. Not only is the building made of durable stone, brick, and cast iron, this central section—which I've always taken as an example of Tweed's zealous overspending—has little to do with him. Most of this is what replacement architect Leopold Eidlitz built after John Kellum had died. By that time, Tweed had already fallen into disgrace. What to me has been the symbol of the building's extravagance was constructed *after* the frauds had ended.

In fact, New York's propensity to build big was only just getting started with Tweed. In the Gilded Age, the era of the so-called "robber barons," New York would build a city Tweed could only dream of. The difference is that the robber barons weren't punished for their building projects—they were crowned captains of industry, their names adorning everything from museums to hospitals to libraries. Carnegie, Frick, Rockefeller, Morgan—all were questioned in their own lives for shady business practices, yet all were destined for greatness. Why has Tweed been consigned solely to the role of villain?

In 1870, Boss Tweed hit the apex of his power and for the next two-and-a-half years, he and his associates plundered the city for millions. As Tammany's Grand Sachem, it was his job to get people elected: aldermen, mayors, the governor. In 1868, Tammany even tried to corner the presidential election, and by some counts as many as sixty thousand New York City immigrants were naturalized in time for the 1868 election. Others were assigned to vote multiple times in different election wards.

US election commissioner John I. Davenport later elaborated on the scheme: Tammany flunkies would be given "a slip of paper containing a fictitious name and residence . . . [and] would register or vote under such name and address. That being done, the 'repeater' would go back to headquarters, return his slip and receive another containing a new name and address. . . ."

In the end, Tweed managed to pull off Tammany victories throughout New York State, but his presidential candidate, Horatio Seymour, lost to Civil War hero Ulysses Grant.

As Tweed's power and wealth grew, so did his ostentation. He joined the Americus Club—founded by old pals from the Big Six fire company—and built them a gorgeous clubhouse in Greenwich, Connecticut. He bought a steam-powered yacht, and then another. Tammany loyalists gave him a diamond shirt pin valued at $15,000.

These conspicuous displays of wealth didn't go unnoticed, nor did Tammany Hall's growing stranglehold on New York politics. Tweed and his three closest political allies—Mayor Oakey Hall, Comptroller Richard Connolly, and City Chamberlain Peter B. Sweeny—had recently started meeting together as an intimate "City Hall Lunch Club." The club soon became known simply as the "Tweed Ring."

At *Harper's Weekly*, Thomas Nast began to draw editorial cartoons lampooning Tweed and the Democratic Party machine. He often depicted Tweed wearing his diamond shirt pin, a demonic smile on his lips. Nast took the Bengal tiger that was the Big Six company's mascot and turned it into the symbol for Tammany Hall—there's no evidence Tweed or Tammany ever used it—and soon the tiger became the stand-in for Tammany Hall's malfeasance. Nast also appropriated the donkey for Democrats (whom he thought of as asses) and the elephant for Republicans, symbols we still use today.

William L. Marcy, another Tammany politician, had coined the famous phrase, "To the victor belong the spoils." To Nast, this epitomized everything that was wrong with the Ring, so he began referring to Tweed in his cartoons as William "Marcy" Tweed and the name stuck. Even today if you browse through Library of Congress subject headings, Tweed is *only* listed as

"Tweed, William Marcy," despite the fact that his actual middle name was Magear. Our vision of Tweed today is so filtered through Thomas Nast's vitriolic drawing board that he's lost his real identity. Facts have been replaced by opinion, flesh and blood by a cartoon character.

In April 1870, with the state and city firmly in Tammany's hands, Tweed (by now a state senator with leverage in Albany) pulled off his biggest coup: a new city charter. Often referred to as the Tweed Charter or the Home Rule Charter, the document transferred much of the power held by Albany to the city itself—which, of course, meant to Tweed and his cronies.

One of Tweed's first acts under the new charter was to dissolve the supposedly bipartisan Board of Supervisors and replace it with a Board of Audit that consisted of him, Hall, and Connolly. Tweed also made himself commissioner of a new Board of Public Works, while Sweeny was appointed head of a Board of Public Parks. Afraid of what Sweeny would do to Central Park, Calvert Vaux and Frederick Law Olmsted resigned, and Jacob Wrey Mould was appointed chief architect in their place.

Strolling through the park today I feel the effects of the Tweed Charter, even though much of the Tweed Ring's "general onslaught on every grove, shrubbery and tree" is no longer evident. It's unclear why—beyond providing Tammany loyalists with jobs—Sweeny felt it necessary to hack away at so much greenery, though it partly reflected a simple clash of tastes. Vaux and Olmsted preferred rustic and overgrown, with circuitous paths that meandered through the park; men like Sweeny, raised on DeWitt Clinton's grid, liked straight lines. They always needed to see where they were going.

Sweeny wasn't all bad. Not only did he allow Mould to finish Belvedere Castle in the wake of Vaux's abrupt departure, but Mould also constructed an elaborate sheepfold on the west side. Ever since Vaux and Olmsted had added sheep to the green in the park in the 1860s, the animals had been housed in temporary pens. Mould built the sheep a huge, gorgeous, Victorian Gothic structure fronting the Sheep Meadow. The barn was designed not only to accommodate two hundred sheep, but also a sheep museum featuring exhibits on animal husbandry, wool samples, and framed portraits of the sheep.

Of course, the building was also oversized because the larger the project, the bigger the payoff. Under the Tweed Ring's watch, no job ever went to the low bidder. Luckily, Jacob Wrey Mould had a design sense as wide-reaching as Tweed's ambitions.

In 1934, at the behest of the new parks commissioner, Robert Moses, the sheep were kicked out and the building was turned into a "popular priced" restaurant called Tavern on the Green. (What we call Sheep Meadow was then "The Green," though I bet few people ever called it that.) Over the years, the restaurant was run by a series of concessionaires, and ultimately became America's highest grossing eatery. In 2009, however, the city declined to renew its agreement with Jennifer LeRoy, whose family had been operating the place for decades.

During the LeRoy era, Tavern on the Green was a popular stop on walking tours. Many people fondly remembered special occasions there, or carboloading before the New York City Marathon. Some would take one look at the Crystal Room on the patio and instantly recall Rick Moranis in *Ghostbusters* banging on the glass as blasé New Yorkers paid no attention.

The Crystal Room—a LeRoy-era addition—is now gone, a victim of the recent renovation, but I hope with the new Tavern that the upstairs bar is intact. Sometimes, in bad weather, clients and I would retreat to what had been the hay loft and grab a drink. It was here that you could get a sense that beneath its trappings, you weren't really in a fancy eatery, just a nineteenth-century barn. Having not seen the plans, I'm curious how far back they have turned the clock—to 1934, when it became a restaurant? To 1870, when Mould built it? I hope it goes back that far; I'm looking forward to the sheep portraits.

A few minutes' walk away is another great example of Mould's keen design sense and the Tweed Ring's incredible overspending: an elaborate watering trough for horses on Cherry Hill. In 1866, at the behest of the newly created ASPCA, the state passed an animal anti-cruelty law. The focus of the law was the health of New York's thousands of horses, which pulled everything from racing carriages to omnibuses to delivery wagons. A blind mule was used to turn the park's carousel (another Sweeny/Tweed addition), and lived its life in deplorable conditions.

Despite the number of horses that brought visitors to the park, Vaux and Olmsted seem not to have turned their attention to the new law. As soon as the Tweed Ring took over, however, Mould outlined his plans for a $5,000 "ornamental terminal and fountain" for the horses near the Mall.

To put that cost in context: An unskilled laborer at the park might make one dollar a day. Figuring a six-day work week and no vacation, that would be just over $300 a year. It would take that workman sixteen years to earn the money that the Tweed Ring was about to spend on a place for horses to drink.

However, it is a gorgeous trough. In spring, the cherries come into bloom, followed by the azaleas, a riot of color framing Mould's work. A utilitarian basin could easily have been placed here—in the same way that the original paddocks could have been left by Sheep Meadow—but today's park would be poorer for it.

This is always the conundrum when thinking about the Tweed Ring. Tweed could have lined the ranks of the city's payroll with dummy jobs and simply skimmed off the top of everyone's paycheck. If he'd done that, we'd have nothing to show for it.

This dilemma isn't new—as long as there have been governments there's been corruption—but the contradiction between Tweed's largesse and his own astronomical theft is worth keeping in mind. Laborers in the park brought home six dollars a week; meanwhile, Tweed wore a $15,000 diamond shirt pin. People in Five Points slept ten to a room. The sheep in Mould's luxurious barn awaited their portrait sessions.

Perhaps the Tweed Ring's most important contribution to the park during Sweeny's tenure was to fight against the idea that the park was merely a rich-person's playground. First came amusements and a Children's District. In 1871, the mule-drawn carousel was added to the park and proved a draw for immigrant New Yorkers. So did the new zoo, located in Mould-designed headquarters behind the Arsenal near Fifth Avenue. These changes started the process of breaking down the barriers that kept the people of the Five Points away. However, the Tweed Ring did not ignore the park's more affluent constituents. The Metropolitan Museum of Art was given land on the east side of the park for a new, permanent home, and the Museum of Natural History was granted a similar tract just outside the park's boundaries on the west side. These two museums are New York treasures, welcoming millions of visitors a year. They both exist, at least in part, thanks to the avarice of the Tweed Ring.

Sometimes, there are no easy answers.

—◦—

Though they did not know it at the time, the beginning of the end of the Tweed Ring came on January 24, 1871. That day James Watson, a New York county auditor, decided to go sleighing in Harlem. On his way home, he was in a bad accident, and died from his injuries a week later. This accident set off a chain of events that would end with Tweed dying in a jail cell on Ludlow Street seven years later.

James Watson played a small, but crucial, role in the Tweed Ring: He distributed the money and hid what was happening from prying eyes. Comptroller Richard Connolly elevated Stephen Lynes, Watson's assistant, to the position, figuring that Lynes could be trusted. To replace Lynes, Connolly found a new accountant named Matthew O'Rourke.

O'Rourke, a budding newspaperman, smelled a story. As his suspicions grew, he began copying ledger entries from the account books. What first worried him was the category called "Armories and Drill Rooms." As far as O'Rourke could tell, tremendous amounts of money were flowing out of the city coffers for the upkeep and furnishing of drill rooms that either weren't used or didn't exist at all—some of the addresses listed were stables or saloons.

When he'd amassed enough evidence, O'Rourke started going to the newspapers, which all turned him away. They were either loyal to Tammany Hall, relied on city advertising dollars, or were afraid of Tweed. The only publications interested in uncovering the Tweed Ring's frauds were *Harper's Weekly*, where Nast already demonized Tweed on a regular basis, and the *New York Times*. On July 8, 1871, the *Times* splashed the headline across the front page: MORE RING VILLAINY: GIGANTIC FRAUDS IN THE RENTAL OF ARMORIES.

Though the news was shocking, it was not yet enough to topple an empire. Unfortunately for Tweed, another former City Hall bookkeeper, William Copeland, had been keeping duplicate ledger books. A former Tammany ally of Tweed's, James O'Brien—who was in his own feud with Tweed—had brought Copeland's ledgers to the *Times* months earlier, but the paper hadn't acted on them. Maybe they were just waiting for the right time. Now, in the light of the Armory scandal, reporters—including Matthew O'Rourke, who'd landed a job at the *Times*—were let loose on the Copeland ledgers.

The details were incredible. Invoices for work at the Tweed Courthouse were astronomical: Garvey's $133,187 for a couple of days of plaster work; $360,752 to a single carpenter—all approved by Tweed, the Commissioner of Public Works. As much as $14 million was siphoned from the city treasury for the courthouse alone, making it, at the time, the most expensive building ever built in the city. It also cost almost twice what Secretary of State William Seward had recently paid for Alaska. Those figures are nearly impossible to translate into modern dollars, but consider that architect Leopold Eidlitz had just finished the massive Temple Emanu-El on Fifth Avenue—which seated eighteen hundred people—for just $800,000, less than 6 percent of the Tweed Courthouse's price tag.

Tweed was arrested in October 1871, released on bail, and promptly won re-election to his state senate seat. To many of Tweed's opponents, this crystallized the problem with Tammany patronage politics, and leading the reform movement was a rising star of the Democratic Party—a party desperately trying to distance itself from Tammany Hall—Samuel J. Tilden. A noted attorney for the railroads, Tilden had long been opposed to the Tammany political machine, and he had an accountant's attention to detail.

With precision, he prepared the case against Tweed. First, he pulled Tweed Ring comptroller Richard Connolly over to his side. Then, he installed Central Park commissioner Andrew Haswell Green as assistant comptroller to keep Connolly honest. With Green and Connolly's help, Tilden spent the next year piecing together the state's case against Tweed, showing exactly how the money had flowed from the city's coffers into the Boss's pockets.

Still, Tweed's first trial, in January 1873, ended in a hung jury. Tilden suspected Tammany Hall had bribed the jurors, so when the case was retried in November, he hired policemen to guard against jury tampering. The second trial, under the direction of chief prosecutor Charles O'Conor, brought a conviction—Tweed was found guilty on 204 counts. Judge Noah Davis, a Republican reformer, sentenced him to twelve years in jail.

Tweed was gone, Tammany Hall was broken, and the city could now finally begin picking up the pieces. As head of the reform movement, Samuel Tilden was suddenly the most famous man in New York. He was nominated to run for governor, an election he won handily in November 1874. From his townhouse on Gramercy Park, Tilden began eyeing the presidency.

Of all the elegant mansions in New York, the one I'm most intimately connected to is Samuel Tilden's on Gramercy Park. Since 1906, it has housed the National Arts Club, a private arts organization, and for many years I worked there. We were married in one of its art galleries; the reception took place in what would have originally been Tilden's front parlors and library.

Though the house has been altered many times over the years, it still bears hallmarks from Tilden's lifetime. In the early 1880s, Tilden hired Calvert Vaux to unite his two townhouses into one massive mansion. Vaux unified the facade in his Gothic style, and oversaw the interior decoration, including stained-glass panels in the parlor by John La Farge and a giant stained-glass dome in the library by Donald MacDonald.

I have spent countless hours in those rooms; I've walked beneath the MacDonald dome so many times that I stopped bothering to look up. Even the remarkable becomes commonplace when you stare at it every day. But I have to remind myself that Tilden's home was anything but commonplace. Even as late as the 1880s, houses all tended to look like Gertrude Tredwell's East Fourth Street home. As Nathaniel Parker Willis wrote, New York homes were so identical that the "proprietor of almost any house in New-York, might wake up in the thousands of other houses, and not recognize for a half hour, that he was not at home."

Walking into Tilden's house in the governor's lifetime, a visitor would have been shocked at how different it was, how lavishly decorated, how decidedly modern. This was the great reformer? Had the Tweed Ring simply been replaced by the Tilden Ring?

Though Tweed had been sentenced to twelve years in prison, he was out in just nineteen months. Judge Davis had overstepped his bounds, misconstruing how he could interpret the various misdemeanor counts of the indictment. (Tweed, incredibly, was never charged with a felony.) Since a misdemeanor, by statute, carries a maximum one-year jail term, Tweed was released in June 1875, as soon as the Court of Appeals overturned Davis's sentence. Thomas Nast commemorated the event with a cartoon on the front page of *Harper's Weekly* entitled *Tweed-le-dee and Tilden-dum*.

Fully aware this might happen, Tilden was ready. He had already filed a $6.3 million civil suit against Tweed, and the moment Tweed was released from prison, a police officer arrested him and hauled him to the Ludlow Street Jail. His bail was set at three million dollars—at the time a record—and Tweed, increasingly isolated, had no way to raise the bond. Tilden was only months away from securing the 1876 Democratic nomination for president; I'm sure he didn't want Tweed out on the campaign trail, reminding voters that the great reformer's biggest triumph was now walking around a free man.

Tweed's life at the Ludlow Street Jail wasn't all bad. He had enough money to install carpeting, drapes—to hide the bars on the windows—and even a piano. His jailers would furlough him on weekends for carriage rides in Central Park or to have dinner with his wife at their home on Fifth Avenue.

On the night of December 4, 1875, Tweed was taken home for dinner; he went upstairs to check on his wife, who was ill, and never came back down. According to more sensational reports, he'd slipped out wearing his wife's dress. Ultimately, he headed for Spain, which had no treaty of extradition with the United States.

Tweed might have lived the rest of his life on the Costa Del Sol, if the Spanish government had not intervened. Maybe they wanted to curry favor with Tilden, the favorite to win the presidential election in a few weeks time. As soon as Tweed stepped off the ship in Vigo, Spain, he was arrested. Evidently, the State Department had transmitted copies of Nast's *Tweed-le-dee and Tilden-dum* drawing so that they'd have a good likeness. I wonder if they were looking for a man wearing a $15,000 pin and a Tammany tiger belt buckle.

After three weeks in a Spanish jail, Tweed was sent back to New York on a US Navy ship. On November 23, 1876, two weeks after the presidential election, Tweed was locked up again at the Ludlow Street Jail. There would be no more furloughs, no more dinners at home.

Tweed was now facing penalties for his escape, but he had most recently been jailed on civil, not criminal charges. He'd served nineteen months after his first conviction. There really was no reason for him not to be a free man. Tilden had just defeated Rutherford B. Hayes in the presidential contest; what damage could Tweed do now?

I don't know if it was any consolation to Tweed, but Samuel Tilden's election victory soon began to unravel. In December, when the Electoral College met, four states—Florida, South Carolina, Louisiana, and Oregon—fraudulently submitted two sets of results: one set showed a Tilden victory, the other set went for Hayes. With neither man the clear victor, the election was shunted to the House of Representatives, who wouldn't touch it. Instead, a fifteen-member bipartisan commission was established to determine the winner. The commission was to have seven Republicans, seven Democrats, and one independent, Supreme Court justice David Davis. When Davis recused himself, he was replaced by a Republican and the vote, split totally along party lines, went to Hayes. Even with Bush v. Gore in 2000, the 1876 election remains the most disputed in American history.

A crushed Tilden returned to his Gramercy Park townhouses to nurse his wounds. Unsubstantiated rumors have long circulated that Tilden became paranoid and built an escape tunnel to make a quick getaway in case the city rioted again. Tilden wasn't paranoid; while the Civil War draft riots are the most famous, New York had a tendency to flare up in violence every few years. There were police riots, bread riots—even a riot over whether an American or an Englishman should play Macbeth on stage.

While Tilden was trapped in a prison of his own design, Tweed was looking for a way out. When he'd been on the lam, a civil jury had found him guilty of stealing more than $6 million from the city. Upon his return, Tweed approached District Attorney Charles Fairchild offering to be the star witness in a case against Peter B. Sweeny. In exchange, Fairchild would let Tweed out of jail. Tweed dictated a confession, but at the last minute Fairchild cut a deal with Sweeny—for $400,000, the state wouldn't press charges. Because Fairchild now didn't need Tweed's confession, he felt no compulsion to let him out of jail.

In the summer of 1877, Tweed again tried to bargain for release. A special committee of the Common Council was "appointed to investigate the fact and circumstances connected with the organization known as the 'Tweed Ring,' and the frauds connected therewith." Tweed was ushered from the jail to City Hall and, over four days, provided compelling testimony outlining the workings of the Ring. He ticked off massive sums of money from invoices laid out before him, affirming that the Ring took "never less than fifteen [percent]."

Reading the testimony today, you can hear the annoyance in Tweed's voice. The Board of Aldermen is hung up on which bills were legitimate and which were bogus and Tweed clearly didn't care, just as long as he got his 15 percent. As irksome as the testimony may have been, it allowed Tweed to come clean, and—he hoped—be rewarded with his freedom.

It was not to be. Tweed was thanked for the information and sent back to the Ludlow Street Jail. He grew sick, despondent, and on April 12, 1878, he passed away, blaming Tilden and Charles Fairchild with his last breath.

Before Central Park was created, the best open space that New Yorkers had to visit was Green-Wood Cemetery in Brooklyn. As I walk into the cemetery on a cold, spring morning, I can see how Frederick Law Olmsted and Calvert Vaux turned to this for inspiration. As in Central Park, the pathways all wend in odd directions—even with a map in hand, it's easy to get lost. I follow paths with bucolic names like Landscape Avenue, past famous names like Louis Comfort Tiffany and Horace Greeley, before finding myself face to face with Boss Tweed.

I push open the low gate emblazoned with a "T," and walk to Tweed's grave marker. For such a big presence, it's a humble memorial: just his name and dates and those of his long-suffering wife, Mary Jane, who died two years after him. He is surrounded by his parents and children, their graves no more remarkable than countless others in the graveyard. There's no mausoleum or statue, which I suppose is appropriate, but I can't help but feel disappointed.

I walk from Tweed over to where a grand figure by Henry Kirke Brown towers over DeWitt Clinton's grave. It's an odd statue—Clinton wears both a suit and a toga—and he casts his glance out toward some distant point on the horizon. I try to imagine what Brown would have done with Tweed. Would he have modeled his statue on a Nast cartoon, complete with buffoonish smile and outsized diamonds? Maybe it's just as well that Tweed's marker remains humble.

I pull out my map of the cemetery and scan it for Thomas Nast, but don't see him listed. A quick Internet search confirms that Nast is interred in Woodlawn, the vast cemetery in the Bronx that serves as New York's other major graveyard. Perhaps that's just as well too.

On Battle Hill, a small rise in the cemetery that was a key position in the Revolutionary War, a statue of Minerva stands looking at New York harbor, her hand pointing straight to the Statue of Liberty. In 1876, when the statue was given to America by the French, Tweed was on the lam. When he sailed back from Spain—a prisoner—the naval vessel that brought him home would have steamed right past Bedloe's Island where, in ten years time, the statue would rise. Had Tweed not fallen victim to his own avarice, who knows how he would have horned in on that project. Maybe we'd stand in Battery Park today, talking about the statue as just another symbol of Tweed's corruption and greed. Or maybe he would have killed the project outright, unable to figure out a way to profit from it.

But I like to think that Tweed, despite his tremendous flaws, would have seen the statue for what it has come to be: a symbol of America's freedoms and a welcoming beacon for the very immigrants who so long kept him in power.

From Battle Hill, I retrace my steps, sloping downward on Vista Avenue to Locust Avenue. On my way toward the exit, I pass Tweed's grave again. Somehow, it—and he—seem even smaller now. And that's all right with me.

Edith Wharton, in an undated photograph from the early 1900s.

CHAPTER 11

Mrs. Astor and Mrs. Wharton:
Tales of the Gilded Age

THE AREA IN AND AROUND UNION SQUARE ISN'T MY FAVORITE part of New York. At one end of the square, the famed green market draws thousands of visitors—chefs, local gourmands, tourists—who clog its narrow aisles in search of unusual vegetables or artisan cheese. At the opposite end, pro-testors and skateboarders jockey for position on the steps, while the stoic equestrian statue of George Washington stands above them, his eyes staring blankly down Broadway, as if he wishes he could be somewhere else.

This was once the most fashionable part of the city. As I walk down Broadway, I pass the cast-iron facade of McCreery's department store, and the upscale St. Denis Hotel where Mary Todd Lincoln once stayed. At the corner of Tenth Street, A. T. Stewart's Cast Iron Palace (the successor to his Marble Palace on Chambers Street) drew a huge clientele. Facing Stewart's, Fleischmann's Model Vienna Bakery served tea and pastries to women tired from their shopping excursions.

Looming above all of it was the spire of Grace Episcopal Church. Origi-nally a chapel of Trinity Church downtown, Grace Church (the debut of architect James Renwick, who would go on to build St. Patrick's Cathedral) opened in 1846, and soon defined elegance and social standing in New York after the Civil War. Its sexton, Isaac Hull Brown, was the social secretary for many of New York's elite. His 1880 *New York Times* obituary noted he "had charge of most of the fashionable weddings and many of the funerals of noted personages among the Knickerbocker families" for years.

Today, this stretch of Broadway has changed almost beyond recognition. Stewart's and Fleischmann's are gone. The St. Denis is an office building; McCreery's houses chain stores. Only Grace Church seems unchanged. A symbol of tradition and permanence, it was built to appear old when it was new, combining European custom with American fashion. It was also a signal that New York's flirtation with living "above Bleecker" (as the neighborhood was characterized) was not a passing fancy. The elite had moved uptown, leaving the old city below Chambers Street to evolve into a purely business district. Grace was the nexus of wealth and, even as people began to move to Fifth Avenue and Central Park in the later decades of the century, this small church continued to have great pull.

Grace Church was the domain of two individuals who would come to symbolize the Gilded Age (as Mark Twain dubbed the era in his 1873 novel of the same name): Caroline Webster Schermerhorn Astor—or "*the* Mrs. Astor" as she was known—and Edith Wharton, the Pulitzer Prize–winning author who is widely regarded as the greatest chronicler of the age.

Mrs. Astor was the doyenne of New York high society. And while Edith Wharton was a member of that same circle, it's in her novels and stories rather than her own life that the era truly comes alive. Biographer Hermione Lee neatly summarized one of Wharton's gifts: "If you were a time-traveller, you could use her books as an unerring etiquette manual, and you would not go wrong." Wharton's novels and stories were about so much more than etiquette; at their best, they capture a social milieu that was on the verge of disappearing, even as Wharton was writing.

On a late summer day, I step into the church's cool vestibule, a sort of air lock between the hustle of Broadway behind me and the sanctuary beyond. Instantly, I'm surrounded by bombastic organ music; a church volunteer informs me that I've arrived in the midst of their Sunday afternoon organ meditation. (I play along, wondering exactly how one meditates to a Bach fugue.)

Had I been visiting in the 1870s, Isaac Brown himself would have been standing here to determine if I was worthy of entry. In his short story "The Two Temples," Herman Melville calls Brown the "disdainful . . . fat-paunched, beadle-faced man" guarding the church entrance. Even though Melville doesn't mention Brown by name, his publisher was leery that Grace Church's parishioners would recognize the target of Melville's ire, and the story was held back from publication.

Though Sexton Brown is long gone, I still get the once-over before I'm allowed in to explore the sanctuary. I walk around the nave, reading names on the pews, and ignoring the occasional concerned look from those there to meditate. Each nameplate denotes to whom a pew belonged. In the nineteenth century, most churches raised revenue through pew rents. When Grace Church opened in 1846, the pews were instead sold at auction and became personal property. Some, recalled former mayor Philip Hone, went for "extravagant prices," as much as $1,400. Annual pew maintenance fees paid for the upkeep of the church.

Today, many of the plaques on the pews are missing, but the names that are left—including Stewart, Remsen, and publisher Clarkson N. Potter—are reminders of the significant New York families who worshiped here. On the front row, which was the most expensive and most desirable, the plaque reads SCHERMERHORN.

Today, the name is vaguely familiar to most New Yorkers—there's the Hoyt-Schermerhorn subway station in Brooklyn, and Schermerhorn Row at South Street Seaport. In 1846, when Grace Church opened, everyone in New York society knew the name—the Schermerhorns were on the top rung of the city's mercantile elite. Abraham and Helen Schermerhorn, who had moved to nearby Bond Street in 1839, purchased this front pew, and from this vantage point they watched their daughter Caroline Webster Schermerhorn marry William B. Astor Jr., in 1853. (Even though William's grandfather, John Jacob Astor, was the richest man in America when he died in 1848, Caroline's marriage to William was seen as elevating the Astors socially.)

Pew 38 was purchased for eight hundred dollars by Abraham Schermerhorn's sister, Elizabeth Jones. Her son, George Frederic Jones, married Lucretia Rhinelander (a descendant of another old New York family), and in 1862, George and Lucretia's youngest child—Edith Newbold Jones—was baptized here at Grace Church. Edith, who was Caroline Schermerhorn Astor's first cousin once removed, would become famous under her married name, Edith Wharton.

Though Grace Church was never Wharton's home parish, its place in New York society made it part of her world, and she followed its parishioners with an anthropologist's gaze. In *The Age of Innocence,* the 1920 novel that won her the Pulitzer Prize, her protagonist, Newland Archer, is married at Grace Church, and contemplates his fate from the chancel step at the front of the sanctuary:

> *Archer had gone through this formality as resignedly as through all the others which made of a nineteenth century New York wedding a rite that seemed to belong to the dawn of history. . . . "How like a first night at the Opera!" he thought, recognising all the same faces in the same boxes (no, pews), and wondering if, when the Last Trump sounded, Mrs. Selfridge Merry would be there with the same towering ostrich feathers in her bonnet, and Mrs. Beaufort with the same diamond earrings and the same*

smile—and whether suitable proscenium seats were already prepared for them in another world.

It can be a bit of a fool's errand to try to align every character in Wharton's works with a flesh-and-blood counterpart, but in her New York novels there are distinct parallels between Wharton's fiction and her real life. Aspects of Mrs. Beaufort, the grand dame of New York Society in *Age of Innocence,* were certainly inspired by Caroline Astor, and many writers see Edith's mother—Lucretia Jones—as the basis for Newland Archer's mother.

If that's the case, Wharton is then casting herself, in an intriguing gender-reversal, as Newland Archer. It seems to fit: Newland isn't looking forward to this marriage (he's in love with Countess Olenska, a married woman), and Edith Jones wasn't necessarily thrilled when she married Teddy Wharton in 1885. In fact, Edith would go on to have an affair of her own and eventually divorce her husband in 1913.

As I pass the chancel step, I imagine the sanctuary filled with Beauforts, Archers, Van der Luydens, and Dagonets—the first families of Wharton's fictional New York—as well as the Joneses, Schermerhorns, Astors, Rhinelanders, and the other society families who might have been in attendance here on Easter Sunday, 1862, to see Edith Newbold Jones baptized. Edith would not officially enter society until she was a teenager, but her christening at Grace Church was a debut of sorts. Throughout her career, Wharton would in turn celebrate and excoriate these "safe, monotonous, and rigidly circumscribed" traditions; her characters are both drawn to, and sometimes shackled by, the class into which she and they were born.

Edith Jones—known as Pussy to her friends—was born January 24, 1862. The family lived at 14 West 23rd Street, just off Fifth Avenue. The house was in the heart of the fashionable area that spanned from Washington Square to 34th Street where William and Caroline Astor's mansion had gone up in the 1850s. Some pioneers lived farther north; for example, in 1870, Edith's aunt, Mary Mason Jones (the basis for Mrs. Manson Mingott in *The Age of Innocence*), built a chateau in the wilderness of Fifth Avenue and 57th Street, near the still unfinished Central Park. However, the Astor home was considered the northernmost reach of polite society. Isaac Brown lamented near the end of his life that he could no longer hope to "control Society above Fiftieth Street."

Edith Wharton's birthplace still stands, though she wouldn't recognize her three-story brownstone behind what is now a five-story commercial building with a cast-iron facade. The ground floor contains a Starbucks, and I walk in one day hoping to find some trace of Wharton, something similar to the commemoration of the Burns Coffee House downtown on the site of the former DeLancey house. Unfortunately, there's nothing to distinguish this Starbucks from any other. I wonder sometimes if a century from now, literary tourists will be searching out these Starbucks outlets in Manhattan, all of which seem to be filled with people writing the great American novel. For all I know, the next Edith Wharton is that young woman typing away in the chair by the window.

In 1879, at the age of seventeen, Edith was "presented to society." She was young—most women debuted at eighteen—and may have entered society early because her father had fallen ill. (Or, as biographer Hermione Lee suggests, her parents may have been concerned Edith was "becoming too shy and intellectual—and therefore unmarriageable.") In either case, Edith was now on the nuptial market, and she began a courtship with Henry Leyden Stevens, whose recently deceased father had run the Fifth Avenue Hotel at Madison Square.

Edith and Henry's relationship was interrupted when the Joneses sailed for Europe in a vain attempt to improve George Jones's failing health. In 1881, he died of a stroke in Cannes, and Edith and her mother moved back to New York, living briefly at 7 Washington Square North on the famous "Row." That summer, *Town Topics*—a gossip magazine that was one part *People,* one part Social Register—announced that Henry and Edith were engaged. This may or may not have been true. Certainly, Henry's mother vigorously opposed the union. Were her son to marry, he—along with his new wife—would inherit his massive trust fund. Edith's mother Lucretia also likely disapproved. Money or no money, Edith would be marrying below her social station.

By October the engagement, if it had ever existed, was over. *Town Topics* reported that Stevens had dropped Edith because of her "preponderance of intellectuality"—just what Lucretia had feared. In 1883, Edith met a friend of her brother's, Teddy Wharton. In early 1885, they announced their engagement, and on April 29 that year—breaking the tradition of a yearlong engagement—they married at Trinity Chapel on West 25th Street across from Edith's house.

From the Starbucks on 23rd Street, I walk up Broadway in search of another of Edith's former homes. Like the block where she was born, the streetscape of 25th Street has been radically altered. Commercial buildings with street-level restaurants and shops stretch west from Madison Square. Her house is long gone, but the church where Teddy and Edith were married still stands. Today, it is home to the Serbian Orthodox Cathedral of St. Sava's, but it retains much of its mid-nineteenth-century architectural charm.

I arrive on a Sunday before the service and I'm warmly welcomed by the parish greeter.

"You know that Edith Wharton was married here?" he says, beaming.

Like Grace Church, this was originally a chapel of Trinity Church, and features a narrow, single-aisle nave. Designed by Richard Upjohn—perhaps the most important figure in the Gothic Revival in New York—it lacks the grandeur of Grace Church or Trinity, but seems more alive, even with water-stains on the stonework and spots of peeling plaster.

"We don't have much money," another parishioner tells me. "But some-how. . . ." He spreads his hands in a gesture of bewildered thanks. "Somehow we have enough money."

We know little about Edith Wharton's wedding day. In her official auto-biography, *A Backward Glance*, Wharton says only, "at the end of my second winter in New York I was married," and moves on. There is a revealing frag-ment from Wharton's unpublished memoir, *Life & I.* In it, Wharton claims she went to her mother before her wedding, "seized with such a dread of the whole dark mystery" of marriage and sex. Wharton's mother dismisses her daughter's fears:

> *"You've seen enough pictures & statues in your life. Haven't you noticed that men are—made differently from women?"*
> *"Yes," I faltered blankly.*
> *"Well, then—?"*

As I did at Grace Church, I try to imagine the view Edith would have seen here on her wedding day. Was cousin Caroline Astor in attendance, like Mrs. Beaufort had been at Newland Archer's wedding? By 1885, Mrs. Astor had firmly established herself as the first lady of New York's high society, so it's hard to imagine that she wouldn't have been invited to her cousin George's daughter's nuptials; still, the wedding was "limited to the immediate relatives of the two families" (according to the *New York Times*), and while it may have included Mrs. Astor, we'll probably never know.

Walking around St. Sava's, I try to picture Mrs. Astor in the front row, dressed as she is in the famous portrait of her by Carolus-Duran. That portrait—owned by the Metropolitan Museum, but off view—originally hung in her mansion, and she would greet her guests at her legendary parties standing in front of it. It's a cherished story of the Gilded Age that Mrs. Astor's ballroom held only (only!) four hundred people. If you weren't a member of that "four hundred" who could fit inside her house, you didn't rate.

By the time Ward McAllister—the successor in society hand-holding to Grace Church's Isaac Brown—began compiling his list of those four hundred, it included various Joneses and Rhinelanders, but not Lucretia Jones. There were no Whartons on it, either. Maybe Mrs. Astor wasn't at the wedding—perhaps Edith wasn't good enough for cousin Caroline, after all.

———

Caroline Webster Schermerhorn was born at One Greenwich Street, steps from Battery Park, in 1830. Nearby Bowling Green was still a fashionable address, but the Tredwells, Astors, and others were moving north of Bleecker Street, as were the Schermerhorns, who relocated to Bond Street in 1839.

Three years after their marriage, William and Caroline Astor built a brownstone mansion at 34th Street on family property. William's brother, John Jacob ("J. J.") Astor III, had married Charlotte Augusta Gibbes a few years earlier, and soon after William and Caroline moved north, J. J. built a similar—slightly more ostentatious—home next door to his brother. It was the beginning of a long feud between Caroline and Charlotte as to who was to be *the* Mrs. Astor. In fact, the battle was passed to their children, and ultimately ended up causing two hotels to be built on the sites of the Astor homes.

The first hotel, the Waldorf, was constructed by J. J.'s son, William Waldorf Astor, simply to force his Aunt Caroline to live next to a commercial establishment. When Caroline Astor decamped for a new, bigger mansion on Fifth Avenue at 65th Street, her son, John Jacob Astor IV, built the Astoria Hotel where her brownstone once stood. Ultimately, the two hotels joined forces as the Waldorf-Astoria, which remained at 34th Street until it sold its land for the construction of the Empire State Building in the 1930s.

It was not a foregone conclusion that Caroline Astor and her ballroom would become the social centerpiece of New York. First of all, as Eric

Homberger argues in *Mrs. Astor's New York: Money and Social Power in the Gilded Age,* 1880s newspapers were more concerned with status and class than the people they covered were. In *The Age of Innocence,* Newland Archer's mother makes a similar point:

> *"Don't tell me," Mrs. Archer would say to her children, "all this modern newspaper rubbish about a New York aristocracy. . . . Our grandfathers and great-grandfathers were just respectable English or Dutch merchants, who came to the colonies to make their fortune, and stayed here because they did so well. . . . "*

Still, while the Archers and Astors might have ignored the gossip pages, they also fed them, and part of Caroline Astor's hold over the press was her utter disdain for it. She never granted interviews, which only made the reading public more keenly interested in her comings and goings. In *House of Mirth,* Wharton's 1905 novel that became her first bestseller, characters like Mrs. Julia Peniston—the aunt of protagonist Lily Bart and a wealthy woman herself—pour over the society pages for tidbits of gossip.

The most closely watched event of the year was Mrs. Astor's annual ball, the toast of the winter social season. In a piece of typical reportage from 1900, the *New York Times* covered the party, the "climax of the season":

> *For last evening, Mrs. Astor issued about 400 invitations, and there were over 300 people present. The cards read "Mrs. Astor at Home, Small Dance, R.S.V.P." The dance last night was "small" only in name. . . . Mrs. Astor received alone in the great drawing room . . . which was filled with vases of American Beauty roses. Along the sides of the hall were branches of flowering almonds, apple and quince blossoms. . . .*

Twenty years later, when Edith Wharton wrote *The Age of Innocence* (set in the 1870s), Mrs. Julius Beaufort's annual ball acts as a stand-in for Caroline Astor's soirees. In both cases, the parties were always held after the opera, which made for a long night. A typical Astor ball would not begin until after 10:00 p.m. Dancing in the picture gallery was followed by dinner, more dancing, and then more food. It wasn't unusual for some guests to head home at dawn. Having a grand ballroom in a mansion was the ultimate marker of success. In *The Age of Innocence,* Wharton keenly describes the

Beauforts—"the first people in New York to own their own red velvet carpet"—as having built one of the few mansions in New York

> *that possessed a ball-room . . . used for no other purpose, and left for three-hundred-and-sixty-four days of the year to shuttered darkness, with its gilt chairs stacked in a corner and its chandelier in a bag; this undoubted superiority was felt to compensate for whatever was regrettable in the Beaufort past. . . .*

The Beauforts' home and party are beautifully shot in Martin Scorsese's 1993 film adaptation of *The Age of Innocence*, starring Daniel Day-Lewis as Newland Archer. While the ballroom itself was built on a soundstage, the entrance to the home was filmed at the National Arts Club, the former Samuel Tilden mansion on Gramercy Park.

I was working at the club at the time, and it was fascinating to watch the crew retrofit the Victorian mansion—it turned out, we had just too many modern alterations for the big screen. For example, since the building was now a working clubhouse, the front reception desk had to be hidden away behind a false marble wall. White, utilitarian walls had to be covered in period-appropriate, bright red wallpaper. Though some club members thought it made the place look like a bordello, the club's administration liked it enough to negotiate to keep the wallpaper when the shoot was over.

Steam pipes had to be hidden in wooden sofits, and paintings were removed from the parlors because they were just not quite old enough. In their place, Scorsese's crew brought in paintings created specifically for the shoot. At first these paintings were jarring—they looked too new. But of course, a painting created in the 1870s would have looked new then.

It took days to transform the club—and more days to shoot—but what ended up on the screen lasts three minutes at best. Still, not only was it fun to play a small part behind the scenes of the tracking shot of Newland entering the Beaufort's home, those few minutes make a wonderful entree into Wharton's world and the splendor of the Gilded Age.

One of the reasons that a meticulously staged film like *The Age of Innocence* can be so instructive is that glimpses of the Gilded Age are harder to come by in real life. For example, all of Mrs. Astor's homes are gone now. Her parents' home on Bond Street came down years ago; her 34th Street mansion was felled for the hotel, and the next one was demolished in the 1920s to make way for Temple Emanu-El.

In the 1890s, tourists would use her mansions as bookends of a mile-and-a-half stroll up Fifth Avenue from 34th Street to 65th Street, gazing on the domiciles of the very rich. One Saturday, I ask Spike to join me on a run to replicate that route, starting at the Empire State Building, to see what traces of Caroline Astor's Fifth Avenue remain.

Since we've actually started our jog farther south, by the time we get to Fifth Avenue it's late enough in the day that the sidewalk is clogged with people. Still, we persevere, weaving our way past the hawkers who sell double-decker bus tours. We pass the old Scribner's Building (Wharton's longtime publisher), and the New York Public Library, and soon we're entangled in Rockefeller Center traffic.

Finally, at 50th Street we begin to see glimpses of Mrs. Astor's New York. Though Mrs. Astor never would have darkened its door, St. Patrick's Roman Catholic Cathedral began construction in 1858, just two years after the Astors moved to 34th Street. Its lofty spires have watched this section of Fifth Avenue transform from suburb to grand residential street to commercial hub.

As Spike and I make our way north of the cathedral, we find two early-twentieth-century mansions built at the end of Mrs. Astor's life that still stand, though both are now stores. The first, built at the corner of Fifth Avenue and 52nd Street in 1902, was home to Morton F. Plant; its next-door neighbor is the only remaining Vanderbilt mansion in what was once a sort of "Vanderbilt Row" that stretched north to 59th Street. Cornelius Vanderbilt II, grandson of railroad and shipping magnate "Commodore" Cornelius Vanderbilt, owned what is still the largest private residence ever built on Manhattan at the corner of Fifth Avenue and 57th Street. His siblings and cousins, including George Washington Vanderbilt (whose North Carolina home, Biltmore, is America's largest mansion), all lived nearby.

When Caroline Astor's parents moved to Bond Street, living above Bleecker had been pioneering; when Caroline and her husband moved to 34th Street, they shifted that border thirty blocks north by sheer force of their social status. By 1895, when Mrs. Astor moved into her home at 65th Street, the lots facing Central Park—once considered too remote for anyone in polite society—were rapidly filling up. One by one, homes south of 59th Street disappeared or turned commercial. The Morton F. Plant house had only been a private residence for fifteen years when the jeweler Cartier bought it in 1917 for one hundred dollars and a pearl necklace. (The store is still there.) The Vanderbilt mansion next door, for years rented to the Goelets, now sells haute couture by Versace.

What ultimately killed the mansions of Fifth Avenue was the apartment building. Once considered the domain of the poor (in tenements) or unmarried men (like Lawrence Selden in Wharton's *House of Mirth*), apartment buildings became all the rage in the first decades of the twentieth century. By World War II, most of the mansions north of St. Patrick's had outlived their usefulness and been torn down. North of 59th Street, the houses were replaced by apartments; south of 59th Street, Fifth Avenue turned into a retail shopping destination. Cornelius Vanderbilt II's enormous townhouse was demolished so that the Bergdorf Goodman department store could go up in its place.

However, one Astor mansion remains: the house of Caroline's daughter, Caroline Astor Orme, built on East 64th Street; it's now owned by the government of India. When apartments began replacing mansions, most of the destruction took place on Fifth Avenue. Side-street mansions like the Orme house were spared, and even today property values on Fifth Avenue outstrip those on any of the nearby streets. The allure of Fifth Avenue is just too strong.

The sudden embrace of apartment living was a symbol of a greater repudiation of the city's Gilded Age past. Some mansions had barely gone up before being torn down. One of the grandest, W. A. Clark's massive 122-room house at the corner of Fifth Avenue and 77th Street, only served as the family's home for fourteen years; by the time it was torn down in 1927, the lifestyle it represented had sunk as surely as the *Titanic* had fifteen years earlier. As Bill Dedman and Paul Clark Newell Jr. write in their book *Empty Mansions,* the family couldn't find buyers for some of the home's most expensive fixtures. The grand marble staircase was dumped into the ocean; the $120,000 pipe organ was ditched in a swamp somewhere in Queens.

A handful of upper Fifth Avenue mansions somehow survived the wrecking ball, and thankfully many of these are now open to the public. Visiting these homes is one way to capture—if only to a small degree—what Caroline Astor's New York would have looked like at the end of her life.

Andrew Carnegie's 1902 home is the Cooper-Hewitt National Design Museum. A block north, Felix Warburg's mansion, completed in 1908, has become the Jewish Museum. At the corner of Fifth Avenue and 86th

Street, William Starr Miller built a gargantuan chateau in 1914 modeled on fifteenth-century French architecture from the Loire Valley. Today, the building houses the Neue Gallery, which displays early-twentieth-century art by noted Austrians and Germans such as Paul Klee, Egon Schiele, and Gustav Klimt. Walking through the galleries gives a terrific taste of the style of interior design that appealed to New Yorkers like Miller (a banker and railroad baron): marble pilasters, gorgeous wrought-iron balustrades, and the veneer of dark wood. In fact, Edith Wharton's first book, the nonfiction *The Decoration of Houses*, written with architect Ogden Codman, advocated exactly this sort of space.

Meanwhile, as rich Americans were throwing themselves into the past, pioneers like Marcel Duchamp were taking the art world by storm. Just a year before Miller moved into his mansion, Duchamp's *Nude Descending a Staircase* had been the talk of the 1913 Armory Show. Of course, part of the city's dynamic has always been the clash between the trailblazers and the conservatives, but at the end of the Gilded Age, the gap between them was growing into a chasm.

One place you would not have found a Duchamp or an Egon Schiele in 1914 was the most famous of the house museums, Henry Clay Frick's full-block mansion at East 70th Street. Designed to open to the public as an art museum after Frick died, the house is the best intact mansion from the end of the era, and was constructed to burnish his legacy.

Today, most visitors are drawn to the mansion's courtyard, or the specially designed rooms like the one that holds the eighteenth-century series of paintings, "The Progress of Love" by Jean-Honore Fragonard (which Frick bought from J. P. Morgan's estate). But what particularly appeals to me is the West Gallery, the closest analog to Caroline Astor's ballroom. All it would take would be a few potted palms, some white lilies, and a small orchestra to turn this room into a space where I can imagine Mrs. Astor holding court. I can see the men in their evening clothes (as Wharton writes in *The Age of Innocence*), "chatting and putting on their dancing-gloves. . . . [before they] joined the line of guests whom Mrs. Beaufort was receiving on the threshold of the crimson drawing-room."

Mrs. Astor didn't live to see William Starr Miller's house or Henry Clay Frick's. In 1908, at the age of 78, she passed away, having spent the last few years of her life in the prison of dementia. In 1928, Edith Wharton published a short story, "After Holbein," whose main character, Evelina Jaspar, is a thinly veiled version of Mrs. Astor.

In the story, Mrs. Jaspar prepares every night for the same fancy dress party—the last one she threw before she had a stroke—that is never going to happen. Wharton writes:

> [T]he poor old lady, who was gently dying of softening of the brain, still imagined herself to be New York's leading hostess, still sent out invitations (which of course were never delivered), still ordered terrapin, champagne and orchids, and still came down every evening to her great shrouded drawing-rooms, with her tiara askew on her purple wig, to receive a stream of imaginary guests. . . .

It was a sad end for the woman who had once held all New York society in thrall, but a perfect subject for Edith Wharton, who was, more than anything else, an astute tragedian. In *The Age of Innocence* lovers are thwarted; in *House of Mirth*, Lily Bart descends from the cusp of high society to working as a milliner and living in the absolute worst room in a boardinghouse, the one that had been created by partitioning one end of a hallway.

Undine Spragg, the never-very-sympathetic lead in *The Custom of the Country*, cycles through husbands looking for a better station in life, and is thwarted at every turn. In her novels and stories, for every witty remark about high society and its trumped-up rituals, Wharton has a shrewd observation of how New York's elite were suffocating in their brocade and their jewels.

The suffocation ultimately led Edith Wharton to leave the city altogether. In 1889, she and Teddy had purchased a home on Fourth Avenue (today's Park Avenue) near the corner of East 78th Street. The house is gone, but its neighbor at 890 Park Avenue still stands; though decrepit and seemingly ready for the wrecking ball, it's one of the only remaining nineteenth-century townhouses on a street better known for its luxury apartments.

Edith and Teddy's choice to live on Fourth Avenue symbolizes a particularly Whartonian relationship between wealth and power. Certainly, the couple had money—not only did they own a townhouse for themselves, but later purchased the house next door for their servants. On 77th Street, the Whartons kept a stable; it still stands, and when I walk by, I'm struck by the fact that a building designed to house one family's horses is many times bigger than an average New Yorker's apartment today.

Still, living on Fourth Avenue was not the same as living on Caroline Astor's Fifth Avenue. For one thing, the open-cut railroad tunnel leading into Grand Central Station had not yet been paved over, which meant that steam trains would have rumbled by just outside their door. The street was also turning commercial; in 1897, the neighbors altered 890 Park Avenue to include a basement storefront. While Wharton came from the same social set as *The Age of Innocence*'s Newland Archer and Mrs. Beaufort, I think she also clearly identified with Undine Spragg from *Custom of the Country*, who is never quite able to step fully into New York society life.

After her first marriage, Undine is forced to live in a house her father had purchased on West End Avenue; as far as Undine is concerned, it could be the other side of the world:

> *[A]fter three years she was still submitting to the incessant pin-pricks inflicted by the incongruity between her social and geographical situation—the need of having to give a west side address to her tradesmen, and the deeper irritation of hearing her friends say: "Do let me give you a lift home, dear—Oh, I'd forgotten! I'm afraid I haven't the time to go so far. . . ." [T]he remoteness of her destination, emphasized the hateful sense of being "out of things."*

Was it Wharton's own sense of being "out of things" that led her to spend more and more time outside of New York? Throughout the 1890s, she traveled in Europe and summered in Maine or Newport. In 1901, the Whartons purchased land in Lenox, Massachusetts, and built a retreat called the Mount. By 1907, Edith had left New York for good, settling in Paris.

The move to France was not simply a shift in geography, but the beginning of a new life for Wharton. In 1913, she divorced Teddy. During World War I, she threw herself into the relief effort, establishing the American Hostels for Refugees, raising money for charities, and writing about the war for an American audience.

After the war came *The Age of Innocence*, an aptly titled look back to New York in the 1870s and Wharton's own youth. Though it would be hard to describe someone with as trenchant a wit as Wharton's as nostalgic, her New York writings after the war do take on a somewhat wistful air, even when they critique. (Wharton later recalled that writing *The Age of Innocence* gave her "a momentary escape" from the aftermath of the war.)

In the world of *The Age of Innocence*, the men have respectable jobs (Newland is an attorney), but rarely seem to go to work. Many make money simply by having money. There's no sense that the world of the novel is also the world of Boss Tweed. Politics is rarely mentioned, though Newland does sigh that "everybody knew the melancholy fate of the few gentlemen who had risked their clean linen in municipal or state politics in New York. The day was past when that sort of thing was possible: the country was in possession of the bosses and the emigrant, and decent people had to fall back on sport or culture."

Also ignored in the world of people like Newland Archer is the real poverty of those immigrants, the same people that reformers Jacob Riis and Lillian Wald (the subjects of the next chapter) were trying to help. In the follow-up to *The Age of Innocence*, 1924's *Old New York*, Wharton examines the city from the 1840s to the 1870s in four novellas. In "New Year's Day," the final novella, Wharton's narrator remembers how the "self-sufficing little society of that vanished New York attached no great importance to wealth, but regarded poverty as so distasteful that it simply took no account of it."

More overtly than *The Age of Innocence*, *Old New York* acknowledges that the city was changing. Wharton writes of Mrs. Struthers, the "Shoe-Polish Queen" who challenges New York society by purchasing a home on Fifth Avenue and greets her guests "plumed and ponderous, with diamond stars studding her black wig like a pin-cushion." When the time-honored tradition of making social calls on New Year's Day begins to fall out of favor, Sillerton Jackson (the stand-in for Grace Church's Isaac Hull Brown and Caroline Astor's flunky, Ward McAllister) mourns its loss—then pretends "never to have observed it." When one character recalls the shock of a couple having an affair at the Fifth Avenue Hotel (which, at the time the story is set, would have been run by the father of Edith Wharton's beau Henry Leyden Stevens), Jackson exclaims, "Fifth Avenue Hotel? They might meet in the middle of Fifth Avenue nowadays, for all that anybody cares."

Wharton opened her autobiography, *A Backward Glance*, with the line: "There's no such thing as old age; there is only sorrow"; at the end, she concludes: "Life is the saddest thing there is, next to death; yet there are always new countries to see, new books to read (and, I hope, to write), a thousand little daily wonders to marvel at. . . . I still warm my hands thankfully at the old fire, though every year it is fed with the dry wood of more old memories."

But even at the beginning of her career, Wharton had seen the inexorable change in the city. Her first published story, 1891's "Mrs. Manstey's View," details an old woman in a boardinghouse looking out at the yards of the houses she can see from her rear window. The view is her constant companion; it shapes "her life as the sea does a lonely island." When a neighbor begins building an extension that will block Mrs. Manstey's view, the loss literally kills the woman.

By the time of Wharton's death in 1937, Mrs. Manstey's New York seemed gone for good. The Gilded Age had ended; the Depression had turned millionaires to paupers. Those who did have money and power were no longer the old Dutch and English families, but the sons of the robber barons, like John D. Rockefeller Jr.—the sort of people the society of Wharton's youth would have politely shut out.

Wharton died at her longtime house in France, and her last words were said to be, "I want to go home." Did she mean to meet her maker? Or back to the New York of her youth, the "life of leisure and amiable hospitality" that she and her most memorable characters were born into?

It's true that when walking up Fifth Avenue today—or standing on Broadway outside Grace Church—the Gilded Age may seem gone, but all it takes is opening the pages of *House of Mirth* or *The Age of Innocence* to bring back the "dry wood of more old memories," and follow Wharton home.

Mulberry Bend Park (now called Columbus Park), ca. 1897.

CHAPTER 12

How the Other Half Lived

THERE'S A SPOT ON THE EDGE OF CHINATOWN, a sliver of open space called Columbus Park, that brings together more of the neighborhood's immigrant history than any other location. Originally known as Mulberry Bend Park, the name was changed in 1911 to reflect the area's Italian heritage. For thirty-seven years, Emma Stebbins's statue of the famed explorer stood in the park, before being moved to Brooklyn in 1971. Most of the Italians were long gone by then too, though traces of Little Italy remain, including the faded sign for Moneta's at 32 Mulberry Street, once a popular eatery.

Born out of the Small Parks Act of 1887, Columbus Park certainly fits the bill: It is one block wide, running between Baxter and Mulberry Streets, and two blocks long, from Worth to Bayard Streets. As I walk north on Mulberry Street, I pass Chinese funeral parlors on the opposite side of the street, side-by-side with stores that sell joss-paper BMWs, cell phones, and elaborate dollhouse-size mansions designed to be burned in funeral pyres. The funeral parlors were once Italian, and some older traditions persist. Sometimes, I'll walk up Mulberry and see a Chinese funeral procession that includes an Italian brass band playing funerary marches.

Just beyond the funeral homes, I come to a small kink in Mulberry Street; this is the bend that gave its name both to the park and the neighborhood surrounding it. When the west side of the street was still packed with tenements, a small alley stood here at 59½ Mulberry. Pioneering photojournalist Jacob Riis immortalized the spot in his photograph "Bandits' Roost." A dozen faces stare out at the intruding viewer, stern and unwelcoming. A man on the right, his eyes locked on the camera, leans on his double-barreled shotgun. Riis described Bandits' Roost as being a fairly benign place—except on Sundays, when "they take to playing cards and generally in the end to the knife; then murder comes in to finish the job."

But I have little time to think about the bandits and their roost. Steps in front of me is a stand of bamboo rippling in the breeze—I am now in the middle of a bustling Chinese community in the park's northern section. Old men sit, their caged songbirds hanging from low tree branches. *Xiangqi* (Chinese chess) players are engaged in closely followed matches; at other tables, card games or mahjong are the favorites. On weekends, if I have a break between tours, sometimes I'll sit here with a cup of coffee or a taro bubble tea and listen to the strains of Chinese opera. I watch the fortune-tellers set up shop along the park fence, waiting to help a bride and groom choose the lucky date for their wedding.

Fronting Bayard Street is a large pavilion designed by Central Park visionary Calvert Vaux that dates back to 1897, when the park first opened. Columbus Park was the last of Vaux's contributions to the city; he'd spent forty years adding to the city's scenic landscape, but did not live to see his final park open. He went for a walk one day in 1895 in Gravesend, Brooklyn, and didn't return. The next day, his body was found in the water. The police initially ruled it a suicide, but then changed the cause of death to "accidental drowning." Vaux, however, had been depressed for some time, and suicide squares with his actions, such as leaving his valuable pocket watch at home. Either way, it was a sad end to the man who had given so much to the city.

I circle Vaux's pavilion and head south on Baxter Street, and within a couple of minutes I'm again at the park's southern edge. I'm now standing at the corner of Baxter and Worth Streets, the only remaining "point" of what was once the notorious Five Points intersection. Five Points was the center of Irish immigrant New York, best known today because of Martin Scorsese's *Gangs of New York*. Opposite me would have been Paradise Square, where the bulk of the action—and fighting—takes place in the film.

My entire circumnavigation of the park has taken me five minutes. Turning around, I have a clear view of Vaux's pavilion and the buildings on Bayard Street. In this small area of Mulberry Bend, Jacob Riis estimated that more than ten thousand people were evicted so that the park could be built.

One day, when I was leading a Five Points tour for a school group from Grant County, Oregon, their teacher interrupted me at this point in my narrative:

"Do you know how many people are in all of Grant County?" he asked his students.

The kids shook their heads.

"Seventy-five hundred."

The students gawked at the park, looked at their teacher, and then stared at the park again as they struggled to comprehend what he was saying. Their entire county *plus* twenty-five hundred people had lived in the slender space of these few blocks. And that wasn't just the population density of Mulberry Bend—it was typical of the streets of what today we'd call Chinatown, Little Italy, and the Lower East Side. At the neighborhood's peak, there were about one thousand people per acre. To put this figure in context, the average number of people per acre citywide today is 41.25—and New York is the most densely populated city in America.

The creation of Mulberry Bend Park—despite the dislocation of so many people—was considered a major victory by the progressive reformers of the day, chief among them Jacob Riis, who had campaigned hard for the park's creation. A year later, an Outdoor Recreation League was started by a group of progressive philanthropists, including Lillian Wald, founder of the Henry Street settlement. The league's first victory was the destruction of tenements along Essex Street and the creation of Seward Park in the heart of the Jewish section of the Lower East Side.

Compared to Columbus Park, Seward Park today is underused. Children play on the equipment and older Chinese residents do Tai Chi in the mornings, but there's an air of benign neglect here. Columbus Park is a spot to take in the sights of a vibrant community; Seward Park comes alive on weekends with the Hester Street Market, then loses its energy again. A century ago, however, both were integral to the life of the city, and their advocates, Lillian

Wald and Jacob Riis, are crucial figures in understanding the largest immigrant neighborhood America has ever seen. More importantly, the work they started over a century ago is still ongoing and this Chinese neighborhood remains a critical starting point for the thousands of immigrants who continue to arrive in New York City each year.

Jacob Riis came to America from Denmark in 1870, hoping to make his fortune and then return home to marry his sweetheart, Elisabeth. Riis's early years in and around New York played out like tragic melodrama. He spent much of his time unemployed and sometimes homeless. His first purchase on arriving in New York was a revolver, having been convinced by stories he'd heard that all of America was essentially the Wild West. That revolver proved handy, but not for self-defense: He pawned it time and again for the money for a meager meal or place to stay. At his lowest point, Riis was forced to lodge in the police station with other homeless men, leaving a stray dog that had befriended him outside. After a scuffle in the jail, Riis was kicked out, but not before the police killed the dog.

Riis's entry into journalism came by happenstance. Desperate for work, he applied to be the city editor of a paper on Long Island. The job turned out to be terrible, and Riis left within two weeks, but it set him on a course toward his future career. In 1874, he joined the staff of the *South Brooklyn News,* only to discover it was on the verge of going out of business. Realizing this might be his only opportunity to make something of himself, Riis somehow scrounged enough money to buy the debt-ridden periodical. He nursed it back to health, and sold it for a large enough profit that he could return to Denmark, wed Elisabeth, and bring her back to New York.

Riis became police reporter for the *New York Tribune,* a job that took him through the very streets he'd once trudged when he was destitute. As he wrote in his autobiography:

> *I went poking about among the foul alleys and fouler tenements of the Bend when they slept in their filth . . . sounding the misery and the depravity of it to their depth. I think a notion of the purpose of it all crept into the office, even while I was only half aware of it myself. . . .*

In 1887, Riis became intrigued with the process of using "flashlight"—an explosive powdered mix of magnesium and potassium chlorate—to take photographs. Immediately sensing the wide-ranging journalistic implications of flash photography, he gathered a team of amateur photographers to help him document conditions in the Five Points and Mulberry Bend.

The photographs became the basis for a slide lecture, an 1889 *Scribner's Magazine* article, and a book called *How the Other Half Lives*, which revolutionized the public's perception of New York's immigrant districts. For many people it was not only the first time they'd seen printed photographs, it was the first time they had been exposed to such abject poverty.

The images in *How the Other Half Lives* range from tenements like Gotham Court, to notorious spots like Bandits' Roost and Bottle Alley, to the crowded market streets of the Lower East Side.

Most of the locations Riis talks about are gone, and as I walk through the streets he describes, I thankfully find few traces of the "vile dens" that Riis so vividly photographed. Gotham Court had started its life as a model tenement. It was built in 1852 by a Quaker named Silas Wood who hoped to rescue "the poor people from the dreadful rookeries they were then living in," but by 1862, nearly one out of every two children born there died in infancy. When cholera struck Gotham Court, 20 percent of the population died. By the end of the century, the entire complex would be torn down.

Today, walking by the spot where Gotham Court once stood, all I see is a different symbol of the city's economic conditions: public housing projects. Though housing projects are ubiquitous in the city—I live near plenty of them—I experience them mainly from the outskirts. On long runs, Spike and I will head north from Wall Street along the East Side. As soon as we pass under the Brooklyn Bridge, our view becomes nothing but these subsidized apartments: the Alfred E. Smith Houses, the Hamilton-Madison Houses, the Rutgers Houses, the Vladeck Houses.

For almost two miles we run. On our right, Chinese men fish the East River; on our left are the looming shadows of these monotonous towers. To many New Yorkers, housing projects are a blight, a symbol not just of poverty but also of a government's inability to cope with its poorest citizens. When you read Riis you're reminded just how bad things used to be. Of Bottle Alley—which would be destroyed to build Columbus Park—Riis writes:

Look into any of these houses, everywhere the same piles of rags, of malodorous bones and musty paper, all of which the sanitary police flatter themselves they have banished to the dumps. . . . One, two, three beds are

there, if the old boxes and heaps of foul straw can be called by that name;
a broken stove with crazy pipe from which the smoke leaks at every joint,
a table of rough boards propped up on boxes, piles of rubbish in the corner.
The closeness and smell are appalling.

With conditions like these, how could the people of New York turn a blind eye?

"Who here has heard of Jacob Riis?"

The question comes from my guide at the Lower East Side Tenement Museum. We are standing in a plain, but nonetheless bright and airy parlor of the Moore apartment on the fourth floor of the tenement at 97 Orchard Street.

There are nods all around. "He wrote *How the Other Half Lives*," says the man to my right.

Our guide smiles. "And what do you remember about how he describes life in a tenement?"

I know where she's going with this. For many people who've never been on the Lower East Side, the area's reputation as a desperately poor and dangerous place is all they know; much of that reputation is thanks to Riis's writing and Herbert Asbury's 1928 book *Gangs of New York: An Informal History of the Underworld*, later turned into a film by Martin Scorsese. Some people are still scared to simply walk down the streets. Not long ago, I had to sit in a Starbucks on Delancey Street for twenty minutes while a client's husband tried to convince her that the neighborhood was safe enough for us to tour.

In *How the Other Half Lives*, Riis condemns the Lower East Side in stark pictures and strong—and often offensive—language. He calls the Lower East Side "Jewtown," and this casual racism is jarring; in part, it is merely the dissonance of archaic terminology, but more often, Riis is looking down on those he'd most like to help.

When considering the Jews, Riis plumbs familiar, anti-Semitic themes: "Money is their God. Life itself is of little value compared with even the leanest bank account." He complains of their "low intellectual status" and their ugly women. He refers to the Italians and the Polish Jews as "the lowest of the whites," and when considering the people moving to the wretched tenements of Gotham Court, he notes it's the "Italian hordes . . . seeking, according to their wont, the lowest level." The Chinese, meanwhile, with their "senseless idolatry" are "a constant and terrible menace to society." Riis uses the word "wretched" a dozen times in *How the Other Half Lives*, "suffering" and "suffer" seventeen times. Places are "vile" and "wicked"; the people who live in them dress in "rags" (which they also peddle on the streets). Riis knew his audience, and most of them were probably as anti-Semitic as he was.

It's little wonder that people stepping inside the tenement museum for the first time are surprised to see scenic landscapes painted in the entrance hallway. In the apartments on view, obvious care has been taken with the household furnishings; there's cheery wallpaper in the parlors. Isn't this supposed to be a wicked dive?

The Lower East Side Tenement Museum serves as a rebuke to Riis's prose. The guides tell stories of the families that lived in the building over time—from the Irish Moore family who moved there in 1869 to the Italian Baldizzis who were forced out of the tenement when it shut down in 1935. They don't underplay the struggles of these Lower East Siders. Indeed, the names of the tours—"Sweatshop Workers," "Hard Times," and "Irish Outsiders"—emphasize that immigrant life was never easy. Still, standing in the Moores' apartment on a warm summer evening, it's not hard to see that a decent life could be made in such small spaces too. Jacob Riis shined a light into the darkest corners of the Lower East Side; the problem was, he never shined a light into the brightest ones.

On the particular tour I'm taking this day, we're exploring behind the scenes, looking at how preservationists took a dilapidated, abandoned tenement building and converted it into a museum.

Originally a tenement was simply any building with multiple dwellings; the only people who were forced to live in such shared space were working-class immigrants. Those with a small amount of money would live in boardinghouses, then hopefully save enough to have their own homes. To those with middle-class aspirations, even a ramshackle, wooden, one-story house was better than the stigma of living in a tenement.

In general, tenements were five or six stories tall with four apartments on each floor—two in the front, with windows overlooking the street, and two in the back, whose windows opened over the outhouses. Prior to 1867, there were no laws requiring any additional windows so the inner rooms were dank; the 1867 Tenement House Law only stipulated ventilation, so transoms or windows *between* rooms were added—the inner rooms still had almost no access to outside air. (At 97 Orchard Street, which was built in 1863, the tenement's owner Lukas Glockner also cut ventilation windows into the hallways, which probably didn't do much good.)

As we stand in a run-down apartment that's not usually open to the public, we are confronted with literal layers of history: nearly two dozen applications of wallpaper—approximately one every two years—on top of multiple coats of cheap paint. I think the wallpaper is a nice touch—until the guide tells us that the law required that the old wallpaper be removed before the new was hung since its paste attracts vermin. Glockner didn't do this. He has left a wonderful historical record for us, but must have fed the roaches for years.

Another aspect of the 1867 law was a privy for every twenty residents. When 97 Orchard Street was constructed in 1863, water and sewer lines had already been laid in the area. However, in keeping with the standards of the time, Glockner put his outhouses in the back, shared not only by all of the building's apartments, but also the customers of the ground-floor saloon.

In 1879, the new Tenement House Act mandated actual outside windows in every room. Architect James Ware's "dumbbell" design, which was soon widely adopted, created air shafts between each building for the required windows, but cut down on a building's floor space. (The name stems from the fact that when viewed from above, the buildings look like dumbbells.) Ware also made provisions for two indoor toilets on every floor, but this innovation—not mandated by law—was usually only found in newly constructed buildings, and even then it was a rarity.

My tour stops out back to look at the four-stall wooden privies that the museum has reconstructed in the rear yard. Until 1888, city laws didn't even require that they flush; someone would have been paid to come and flush the contents of the outhouses into the sewer system. Steps from the outhouses is a spigot that provided the fresh water for the building. It was here that tenants would have filled jugs and buckets to carry water upstairs—sixty-one steps to the fourth floor—for cooking, house cleaning, and bathing. Just hauling the water was back-breaking work, even before the actual chores had begun.

Sometimes on these tours, you can see people thinking, *I could live in a space like this.* But as I stand in the rear yard next to the common spigot and the outhouses, I know that just isn't true. The conditions, even in the "model" tenements, are beyond most of our experience. Sometimes more than one family shared three rooms—and they weren't the only tenants. Many families kept animals, either as pets or for food. Chickens often roamed the halls as part of tenement poultry farms, as did geese whose fat was a staple of Jewish cooking. As Tenement Museum scholar Jane Ziegelman has pointed out, Jewish goose-farming was so important it "expanded from a cottage industry to a major commercial enterprise, with large poultry yards lining the East River."

Incredibly, the conditions Riis railed against in the 1890s are still to be found in today's Lower East Side. Granted, they are more hidden, but apparent if you know where to look.

For a long time, one of the most startling moments on tours of the area near the tenement museum—the only thing that's made clients shriek—was the rooster that lived at a makeshift auto mechanic's shop on Ludlow Street. He appeared at the beginning of the Year of the Rooster as a good luck charm. When we walked a few blocks to Broome Street, we came nose-to-nose with a different form of urban animal husbandry. There, across the street from the old Greek synagogue, the basement of a tenement had been given over to either a chicken farm or, more likely, a chicken rendering plant. The stench was so strong that we could barely take the time to look at the synagogue before being chased away. That poultry plant is gone, but others certainly still exist, as I'm sure people are still keeping domestic farm animals in their apartments.

～～

Jacob Riis's solution to the problems of the Lower East Side was private enterprise: new tenements, an "investment . . . in hard cash," along with better planning and stricter enforcement. Riis had a strong distrust of government programs—or, at least, of the ability of a Tammany-dominated City Hall to get things done. While it seems like the audience for Edith Wharton and Jacob Riis might be as different as their subject matter, in fact it was exactly Wharton's society that *How the Other Half Lives* was intended to influence. They were the ones who had money and could make a real impact in the lives of Lower East Siders.

Riis's contemporary, Lillian Wald, took a different approach: bring professional health care directly to the people. Wald was born in Ohio in 1867, three years before Jacob Riis landed in America. She came to New York City in 1889 to study nursing; three years later, having worked for a time in the overcrowded conditions at New York's Juvenile Asylum on Tenth Avenue, Wald decided to improve her training, enrolling in medical school.

While studying, Wald also volunteered at a school on Henry Street; it was there that an encounter with a young girl—in the midst of a lesson on how to make a bed—changed her life. As Wald recalled in her memoir:

The child led me over broken roadways—there was no asphalt, although its use was well established in other parts of the city—over dirty mattresses and heaps of refuse . . . through a tenement hallway, across a court where open and unscreened [water] closets were promiscuously used by men and women . . . and finally into the sickroom. . . . That morning's experience was a baptism of fire. Deserted were the laboratory and the academic work of the college.

It wasn't long before Wald hit upon the notion of a "settlement" house—unaware that other progressive health professionals were having the same idea. The idea was simple: Too often, charity work consisted of throwing money at the poor, or convening panels or government agencies to study a problem. There was also a strong undercurrent of moralistic paternalism, a suggestion that simply converting to Protestantism would lift Lower East Siders out of the mess they were in.

Riis's work was layered with this. When he took *How the Other Half Lives* on the road as a "magic lantern" slide show, he would address church groups and intersperse the presentation with hymns. The penultimate slide in the show showed poor tenement dwellers unceremoniously dumped in a potter's field; the final slide was Jesus.

Wald wanted something different—a place where professionals would actually help the poor on an ongoing basis. In order to do that, they would need to live, or "settle" in the neighborhood. Wald and her friend, a fellow nurse named Mary Brewster, moved to a tenement on Jefferson Street, originally dubbed Nurses' Settlement.

It's refreshing how remarkably different Wald's attitude was from that of Jacob Riis. She writes that "the mere fact of living in the tenement brought undreamed-of opportunity for widening our knowledge and extending our human relationships. That we were Americans was wonderful to our fellow-tenants. They were all immigrants—Jews from Russia or Roumania." Later, when Wald recalls the "pain and poverty" of the winter of 1893, it is to remember with fondness the kindnesses of the poor to each other—and her. For every "vile den" in *How the Other Half Lives,* Wald's memoir finds "two rooms scrubbed clean." Also, within the immigrant community, there was a realization that some people were better off than others. In his oral history of New York, *You Must Remember This,* Jeff Kisseloff interviews Robert Leslie, who grew up on the Lower East Side and would tag along with Jacob Riis "on his rounds to see the poverty." Leslie realized during those walks how lucky he was—compared to "how the other people lived, we were rich."

There were few doctors on the Lower East Side, and most tenement dwellers would not have been able to afford them anyway. Wald's team of nurses made the rounds to the tenements (today's Visiting Nurse Service of New York is the direct descendant of Wald's settlement house), helping expectant mothers, acting as midwives, and focusing on preventative care. Wald coined the term "public health nurse" to describe her work, and over the course of her lifetime, thousands of families benefited from her care. In 1895, financier Jacob Schiff bought Wald an old townhouse at 265 Henry Street as the settlement's new headquarters. Over a century later, the organization is still there.

Sometimes when I'm leading tours of the heart of the Lower East Side, it can be disheartening, especially when visitors with ancestors from the area are looking for something I can't show them. We go by the former home of the First Roumanian-American Congregation, now an empty lot; the building, suffering from a neglected roof, partially collapsed in 2006 and was demolished. Nearby, we stop at Economy Candy, the venerable old sweets shop, but visitors look in dismay at the boutique hotel and raw juice bar across the street. None of this is what they'd hoped to find: the bustling street scenes of a century ago that their grandparents and great-grandparents knew.

Still, what remains has deep roots: we stop for Kossar's bialys, serving the staple bread that once rivaled the bagel in popularity, and then visit the Pickle Guys, who still slow-brine and sell straight from the barrel. Then, we come to Seward Park. Not only was this the first public playground in America, giving working-class children—many of them *working* children—a place to blow off steam, it became a rallying point for the community. The problem with Jacob Riis's version of the Lower East Side was that its residents lacked agency. The tenements laid the poor so low, they were unable to pull themselves back up again. Wald saw things more accurately, and knew a place like Seward Park could provide the impetus for people to work toward change.

That change, of course, has been hard to come by. When people sigh about the lack of street life in the area around Seward Park, I make a course correction in the tour, and we veer down Canal Street toward the heart of modern Chinatown. The streets here can be as densely packed today as they would have been on the Lower East Side a century ago. Fruit and vegetable vendors hawk their goods from sidewalk stands that are the direct heirs to the pushcarts that would have clogged these streets in the nineteenth century. For those whose only experience of shopping is the air-conditioned grocery store, seeing fish vendors proudly displaying the fresh catch in tubs of ice on the sidewalk can be jarring. We walk by storefronts selling dried shrimp, mushrooms, and Chinese herbs and roots that most Westerners don't recognize. This food is as foreign to most of my clients today as a pickle from a barrel would have been to an Edith Wharton character slumming it on the Lower East Side.

There are other parallels hidden behind the tenement walls—and, in most cases, the Chinese are living in the exact same tenements that were built in the 1880s for Italian and Jewish families. For one, there is immense overcrowding. In some tenement apartments, as many as two dozen single men live in three rooms; in August 2013, the *New York Post* ran an exposé on a flop house on Hester Street where ten dollars a night buys a stay in a seven-by-five-foot cubicle surrounded by chicken wire. Its residents could have stepped out of a photograph in *How the Other Half Lives*.

Having given my clients a taste of Chinatown, we turn and head back into the Lower East Side. The deeper we walk down Grand or Henry Streets or East Broadway, the more signs we see for the Henry Street settlement: the Abrons Arts Center, offering instruction in everything from painting to theater; the Neighborhood Resource Center, which helps residents with legal advice; the Youth Services Headquarters and computer lab.

Over the years, Wald's reputation grew. On her seventieth birthday in 1937, she was presented with a silver platter engraved with the signatures of her admirers, including John D. Rockefeller Jr., Franklin and Eleanor Roosevelt, and dozens of Henry Street Settlement employees.

On a run around Lower Manhattan one Sunday morning, Spike and I find ourselves crossing Houston Street and wending our way into Alphabet City. First, we pass the Lillian Wald and Jacob Riis Houses, a gargantuan complex running north from East Sixth Street. Built just after World War II, they are the culmination of Riis's desire to see the tenement destroyed and replaced by better housing stock. Opened in 1949 as the solution to New York's housing problem, the Riis Houses soon began a downward spiral. As Philip Lopate notes in *Waterfront: A Walk Around Manhattan*:

> *During the mid-1970s, when New York was going through its fiscal crisis, the city had no money for maintenance or landscaping and simply paved over everything with asphalt . . . [which] invited antisocial loitering and criminal behavior such as drug deals, robberies, and violent assaults, which peaked during the crack cocaine epidemic of the 1980s.*

One bright spot was M. Paul Friedberg's central playground, Riis Plaza, a "total play environment" with a treehouse, mounds, paths, swings, and a constantly varied terrain. For Jacob Riis, such a space would have been a vindication of his vision. No dark alleys, more open sky. Today, as Spike and I jog west on Tenth Street through the middle of the complex, signs of play are scarce. Riis Plaza, like the rest of the Riis Houses, fell into disrepair. Beloved features like the "igloo" were easier to knock down than fix. Crime is down in this area, but not eradicated. During the post–Hurricane Sandy blackout in 2012, the complex lost power, trapping people in the high-rises when Avenue D flooded and the elevators quit working.

Traces of the storm are gone now, but the deeper problems remain. New York keeps getting more expensive—median rent in Manhattan today hovers around $3,200—and the city's population is only growing. We will never again see the numbers that Riis and Wald encountered on these streets on a daily basis, but nearly a century-and-a-quarter after their pioneering work, many of the challenges they faced are the ones we must confront today. The city has $100 million apartments (that's not a typo) and $10 flophouses; it's hard to see, sometimes, how all the Lillian Walds or Jacob Riises in the world will ever bridge that divide.

The Brooklyn Bridge, ca. 1896.

CHAPTER 13

Seth Low:
From the Brooklyn Bridge to the Big City

I'M STANDING ON THE BROOKLYN BRIDGE. It's pouring rain, I'm freezing, and the woman next to me keeps trying to take my picture. She's been told it is part of the "mission," but her enthusiasm is beginning to wear on me. There's a line of us stretching all the way across the bridge from Manhattan to Brooklyn on this unseasonably cold May night. We're there to help celebrate the bridge's 125th anniversary by taking part in a collective prank/art project with Improv Everywhere.

Just as I'm losing patience, Improv Everywhere's founder, Charlie Todd, suddenly runs in front of me yelling, "Go! Go! Go!" I point my disposable Kodak camera through the raindrops and take a photo into the darkness. Then the woman to my right takes her picture, and so on down the line. That's our "mission" for the night: to create a cascade of light across the bridge. Other Improv Everywhere "agents" are on the Manhattan Bridge filming us.

Charlie Todd describes what Improv Everywhere does as "scenes of chaos and joy," and on this night, chaos is the right word. Despite the forbidding forecast, more than seven hundred volunteers have shown up. A few haven't bothered to bring umbrellas, and as the evening stretches on, the logistics of trying to create a wave of light prove harder than expected. Some people—wet, tired, and unsure they're having fun—give up and disappear into the night.

That seven hundred people would turn out on such a terrible night says a lot about the popularity of Improv Everywhere—and of the Brooklyn Bridge. Agents don't know what the mission is going to be in advance; but if we'd all shown up on this miserable night and it had turned out to be a mission to light up the Queensboro Bridge, I don't think so many people would have stuck around.

Celebrated in song, story, poetry, photography, and the artwork of everyone from Joseph Stella to Andy Warhol to Georgia O'Keeffe, the Brooklyn Bridge isn't merely a bridge, it's a symbol of the city. Perhaps it's not as famous as the Empire State Building or Statue of Liberty, but those spots aren't as integral to a New Yorker's daily life—they're the places New Yorkers are dragged to when visitors come from out of town. The Brooklyn Bridge is a real part of the fabric of the city, and its mundane purpose does nothing to dampen its appeal.

The rain, however, finally causes Improv Everywhere's project to fall apart. More and more people are on their way home. Some, like me, retrace their steps back to Manhattan and the warmth of the subway. Others head east. They'll be deposited near Cadman Plaza, home of Brooklyn Borough Hall, which was—before 1898—Brooklyn City Hall.

I leave the bridge and cross City Hall Park to get to the express train; as I pass through the park, I glance up at the lights shining atop the dome of City Hall. While the location of the bridge was based on the width and course of the river, I'm sure the terminus on either end played a role too. On the Manhattan side: New York City Hall, Newspaper Row, and—just a few minutes south— Wall Street. On the Brooklyn side: Brooklyn City Hall, the banks and office buildings of Montague Street, and the prosperous suburb of Brooklyn Heights.

Throughout the nineteenth century, Brooklyn had defined itself as something different, set apart from New York. Sure, Brooklynites might go to New York for work; but as one writer later observed, they "left business at half after three; crossed the East River on the Wall Street Ferry; dined at four, and then, in the long spring twilights, sedately went driving in Prospect Park."

That was all about to change.

⚊⚊

The Brooklyn Bridge opened on May 24, 1883, with great fanfare. The newspapers dubbed it the Eighth Wonder of the World. The bridge was an engineering marvel, a steel suspension roadway spanning over a mile from New York to Brooklyn. No longer would people be dependent on ferries for transport. Seven days a week, twenty-four hours a day, the hearts of these two great cities would be connected.

Leading the procession across the bridge on opening day was Emily Roebling. Her husband, Washington, and father-in-law, John, had designed and built the bridge, but neither man was present at its completion. John Roebling had died in a tragic accident in 1869, just as construction was getting underway. After his passing, the role of chief engineer fell to his son, Washington, who soon became paralyzed. Washington spent too much time in the pressurized caissons underneath the East River where the workers were digging out the foundations for the bridge towers, which caused him to get the bends. Unable to walk and in crippling pain, Washington had to be content watching through a spyglass from their Brooklyn Heights apartment as his wife became the first person to travel across the bridge.

Emily Roebling wasn't the only one leading the procession. Riding along with her in the front carriage was a live rooster, a symbol of victory and triumph. Behind Roebling came the brass band and the dignitaries: President Chester Arthur, Governor Grover Cleveland (who would soon succeed Arthur), and New York's new mayor, Franklin Edson. As the group neared Brooklyn, they were greeted by that city's young mayor, Seth Low, who ushered them to the stage for the formal dedication. Later, Low would entertain the president and governor at his house, which had gorgeous views of the new bridge.

Like Franklin Edson, Low came to the bridge project late in its construction. He had been elected mayor of Brooklyn less than two years earlier, but he'd immediately immersed himself in tackling what he thought were the causes of the bridge's costly delays, chief among them Washington Roebling. Though he was unsuccessful in his campaign to have Roebling removed as chief engineer, Low took pride in his role in shepherding the bridge to its conclusion. He declared opening day a holiday in Brooklyn, encouraging every house to hang bunting and every citizen to turn out for the festivities.

In his remarks at the opening ceremonies, Low first praised Washington Roebling (whom he'd so recently tried to fire), before focusing on a theme that preoccupied Gilded Age New Yorkers: engineering as a sign of progress and superiority. Low called the bridge "graceful, and yet majestic," noting how "it clings to the land like a thing that has taken root. . . . Not one shall see it and not feel prouder to be a man."

He then turned his attention to the economic boon the bridge would bring to Brooklyn. Like many of the other speakers, he compared it to DeWitt Clinton's Erie Canal. The same fortunes that the canal had brought to New York in the 1820s, the bridge would now generate. Time, Low noted, is "not only money—it is opportunity. . . . The certainty of communication with New York afforded by the Bridge is the fundamental benefit it confers."

However, some Brooklynites now worried their city would become a dumping ground for New York's undesirables. In its coverage of the opening ceremonies, the *Brooklyn Daily Eagle* noted that one could tell which members of the crowd were local Brooklynites by their "sedate, complacent" faces. By contrast, the Manhattan residents stood out with their "quick, nervous, restless" expressions.

As the *Eagle* had already written a few years earlier, "the narrow island of Manhattan can never supply [enough housing], and can never be made to do so." Instead, "the future of New York, as the commercial metropolis of the Union [is] contingent upon . . . cheap, commodious and desirable homes within reach of their business."

How long would it be until those nervous New Yorkers came over the bridge to stay?

New York's Mayor Edson probably scared Brooklynites by invoking a marriage metaphor: "What has thus been joined together shall never be put asunder." Edson then peered twenty-five years into the future to 1908: "Will these two cities ere then have been consolidated into one great municipality, numbering within its limits more than five millions of people?"

The consolidation of the two cities would happen even quicker, on January 1, 1898, but Edson was very close on the population. In the 1910 census, the population of the new City of New York—which, in addition to Brooklyn and Manhattan, included the Bronx, Queens, and Staten Island—was 4.76 million.

The fifteen years between the bridge's opening day and five-borough consolidation were ones of great change for Brooklyn and New York. Some were eager to see the two cities join together. Others had to be reluctantly cajoled into the relationship.

In the end, the man who would do much of that cajoling would be Seth Low.

———

Seth Low was born in 1850 on Washington Street in Brooklyn Heights; Low's father, shipping magnate Abiel Abbot Low, moved the family to 3 Pierrepont Place—still one of the most distinguished townhouses in all of Brooklyn—when Seth was still a child.

From their back porch, young Seth could watch the boats lining the Brooklyn and Manhattan piers. Many of those ships were owned by his father, who had pioneered the South American route to China. Across the river in Manhattan, A. A. Low ran his shipping empire from Burling Slip and Schermerhorn Row, today the heart of the South Street Seaport complex.

In Seth's childhood, his house would have backed onto a garden that ran along the edge of the steep cliff that gave Brooklyn Heights its name. Since the 1950s, however, a pedestrian path has skirted the backyard of the Low house, which allows me to bring visitors to see the view from Low's perspective—not that he would recognize much of the current skyline.

Today, skyscrapers fill the frame, from classics such as the Woolworth Building, to the new World Trade Center complex, to residential behemoths like the new "New York by Gehry." In the 1850s, Low's eyes would have immediately been drawn to the water. Not only would clipper ships have lined the piers, the East River would have been choked with local traffic.

Looking across to Pier 17, the main shopping area of South Street Seaport, I can still see a few old ships, including the four-masted barque *Peking*, riding empty at the water's edge. These ships are a part of the South Street Seaport museum, an institution whose future looks grim. It was devastated by the loss of tourism in Lower Manhattan following the 9/11 terrorist attacks, and after inching back over the course of a decade, the museum's holdings were swamped by Hurricane Sandy in 2012. Losing the museum would be a blow, because New York's maritime history is too often given short shrift. From the Dutch era until the early twentieth century, the port of New York dominated the city's economy as much as Wall Street controls it today. Unfortunately, few New Yorkers think about the economic impact of the sea anymore. Shuttling back and forth between work and home in the subway, there are some Manhattanites who are only dimly aware they live on an island. In Seth Low's day, every aspect of his life was in some way tied to the sea.

Even in Low's early life, he would have seen changes in the city's maritime economy. He was just eleven years old when the Civil War began, limiting trade in the city. By the time Low graduated as Columbia College's valedictorian in 1870 and began commuting by ferry to his father's firm in Lower Manhattan, maritime trade was beginning to decline. Brooklyn, Manhattan, and—to a lesser extent—New Jersey competed for the business of unloading ships, and the system, as Central Park commissioner Andrew Haswell Green would note when pushing for five-borough consolidation, was plagued by what he called "governmental antagonisms."

After nearly a decade in his father's employ, Seth Low decided to run for mayor of Brooklyn. He had never held elected office, but came from a political family, his grandfather having been president of the trustees of Brooklyn when it was still a village. As a member of the Young Republican Club, Low had worked on the 1880 presidential campaign of James Garfield. The next year, Brooklyn was poised to elect a mayor who would have broad new powers under a revised city charter. When the Young Republicans clashed with the old guard of the party, Low emerged as the fusion candidate. At age thirty-one, he was carried into office with a comfortable margin of victory.

During Low's two terms as mayor, his achievements included not only presiding over the opening of the Brooklyn Bridge, but also minimizing state interference with Brooklyn's domestic politics—thus strengthening home rule—and modernizing the city's school system. Crucially, as biographer Gerald Kurland has noted, Low integrated the city's school system and provided city money to purchase textbooks for all students, not just those willing to take a "pauper's oath."

Low could probably have served a third term as mayor, but his support for Democratic presidential candidate Grover Cleveland alienated him from his own party. Instead, he returned to civilian life. Having served for many years as a trustee of Columbia College, he became that institution's president in 1890. For the next twelve years, Low would guide Columbia through an extraordinary change, turning the college into a true university, and spearheading the school's move from cramped quarters in midtown to Charles McKim's master-planned campus in Morningside Heights.

Most people don't know who Seth Low is anymore. But once I mention Columbia, I can always pick out the alumni in the crowd. They nod in recognition; there's a half smile that says, *That* Seth Low.

On a sunny fall morning during the first week of classes, Spike and I are running along College Walk, the center of Columbia's campus. We're both alumni, but we're not here to reminisce; we're trying to get from Riverside Park over to Morningside Park and the campus—which spans from 114th Street to 120th Street between Broadway and Amsterdam—stands between us and our destination.

Entering from the Broadway side of the campus, Charles McKim's monumental classroom buildings—limestone on the street level, brick above—turn this passageway into a narrow corridor, blocking any view of the center of campus. It's only when we reach the middle of the walk that the campus opens up before us, almost cinematically. (In fact, this view has been used in movies many times, from *Ghostbusters* to *Marathon Man* to a host of Woody Allen films.)

Up a flight of steps to our left is Low Library, named in honor of Seth Low's father, which today serves as the university's administration building; it was the president's office here that was famously occupied in 1968 during Columbia's student takeover. It hasn't been a library for decades. Within a few years of its opening, the trustees realized it was inadequate to the task; in 1910, the *Architectural Record* quipped that it was "a library de luxe and not de books."

Such peevishness aside, McKim's master plan for Columbia is a remarkable achievement; taken in its entirety, the campus can somehow simultaneously seem grandiose and intimate, inspired by the past and yet unique to its time.

Spike and I run past Rodin's "Thinker," St. Paul's Chapel, the Avery Library, and Schermerhorn Hall, the names representing the New York families whose money went to ensure Low's vision of a grand university. Size mattered, not simply because the school had outgrown its midtown campus, but because Low knew that New York City was on the cusp of great change. Already the largest city in America, it was on the threshold of becoming a world economic power. As another biographer, his nephew Benjamin R. C. Low, put it, Seth Low "never forgot that Columbia belonged to New York, and his vision of the future, outreaching that of most of his contemporaries, was part of what he foresaw for the great city of which he was now one of the leading citizens."

Having circled Low Library, Spike and I head back down the steps; we face Butler Library (the current repository of most of the university's holdings, including Seth Low's papers), continue across College Walk, and pause at the president's house on Morningside Drive at 116th Street. It was built too late for Seth Low to occupy, but was home to Dwight D. Eisenhower during his tenure as the university's president. Then, we turn south toward St. Luke's Hospital and the Cathedral of St. John the Divine. Originally, all of these institutions were affiliated with the Episcopal Church; Columbia broke longstanding tradition when it appointed Eisenhower, a Presbyterian, to head the school.

Seth Low had converted from Unitarianism to being an Episcopalian soon after his Columbia graduation. He came from a long line of New Englanders, and Unitarianism was in keeping with his New England and Brooklyn roots. Low's switch to the Episcopal Church can be framed as the first step in his conversion from being a sedate, complacent Brooklynite to a quick, restless New Yorker.

Having spearheaded the campaign to make Columbia a great school for a great city, Low turned his attention to his next project: creating that great city.

—◆—

On December 31, 1897, an electric trolley car wended its way across the span of the Brooklyn Bridge for the first time. Employees of the trolley company made last-minute adjustments to the electric cabling and then, a few minutes before midnight, the *Columbia* and the *Amphion*—two "sumptuous" trolley cars (in the words of the *New York Times*)—ferried a delegation of Brooklyn dignitaries to Manhattan to celebrate New Year's Eve. When the trolleys took them home again at the end of the party, their city was gone. At the stroke of midnight, Brooklyn had ceased to exist as an independent entity. It was now just one of five boroughs.

On the Manhattan side, a celebration thrown by William Randolph Hearst's *New York Journal* was hampered by rain that turned to snow by midnight; still, an estimated 100,000 people came out to cheer the beginning of the new city.

In Brooklyn, things were much more somber. Mayor Frederick Wurster welcomed Seth Low and other former mayors for an "observance" at Brooklyn City Hall. Though the reception was held for pro-consolidation advocates, it can't have been a cheery occasion. The official poem written for the festivities ends its first stanza with "You, with me, must die."

The desire to unite Brooklyn and Manhattan predated the construction of the Brooklyn Bridge by decades. It was first suggested in the 1820s, and by the time of the Civil War, New York had already seriously considered annexing Brooklyn, if only to bolster its revenues. In 1868, Central Park commissioner Andrew Haswell Green proposed a consolidation of "New York and Kings County [Brooklyn], a part of Westchester County [the Bronx], and a part of Queens and Richmond [Staten Island], including the various suburbs of the city...."

As Green noted in his proposal, the more than 1.5 million people in New York's environs were "all drawing sustenance from the commerce of New York" while "contributing but little toward the support of its government." It's a problem that still vexes the city to this day—thousands of people come into New York to earn money, then retreat to the suburbs to spend that money and contribute to another municipality's tax base. In the nineteenth century, the primary suburb was Brooklyn, and New York wanted its piece of the pie.

Green made little headway. While other people were clearly thinking along the same lines, his proposal was too unwieldy to attract widespread support, especially from New York's Tammany-dominated government. After Boss Tweed's downfall—when Green was installed as city comptroller to sort through the city's financial mess—Green did achieve one small victory: the annexation of parts of Westchester County in 1874 into what was known as the "Annexed District of the Bronx," or the more poetic "Great North Side." The areas of Morrisania, West Farms, and Kingsbridge were supposed to become prosperous residential districts, adding to the city's tax base, and helping to alleviate the city's housing crisis.

However, these Bronx neighborhoods were simply too far north to appeal to most downtown New Yorkers. Though New York's newest form of public transit, the elevated railroad, began operation in 1878, it would not reach the Bronx until 1886, and without an easy commute to and from the Bronx, development stalled.

Then, in 1889, the Washington Bridge opened, connecting Manhattan to the Bronx at 181st Street. Andrew Haswell Green saw the bridge as integral to the opening up of the Great North Side, and following its completion, he again set his sights on creating a consolidated New York City. At Green's urging, the New York State legislature appointed him to head a commission to explore unifying Brooklyn and New York with the other nearby counties. Green chose J. S. T. Stranahan of Brooklyn, a Brooklyn Bridge trustee and former Brooklyn Park commissioner, as vice chairman, and placed renowned architect Calvert Vaux on the commission for increased gravitas.

The timing finally seemed right: the Bronx and Brooklyn were inextricably linked to Manhattan. Queens was growing in stature and population, including the new Long Island City on the East River. Tammany Hall, initially weakened by the Tweed scandals, had bounced back. Reformers like Green saw the possibility in the Greater City of New York as a Republican check to Tammany's power. Meanwhile, New York's port—the largest in America—was also riddled with corruption. Some said, only half jokingly, that the job of port collector was the second most powerful position in America. Could a new, consolidated New York reform the port, too?

If Green thought that having strong New York and Brooklyn proponents chair the committee would lessen resistance to consolidation, he was sorely mistaken. Opposition sprung up on both sides of the river. As Green's effort picked up steam, a League of Loyal Citizens was founded in Brooklyn to oppose consolidation and that city's loss of identity. While Green tapped Seth Low to help him spread his gospel of consolidation, Low's brother Abbot joined the League to register his opposition. They wrote a new anthem for Brooklyn, "Up with the Flag," which began:

> *Up with the flag!*
> *The flag that long*
> *Has waved o'er Brooklyn's city fair,*
> *To keep her sons in union strong*
> *To bid them heed the motto there:*
> *"Right makes Might."*

Brooklyn's motto—in Dutch *Eendracht maakt macht*—not only rooted the city to its colonial heritage, but "Right makes Might" were the same words used by Abraham Lincoln, the Great Emancipator. Lincoln's armies had fought for freedom—should Brooklynites give their precious rights up so easily?

In 1894, Green had the legislature put the idea of consolidation to a vote; in order to convince everyone to go along with the plan, the legislature agreed that the outcome would be non-binding.

Seth Low began stumping for consolidation. In a speech to the City Club, a good government group, he argued that unification would bolster Brooklyn's middle class. This was a direct challenge to the often unspoken fear that Brooklyn would become the dumping ground for Manhattan's hordes of Lower East Side immigrants.

In general, the tide seemed to be moving toward unification, and when the votes were tallied, every borough had cast its lot with consolidation. In Brooklyn, the margin of victory was slim: Out of the nearly 130,000 ballots cast in Brooklyn, the pro-consolidation faction only won by 277 votes. In Queens, Flushing voted down the measure, fearing that a greater New York would be in thrall to Tammany Hall. However, the rest of Queens was in favor of consolidation and so Flushing was dragged unwillingly into the city.

The only major area that ended up keeping its autonomy was Mount Vernon in Westchester County.

Despite the fact that the referendum was supposed to be non-binding, the state legislature set a date for five-borough unification: January 1, 1898. This sparked a flurry of activity. With no city charter, how would this new municipality function? Seth Low, despite being an advocate of consolidation, urged New York's mayor William K. Strong to veto the state's measure. Both Strong and Brooklyn's mayor did veto, but the legislature simply overrode their vetoes.

Now faced with the prospect of this new city taking shape in less than two years, Seth Low appealed to New York's governor, Levi P. Morton, to appoint him head of the New York Charter Commission. The resulting city charter, a 1,000-page document, dealt with everything from port taxes to street paving, and Low found himself in the unique position of being intimately familiar with every aspect of this new city's government. It's not surprising that he was soon drafted to run to become the first mayor of the unified city.

Unfortunately, it wasn't the Republicans that drafted him. With his own party throwing its weight behind former Secretary of the Navy Benjamin F. Tracy, Low had to settle for being the candidate of the Citizens' Union, another good government group. He campaigned hard on his record as a reformer who was willing to stand up to Tammany Hall, but the deck was stacked against him. Not only did he and Tracy split the Republican vote, but Tammany Democrats turned out in force to elect Robert A. Van Wyck (the namesake of the expressway in Queens), robbing Low of the honor of being the unified city's first mayor.

Van Wyck's administration, though not the Tammany disaster that some Republicans feared, was mired in scandal. Low was able to handily win the election of 1901, but that made him the city's *second* mayor—the namesake of no expressways.

Andrew Haswell Green's fate is even more tragic. On his way home in November 1903, Green paused near his front door; a man approached him and shot him five times—a case of mistaken identity. In 1929, the Andrew Haswell Green memorial bench was erected in Central Park. Originally more prominent, it was moved to a side path near the 102nd Street transverse road in the 1980s and was essentially forgotten.

The city that Green and Low—and countless others—created is almost impossible to take in. I tell people it has nearly 8.5 million people, but that number is so large as to be meaningless. That makes it smaller than

Azerbaijan but slightly bigger than Austria; or, put another way, just slightly smaller than the entire population of New Jersey.

The city's physical size, too, is hard to comprehend. The best way to do it is on foot, but the only people crazy enough to do that are the occasional urban explorers who set out to walk all its streets (most recently William Helmreich, who traversed almost 120,000 city blocks), and the more than forty thousand runners who complete the New York City Marathon each November. Starting on the edge of Staten Island, the race course snakes 26.2 miles through each of the five boroughs, ending at Tavern on the Green in Central Park.

My first experience running the marathon was in 2001, just two months after the World Trade Center attack. It was, all at once, a somber and exhilarating experience. Many of us ran in memory of those we knew who'd been killed that day, but the event was far from funereal. In every borough, crowds of people—some visitors, but mostly locals—lined the streets to cheer us on. This happens every year, of course, but for a city still reeling in shock, it was a transformative event. While I can't say I remember every one of my fifty-two thousand steps, moments stand out clearly: the famous recording of Frank Sinatra crooning the "Theme from *New York, New York*" at the starting line; the red-white-and-blue streams of water from the fire boats beneath the Verrazano-Narrows bridge; the roar of people greeting us on the Brooklyn side of the bridge.

The course knit its way through areas that were rural when Manhattan and Brooklyn merged, such as Dyker Heights and Bay Ridge. A century ago, these Brooklynites were strongly in favor of unification; they looked at Manhattan with its paved streets, adequate water supply, and burgeoning transit system and decided to cast their lot with a city that could get things done.

My fellow runners and I then made our way toward downtown Brooklyn, through Clinton Hill and Williamsburg where, all of a sudden, every face on the street was an Orthodox or Hasidic Jew, the rows of young girls standing in identical skirts and tops. At the halfway point, we crossed the Pulaski Bridge (where followers of guru Sri Chimnoy handed out oranges) and ran through industrial Queens. After less than three miles, I found myself facing a wall of sound: the thousands of people on the Manhattan side of the Queensboro Bridge.

When the Brooklyn Bridge opened only two other bridges linked Manhattan to the outside world, the ancient Kings Bridge to the Bronx (demolished in 1917) and the High Bridge of the Croton Aqueduct system. Today, twenty-two bridges ring the island, along with car, train, and subway tunnels. Five-borough consolidation brought improvements in mass transit, including, under mayors Van Wyck, Low, and George B. McClellan, the construction of the first subways, which reached Brooklyn in 1908.

Having run up First Avenue, I crossed into the Great North Side of the Bronx on the Willis Avenue Bridge, back to Manhattan on the Madison Avenue Bridge, and finally into Central Park and the finish line.

I don't know what Seth Low and Andrew Haswell Green would think about all this. Our running outfits alone would probably cause them to faint. (As Miss Manners wrote in 2011: "No city can keep its self-respect if its streets are filled with citizens who appear to be running around in their underwear.") Green, the one-time Central Park commissioner, might applaud the democratic nature of the event, even if he couldn't understand why people would put themselves through such misery for a medal and a Mylar blanket.

The marathon is the single biggest one-day event on the city's calendar. Every year millions of people come to the city—not to see the Empire State Building, Statue of Liberty, or even the mighty Brooklyn Bridge, but to stand on a random street corner in Queens to shout encouragement at total strangers. I hope Green and Low would see it as a testament to their hard work—all of these diverse communities coming together as one unified city.

There's one final place where New York's unification is celebrated, the Surrogate's Courthouse in Lower Manhattan, but most visitors would be hard-pressed to find it.

The building itself was designed by John Rochester Thomas, who beat out 133 other architects for the honor of building a new city hall for the unified Greater City of New York. However, when Andrew Haswell Green got word of the plan to tear down the 1811 city hall, he rallied public support to save the DeWitt Clinton–era building.

Green, a friend and former colleague of Samuel Tilden, was also a trustee of the newly formed New York Public Library, which had been created through a bequest in Tilden's will. For a brief moment, the library considered moving the old city hall to a new location and using it as the library's main building, but ultimately the city decided it should stay put. Meanwhile, John Rochester Thomas made a few minor revisions to his Beaux-Arts building to house the city's Hall of Records and Surrogate's Court.

Thomas died just as construction was beginning, and Mayor Van Wyck handed the project over to a Tammany-affiliated firm, Horgan & Slattery. At the attic level of the building, facing Chambers Street, are statues of eight men deemed worthy to represent New York's municipal history, including DeWitt Clinton, Philip Hone, and Peter Stuyvesant.

As a working government office building, Surrogate's Court doesn't really welcome casual visitors. Still, I'll sometimes show people the lobby, because it is a knockout of Parisian-influenced design. Over one door is a marble sculpture by Albert Weinert, an allegorical piece entitled *The Consolidation of Greater New York*. In it, a smaller, central figure reaches out to two larger individuals—I'm guessing New York and Brooklyn—to join them together. The piece is overwhelmed by the opulence around it, but it is at least a token acknowledgment of men like Andrew Haswell Green and Seth Low, and their new, mighty metropolis.

Leaving the courthouse, I walk just a few steps south and I come face to face with the Brooklyn Bridge. Somewhere near this spot on May 24, 1883, Emily Roebling and her rooster sat waiting to make the first bridge crossing. On the other side, Seth Low stood in his topcoat and hat waiting to greet her. Just two decades—and countless trips across the bridge—later, Low would be sitting in his office on this side of the bridge as mayor of a five-borough New York.

Where I'm standing was also the place where trolley cars began running on the day of five-borough consolidation. Today, with 656 miles of subway connecting most of the city, it's easy to forget how crucial transport across this bridge was. With the advent of the trolley system, passengers could cross the bridge and be whisked in 25-cent parlor cars like the *Amphion* and *Columbia* all the way to the pleasure grounds of Coney Island. Once Brooklyn's best-kept secret, Coney Island was soon the most popular leisure spot in all of New York City.

With Manhattan at my back and Brooklyn in front of me, I walk onto the bridge, arcing upward toward its Gothic towers that stand "sleepless as the river under thee," as Hart Crane wrote in his epic poem "The Bridge." In an instant, I'm engulfed by people: tourists walking too slow, bike riders out for a late-day ride, office workers commuting home to Brooklyn Heights. There's a buzz—the sound of the wind through the steel cables, the hum of traffic on the roadbed below me—but it sounds from up here like I've tapped directly into the energy of the big city itself.

J. Pierpont Morgan, ca. 1902.

CHAPTER 14

The City of Morgan

Of all the robber barons, bankers, railroad tycoons, and stock market speculators whose wealth drove New York at the end of the Gilded Age, J. P. Morgan seems the most important—and the least known. When I say Andrew Carnegie, people immediately know of his philanthropy and Carnegie Hall. The name Rockefeller has been synonymous with success for decades. But Pierpont Morgan, as he liked to be called, is a bit of an enigma, always a little out of focus or just outside the frame.

For example, many visitors to the city put the Frick Collection on their itineraries, but they're less familiar with the Morgan Library; they flock to St. Patrick's Cathedral, but haven't heard of St. John the Divine. Few who go to the Museum of Natural History realize that Morgan was a founding trustee and that his gifts of gems were once the stars in the museum's firmament—or that the Metropolitan Museum of Art owed much to him as well.

This lack of regard for Morgan may simply stem from the fact that he was a banker, and bankers have long wielded power but received little respect in return. In his obituary, the *New York Times* described Morgan as "the greatest figure in finance that this country has ever produced." Not only had his "House of Morgan" become the most influential firm on Wall Street, he had used his fortune in myriad ways to bolster the city, from the arts to science to infrastructure to transportation to religion. The man himself may be fading into history, but in many ways, New York truly is a City of Morgan.

When plotting out how to do justice to that city, I kept bumping up against the same constraints: There's simply too much that's tied to Morgan in the city—and his life covers too wide a swath of time and geography—to neatly encapsulate. Ticking off the places that are associated with him, I realized I'd have to trek fifteen miles just to visit all the sites I wanted to include.

So I texted Spike.

"How far would you be willing to run on Saturday?"

"Between one and twenty miles," he replied.

"Meet me at 7:00 a.m. at Fulton Street and Broadway in front of St. Paul's Chapel."

Long ago, Spike learned not to question these things.

On Saturday, he walked up to St. Paul's a couple of minutes before seven.

"So," he asked, "where are we going?"

"We're tracing the life and work of J. P. Morgan." I said. "And there will be doughnuts."

"Doughnuts? Let's go."

It makes sense to start any exploration of Pierpont Morgan in Lower Manhattan; it was the nucleus of his world, and—for many years—he was the gravitational center of the Financial District. The House of Morgan at 23 Wall Street was the undisputed king of American banks.

But as Spike and I run south from St. Paul's, our first stops are just as tied to Morgan as the bank. First, we pass the former headquarters of the White Star Line and International Mercantile Marine (IMM), a vast transatlantic shipping cartel that Morgan formed in 1901. Not only did IMM own White Star, Morgan was slated to return from a trip abroad in 1912 on its new flagship, *Titanic*. Due to illness—Morgan was often in poor health—he canceled at the last minute, and thus lived to see IMM enmeshed in the investigation of the ship's sinking.

The building at One Broadway was remodeled as IMM after Morgan's death, but it is nevertheless a terrific example of how Lower Broadway used to be dominated by shipping companies. On the Battery Place side of the building, I point to the entrances: The one closest to Broadway reads FIRST CLASS, while the one at the rear of the building is marked CABIN CLASS. Even when purchasing tickets, the passengers had to be kept in their place.

Across the street, the ornate Alexander Hamilton United States Custom House dominates Bowling Green Park. Designed by Cass Gilbert and erected between 1900 and 1907, it went up during the period before federal income tax, when tariffs and customs duties accounted for the bulk of the government's revenue. Morgan despised the place. A great collector of art and antiques, Morgan wouldn't bring them into the United States because of an 1897 law that imposed a 20 percent tariff on works of art. Instead, he kept them in his houses in Putney and Grosvenor Square, London. Only books—which were deemed "educational" and therefore not subject to the same taxes—made their way to Morgan's home on Madison Avenue.

From Bowling Green, Spike and I head up to Wall Street and Morgan's Bank. It's still very early on Saturday, and for the most part, we are the only people on the street until we reach Federal Hall National Memorial, where a boot camp fitness group has taken over the steps. When we get there, they are in the middle of a drill that has them putting on and taking off their backpacks over and over again, all under the watchful gaze of George Washington.

"Pick it up!" the drill instructor yells behind us as we jog further down Wall Street. His charges dutifully grab their backpacks from the sidewalk and hurry to put them on.

Spike points to the pockmarks on the wall. "Are those the marks from the bomb?"

Of all the stories associated with the House of Morgan, the most famous is the most tragic—the September 16, 1920 bombing that left thirty-eight people dead and more than four hundred injured. The shrapnel marks, some bigger than my fist, are the only indication that anything happened here at all.

After Pierpont Morgan's death, J. P. Morgan & Co. was taken over by his son, Jack. At the time, the bank was in the process of replacing its old headquarters at 23 Wall Street with a reserved, four-story building by the architects Trowbridge & Livingston. By this point, the bank was so famous that they didn't bother to put their name on the door: everyone simply knew where it was.

At about noon on the day of the blast, a horse-drawn wagon pulled up on the opposite side of Wall Street. It was just the beginning of the lunch-hour rush, and bankers, stockbrokers, and traders on the outdoor curb market were all on the street. At 12:01 p.m., the horse cart exploded, sending five hundred pounds of metal sash-weights into the air; many of the victims died instantly.

Considering how quick we are today to blame an attack like this on terrorism—and knowing how much anarchist activity there was in 1920—it's amazing that the police didn't think the crime was politically motivated. But anarchists tended to choose individual, well-known targets, not random strangers on the street. No one was even sure what the target was supposed to be: the House of Morgan, the Federal sub-treasury building, or the Stock Exchange itself.

However, the police soon found fliers in a nearby mailbox signed by the "American Anarchist Fighters" demanding the release of political prisoners—probably Sacco and Vanzetti, who'd recently been arrested. Many historians think Mario Buda, an associate of Sacco and Vanzetti's, planted the bomb, but he was never questioned and his role remains a mystery. In fact, the Wall Street bombing is the most significant unsolved case of the twentieth century.

It was Jack Morgan who decided that in remembrance of the victims, some of whom were House of Morgan employees, the shrapnel marks shouldn't be filled. It was the worst terrorist attack in America until the 1995 Oklahoma City bombing, yet there is no memorial other than these holes in the side of the bank: no plaque, no list of names of the victims. In 1920, they may have figured, *Who will ever forget this day?* Yet, a few years later, a *Wall Street Journal* reporter took to the streets to ask people about the event. Some remembered, some had no idea what he was talking about. Today, even fewer know this story.

Spike and I take a moment to gaze at the pockmarks before I guide our discussion to a happier subject. "You know, this was the first place downtown to be lit with electricity."

Behind us, the drill instructor's aide de camp has unfurled a giant American flag. The whole scene is weird—and we've been paused long enough—so we take off running again in search of a site on Pearl Street. As we go, I tell Spike the importance of our next destination. First, coffee (we drink espresso instead of Gatorade); then, we cut east across the island toward Pearl Street in search of Edison's original power plant.

On September 4, 1882, at three o'clock in the afternoon, the dynamos at 255–257 Pearl Street rumbled to life, under the watchful eyes of engineers from Thomas Edison's Illuminating Company. A half a mile away, at the corner of Wall and Broad Streets where Spike and I have just been standing, Thomas Edison flipped the switch. In a moment, electric lights in the headquarters of Drexel, Morgan & Co. (the precursor to J. P. Morgan & Company) blazed on. Despite the round of applause, it was actually a bit of an anti-climax. Compared to the natural light streaming in the building, Edison's incandescent bulbs weren't that bright.

But Pierpont Morgan knew they were on the cusp of a revolution. A year earlier, Edison had installed electric lights in Morgan's mansion, run from a steam-powered generator built in a basement below Morgan's stables. It was an awkward system—the generator was too loud, the current sometimes spotty—but Morgan was the first man in America to have electric lights at home. He knew it would only be a matter of time before Edison's technology hit the mainstream.

A year later, that moment had arrived. As the sun began to dip, the Drexel Morgan offices grew brighter and brighter. Uptown on Nassau Street, lightbulbs burned in the *New York Times* editorial offices, so "brilliant that it would be unpleasant to look at." By 1889, Morgan had shepherded together all of Edison's various small companies under the banner of Edison General Electric; in 1892, Morgan merged that company with Thomson-Houston Electric Company, dropping the name Edison and forming the General Electric that still thrives today.

Spike and I reach the former site of the power plant, where a plaque reminds passersby of Edison's pioneering work. We then pause next door in front of a pair of old, three-story brick houses. These homes would have been here when Edison was installing his dynamos—were they wired for electricity that year by Edison? Though I know businesses were the early adopters of the technology, I try to imagine Edison himself rigging incandescent bulbs—usually fitted to the pre-existing gas fixtures—in these buildings.

That night, as Edison walked back to the power plant from Drexel Morgan, he might have stood where we are now standing, looked up, and seen someone reading by the bright light of their brand new electric bulb. Pierpont Morgan was right—it was the start of a revolution.

Our next stop, St. George's Church, Stuyvesant Square, was both Morgan's parish for much of his life, and the site of his funeral on April 14, 1913. We weave through Tribeca, Soho, and the Village until—after the first promised doughnut stop—we arrive at Gertrude Vanderbilt Whitney's statue of Governor Peter Stuyvesant in the square that bears his name.

By ten o'clock in the morning on the day of Morgan's funeral, most of the pews at St. George's were filled. In the front rows, luminaries such as John D. Rockefeller Jr. and William K. Vanderbilt turned to see a coffin covered in roses being carried down the center aisle. Among the pallbearers were Senator Elihu Root, and the city's former mayor, Seth Low.

Morgan had passed away two weeks earlier at the Grand Hotel in Rome. When he'd arrived for his annual stay in Italy in March, art and antiques dealers had flocked to his rooms, as they did every year. When word spread that Morgan was ill, London's *Daily Mail* reported that the hotel became a *besieged fortress. There is not an art-dealer or antiquary in Rome who is not making desperate efforts to approach the financier with the offer of some extraordinary bargain. . . . Waves of these amateur art-dealers . . . sweep up on the hotel from early morning till late at night and are repulsed with the regularity of surf on the beach. . . .*

When Morgan's body returned to New York, flags at the New York Stock Exchange flew at half-staff for days. Morgan lay in state at his gorgeous library on East 36th Street before the hearse made its journey to St. George's, where Morgan had served as a vestryman for forty-three years. In keeping with Morgan's unbridled ambition, St. George's had grown to be the largest Protestant church in the world.

During Morgan's time on the vestry, the Stuyvesant Square area changed radically. Established in 1836 through a gift from the Stuyvesant family, the square had fallen on hard times. William Rainsford, who became St. George's rector in 1883, later recalled it as "a dirty, neglected mockery of what a city park might be. Its fountains were waterless, the basins filled with rubbish from the street. I myself saw dead cats and empty tomato cans piled in them."

With Morgan's support, it was Rainsford who turned the church and square around. As wealthier New Yorkers moved farther uptown, St. George's pew rents declined precipitously. Instead of charging more money to make up for the lost revenue, Rainsford instead abolished pew rent entirely—one of the first major parishes to do so—and turned the church's ministry toward the poor and the immigrants in the neighborhood. Membership rebounded under Rainsford's guidance, and three years later, in 1886, Morgan paid for a gigantic new parish house to be built on Sixteenth Street.

St. George's was a trailblazing church in other ways. In 1894, Morgan cast the deciding vote for hiring African-American baritone Harry Burleigh as the church's soloist, a position he would hold for forty years. Burleigh, a gifted composer and arranger, helped popularize spirituals through his work at St. George's. His friendship with Antonin Dvorak, who lived nearby, deeply influenced Dvorak's *New World Symphony*. When Morgan made out his will a few months before he died, he not only specified exactly which hymns should be sung at his funeral, but also that Burleigh should sing them.

St. George's is still an imposing architectural presence on the square, but it's a much smaller parish. Like many other churches in the twentieth century, it could not afford to remain independent, and merged with Calvary on Gramercy Park and the Church of the Holy Communion on Sixth

Avenue. Strapped for cash, the church ultimately sold Holy Communion; it was converted into the Limelight, a notorious nightclub, and then into a shopping arcade.

Spike urges us onward. We still have many miles to go.

———

After more doughnuts, we run up Madison Avenue to the Morgan Library. In 1903, Morgan turned to leading architect Charles Follen McKim to build him a library next door to his house. When McKim was finished he'd created what the *London Times* called "the most carefully guarded treasure house in the world." The paper went on to call Pierpont "the greatest collector of things splendid and beautiful and rare who has ever lived," surpassing even Renaissance art patron Lorenzo de Medici.

For those of us who swoon in the aisles of the local bookstore, Morgan's Library is a paradise. The museum, which now encompasses an annex, a modern addition by Renzo Piano, and Pierpont's son Jack's house, is a fascinating blending of old and new styles, and there's a great contrast between the soaring glass tower of Piano's new lobby and the old-world decadence of McKim's Renaissance Revival library, based on sixteenth-century buildings in Italy.

The main library is three stories high, and is lined with bookcases, above which are paintings of great figures from literature, art, and science, including Dante, Michelangelo, and Galileo. Signs of the zodiac are arranged throughout the ceiling, and over the mantelpiece hangs a Renaissance tapestry depicting *The Triumph of Avarice*. Beneath it is inscribed in Latin, As TANTALUS IS EVER THIRSTY AMIDST WATER, SO DOES THE MISER ALWAYS DESIRE RICHES. Morgan's generosity aside, he suffered—like most of his compatriots—from the Gilded Age disease of greed. I wonder if he had the inscription put there as a warning to himself or a rebuke.

Morgan's role in shaping America's financial health from the 1890s through his death can't be understated. After J. P. Morgan & Co. propped up the failing United States Treasury and ended the Panic of 1893, the Dow Jones continued to rise, reaching a peak of 103 in January 1906 (the first time the twenty-year-old Dow had broken a hundred).

However, over the next two years, the market would falter, and lose almost half its value. In 1907, there was another panic that began when United Copper Company tried—and failed—to corner the copper market. Banks and trust companies associated with the copper company began to fail, and again it was

Pierpont Morgan who stepped in. On Saturday, November 2, 1907, he gathered the city's bankers in the library—underneath *The Triumph of Avarice*—and placed presidents from trust companies in his nearby study, a room I love even more than the library itself. It was here that Morgan in his later years did most of his official business. The room is both beautiful and drives home Morgan's staggering wealth. Perusing one shelf, I see nothing but early editions of Shakespeare. That shelf alone represents a lifetime of income for many people.

Once the bankers and trust company presidents were ensconced in their respective rooms, Morgan locked the doors and went to play solitaire until an agreement could be reached. By three in the morning, a deal had been struck to bail out the failing trusts.

In the aftermath of Morgan's rescue, politicians began to reconsider the fact that America lacked a central bank; ultimately, the Federal Reserve was chartered to take the burden of shoring up financial markets away from people like Morgan. Morgan's opponents wondered if the panic had been manufactured so that Morgan's U.S. Steel could acquire the failing Tennessee Coal at a bargain price. Congressman Arsene Pujo, the chairman of the House Committee on Banking, created a special investigative committee to look into any wrongdoing. While Morgan was not sanctioned, the often testy committee hearings exacerbated his declining health. In the spring of 1913, he left for his annual trip to Europe; he returned in his casket.

~

Spike and I bid farewell to the library and run over to Fifth Avenue; our next stop, uptown at East 60th Street, is the Metropolitan Club, one of New York's many private membership clubs. As we jog there, we're covering the same ground—and roughly the same time period—as our run where we looked for Caroline Astor's New York. But her world and Morgan's rarely collided. Only toward the end of her life, when Mrs. Astor decided to host a "Bohemian" (read: down-market) ball did she deign to invite people like her cousin Edith Wharton and a mere banker like Pierpont Morgan.

When Spike and I reach 60th Street, I can't help but think of Morgan's alleged instructions to his architect, Charles McKim's partner Stanford White: "Build a club fit for gentlemen. Damn the expense!"

This exhortation is almost a parody, too much the embodiment of what outsiders thought rich people should sound like. Then again, Morgan was building the Metropolitan Club simply because he was irked at the membership policies at the rival Union Club, so, maybe "damn the expense" was the order of the day.

Private clubs were the place where gentlemen did business—the Gilded Age equivalent of the golf course—and it made sense that Morgan would want his business associates to have access to these vital spaces. Morgan's business interests had long been intertwined with the railroads and, in 1899, he proposed John King, the president of the Erie Railroad, for admission to the Union Club. The Union Club's membership committee turned King down. When two more of Morgan's friends were blackballed, he organized a revolt. Prominent members of the Union Club walked out (though, hedging their bets, didn't resign), and on February 20, 1891, met to found the Metropolitan Club.

Among the attendees at that first meeting were William K. Vanderbilt, Cornelius Vanderbilt II, Samuel D. Babcock, and Robert Goelet. Morgan couldn't attend, but they voted him in as president of the new club anyway. Twenty-five men were elected to the club's board of governors and each put forward five thousand dollars for the construction of a new clubhouse. They quickly acquired this choice lot on Fifth Avenue at 60th Street, hired Stanford White, and got to work.

White is often the architect most associated with the Gilded Age. His other work around the city includes the memorial arch in Washington Square, private mansions, other private clubs, and the old Madison Square Garden—of which Morgan was a major backer—where the architect would be murdered in 1906.

For Morgan, White created soaring interior spaces for the new clubhouse. On February 20, 1894, the board of governors met there for the first time. A few days later, the doors were thrown open to the press. The *New York Times* called it "a well-behaved and most respectable palace" but critiqued it for being too outsized: "It is difficult to imagine this interior restful and companionable."

Beyond this press preview, few who were non-members would ever get beyond the front door. To them, and to most of us today, the only visible part of the club is the outside. On the 60th Street side of the clubhouse is a recessed carriageway, closed off with forbidding, wrought-iron gates. (As Edith Wharton would write in *The Decoration of Houses* in 1898: "While the main purpose of a door is to admit, its secondary purpose is to exclude.") On each gate, a gold "M" is emblazoned; at face value, these "M"s—which are also on oval embossed keystones above the windows and worked into the banister—stand for Metropolitan, but I'm sure members of the club knew who they actually stood for.

By now, Spike and I have run over ten miles. The end is in sight, but first we need to cross Central Park to the American Museum of Natural History.

In 1869, J. P. Morgan was one of the founding trustees of the Museum of Natural History, which had its first, temporary, home inside the Central Park arsenal. Throughout the museum's early life, Morgan was an important benefactor, donating precious gems and minerals to the collection. Of these, the most significant—and largest—was the Star of India, a 563-carat sapphire Morgan bought in London in 1902. When the jewel first went on display, it immediately became one of the museum's biggest attractions; it is still the largest sapphire on public view.

Today, the Star of India seems tucked away, far from the dinosaurs and planetarium that draw so many museumgoers. Perhaps that's just as well—the gem has long drawn admirers, not all of them with the best intentions. On the night of October 29, 1964, in a daring heist, the Star of India was stolen by Jack "Murph the Surf" Murphy, a former surfing champion turned cat burglar. Murphy and his crew were able to climb in an unlocked window, open the jewel cases—which weren't alarmed—and make off with the Star of India, the DeLong Star Ruby, and the Eagle Diamond (another gift from Morgan). Murphy was arrested two days later, which led to the recovery of the Star of India and DeLong Star Ruby. Alas, the Eagle Diamond was never recovered; it may be in private hands or might have been cut down and sold in pieces.

Across the park, traces of the Metropolitan Museum of Art as Morgan would have known it also remain. Both museums were founded about the same time, and both were built by Calvert Vaux and Jacob Wrey Mould. For years, the Metropolitan Museum tried to woo Morgan away from his trusteeship at the Museum of Natural History; Morgan resisted, and since the institutions' bylaws specified that the two museums could not share trustees, the Metropolitan bided its time for one of New York's premier collectors to join its family.

Morgan's art collection had started on his honeymoon. In 1861, he had married Amelia Sturges in her family's home on East 14th Street, a house filled with Hudson River School art. Amelia's father, Jonathan, had commissioned Asher Durand's *Kindred Spirits*, and had paid for Durand's sketching trips to Europe. Whether Morgan was influenced by Jonathan Sturges's taste is unclear, but his brief first marriage did inspire Morgan to acquire his first painting.

Morgan married Amelia knowing she was ill, probably with tuberculosis. Immediately following the wedding in October 1861, they took an extended honeymoon to the Mediterranean, hoping the climate would improve her condition. However, on February 17, 1862, Amelia died in France; soon after, Morgan purchased his first painting, a "young fey woman," which he hung in a place of honor over his fireplace. It was the beginning of Morgan's private collection and his yearly pilgrimages to purchase art.

In 1888, Morgan was finally convinced to join the Metropolitan's board, and two years later, when Pierpont took over his father's company, he began collecting in earnest. In one story—perhaps apocryphal—a dealer approached Morgan with Vermeer's *Lady Writing*, hoping to get $100,000 for it.

"Who is Vermeer?" Morgan asked. After he'd listened—and realized how rare a painting it was—he simply said, "I'll take it," and handed over the $100,000. That time, he got lucky, and the painting now hangs at the National Gallery in Washington, one of only about three dozen surviving Vermeer canvases. Other times he wasn't as fortunate, but all the big-time collectors of his era were fooled by unscrupulous dealers and forgers. To that end, Morgan employed art connoisseurs and dealers like Bernard Berenson and Joseph Duveen to advise him; in doing so, he was able to purchase pieces like a Raphael altarpiece (now in the Metropolitan Museum), a Gainsborough, and an entire room of panels by Fragonard. It was this art that Morgan kept in London to avoid American taxes; when the tax codes were rewritten after Morgan's death, much of his private collection finally came to the United States.

It's remarkable how small the original Metropolitan Museum was. Today's medieval hall was essentially the entire museum. In a few places, Vaux and Mould's architectural details peek through: One wall of the Lehman wing is the original Central Park facade. Upstairs, in a second floor hallway, a similar remnant of the Fifth Avenue side of the building remains—just the top of one arch peeking through. But my favorite part of the Morgan-era museum is a Vaux and Mould staircase, complete with beautiful columns and quadrafoil arches in the banisters, that leads from the second floor down to the gift shop. These must be the most seldom-used stairs in the whole museum, and I always love finding places in the museum—the most heavily visited spot in the city—where I can stand and be completely alone.

—◦—

The sun is getting high as Spike and I finally crest the hill in Morningside Heights that brings us to the Cathedral of St. John the Divine and the end of our run. Having come all the way from Battery Park, I have a sense now of just how far away this church must have seemed from the rest of the city when its cornerstone was laid on December 27, 1892.

Considering the fact that the Episcopal Church had been the denomination of New York's elite for nearly two centuries, it's a little surprising that work did not begin on a cathedral until the close of the nineteenth century. Initial reluctance stemmed from the church's anti-English bias, but even as that waned, it took a long time for plans for the cathedral to crystallize. Perhaps they were just waiting for the money.

Certainly, by 1892 New York's Episcopalians were richer than they'd ever been, and the cathedral's trustees included J. Roosevelt Roosevelt, Cornelius Vanderbilt, and Morgan. On that cold December day, the trustees paraded into the tent behind the cathedral's architect, George Heins, with an array of bishops trailing behind them. It was a day full of hope and exuberance. Certainly no one there realized that nearly 125 years later, the great cathedral would still not be finished.

The building of St. John the Divine was plagued with problems from the start. The trustees, under Morgan's guidance, hosted a design competition, ultimately selecting the firm of Heins & La Farge, even though their design was no one's first choice.

Work on the cathedral didn't begin until the spring of 1893, and immediately the crew ran into trouble. A foundation that should have taken months to lay ended up taking years. Without anything to show for it, the cathedral was already over budget, so Morgan wrote a check for $500,000, "to get us out of the hole"—literally and figuratively. In 1903, the giant granite columns of the apse were hoisted into place, but by 1905, only one chapel had been completed. Then, in 1907, George Heins died of meningitis. Though the trustees were legally able to break their contract, they allowed La Farge to continue until the apsidal end of the church was complete. This small portion of the cathedral, known as the choir, was consecrated on April 19, 1911. With this milestone behind them, the trustees ended their relationship with Heins & La Farge and hired Ralph Adams Cram to finish the church.

Over the next three decades, Cram would erect the bulk of the cathedral, along with the synod house, the cathedral school, and the bishop's residence and deanery, which looks like a French chateau. Though Morgan didn't live to see this impressive edifice finished, he left his mark on it. As the large building was going up, there were rumblings that it was too grandiose a home for a member of the clergy. Morgan allegedly retorted: "Bishops should live just like everyone else."

Today, while the cathedral performs a vital mission in the neighborhood as a religious space, it is an odd tourist attraction. Students of architecture mingle with Japanese tour groups. As Spike and I run past, a dozen buses are all simultaneously disgorging passengers, but sometimes I go inside to lead a tour and virtually have the place to myself.

The cathedral overwhelms in its massiveness. At 601 feet long and 121,000 square feet of floor space, it is the world's largest cathedral and fourth largest church, but it's the details that define the experience: In one window, dedicated to John Jacob Astor IV, there's a small image of the *Titanic* sinking. In another, the Civil War generals Ulysses S. Grant and Robert E. Lee face off against each other; nearby, images trace the evolution of communication from the printing press to the television, a technology still basically on the drawing board when this stained glass was designed.

I was touring with a couple from London once, pointing out all these oddities, when the husband remarked, "That's so very American." And I suppose it is. The images seem a little random, a little eccentric, and maybe that's a proper metaphor for our country. I don't think my visitor meant it as a compliment, but I'm taking it as one.

Outside, we visit Cram's magnificent Synod House. In front, there's a central jamb figure that on a European cathedral would likely be Christ or the church's patron saint. Here, it's George Washington, the patron saint of our country. In the figures that adorn the archway, Cram has carved New York's merchants and tradesmen, including himself, clutching a small model of the cathedral. I search the faces for J. P. Morgan or anyone recognizable from the world of high finance, but come up short.

Spike looks at his watch and I know I need to let him go. We've covered nearly five decades in our fifteen miles and haven't even visited every place we could have. Morgan served on the board of the Vanderbilts' New York Central Railroad, but we've left Grand Central Terminal off our route; we jogged by the Union Club—which blackballed Morgan's friends—without stopping, and there are countless other spots associated with Morgan that we've skipped as well.

But Spike doesn't seem to mind. He tells me this has been one of his favorite runs, and as we say goodbye, he's already trying to remember all the things we've talked about so that he can share it with other people.

"You can just buy my book," I tell him.

"Geez. I have to buy the book?"

Portrait of Langston Hughes by Carl Van Vechten, 1936.

CHAPTER 15

The Liberators:
Harlem, Greenwich Village, and the American Left

NEW YORK BEFORE WORLD WAR II IS OFTEN VIEWED through a veil of alcohol. It's the world of F. Scott Fitzgerald's *The Great Gatsby*, Dorothy Parker's Algonquin Round Table, bathtub gin, and—more recently—HBO's *Boardwalk Empire*. There's a pop and fizz to our cultural depictions of the time, despite the violent lawlessness that sometimes characterized the period.

In New York, two neighborhoods were most associated with speakeasy culture: downtown, the quiet byways of Greenwich Village were taken over by cabarets and illegal bars; uptown, Harlem prospered as a place for jazz and sweet cocktails, the sugar added to hide how vile the liquor was. In both cases, outsiders traveled to these areas to be transgressive—not just to break the law by drinking, but to mix with bohemians and African Americans. These neighborhoods were places where, for a night, New Yorkers could escape their mundane lives.

What speakeasy tourists rarely saw were the real outsiders, the radicals who had long made Greenwich Village an actual haven for intellectual bohemianism, or the Harlem writers whose output in the 1920s and '30s would come to be known as the Harlem Renaissance. Harlem and Greenwich Village had much more in common than just cheap booze; these were the bastions of the American intellectual left. However, despite the fact that the express subway hurtled passengers from 135th Street to 14th Street in less than half an hour, Harlem and the Village were worlds apart.

~~~

By the time Prohibition went into effect on January 17, 1920, many old-time residents of Greenwich Village thought its bohemian heyday had already passed. Ever since the days of Edgar Allan Poe, the area's low rents had drawn writers and artists. Then, in 1858, Richard Morris Hunt's Tenth Street Studio building opened just east of Sixth Avenue, becoming the home to generations of American artists; it planted the seed that the Village was the place to be for creative people—an American "Left Bank," like Paris's bohemian quarter.

Even before the speakeasies, this notoriety drew tourists. There were "goofy" clubs, like the Pirate's Den, where the waiters dressed up in costume. At Polly's Restaurant on MacDougal Street or Bruno's Garret (part publishing enterprise, part tourist trap), visitors might get a glimpse of a real bohemian—or someone posing as one. In 1913, John Reed, better known for his political journalism, lampooned Village life in *A Day in Bohemia;* in the same vein, Sinclair Lewis's *Hobohemia* satirized the inability of most Villagers to make money off their lifestyle.

Once the speakeasies opened, the popularity of the Village skyrocketed. When the Eighteenth Amendment prohibiting the sale and manufacture of alcohol went into effect, it forced fifteen thousand bars in New York to close; within a decade, there were thirty-two thousand speakeasies. This is a staggering amount of drinking—today, the city doesn't even have three thousand stand-alone bars.

As the song "Down in Old Greenwich Village" proclaimed:

> *Way down south in Greenwich Village*
> *Comes a bunch of uptown swillage*
> *Folk from the Lenox subway stations*
> *Come with lurid expectations.*

But while tourists might flock to Sheridan Square looking for a stiff drink and a "real" bohemian, the genuine Greenwich Village counterculture continued away from public view, in tiny apartments and blind alleys.

Socialist John Reed—the only American buried in the Kremlin wall—worked on his history of the Bolshevik revolution, *Ten Days that Shook the World,* from his flat on Patchin Place. Birth control advocate Margaret Sanger moved into a lower Fifth Avenue apartment in 1922. The Provincetown Players, home to Eugene O'Neill and pioneers of Off-Broadway theater, set up shop on MacDougal Street south of Washington Square in 1918. A decade earlier, sculptor and arts patron Gertrude Vanderbilt Whitney bought a carriage house on MacDougal Alley for her studio, confirming her bohemian credentials. Over the next two decades, her commitment to collecting the work of her artist friends and neighbors eventually led to the opening of the Whitney Museum of American Art.

These people didn't all travel in the same circles, but one man who often brought these disparate strands of Village life together was Max Eastman, the charismatic editor of the socialist magazines *The Masses* and, later, *The Liberator*. Eastman isn't a household name today, but in many ways he was the patron saint of the Village bohemians.

Max Eastman arrived in Greenwich Village in 1907, and soon fell in with Mabel Dodge, whose salons in her lower Fifth Avenue home were legendary. Described as both a "dynamo" and "sphinx-like," Dodge had set out to create an atmosphere in New York like that in Gertrude Stein's home in Paris.

Dodge's salon drew people from every walk of life: anarchists Andrew Berkman and Emma Goldman, muckraking journalist Lincoln Steffens, photographer Alfred Stieglitz, as well as Eastman, Reed, Lewis, Floyd Dell, and most of the other people who would end up writing for *The Masses* or Greenwich Village's famed literary journal, *The Dial*. Eastman later said that Dodge's salons were a "magnetic field." Men fell under Dodge's spell, including Eastman and Reed, the latter of which had an affair with her before meeting his future wife, Louise Bryant.

In 1912, Eastman was made editor of *The Masses* (for "no pay"), taking over a magazine with a dwindling subscription base and poor finances. Bailed out by Alva Vanderbilt Belmont (Gertrude Vanderbilt Whitney's aunt), Eastman made the magazine the toast of the "lyrical Left." Among those *The Masses* published were Reed, Bryant, Dell, Dorothy Day, Sherwood Anderson, Upton Sinclair, and realist artist John Sloan.

The Masses aimed to encapsulate not just the left-leaning ideology of the Village writers, but to capture the zeitgeist of the neighborhood: "Fun, truth, beauty, realism, freedom, peace, feminism, revolution." It was a tall order, and some readers were baffled by the magazine's broad-minded agenda, but under Eastman it grew in prestige—if not in circulation.

People who take Greenwich Village tours—when they're not specifically hunting down the haunts of their favorite writers or following in the footsteps of Bob Dylan—are often hoping to find some traces of this bohemianism. Alas, I can't even show them a real speakeasy anymore.

For years, as I led groups through the West Village, I would see visitors doing a ritualistic dance outside the plain townhouse at 86 Bedford Street. They'd consult their guidebooks and shake their heads. When they looked like they were giving up, I'd cross the road to ask, "Are you looking for Chumley's?"

"Yes!"

I'd push open the door of the house and gesture to the dark interior. "Up these four stairs, down the ones on the other side and there you are."

They'd freeze.

"Trust me—you're in the right place."

New York has had a proliferation of faux speakeasies in the past decade, but none compare to Chumley's, which was the real deal. Established as a bar in 1928, Chumley's began pouring drinks almost a decade into America's fourteen-year "noble experiment" with Prohibition. It was a focal point of the Greenwich Village literary scene, both in the downstairs bar and an upstairs gathering spot for writers and intellectuals known simply as "The Meeting Place." Like most illegal bars, it didn't bother with a password; it simply hid in plain sight.

The saloon's "back" door was actually its Bedford Street entrance (the front door was in a courtyard around the corner). Inside the back entrance, proprietor Leland Chumley installed a tricky set of steps to trip up Prohibition inspectors if they happened to come in that way.

After Prohibition was lifted in 1933, Chumley declined to install a sign over the door or advertise. You either knew where the place was or you didn't. That's how things remained until 2007. Despite befuddled tourists pacing on the sidewalk, Chumley's held onto its history.

Then, disaster struck. Workers doing unauthorized repairs caused the house's ancient chimney to collapse, destabilizing the wall and roof. The owners of the bar packed away a trove of memorabilia—paintings, photographs, and first-edition dust jackets of famous authors who drank and worked there—and began the laborious work of restoring the bar. Restoring turned into rebuilding. Today, over six years after the chimney collapse, the reopening of Chumley's always seems to be just around the corner—but never quite arrives.

Some people have written Chumley's off, but not me. If even half the stories of the people who walked through that courtyard door are true, it remains an important touchstone of the Village's bohemian past. F. Scott Fitzgerald and Ernest Hemingway were both said to have imbibed there, but many of the other writers whose dust jackets were memorialized on Chumley's walls fail to impress my clients. Names like Max Eastman and Floyd Dell elicit no response. Even Emma Goldman, the most radical revolutionary in America, has seen her reputation fall by the wayside. A few people read Edna St. Vincent Millay, and know that Eugene O'Neill gets revived on Broadway every now and again. But most of the others are ghosts.

One name I sometimes see connected to Chumley's—though he was long dead by the time it opened—is John Reed. Maybe that's because people link him to the area having seen the Warren Beatty film *Reds*. Just around the corner from Chumley's is the Grove Street house Beatty used as the stand-in for Reed's address in *Reds*. I appreciate the fact that Beatty not only picked Grove Street because it could reasonably pass for 1915–20, but also because it's a street all his characters would have known in real life.

When I walk by the old Whittemore mansion—which Beatty used as the stand-in for Eugene O'Neill's house—I know this is a street the real O'Neill walked on. Max Eastman, played by Edward Herrmann in the film, would have journeyed this way too, heading to Chumley's or to see a play at the Cherry Lane Theatre. Very little has changed in the past century in this section of Greenwich Village, and even though traffic hurtles by on nearby Hudson Street and Seventh Avenue South, all it takes is a few steps on Grove Street to really feel like you've discovered Eastman's world.

As America moved toward entering World War I, Max Eastman found himself in trouble. He was passionately opposed to the war, and *The Masses* became increasingly vocal in its denouncements of military recruiting. As a result, the US Post Office canceled the magazine's second-class postal privileges, effectively silencing it. Eastman, Dell, Reed, and other contributors were charged with violating the Espionage Act. Two trials ended in hung juries and Eastman was never convicted—but *The Masses* was dead.

In its place, Eastman founded *The Liberator* with his sister, Crystal. In its pages, John Reed reported directly from Russia as the Bolshevik Revolution unfolded. Another contributor, Helen Keller, passionately defended America's most radical labor union, the IWW. It was through the union that Eastman met Lee Chumley, and the spirit of radicalism from the IWW infused both Chumley's and the upstairs Meeting Place.

In addition to political coverage, *The Liberator* also published poetry. In the first issue, Floyd Dell wrote a critique of James Weldon Johnson's new book of poems, accusing it of not sounding "Negro" enough for a black poet. To his credit, not only did Eastman print Johnson's lengthy rebuttal in the next issue, he asked Johnson to write about African-American struggles for equality. *The Liberator* began publishing black poets, such as Fenton Johnson and Claude McKay, who would later be considered one of the great figures of the Harlem Renaissance.

In 1919, the magazine published McKay's sonnet "If We Must Die," inspired by an outbreak of lynchings and racial violence that year dubbed the "Red Summer" by James Weldon Johnson. McKay wrote:

If we must die—let it not be like hogs
Hunted and penned in an inglorious spot,
While round us bark the mad and hungry dogs,
Making their mock at our accursed lot.
If we must die—oh, let us nobly die. . . .

In 1921, Eastman asked McKay, who had fully embraced socialism, to join *The Liberator*'s staff, forging a tentative bridge between the activist community in the Village and the burgeoning Harlem left. The next year, Eastman left the editorship in the hands of McKay and another colleague, Michael Gold, so that Eastman could travel to Russia to see the results of the Bolshevik Revolution firsthand.

However, McKay soon clashed with Gold over how to cover race in the magazine, and he resigned in July 1922. With Eastman and McKay gone, *The Liberator* limped along; in 1924 it was folded into the Communist Party's official magazine.

In 1927, Eastman returned to America disillusioned with Stalin, who had turned against Eastman's friend Leon Trotsky, and began to disassociate himself from socialist causes. He spent much of his time at his house in Croton-on-Hudson. Biographer William L. O'Neill later noted that Eastman had "always looked down on Greenwich Village bohemianism. He preferred to live in Croton near other serious radicals." This doesn't exactly square with the idea that *The Masses* celebrated the "fun, truth, beauty, realism, freedom, peace, feminism, revolution" of the Greenwich Village milieu, but perhaps it was simply that the "old Village" was gone.

Fun, truth, beauty? The bars and cafes where Max Eastman and his friends passionately debated everything from music to politics to art were being overwhelmed by cheap speakeasies, Chumley's notwithstanding. Realism, freedom, and peace? As a new war in Europe loomed, America was faced with the dilemma of whether or not to join the European conflict. Feminism? Yes, significant battles had been won—the Nineteenth Amendment gave women the right to vote in 1920—but outside of neighborhoods like Greenwich Village, true equality seemed like a distant dream.

Revolution? In so many ways, the revolution had never arrived.

When Claude McKay resigned from *The Liberator,* he followed in Eastman's footsteps to Russia. While Eastman's trip sparked his gradual shift toward conservatism, Claude McKay's was a "magical pilgrimage." He embraced Communist Russia's "atmosphere . . . all that Byzantine conglomeration of form and color, shedding down its radiance upon the proletarian masses." While McKay, too, would eventually repudiate Communism, his writings from this period—the novels *Home to Harlem, Banjo: A Story without a Plot,* and *Banana Boat*—all weave together subjects of class, race, and socialist politics.

Today, while McKay's name is no longer as familiar as those of Langston Hughes, Richard Wright, or Zora Neale Hurston, he was a key figure in the development of the African-American literature that put Harlem on the map as a cultural center in the 1920s and '30s. Unlike many of his peers, McKay would shuttle back and forth between uptown and downtown, putting him in the position of being what he called "the contact man between Harlem and the Village."

However, there were other points of contact between Harlem and Greenwich Village—and they had very little to do with socialism or literature. Many of the same faux-bohemians who went to the Village to drink also traveled to Harlem for booze, dancing, and jazz.

A handful of clubs dominated the scene: the Cotton Club, Savoy Ballroom, Small's Paradise, Barron Wilkins's Exclusive Club, and Connie's Inn were all draws in what came to be known as "Jungle Alley." As scholar Steven Watson put it, the "major element of Uptown allure was its enormous social fluidity; in this urban free zone . . . the Social Register and Emily Post held no sway."

Most of these clubs were segregated. Langston Hughes called the Cotton Club a "Jim Crow club for gangsters and monied whites"; they listened to Duke Ellington while surrounded by racist caricatures of black field hands. The segregation went both ways—when Claude McKay tried to take Max Eastman to Ned's, an all-black cabaret where he was a regular, Eastman and McKay were both turned away.

The cabarets that served only blacks became "a refuge for local residents seeking to escape white voyeurs" in the words of historian Kathleen Morgan Drowne. As in Greenwich Village, there came to be two Harlems: the one visited by urban adventurers that was marketed, packaged, and sanitized for the tourist trade, and a second Harlem, where people worked, worshiped, ate, and drank—apart from these white visitors.

Only a few decades earlier, Harlem had been almost exclusively white. In the late nineteenth century, as the pace of real estate development increased, rows of identical townhouses had been erected in Harlem in the hopes of luring the Gilded Age middle class northward.

When that middle class failed to materialize, Harlem's real estate market collapsed. In 1904, when the first line of the subway opened, Lower East Side Jewish families flocked to Harlem to be closer to City College, the city's free university built high on Hamilton Heights. For awhile, Harlem was the second-largest Jewish neighborhood in New York.

In 1891, contractor David King invested in a series of 146 townhouses and three apartment buildings along 138th and 139th Streets between Adam Clayton Powell Jr. Boulevard and Frederick Douglass Boulevard. The development was a spectacular failure, and by the time of its foreclosure, only nine of the homes had sold. Meanwhile, the main African-American area of the city, known as the Tenderloin, was about to experience a great upheaval. In 1901, when the Pennsylvania Railroad was given the right to build their massive new rail yards and Penn Station in the midst of the black community, Tenderloin residents began filtering up to Harlem, where the real estate glut had made landlords desperate for tenants. In 1919, King's mortgage company started renting his houses to black families, and soon the development took on the name "Striver's Row."

When Claude McKay arrived in New York from Jamaica in 1914, by way of Alabama and Kansas, he found Harlem on the cusp of change. In 1910, only 10 percent of the area's population had been black; by the time McKay's novel *Home to Harlem* came out in 1928, that figure had risen to almost 70 percent.

What made Harlem different from other major black cities, such as Chicago, was the diversity within its population. While the Great Migration brought some blacks from the South, others—like McKay and scholar Arturo Schomburg—came from the Caribbean. Some had deep roots in New York City, where the African-American population stretched back all the way to Peter Stuyvesant's era. Some migrants had been enslaved; others came from families that never knew slavery.

As the population in Harlem grew, the neighborhood galvanized the activism of people as diverse as McKay, W. E. B. DuBois, Marcus Garvey, and A. Philip Randolph. That activism would soon influence the man who is perhaps the best-known symbol of the Harlem Renaissance—Langston Hughes.

Born in Kansas and raised in the Midwest, Langston Hughes came to New York in 1921 to attend Columbia University. He was already a budding poet—inspired, he later said, by reading Claude McKay in *The Liberator*. He was also inculcated in socialism. At his high school in Cleveland, "red flags lined the hallways and John Reed's *Ten Days That Shook the World* was required reading," according to critic Jonathan Scott. (Ironically, Central High was also the alma mater of John D. Rockefeller, America's richest capitalist.)

Hughes lasted one year at Columbia, dismayed at the racism he encountered. After a sojourn in Paris and Africa, Hughes returned to the United States, published his first collection of poetry, finished his degree at Lincoln University in Pennsylvania, and returned to New York as the Harlem Renaissance was in full bloom.

Many people date the beginning of the Harlem Renaissance to Alain Locke's 1925 volume, *The New Negro,* an anthology that brought together some of the best writing coming out of Harlem. But what really riled the waters was Carl Van Vechten's novel *Nigger Heaven,* released a year later. Van Vechten, a white photographer and journalist, had established himself as the "downtown" expert on the neighborhood and its denizens. Having first ventured into Harlem in 1924, he began spending all his free time there, wrote articles for *Vanity Fair,* and brought downtown friends (like F. Scott Fitzgerald) to Harlem.

Though fiction, *Nigger Heaven* was seen by many as a realistic portrait of the neighborhood. It sparked a Harlem craze among downtown whites, and though many Harlem writers, including Hughes, praised the book's honesty, Van Vechten was also lambasted by African-American critics for the book's lurid sex and emphasis on crime. Its title—a common epithet for the racially segregated balconies of many theaters, and a metaphor for Harlem's place in the city—was also seen as an affront.

But Van Vechten had pushed open an important door. Two years later, those same critics would dismiss Claude McKay's *Home to Harlem,* another work of neo-realism, for similar offenses. As W. E. B. Du Bois wrote, "after the dirtier parts of its filth, I feel distinctly like taking a bath."

This type of criticism only fueled sales. Van Vechten outsold all Harlem's black writers; *Home to Harlem* was McKay's only unqualified success. When Langston Hughes returned to New York, he found Harlem both reveling in and worried by its own prosperity. There had been, indeed, a Harlem Renaissance. The question for Hughes was: Was there now going to be a Harlem Enlightenment?

Harlem draws an eclectic cross-section of tourists. Europeans often come because they feel it's one of the only places that they can experience a truly authentic slice of urban American life. New Yorkers want to experience something off the beaten path—a neighborhood that's so close, yet still undiscovered. But I can tell when people are there because they want to go slumming. After we've seen the multimillion-dollar townhouses on Convent Avenue or the beauty of Stanford White's homes on Striver's Row, someone will sidle up and say, "I thought this area was going to be more. . . ." They let it hang there, allowing me to fill in the blank.

What even New Yorkers aren't expecting is the peaceful, almost suburban feel of some of these streets. When we walk down Striver's Row, people are as impressed by the architectural grandeur as they are by the signs urging residents to walk their horses to the rear stables. In many ways, it's a street that remains virtually unchanged from when Claude McKay and Langston Hughes would have walked here, or when famous Harlemites like Bill "Bojangles" Robinson, architect Vertner Tandy, or bluesman W. C. Handy lived in these homes. I wonder if Langston Hughes appreciated this quiet, unhurried feeling as well. Or are we not experiencing what Hughes knew at all? Was the pace of his Harlem in the 1920s and 1930s so much more frenetic that it energized these peaceful streets?

If Hughes were to revisit the neighborhood today, he'd find familiar sites: His house on West 127th Street is still there, as is the famous YMCA (now named for Claude McKay) where many Harlem Renaissance figures once roomed. The old churches—Harlem has one every few blocks—stand as sentries, watching over the area.

At the corner of Adam Clayton Powell Jr. Boulevard and West 135th Street, Hughes might do a double-take when he saw that the building he knew as a nightclub called Small's Paradise is now an IHOP. If he walked a few blocks north, he'd find the shell of the Renaissance Ballroom and Casino next to Abyssinian Baptist Church. Trees grow from its roof and it looks like it could collapse in on itself any minute.

In fact, the more Hughes looked around, the more he'd realize that Harlem is only the same in a superficial way. The Cotton Club and Savoy Ballroom are gone; the blocks where the clubs once stood were razed for apartment buildings. The Lafayette Theater—where Orson Welles's WPA theater troupe performed an all-black, "Voodoo" *Macbeth* in 1936—only recently fell to the wrecking ball. In place of these iconic Harlem Renaissance spots are everything from 1950s Title I housing to modern, sleek glass condominiums. On 125th Street near the Apollo Theater is an H&M clothing store and a Starbucks.

To people who've never been to Harlem, I think that's the part that erases whatever mystique they may have about the neighborhood. It's not the Starbucks or the IHOP—though they do burst some illusions—it's the fact that Harlem is no longer an enclave that stands apart from the market forces that shape the rest of New York City. The Harlem Renaissance couldn't have happened in any other place in the world—there was nowhere quite like it. Today, Harlem is in real danger of becoming just like everywhere else.

Having already made a name for himself as a poet, Langston Hughes's debut novel, *Not Without Laughter,* garnered acclaim upon its release in 1930. That same year, Hughes became head of the League of Struggle for Negro Rights, a Communist organization. The move galvanized Hughes's political thinking and was a coup for the Communists, who now had a leader of the Harlem Renaissance as a visible promoter of the cause.

In 1932, Hughes was invited to Russia by the Soviet government. He and other African Americans had been asked to participate in a propaganda film about race relations and labor strife in America. The journey had a profound effect; as Hughes later recalled in his autobiography, "When the train [to Russia] stopped . . . for passports to be checked, a few of the young black men and women left the train to touch their hands to the Soviet soil, lift the new earth in their palms, and kiss it."

However, the Russian director lacked any real knowledge of the African-American situation in the United States and Hughes was unable to help salvage the script. When the project fell apart, Hughes stayed in the Soviet Union, traveling to Central Asia (then off limits to foreigners) before returning to the States in 1933 to live in Carmel, California. There, he wrote his finest short story collection, *The Way of White Folks,* heavily imbued with socialist outrage.

In 1935, his first Broadway play, *Mulatto,* debuted, which dealt with miscegenation and white-on-black violence in the South. Despite the controversial themes, it ran for over a year and held the record of the longest-running Broadway show by an African-American writer until Lorraine Hansberry's *Raisin in the Sun* in 1959 (named for a line in Hughes's poem "Harlem").

Today Hughes's more overtly political works are often glossed over, but this is a man who wrote a poem called "One more 'S' in the USA," challenging readers to "put one more S in the U.S.A./To make it Soviet." He served as a war correspondent during the Spanish Civil War, but also wrote a column beginning in 1943 to bolster American support for World War II. The column was centered on a character named Jesse B. Semple, who dispensed homespun wisdom in a Harlem bar in exchange for a beer. Hughes continued writing about Semple until 1965, and the column is considered by some to be Hughes's finest contribution to American letters.

Like Claude McKay and Max Eastman, Hughes's politics eventually shifted rightward, though he never gave up on socialism. In 1953, he was brought before Joseph McCarthy's Senate committee, and had to disavow any ties to the Communists. I wonder what Hughes thought of Max Eastman during this time. Hughes, as a young man, had been so influenced by reading *The Masses* and *The Liberator*. Now Eastman had become a conservative *Reader's Digest* columnist and backer of McCarthy's witch hunt.

After Hughes died and was cremated, his ashes were buried under the floor in the Schomburg Center for Research in Black Culture on Malcolm X Boulevard. His remains lie beneath a mosaic of rivers that come together at the words, "My soul has grown deep like the rivers." The line comes from "The Negro Speaks of Rivers," a poem from Hughes's first collection.

When I finish a tour near the Schomburg Center, I'll take visitors inside to show them Hughes's final resting spot and read from the poem. On my most recent trip, the room—known as the Langston Hughes Auditorium— was in use. A card table with name tags and gift bags sat on top of the mosaic.

"Can we help you?" the young woman behind the table asked with some incredulity. Clearly, we were not on her guest list.

I pointed at the artwork at her feet. "We're just taking a quick look at the design. Did you know that's Langston Hughes's grave?"

Her eyes widened; obviously, she didn't know.

"Right there?"

I nodded and read an excerpt from the poem—loud enough for her to hear—in which Hughes ties his own experience both to his ancestors who toiled on the banks of the Nile and to Abraham Lincoln, whose 1831 trip down the "muddy bosom" of the Mississippi to New Orleans was a crucial moment in shaping his abolitionist views.

She thanked us and, as we turned to leave, I could see she was moving her table.

CHAPTER 16

Peace through Trade:
The Rockefellers and the Modern City

THERE'S SOMETHING ABOUT THE NAME ROCKEFELLER. Sure, the Vanderbilts and Whitneys and Carnegies and Astors were all rich, but none of them ever captured the public's attention in quite the same way John D. Rockefeller did. Just look at popular American songs: from Irving Berlin to Bette Midler to Bob Dylan to Jay Z, the word Rockefeller (or "Roc-a-fella," in Jay Z's case) has become synonymous with wealth and success. In 1930, Dorothy Fields and Harry Richman's "On the Sunny Side of the Street" summed up the sentiment: the ultimate satisfaction was to be "rich as Rockefeller"—even if you didn't have a cent.

This perception was partly because the Rockefellers really did have more money than anyone else. As the *New York Times* noted in 2007, "when wealth is measured as a percentage of the economy, John D. Rockefeller was the wealthiest American ever." Rockefeller's fortune came—at age thirty-one—from founding Standard Oil, which monopolized America's drilling and refining. In 1911 Standard Oil was found to be in violation of the Sherman Antitrust Act and carved into dozens of different companies. Since John D. Rockefeller held shares in most of these offshoots (including Exxon and Mobil), his wealth only increased after the government's intervention.

While John D. Rockefeller was a philanthropist, it's his son John D. Rockefeller Jr. whose mark on New York City is more keenly felt. Not only was he the force behind Rockefeller Center—today, one of the most visited spots in the city—his philosophy of internationalism and his pursuit of "world peace through trade" left its stamp on everything from the United Nations to Riverside Church to the World Trade Center.

Junior (as he was often called) summarized his philosophy in a radio broadcast in 1941, just as America was being pulled toward World War II. The speech, emblazoned on a plaque at Rockefeller Center, enumerated ten philosophical principles, including:

Rockefeller Center, ca. 1940. La Maison Francaise and British Empire Building are in the foreground.

I believe that every right implies a responsibility; every opportunity, an obligation; every possession, a duty.

I believe that the law was made for man and not man for the law; that government is the servant of the people and not their master.

I believe that truth and justice are fundamental to an enduring social order.

I believe that love is the greatest thing in the world; that it alone can overcome hate; that right can and will triumph over might.

Today, the name Rockefeller may still be synonymous with phenomenal wealth, but from Battery Park to the Cloisters, even a casual encounter with the Rockefellers' New York shows that Junior and his sons really did see in "every opportunity, an obligation," which they took very seriously. As with J. Pierpont Morgan, whose influence in New York was fading as Junior's was rising, it is hard not to spend time in New York without benefiting from Rockefeller's vision.

John D. Rockefeller Jr., born in 1874, began working in his father's office at 26 Broadway in 1897, a stone's throw from the New York Stock Exchange and the famed "House of Morgan." In the 1920s, the Rockefeller headquarters was overhauled, gaining a giant tower and expanding its footprint northward. When the refit was completed in 1926, Standard Oil was one of the most imposing skyscrapers in the Financial District. At the top of the new tower was a giant aluminum brazier—ignited at night as a beacon for ships—that reminded everyone that the cornerstone of Standard Oil's success was the kerosene business. Today, most passersby pay the Standard Oil building little mind, but it's a terrific edifice, one of the last of its era before the rise of Art Deco. The decorative scheme features torches, oil lamps, and keystones with an "SO" logo.

Though Junior resigned his seat on Standard Oil's board in 1910 to focus on his other commitments, he remained a major stockholder, continued to keep an office at 26 Broadway, and served on the boards of various companies, including Pierpont Morgan's U.S. Steel.

Among the many Rockefeller offshoots that Junior owned stock in was Colorado Fuel and Iron (CFI), a mining company that went on strike in 1913. After strike breakers tried to intimidate the miners, the governor of Colorado called in the National Guard. On April 20, 1914, the guardsmen attacked the mining camp in Ludlow, Colorado, burning it to the ground. Two women and eleven children, trapped in an underground bunker beneath one of the tents, were asphyxiated.

The International Workers of the World (IWW) began calling the event the "Ludlow Massacre," and laid blame directly at the feet of Junior Rockefeller, the company's largest single stockholder. Upton Sinclair, whose book *The Jungle* had directly led to the passage of the Pure Food and Drug Act in 1906, organized a silent protest outside 26 Broadway, where demonstrators wore black crepe in mourning. Not everyone was so peaceful. Marie Ganz, a Lower East Side labor activist, was arrested for threatening to "shoot down John D. Rockefeller, Jr., like a dog." On July 4, 1914, a tenement on Lexington Avenue blew up, the bomb being manufactured inside likely meant for Rockefeller's West 54th Street house.

From the beginning, Rockefeller maintained his innocence in the events in Ludlow. He was just a shareholder, after all. As far as he knew, CFI had been doing its best to meet worker demands (though not the demand to unionize), and once the National Guard had been called in, he wouldn't have been able to interfere with a military matter anyway. But the more Junior protested, the more culpable he seemed.

In an attempt to repair his image, Junior met with Mary Harris "Mother" Jones, the IWW co-founder and the "grandmother of all agitators." After the meeting, Jones told the *New York Times* that Rockefeller's opponents had "been misrepresenting him terribly." Rockefeller then traveled to Colorado to meet with the miners and hear their demands firsthand. He endorsed a (company-run) union, along with efforts to improve the mining towns. Many of the workers' concerns, including an eight-hour work day and the abolition of child labor, soon became part of the national conversation.

Mostly, Rockefeller charmed them. After a dinner in the mining town of Cameron, Junior gave a short speech, and then asked if the tables and chairs might be cleared for a dance. After a spin across the dance floor with the superintendent's wife, Rockefeller danced with all the women. Throughout his trip to Colorado, he ate with the workers, descended into mine shafts, and left with a different view of CFI—and of himself.

The Ludlow Massacre was a watershed moment for Rockefeller. He had grown up in the shadow of a domineering, supremely successful father whom he tried to emulate and please. He had been routinely rewarded for it, but it had given him a blinkered view. Ludlow opened his eyes to the world beyond the scope of 26 Broadway. It would permanently change the trajectory of his life.

John D. Rockefeller Jr. would inherit from his parents a plain-spoken faith. Raised a Baptist, Junior came from a home where smoking and drinking were forbidden and church attendance was mandatory. His parents disapproved of gambling, dancing, and going to the theater, and though Junior attempted to follow their example, he rebelled in his own ways.

Rockefeller's religious leanings were decidedly progressive. After World War I, he embraced the Interchurch World Movement, a short-lived organization focused on promoting harmony within American churches and in Rockefeller's words, "molding the thought of the world as [the church] has never done before." When the Interchurch World Movement folded, Rockefeller turned his attention to other religious ventures, including underwriting a study, *Rethinking Missions,* which recommended less religious zeal in missionary work and more social justice.

In 1922, the Rev. Harry Emerson Fosdick—brother to longtime Rockefeller adviser Raymond Fosdick—preached a sermon at First Presbyterian Church titled "Shall the Fundamentalists Win?" which made a case that the Fundamentalists' "apparent intention is to drive out of the evangelical churches men and women of liberal opinions. . . . The best conservatives can often give lessons to the liberals in true liberality of spirit, but the Fundamentalist program is essentially illiberal and intolerant."

Junior, who clearly thought of himself as a "best conservative," was impressed by Fosdick and invited him to take over the pulpit at Rockefeller's Park Avenue Baptist Church, forging a longstanding alliance between the two men.

Then, in 1925, Junior approached the Episcopal Cathedral of St. John the Divine with a check for $500,000—just as Pierpont Morgan had done a generation earlier. The cathedral was in dire financial straits, and even though he was a Baptist, Rockefeller was prepared to help. The Episcopal bishop, William T. Manning, had spoken of making the church "into an *ecumenical* force for Protestant unity," which aligned perfectly with Rockefeller's goals.

In a note attached to the check, Rockefeller told Bishop Manning it was his "hope that, if not now, in the near future it may be deemed right and fitting to invite representatives of Protestant communions other than the Protestant Episcopal Church to share in the control and direction . . . of St. John the Divine."

Manning publicly thanked Rockefeller for the money—so Junior couldn't take it back—but ignored the request. Whatever ecumenical outreach the church planned to do, it didn't include having a Baptist millionaire serve on its vestry.

Rockefeller, undoubtedly hurt, decided to embark on a game of one-upmanship, uncharacteristic for him. Since the Episcopal Church didn't want him, he would build his own church in the same neighborhood—bigger, better, and faster—with Harry Emerson Fosdick at the helm.

Rockefeller selected a nearby site on the edge of Riverside Park near Grant's Tomb, about ten blocks from the cathedral. The non-denominational Riverside Church would sport the world's tallest church tower, visible from the Hudson River and for miles around. It not only dwarfed its surroundings, it completely overshadowed St. John the Divine, still struggling to finish its nave.

Construction on Riverside Church began in 1927, and took just three years. Like St. John the Divine, it was styled as a Gothic church, but there the similarities ended. The Episcopalians were building in a medieval fashion, stone upon stone. Riverside Church was a skyscraper, its stone facade masking a steel-frame skeleton. Building out of steel not only allowed the tower to hold a seventy-two-bell carillon (the world's largest), but also offices, meeting rooms, even a radio station.

What was most different about Riverside Church was the way its decorative scheme—while still hewing to Gothic templates—spoke to the parish's mission. St. John the Divine may have included whimsical stained-glass windows, but the iconography at Riverside Church emphasized the parish's inclusive nature and its humanism.

When I give tours of Morningside Heights, I usually start at St. John the Divine and end at Riverside Church, using the two religious spaces as bookends to show the neighborhood's role as home to so many great New York institutions. Sometimes called the Acropolis of New York, Morningside Heights also includes Columbia University, Barnard College, the Manhattan School of Music, the Interchurch Center, Union Theological Seminary, and International House—these last three also Rockefeller-funded. Unfortunately, I often spend so much time in the gargantuan Episcopal cathedral that by the time I reach Riverside Church, I'm either pressed for time, or my companions are suffering ecclesiastical fatigue. (Sometimes we simply can't get in. St. John the Divine is set up for the tourist trade; Riverside Church is not.)

Even if we don't go inside Riverside Church, I can point out highlights: on the west portal (modeled by architects Collens & Pelton on Chartres Cathedral), fourteen scientists are among the figures above the door. When the church circulated a list of the scientists it was thinking about including, the scholars they consulted all said the same thing: *Where's Einstein?*

The church hadn't really been considering him—if he were included, it would make him the only living figure represented—but the consultants insisted that the church couldn't depict great scientists without him. When the famed physicist found out, he paid a visit to the church. He was a little taken aback to see his Jewish self over the main entrance to a Protestant church.

On the tour of the sanctuary, however, Einstein was impressed by the cathedral's wide-ranging imagery. As church historian Eugene C. Carder noted, Einstein stood "before the Philosopher's Window in the east aisle, [where] his eye was caught by the portraiture there of Emanuel Kant, the great German philosopher, walking in his garden. . . . 'This could not happen in Europe. I am afraid it may never happen there.'"

At the front of the church, a white limestone chancel screen features seventy-two figures that run the gamut from artists such as Leonardo, Michelangelo, and Fra Angelico, to Abraham Lincoln, Booker T. Washington, and Florence Nightingale. In keeping with Rockefeller's desire to unite Protestant sects, the screen also depicts George Fox, founder of the Quakers, standing near theologians John Calvin, John Wesley, and Martin Luther. When the church opened, it had been two-and-a-half centuries since John Bowne had secured freedom of worship for the Quakers—and all New Yorkers. Rockefeller hoped Riverside Church might emphasize common ground, instead of the divisions that had caused people like Peter Stuyvesant to persecute fellow Christians like Bowne.

Sometimes when I'm guiding tours, I'll be lucky enough to arrive at Riverside Church on a Sunday morning just as services are finishing. As we step inside the doors, it seems like Rockefeller's plan is working. The congregation brings together people of many different races and backgrounds. It draws from Harlem, the neighborhood just north of the church, as well as Morningside Heights. Some people travel from the other side of the city or drive down from Westchester County to worship here, and the feeling of fellowship can't be denied.

But then I'll take my clients back outside and point out the figures on the church's exterior: Ralph Waldo Emerson, Charles Darwin, Galileo, Buddha, and Hippocrates. Some visitors smirk at the depiction of Einstein or Galileo, but can get hostile when I point out Buddha and Confucius.

"Why is Buddha on a church?" I was asked at the end of a tour.

"Rockefeller wanted to show the commonality of all religion," I responded.

Any warmth of feeling from inside vanished. As Rockefeller was to find out time and again in his life, the spirit of ecumenism only goes so far.

In the midst of the construction of Riverside Church, John D. Rockefeller Jr. involved himself in a project of such massive scale that it would forever dwarf his contributions to Morningside Heights. That project, of course, was Rockefeller Center, though originally Junior had no plans to have the family name attached to it.

Even before the Ludlow Massacre, the name Rockefeller often caused intense negative reaction. When his father attempted to give money to the Board of Foreign Missions, one member wondered, "Is this clean money? Can any man . . . touch it without being defiled?"

By the time Riverside Church opened, Junior had done much to resuscitate the Rockefeller name, but he was still wary of using it. In part, he wanted projects to stand on their own. For example, he didn't even attend Riverside Church's first services—he wanted the publicity to be about the parish and its mission, not the rich man sitting up front who had bankrolled it.

In the 1920s, the Metropolitan Opera approached Rockefeller to help them lease a tract of land in Midtown owned by Columbia University. The idea was to erect a unique retail/office/arts complex, at the heart of which would be a new opera house. Junior agreed to help, but only because he felt the proposed real estate venture would be a money-maker.

Then, the stock market crashed and the project—which Junior was already committed to financially—was in jeopardy. One casualty was the Metropolitan Opera, which was forced to stay in its inadequate home on Broadway until moving to Lincoln Center in 1966. By that point, Rockefeller was already in too deep, and the center's construction moved forward.

Rockefeller hired the firm Todd, Robertson & Todd to oversee many aspects of construction, including renting out the buildings, even though they hadn't been built yet. As the project grew in the 1930s, Rockefeller thought about how the complex could be built to reflect his worldview. Yes, there would be shopping, live theater, and—with the addition of radio giant RCA to the main building—the replacement for the opera that gave the center its initial name, "Radio City." But those elements didn't concern Junior as much as the office tenants. RCA and the RKO movie house were just style; the businesses at Rockefeller Center were to be the Center's real substance. In the end, this division between style and substance was likely what convinced Rockefeller to drop the Radio City moniker and name the complex after himself.

Much of the task of finding potential tenants fell to Hugh Sterling Robertson, who hit upon the idea of erecting two low buildings fronting Fifth

Avenue—hastily designed to replace the missing opera house—and show-casing in them exclusively British and French tenants. One office tower he dubbed the "British Empire Building," the other "La Maison Francaise."

Junior instantly embraced the plan, even quipping that the planted walk-way between the two buildings should be called the "Channel Gardens." The same ecumenical spirit he was trying to foster in Riverside Church could now also play out at Rockefeller Center in the world of commerce. As he later wrote, the buildings would be "symbols in stone and steel of the com-mon interests . . . and good will of three great powers."

Through an act of Congress finagled by Robertson, goods sold at Rock-feller Center by French and British merchants would be duty free. Junior also hoped to attract more than retail: He wanted to draw consulates, diplomatic offices, and other national interests—to make the buildings their own sort of business League of Nations. The French consul relocated to La Maison Francaise when it opened in 1933, but the Center could never convince the British to move there. However, both buildings still strongly reflected each nation's heritage. On the front of the British Empire Building, nine gilded bronze figures were installed to represent major British industries; similarly, on the French building, an allegory of Franco-American friendship was placed above the Fifth Avenue entrance.

Much of the iconography of Rockefeller Center can be obscure, but the message of these buildings was clear: The League of Nations had fallen down on the job of fostering world harmony; perhaps, Rockefeller reasoned, the internationalism of these commercial buildings would have a better chance of bringing about world peace.

Visiting Rockefeller Center today can feel like a chore. It's one of the places—like Times Square—that locals avoid and that many tourists give a perfunctory once-over, checking it off their lists. That's too bad. Especially during the less crowded eleven months of the year *sans* Christmas tree, it is one of the most delightful urban spaces in America—a pioneer of mixing retail, business, entertainment, dining, and sightseeing. It's massive (origi-nally six million square feet that was later doubled) but it manages to bring everything to a human scale. It even has the best rooftop observatory in the city, Top of the Rock, which, in Junior's day, was set up to look like a luxury steamship, complete with Adirondack deck chairs.

Yet even as much as I admire it, I too am guilty of giving the place short shrift. When touring there, I'll explain how Rockefeller Center was a driving force in creating modern Midtown as a business district; I talk about Junior's desire to foster "world peace through trade"—a phrase that would be introduced at the 1939 World's Fair and later adopted by his son David at the World Trade Center. I go inside to show them Jose Maria Sert's *American Progress* mural in the lobby of 30 Rockefeller Plaza—which famously replaced Diego Rivera's objectionable, Leninist original.

But, to me, none of this captures the spirit of Rockefeller Center as much as an overlooked series of carvings on the International Building North, opposite St. Patrick's Cathedral, Leo Lentelli's *Four Continents*. In each piece, Lentelli draws on familiar iconography. To represent the Americas, Lentelli chooses a Mayan, a buffalo, and corn; for Europe, Neptune, god of maritime trade; for Africa, a chief with his scepter; and for Asia, a figure of Buddha.

These are a striking contrast to these same continents as they are depicted downtown at the Custom House on Bowling Green. There, massive statues by Daniel Chester French from 1907 are designed to bolster America's claim to world domination. French's Africa and Asia statues, if not overtly racist, are at least symbolically charged with racial antipathy. Lentelli's work avoids French's editorializing, striving for what has always struck me as a particularly Rockefellerian balance.

Junior didn't care for some of the art at the Center, including, as journalist Daniel Okrent has pointed out, Leo Friedlander's mannerist nudes above the side entrance to 30 Rockefeller Plaza. But I wonder if he approved of Lentelli's *Continents*. So much of the Center's iconography is bombastic or obscure, but to me these four carvings speak to Junior's real faith that these international tenants might be the world's best hope for a better world.

After a rough start, Rockefeller Center did end up a success. In 1933, the Rockefellers relocated their own offices from 26 Broadway to the Center. Since renting office space in the Depression was difficult—the Empire State Building was dubbed the "Empty State Building"—the move was a show of confidence. Rockefeller's new headquarters was "Room 5600" (the entire 56th floor) of 30 Rockefeller Plaza; by this time, his eldest sons, John III and Nelson, had joined the family business, and, in time, younger sons Laurence, Winthrop, and David would all be included as well.

After the construction of the British Empire Building and La Maison Francaise, Rockefeller Center embraced other foreign tenants, but Rockefeller's vision of the center as an international commercial hub never materialized. In part, this was because Europe was already sliding toward World

War II. The International Building, just north of 51st Street, welcomed the Italians in the Palazzo d'Italia (with the approval of Mussolini, to whom Hugh Robertson made a personal pitch), but while Rockefeller's agents flew to Germany to talk to Hitler's new government about a planned Deutsches Haus, it never materialized. As it was, the original art on the Palazzo d'Italia, a sculpture by Attilio Piccirilli promoting fascist values, was boarded over during the war and then removed.

Other international tenants moved in, but some were short lived. Holland House, which included offices for the airline KLM and the Dutch government, opened in 1940, only a few months before Hitler invaded the Netherlands, at which point they were forced to close. During the war, the French consulate would also shutter; at the war's end, they moved uptown. (In a good example of how real estate values had changed, the French consulate moved to a Gilded Age mansion on Fifth Avenue, which they purchased and converted into offices. Fifth Avenue houses were so old-fashioned by the 1940s that it was cheaper for France to purchase an entire mansion than to continue renting at Rockefeller Center.)

By the 1950s, Rockefeller Center was a thriving place—Radio City Music Hall brought in the crowds to see the Rockettes; the skating rink and Christmas tree were already fixtures. But the international character of the buildings continued to suffer, and while La Maison Francaise and the British Empire building attracted international firms—and continue to today—Rockefeller's vision of peace through trade would have to wait.

⌁

By the end of World War II, Junior had successfully convinced Americans that the Rockefeller name no longer meant just money and power, it also meant art (he had paid for the Cloisters in Fort Tryon Park, and his wife, Abby, and son, Nelson, were founders of the Museum of Modern Art), commercial real estate, and—because of the iconic Christmas tree—even family fun.

But in the post-war years, as the Rockefeller sons began to take on the mantle of responsibility, the family name became more closely aligned with politics. There had always been people who were anti-Rockefeller, but now a whole cottage industry of Rockefeller-based conspiracy theories surfaced. Books, papers, and blogs continue to abound about the family's ongoing, sinister quest for a global government either run by or financed by the Rockefellers.

These conspiracies were fueled by the family's continued commitment to Junior's pursuit of international cooperation, which became entwined with

Nelson's political ambitions. When the United Nations was being formed, Nelson worked hard to make sure that the new body's headquarters was located in New York. After the city's first choice, the site of the 1939 World's Fair in Flushing Meadows, Queens, was rejected, Nelson scrambled to find an alternative. With the UN's deadline for finding a home looming, he suggested the family's Hudson Valley estate, Pocantico, but that was deemed too far from the city.

Then, Nelson convinced his father to purchase a site on the East River that the family could donate to the UN. The area, stretching north from 42nd Street along Turtle Bay, was owned by real estate developer William Zeckendorf, who planned to build a commercial complex to rival Rockefeller Center. By convincing Zeckendorf to sell, the Rockefellers not only secured a home for the United Nations, they undercut any serious competition.

Among the many 1939 World's Fair pavilions, one minor contributor had been the International Chamber of Commerce's "World Trade Center," a showcase for the idea of "world peace through trade."

The World Trade Center didn't make much of a splash. However, one member of the International Chamber of Commerce was Winthrop W. Aldrich, the chairman of Chase Bank and Junior's brother-in-law. Aldrich possessed the keen sense that keeping Chase Bank, the City of New York, and America thriving—in that order—would require a global outlook. And despite the old adage that war was good for business, Aldrich was betting that peace was even better.

In the wake of World War II, as Nelson Rockefeller was working to find a home for the United Nations, Winthrop Aldrich was appointed to a new World Trade Corporation to revive the ideas put forward at the World's Fair. Perhaps there could be a permanent World Trade Center as a hub for international commerce in New York. Though Aldrich's corporation made little headway in the 1940s, the idea was resuscitated a decade later by Chase Bank's new chairman, David Rockefeller—Junior's youngest son—who saw the World Trade Center as the key to revitalizing the moribund Financial District.

One of the unintended consequences of the opening of Rockefeller Center was the establishment of a Midtown business district and the general exodus of companies from downtown. In the years immediately following World War II, new skyscrapers began to line Park Avenue and Sixth Avenue, including such gems as Lever House and the Seagram Building. In 1955, when Chase Bank decided it had outgrown its downtown home, David

Rockefeller had a hard choice to make: follow his family to Midtown or stay put? Ultimately, Rockefeller made the decision to remain in the Financial District, using his uncle's World Trade Center concept as the anchor of a new downtown real estate market.

This time, the idea stuck—in part because David's brother Nelson was now New York's governor. In 1966, after about six years of feasibility studies, legal wrangling, and evictions, construction began on the huge office complex that would house what would briefly be the world's tallest buildings.

The earliest plans for the World Trade Center complex called for hotels, residential areas, and a new home for the New York Stock Exchange. Major companies from around the world would be enticed to locate their offices there, producing the same sort of commercial synergy that Junior had hoped for at Rockefeller Center. Meanwhile, as New York's manufacturing and shipping businesses were shrinking, it would give the city the opportunity to engage in a radical revision of the area, getting rid of the old, rusting piers, the smelly produce and fish markets, and "Radio Row" (a mostly Arab ethnic neighborhood) in favor of state-of-the-art financial services.

The complex grew to include seven towers: the 1250-foot Twin Towers (WTC 1 and 2) anchored the complex; shorter skyscrapers, including the Vista (later Marriott) Hotel in WTC 3, and the United States Custom House—relocated from Bowling Green—in WTC 6. By the time the final building, WTC 7, had been completed in 1987, over 13.4 million square feet of office space had been added downtown.

Along the way, the underlying theme of peace through trade was sublimated, but never entirely erased. Austin J. Tobin, the head of the Port Authority of New York and New Jersey, whose agency owned the land on which the Trade Center was being built, attached great symbolic meaning to the sculptural centerpiece of the center's plaza, Fritz Koenig's twenty-five-foot-tall globe called *Grosse Kugelkaryatid* ("large spherical caryatid"), known to everyone as "Sphere." There's some debate whether Koenig ever saw the piece as an evocation of "peace through trade," but after the 9/11 attacks felled the complex—and the sculpture—it took on deeper shades of meaning.

Despite the devastation of the site that September day, Koenig's Sphere was found a few weeks into the recovery operation. Badly dented but mostly intact, it almost immediately came to stand as not only a vivid reminder of the buildings that were gone but also a testament to the resilience of New Yorkers.

On March 11, 2002, six months after the attack, the Sphere was unveiled in Battery Park, a few blocks south of the complex. Six months later, on

September 11, 2002, an eternal flame was added along with an official sign to remind visitors that the sculpture had originally been conceived by Koenig as a symbol of world peace—even if that wasn't necessarily true.

"Sphere" has now resided in Battery Park for over a decade, making it not only a symbol (as the sign says) of "the indestructible spirit of this country," but of the often intractable positions taken up by all parties involved in the new Trade Center. Should "Sphere" remain in Battery Park, which was meant to be a temporary location? Or should it go to the plaza that surrounds the twin pools of Daniel Arad's poignant commemoration, "Reflecting Absence"? Or, as some argue, should it instead be placed in the museum beneath the memorial?

Personally, I would leave it where it is. It allows people to memorialize the events of 9/11 without the crowds associated with Ground Zero. The sculpture also now sits only steps away from the old Standard Oil tower at 26 Broadway. Standing on the threshold of Castle Clinton in Battery Park, I can look back at "Sphere" and then cast my eyes upward to see Standard Oil's stylized kerosene brazier. I like this connection between John D. Rockefeller's mercantile empire and this broken symbol of America's global reach.

Was John D. Rockefeller Jr.'s vision of international peace and understanding realized at the World Trade Center? That's hard to square with the events that brought down the complex in 2001. While Junior—who died in 1960, before the complex was built—may have seen commerce as a force for positive good in the world, it's also easy to understand how the Twin Towers came to be seen as symbols of American hubris.

Still, while Americans made up the bulk of the nearly three thousand people killed that September morning, I'm often reminded of the Trade Center's—and New York's—true reach: People of seventy-one nationalities were killed that day, from almost every corner of the globe.

Can world trade and world peace ever be synonymous? Or will this bent Sphere stand not just as a memorial to those who died so tragically in 2001, but to the very idea of a Rockefellerian world where money can create a just world? In his credo, Junior wrote that "love is the greatest thing in the world. . . . [I]t alone can overcome hate."

More than anything else, the Sphere is really a symbol that we have a lot of work to do.

Left: Robert Moses admires a model of the proposed Brooklyn-Battery Bridge, 1939.
Right: Jane Jacobs at a meeting of the Committee to Save the West Village, 1961.

CHAPTER 17

The Battle for New York:
Jane Jacobs vs. Robert Moses

I LIKE TO SAY "ROBERT MOSES" TO PEOPLE FAMILIAR with New York history
to see what kind of reaction I get.

I'll be strolling through Washington Square on a gorgeous afternoon,
past the jazz musicians and chess players, and pause to point out where
Moses once wanted to run a highway. That's usually enough to elicit a
grumble.

In Central Park, when we look at the forlorn Rumsey playfield that
replaced the Casino restaurant—Moses bulldozed it mostly to spite Mayor
Jimmy Walker—there's often a deep sigh. Or I'll mention Moses's desire
to make Cadman Plaza the "Piazza San Marco" of Brooklyn. That brings a
distinct eye roll or a smirk.

What is it about Robert Moses that makes tempers rise? He was the most important American urban planner in the twentieth century, and his mark can be felt across all five boroughs. He constructed swimming pools, improved public parks, created beach access for working-class New Yorkers, built highways, housing projects, and bridges. He was the driving force behind both the 1939 and the 1964 World's Fairs. The list of Moses's accomplishments can fill volumes.

Yet people can't stand him.

Over the course of his tenure in public service, Moses was known for his dictatorial style. He didn't take criticism well, nor was he a fan of consensus building. Having chosen a course of action, he pursued it relentlessly, even when public or expert opinion turned against him. He famously said, "When you operate in an overbuilt metropolis you have to hack your way with a meat ax." (There being an exception to every rule, one client responds to this meat ax line with a rousing "Exactly!")

Certainly, Moses had blind spots. His love of the automobile meant that he rarely considered the benefits of public transportation. His view that any remotely dilapidated place was a slum was short-sighted. For example, it's hard to envision Soho today—full of high-end boutiques and luxury lofts—as a slum waiting to be bulldozed. Apartments in the area have some of the highest average rents in the city. It has become the number one shopping destination in New York. If you'd predicted Soho's renaissance to Robert Moses in the 1950s, he would have laughed you out of the room.

Because Robert Moses was so controversial—and because he lost some surprising battles—his story is often told as a David and Goliath tale. Cast in the heroic underdog role is urban activist Jane Jacobs. Jacobs repudiated many of the beliefs behind Moses's urban renewal in her landmark book, *The Death and Life of Great American Cities.* She even fought Moses on a personal level, getting arrested at a public hearing about Moses's proposed Lower Manhattan Expressway that would have destroyed much of Soho.

The clash between Moses and Jacobs has literary, even operatic, overtones; indeed, I wasn't surprised to recently discover that a Moses/Jacobs opera is in the works. While I don't know how the composers are planning to tell the tale, the story has shades of Greek tragedy: the powerful politician laid low both by the unassuming writer and his own overarching ambition.

Robert Moses was born in New Haven, Connecticut, in 1888, the son of successful German Jewish immigrants. In 1897, the family moved to New York. Moses grew up in an Upper East Side townhouse with a cook, servants, and a chauffeur; it's hard not to think that his upbringing influenced his later thinking. Though he will forever be associated with projects like the Triborough Bridge and the Cross-Bronx Expressway, Moses never learned to drive—he didn't have to. For his entire life he was a passenger, luxuriating in the back seat. No wonder he thought cars and highways were such a great idea.

After attending Yale, Oxford, and Columbia (where he was awarded a PhD in 1914), Moses was tapped to draft a report on how to reorganize New York City government. The plan went nowhere—Tammany Hall was still too powerful to allow civil service reform—but it launched Moses's career. He soon secured a job in the administration of Governor Al Smith.

By 1924, Moses had scored his first big victory, convincing the legislature to create and fund a New York State Council of Parks. This new agency, designed to regularize and improve New York's vast parkland, established Moses's *modus operandi:* discover a problem (poor management of parks that had little public access); propose a solution (a wide-reaching agency that had the power to acquire land *and* build roads); and make sure that the agency (always run by Moses) was subject to as little oversight as possible.

In 1928, Smith ran for president, losing badly to Herbert Hoover. The new governor, Franklin Delano Roosevelt, detested Moses. A few years earlier, Roosevelt had asked Moses to find a job for his friend Louis Howe; Moses, who hated granting political favors, had turned him down. Still, Moses kept his job, and created one of his best-loved projects, Jones Beach, a public recreation area on the south shore of Long Island. The building of Jones Beach revealed another hallmark of Moses's style: incredible attention to detail. From the number of lockers and parking spaces to the colors of the beach umbrellas, there was no decision too small for Moses. He micromanaged his projects; when they were successful, he could rightfully take all the credit.

Moses's success at the Council for Parks and at Jones Beach—it drew over 1.5 million people its first year, 1930—led to two important new positions. Because one of Moses's key innovations was to create a series of bucolic, two-lane parkways to allow better access to his parks, Moses was appointed head of the Triborough Bridge and Tunnel Authority in 1933, a commission that not only built the Triborough Bridge, connecting Manhattan, the Bronx, and Queens, but also became Moses's self-financing fiefdom. That same year,

Fiorello La Guardia was elected mayor of New York City, and Moses was named commissioner of a newly consolidated, five-borough parks system— never relinquishing any of his other jobs. At the peak of his career, Moses simultaneously ran a dozen separate city and state agencies. No man in New York—not even Boss Tweed—has wielded more power than Moses.

Often, the goals of Moses's agencies converged. In order to build new homes as New York City's housing commissioner, Moses needed the authority to tear down what was in the way. So, it's a good thing he was also slum clearance commissioner, with the ability to condemn entire neighborhoods as his vision saw fit. Moses followed the same pattern with parks, bridges, cultural centers, and anything else that needed to get built on his watch. If it was in the way, he just tore it down.

After all, who was going to stop him?

One of Moses's less famous confrontations encapsulates his style—the fight over Castle Clinton in Battery Park. I like to bring visitors into the old fort, first listing the building's various incarnations: defensive position, reception hall, theater, and immigrant processing station—all of which happened before it was turned into the city's aquarium.

Despite this long history, Robert Moses wanted to tear down Castle Clinton in 1939 to build the world's longest suspension bridge, connecting Battery Park to Brooklyn. At this point, I'll guide my visitors out to the water's edge, past the big white Statue of Liberty security tent, so that we can see Governors Island and Red Hook, Brooklyn.

"The bridge would have run directly over our heads," I say, drawing an imaginary line in the sky. "It would have followed the basic path of the Brooklyn-Battery Tunnel, which is underneath our feet."

Though public opposition to the bridge was immediate, Moses pushed forward as if there were none. Ultimately, it was President Roosevelt, Moses's old antagonist, who nixed the bridge for reasons of national security.

In response, Moses turned the bridge into a tunnel—and Castle Clinton still stood in the way. When historic preservationists complained, Moses shot off a lengthy letter to the *New York Times*, chastising his detractors who were "woozy with sentiment":

Castle Clinton, which was a post–Revolutionary affair, has no history worth writing about. Various personages landed there, but the same distinguished people landed at many other places in the course of their careers. . . . [T]he

Aquarium is an ugly wart on the main axis leading straight to the Statue of Liberty—a vista of which future New Yorkers some day will justly be proud.

He then quoted an 1860 *New York Daily Tribune* story that called the place a "dirty and noisesome dumping ground." It had been terrible eighty years ago, he seemed to suggest, so it must still be terrible now.

More to the point—and here Moses actually had a point—the fort was "wholly unsuited to a modern aquarium." As parks commissioner, Moses had a plan to move the fish to a state-of-the-art facility at the Bronx Zoo.

And that was that. If any of the "stuffed shirts" complaining about the castle's demolition had an idea about how to restore and run the building without it costing the city an arm and a leg, Moses promised to be receptive. In Moses's mind, the fort was as good as gone.

To Moses's chagrin, the city's preservationists weren't going down without a fight. And while saving Castle Clinton ultimately took an act of Congress, it was one of the first indications that Moses could, in fact, be stopped.

By 1950, when control of Castle Clinton was ceded to the federal government, the Brooklyn-Battery Tunnel was on the verge of opening; Moses, in typical fashion, had shrugged and moved on. He didn't even consider it a defeat. After all, *he* wasn't the one standing in the way of progress. No—it was preservationists, the idle rich, and sentimental scribblers who were preventing New York from recapturing its glory as America's greatest city.

People like Jane Jacobs.

<hr />

Jane Jacobs moved to New York in 1934, hoping to be a writer. As she looked for a stenography job (her fallback career), she observed the city around her, and began pitching stories about New York's neighborhoods; her first article, on the fur district, was published in *Vogue.*

After a short stint at Columbia's School of General Studies, Jacobs got a job at the State Department, writing articles for overseas publications. In 1947, she and her husband purchased a rundown townhouse at 555 Hudson Street in the West Village for $7,000, and began fixing it up. At the time the industrial western section of the neighborhood was in decline. Shipping and manufacturing were gradually moving outside the city, and much of the area between the Jacobs' house and the Hudson River was underused.

In 1955, when she was writing for *Architectural Forum,* Jacobs was approached by Rev. William Kirk, a minister from Harlem, who was alarmed

at the Title I housing going up in his neighborhood. Title I was a federal program, under the Housing Act of 1949, that gave cities wide leeway for slum
clearance so that older, poorer housing stock could be replaced with middle-
income developments. In New York, Title I was the domain of Robert Moses.

Jacobs went to Harlem with Kirk to see the destruction that these huge
developments had wrought. Despite rental brochures that promised that
tenants at Lenox Terrace—the mega-project spanning 132nd to 135th
Streets between Fifth Avenue and Lenox—would be "Surrounded by spa-
ciousness . . . Encircled by convenience," locals were distraught. Not only
had the project destroyed Harlem landmarks like the Savoy Ballroom and
the original Cotton Club, it was unraveling the entire fabric of the neighborhood. To Moses and the developers, what the community had lost was
more than made up for by the new buildings and—the big selling point—
beautiful green lawns.

As one Harlemite told Jacobs:

*Nobody cared what we wanted when they built this place. . . . We don't
have a place around here to get a cup of coffee or a newspaper, even. . . .
But the big men come and look at that grass and say, "Isn't that wonderful! Now the poor have everything!"*

In 1958, with her experience in Harlem as a springboard, Jacobs penned
her most influential article, "Downtown is for People," for *Fortune* magazine, claiming bluntly: "These projects will not revitalize downtown; they
will deaden it."

While the article discussed cities across America, Jacobs set her sights
on New York's Upper West Side, where Robert Moses was razing the neighborhood of San Juan Hill to make room for a project called Lincoln Square:
Title I housing, a new campus for Fordham University, and, at its center,
what was to be America's largest performing arts complex, Lincoln Center.
In "Downtown is for People," Jacobs pointed out that Lincoln Center was
"intended to be very grand and the focus of the whole music and dance
world of New York. But its streets will be able to give it no support whatever."

The article caught the attention of the Rockefeller Foundation, who
awarded Jacobs a grant to expand her observations into a book. The result
was *The Death and Life of Great American Cities,* still to this day an iconic
work of urban thinking. Much of what Jacobs wrote in *Death and Life* is now
considered gospel; her chapter titles alone—"The Generators of Diversity,"

"The Need for Small Blocks," "The Need for Aged Buildings"—are the bywords of smart urban planning. With one book, she rewrote the entire philosophy of what a city should be.

But as I stood in the middle of Lincoln Center on a recent evening waiting to go into a performance, I looked around me at the vibrant cultural center and I wondered: *Why did she think this was going to be so terrible?*

I happen to love Lincoln Center. In part, that's because I'm an Upper West Sider, and while I don't suffer from the same parochialism as a lot of New Yorkers (who won't leave their own neighborhoods unless forced), I am proud that such an incredible place is in *my* neighborhood.

But I also just love the space itself, and in this I'm a bit of an outlier. Most people tolerate Lincoln Center. The ongoing renovations to the complex, started in 2005, have made it a warmer, friendlier place to hang out—there's a lawn now, which would probably please Robert Moses—but even when it was nothing but stark lines and cold marble, there was something appealingly monumental about the place. Which, of course, was the point.

As plans for Lincoln Center began to take shape, Robert Moses invited Harry Guggenheim to build his new museum at the complex. When Guggenheim declined, the anchor tenant instead became the Metropolitan Opera. Around the same time, the New York Philharmonic was losing its lease at Carnegie Hall, and the idea for a grand, all-encompassing arts complex began to take shape. In addition to the Met and the Philharmonic, Lincoln Center would house a Broadway theater, Juilliard, the New York City Ballet, and the performing arts branch of the New York Public Library.

To spearhead the new venture, Moses tapped John D. Rockefeller III as Lincoln Center's president. The center hired Wallace K. Harrison—one of Rockefeller Center's architects—to oversee the master plan. The first building to open was Philharmonic Hall (now Avery Fisher Hall) in 1962. The New York State Theater followed in 1964, and its grand centerpiece, the Harrison-designed opera house, in 1966.

Set back from the street by a series of steps and a broad plaza, the Metropolitan Opera can only be described as a temple to music. Pilgrims must ascend the stairs to the public plaza, with its Philip Johnson–designed fountain, before entering the temple precincts themselves. Then, if you're like me and sit in the cheap seats, the journey continues up and up and up until finally ending at what seems like the loftiest perch in New York. It's a kind of symbolic journey that is common in other New York institutions, including the New York Public Library, and the Metropolitan Museum of Art; this ceremonial path is programmed for the pedestrian who walks over from Broadway—be that from the subway station, a taxi stand, or just somewhere else in the neighborhood.

Jane Jacobs didn't think this was going to happen. I take it for granted that New York is a city of walkers—it's what I do, not just vocationally, but as a matter of course. As Jacobs rightly pointed out, the lifeblood of cities are its streets, referring to the "banquet and social life of city sidewalks."

But the Lincoln Center plaza threw her for a loop. In "Downtown is for People," she wrote that patrons would be forced to arrive at the complex's bleak Amsterdam Avenue side, because it was the only part of the center where a building touched the sidewalk, and "the only place where the building will be convenient to the street and . . . where opera-goers will disembark from taxis and cars."

Did she really think no one would get out of a taxi on the Broadway side and walk across the plaza?

Jacobs wasn't alone—Lincoln Center's planners had similar concerns. Architectural historian Hilary Ballon has noted that the developers thought that in a city where people "do not walk generally because the city is generally not a pleasant place for people to stroll," the plaza would act as a barrier. They toyed with the idea of a driveway leading to the opera house's front door before reverting to the open pedestrian plan. In the same way it's hard to imagine today's Soho as the rundown area it was fifty years ago, it boggles the mind to think of the Lincoln Square area being so bleak that no one would walk its streets.

Jane Jacobs's other major complaint was that the city didn't need to concentrate all its cultural resources in one place, remarking that Lincoln Center was being "planned on the idiotic assumption that the natural neighbor of a hall is another hall." She felt Moses should be making room for "restaurants, bars, florist shops . . . all sorts of interesting places."

Today, all of those interesting places do surround Lincoln Center, without Moses providing them. By the time the complex was finished in the late 1960s, it had jump-started the Upper West Side real estate market that had remained moribund since the Depression. Apartment towers rose with restaurants and bars occupying the retail space. Grocery stores and movie theaters followed and then, more recently, chain stores like Lululemon and Starbucks. Would so much development have happened if Lincoln Center had been just an opera house, with the other venues scattered across the city? Or did the neighborhood need such a strong mix of arts organizations to be a success?

On summer evenings, I'll walk by the center just as the band strikes up and swing dancers take to the plaza. Crowds are drawn by the music, wandering in from Broadway and Columbus Avenue to watch and listen. In tiny Dante Park across the street, couples sit on benches sipping coffee. Isn't this the sort of street life that Moses's Title I projects were supposed to destroy?

Well—yes, and no. The Lincoln Square project *did* destroy street life. Rows of San Juan Hill tenements were torn down (they live on in the opening sequence of *West Side Story*), and the stoop life of the neighborhood with them. Tobacconists, corner bodegas, and soda fountains were all bulldozed in the name of progress. While it can be argued that Lincoln Center opened up access to the arts, that doesn't negate the fact that thousands of tenement dwellers were uprooted to make it happen.

Do the positive benefits of Lincoln Center make it a success? Or does the destruction of San Juan Hill mean it was a failure?

———

For a long time, Robert Moses has had a reputation of being anti-poor, a view fostered by Robert Caro's monumental biography, *The Power Broker*. But the case that Moses was against the working class isn't clear-cut. Yes, his slum clearance projects uprooted communities, but were those people always worse off? Many of the tenements Moses tore down had no heat or hot water. There's no denying that the places people moved to were more expensive, but they were also higher quality.

And, no matter his reputation, Moses did more than any other figure from the Depression onward to expand recreational access for average New Yorkers: swimming pools (including Brooklyn's massive McCarren Park pool, which held over 6,500 people), playgrounds, new parks, and waterfront access. Long Island's Jones Beach was the crown jewel of Moses's beach developments, but closer to home, he was responsible for Orchard Beach in the Bronx, changes to Coney Island in Brooklyn, and Rockaway Beach and Jacob Riis Park in Queens.

It's a week after Labor Day when I decide to explore Jacob Riis Park for the first time. Named for the author after his death in 1914, the park grew considerably under Moses. Alas, the wonderful Art Deco bathhouse was poorly truncated by architect Aymar Embury II because Moses thought it extended too close to the ocean, but Embury also built the charming Central Mall Building with its semi-circular patio that opens to the sea.

On summer weekends, ferries bring beachgoers from Manhattan directly to the park, but I decide, instead, to take the two-dollar commuter ferry early one weekday morning. There are a total of six of us on board as we glide out from the Wall Street slip and begin heading toward the harbor. We go beneath Moses's Verrazano-Narrows Bridge, which connected Staten Island to Brooklyn in 1964, then glide by Coney Island—where Castle Clinton's aquarium finally found a home—before heading under the Marine Parkway Bridge (also by Moses) and arriving in the Rockaways. When the Marine Parkway Bridge was finished in 1937, it opened up Jacob Riis Park to everyone in Queens and Brooklyn, who could easily catch a city bus to the beach. Later, the IND subway extension to the Rockaways made access even easier.

A ten-minute walk from the ferry slip brings me to the bus stop, and another fifteen minutes on the bus deposits me on the edge of Jacob Riis Park. It's a bleak day; the only people on the boardwalk are a few locals out for a walk and a trio of men with golf clubs in search of the nearby links. The sea crashes into the beach with a constant roar that's drowned out only by the occasional cry of a seagull. It seems Fellini-esque. Had I been here a week earlier, this beach would have been teeming with people enjoying the last hurrah of summer. Even as I brace against the wind, I still feel their spirits here. A beer bottle sticks up from the sand; an ice cream wrapper flits by.

Jane Jacobs didn't talk much about beaches, perhaps because they seem the antithesis of the urban experience. Yet here I am at the beach and this is still New York City; these Rockaway residents who wave as they walk by or stop to chat are just as much New Yorkers as Jacobs's Greenwich Village neighbors.

Being out here crystallizes a significant difference between Robert Moses and Jane Jacobs. Moses always thought of the big picture. His hunger for power was driven by ego, but also by the idea that only by controlling twelve different agencies could he effect real change. He was as concerned with a highway in the Bronx as a beach in Queens and, more to the point, saw how those things were interconnected—how a resident of Pelham Bay in the Bronx could hop in the car and be at Jacob Riis Park in less than an hour.

Jane Jacobs, by contrast, celebrated thinking local. What worked in Greenwich Village might not be best somewhere else. In her eyes, a great failure of urban planning was its one-size-fits-all approach. Most importantly, the people whose lives were being turned upside down needed to be a part of the process. Robert Moses hated process—dealing with all those people kept getting him into trouble.

The downside of local thinking, however, is that it can lead to a "not in my backyard" mentality, an attitude that has become too prevalent in New York. The preservation movement, which scored a major victory with the creation of the city's landmarking laws in 1965, helped protect the older buildings and mixed-use neighborhoods that were central to Jacobs's thesis. But preservation exists to celebrate the status quo, and can stifle new growth. I think it's important to acknowledge that saving one type of neighborhood can shut the door on creating a different cityscape that might be just as vibrant as what it has replaced.

In the 1960s, this clash between preservation and construction came to a head with the fight over "Lomex"—the Lower Manhattan Expressway—the last major fight between Moses and Jacobs. It was a bruising battle that set the stage for changes in Soho and environs that neither could have predicted.

In 1951, a Title I project called Washington Square South promised to completely remake Greenwich Village. From Sixth Avenue to Mercer Street, all the old buildings south of Washington Square would be torn down for forty acres of housing and an expansion of New York University. West Broadway—to be renamed Fifth Avenue South in a revival of a failed Tweed-era experiment—would run through the middle of the development. It would be connected to the actual Fifth Avenue by going straight through Washington Square.

Even after the Title I project shrank to only include the area east of West Broadway, Moses persisted in trying to connect Fifth Avenue through the square. That plan was finally defeated in 1959 by a group of Village residents that included Jane Jacobs and was led by Shirley Hayes, whose children relied on the park for its open space. Not only was the new road kept from the park, but Hayes had managed to ban all traffic from the square, ending the city's longtime use of the area around the fountain as a de facto bus depot.

That Moses should lose to what he called "a bunch of mothers" was galling. Even more upsetting was that his opponents didn't seem to understand two crucial facts. First, Moses truly believed that "cities are created by and for traffic." Without a road in Washington Square, the neighborhood would descend into chaos. Second, Robert Moses had created more ways for city children to get out in the fresh air than anyone in history. Why cling to the nostalgia of Washington Square when Washington Square Village was going to have plenty of open space?

Then, in 1961, just as *Death and Life* was being readied for publication, Jane Jacobs discovered that the city had selected her section of the West Village as the next slum to be cleared in urban renewal. Jacobs, who'd been painstakingly restoring her Hudson Street townhouse, looked around and wondered: *What slum?* It was one thing for Jacobs to rail against Lincoln Center on an intellectual level; now, Robert Moses had put her home in the path of the wrecking ball.

Jacobs quickly formed the Committee to Save the West Village, which would meet at local watering holes like the Lion's Den and the White Horse Tavern, just up the street from her house. She organized neighborhood residents to attend planning meetings and public forums to speak against the slum designation. The committee painstakingly documented the buildings in the designated area, finding little evidence of urban blight. Meanwhile, Jacobs examined every person who stood to benefit from the slum designation, eventually discovering that the pro–urban renewal groups were in the pockets of the developers. (Today, that seems par for the course; in 1961, it was shocking.) Ultimately, New York's mayor, Robert Wagner, saw the controversy as affecting his re-election prospects, and the slum designation was revoked.

Walking today from the Village to Soho, I sometimes pass through Washington Square Village, and the contrast between it and the park just to the north couldn't be greater. The actual Washington Square is alive with activity; on a sunny day, in fact, it is such a jumble of NYU students, children, musicians, and tourists that it can feel like a smaller, hipper, Times Square.

A few minutes away, I pass into the confines of Washington Square Village and all that hubbub is instantly gone. The buildings are constructed around large, central open green areas—which are completely empty. The play areas are devoid of children; no one sits admiring the foliage. It's like a dystopian vision of the future. The buildings must house thousands of people, but none of them are to be seen. I move on quickly, passing through the equally empty I. M. Pei buildings that formed the second part of this Title I project, and only when I plunge into the crowded streets of Soho do I begin to relax again.

It's an almost textbook example of what was wrong with Robert Moses. He killed the street. He may have been right that the city was created for traffic—it's hard to argue that DeWitt Clinton's grid was not about vehicular motion—but pedestrians have always outnumbered vehicles and I think they always will. Conscious of it or not, people are drawn to New York because that grid has made walking, all these centuries later, the best way to experience the city.

I walk south on West Broadway to Broome Street and then head east. This would have been the path of Lomex, the super highway first sketched out by Moses in 1940 to connect the Holland Tunnel to the Williamsburg and Manhattan Bridges. Not only would it shuttle traffic between Long Island and New Jersey, it would provide the impetus for dealing with the failing manufacturing area along Broadway.

In 1962, a report on the area prepared by the City Club, *The Wastelands of New York City*, coined the term "South of Houston Industrial District," later shortened to Soho. In the report, the City Club saw little in the area worth saving, and Moses seized on the idea of creating a new neighborhood with modern Title I housing built surrounding the highway.

Though some artists were living and working in Soho loft buildings, there was little to attract the average New Yorker. The streets were dirty; the buildings were covered in graffiti. A few factories soldiered on, but most had shut down, and there was very little of the street life that *The Death and Life of Great American Cities* accused Moses of setting out to destroy.

And yet, suddenly Jane Jacobs was there to oppose Lomex. A Joint Committee to Stop the Lower Manhattan Expressway was formed and, using the same tactics as her Greenwich Village group, the committee launched a campaign to derail the highway. As Lomex's costs skyrocketed, the committee managed to get the city's Board of Estimate to delay funding. Jacobs continued to build a coalition, and by 1967, two hundred different civic groups had joined in opposition to the plan. That was in addition to the thousands of families and hundreds of businesses whose homes and buildings would be destroyed to make way for the highway.

Yet Moses persisted. His office produced a short film, *This Urgent Need*, showing the "slow strangulation" of the area by traffic. Once the World Trade Center complex was finished, Moses thought, things would only get worse. When Mayor Wagner left office and was replaced by John Lindsay, the new mayor—who'd campaigned against Lomex—was now suddenly for it. As far as Moses was concerned, mayors came and went. With enough persistence and time, he could see any project through.

The turning point came in 1968, at a hastily convened public hearing at Seward Park High School. At the meeting, Jane Jacobs and other Lomex opponents, aware that the meeting would do little to sway Moses, decided to storm the stage. Jacobs was arrested, and charged with disturbing the peace. Though the press, from the *New York Times* to the *New Yorker,* had covered the highway's tortuous development for years, Jane Jacobs in the back of a squad car made for good copy. If New York's leading urban theorist was willing to be arrested, could this highway really be such a good idea?

Mayor Lindsay began to see that it wasn't worth the effort; in July 1969, he finally declared the Lower Manhattan Expressway dead.

Robert Moses, then eighty years old, had seen his final projects undone by well-organized, grassroots campaigns. The visionary planner was unable to imagine that someplace like Soho could thrive without ten lanes of speeding cross-city traffic. Moses left city government, and while he continued to be a presence at the fringes of city life until his death in 1981, his era was definitely over. In 1968, Jane Jacobs moved to Toronto, never to return to the Village she'd fought so hard to save.

What happened next was nearly two decades of spiraling crime rates, ballooning debts, and infrastructural decay. Projects that Moses had spearheaded in the 1930s, like his public pools and improvements to city parks, fell apart. Highways and bridges needed maintenance dollars that weren't there. When New York finally began to bounce back financially in the 1980s, Moses was no longer seen as a hero but as an egotistical failure. While his great successes, like Jones Beach, weren't exactly forgotten, people focused on the anti-urban, tower-in-a-park Title I houses, castigated as banal spaces that deadened city life.

Jane Jacobs's view of close-knit neighborhoods with varied street life was in its ascendency, and cities and suburbs around the country tried to emulate her mixed-use, human-scaled West Village neighborhood. Today, walking past Jacobs's old house on Hudson Street, which now houses a cute boutique store at street level, Hudson Street is alive with people. I pass the White Horse Tavern—home to drinkers as varied as Dylan Thomas, Bob Dylan, and supposedly Edith Wharton—and brunch crowds fill the sidewalk tables.

Later, I return to Soho and walk along the path of Lomex. As I stand on the corner of Broome Street and Broadway looking at E. V. Haughwout's cast-iron department store, I think how strange it would be if all of this was gone.

Certainly, one thing that helped quash Moses's Lomex plans was the Landmarks Preservation Commission's newly vested power to protect buildings with historical and architectural merit. When buildings like

Haughwout's were designated landmarks, it became much harder for people like Moses to push through slum clearance projects with impunity.

Walking along Broome Street, I start to think how different this street must have seemed to Robert Moses as he walked its blocks. Then, I remember something. He probably *never* walked these streets. Driven across Broome Street on his way to the Holland Tunnel, he could look out the window of his limousine and see nothing but blight. He never interacted with the store owners; he never took the time to talk to the immigrants who were in the factories that survived in the area, even as manufacturing fled the city. He certainly didn't hang out in artists' lofts or visit the galleries that slowly began to occupy the former ground-floor retail level. Moses knew Soho on paper. He knew Lomex as a line on a map and a Lucite model that he stored in his office.

Jane Jacobs, by contrast, knew people. She knew the priest of the parish on Broome Street that knocked on her door one day, soliciting her help in fighting Lomex; she knew the longshoremen at the White Horse Tavern whose livelihoods were threatened by the West Village slum designation. She knew the "bunch of mothers" whose children gathered to play in Washington Square Park.

Standing on this street corner, engulfed in Saturday afternoon Soho shoppers, I realize—as Jane Jacobs did before me—that cities work because their life blood is people—not the faceless, nameless people of architectural drawings and fact-finding studies, but actual individuals with homes and jobs and dreams. Robert Moses saw New Yorkers in the abstract, consumers of his products; Jane Jacobs fought battles on the ground to save family-run corner stores and parks for neighborhood children.

In the end, do cities need both a Moses and a Jacobs to succeed? A government's power derives from its ability to think big—a Jane Jacobs couldn't build something like the Triborough Bridge. But neither could Robert Moses renovate Jane Jacobs's—or anyone's—individual brownstone. It may not make for a very good opera, but somewhere between them is the middle ground that makes New York work.

Cafe Wha? on MacDougal Street.

CHAPTER 18

"City Like a Web":
Bob Dylan and MacDougal Street

NOTHING WITH BOB DYLAN IS EVER EXACTLY WHAT it appears to be. If you're a Dylan fan, that's not news, but it's worth noting that Dylan's New York is as hard to pin down as Dylan himself. Facts and half-truths rub shoulders with myths and legends. A dozen sources might provide conflicting versions of the same story. I walk down the streets that Dylan roamed in the early sixties looking for traces of his city, but they are elusive. Some are gone, some are forgotten, some never existed in the first place.

Even Dylan himself never gets the story straight. In his autobiography, *Chronicles, Volume One* (a long-promised second installment has yet to materialize), Dylan says he rolled into town in January 1961 in a 1957 Chevy Impala—a year before the Impala went into production. Was it a '58 and Dylan simply forgot? Or was he deliberately creating a narrative that, even at its most mundane level, literally can't be true?

Scott Warmuth has compellingly argued in his essay "Bob Charlatan" that whatever truth there may be in *Chronicles, Volume One* has been woven from an amazing pastiche of materials—literally hundreds of disparate sources. For example, when Dylan talks about Cafe Wha?, the first place he played in New York City, one of his fellow performers is described as a man in "a priest's outfit and red-topped boots with little bells." Warmuth traces that factoid to Luc Sante's book *Low Life*, in which the thug John Allen employed women wearing "red-topped boots festooned with little bells." But, I've discovered that Sante's description isn't original either—he's paraphrasing gang aficionado Herbert Asbury's *All Around the Town*, which talks about Allen's girls with their "red-topped black boots, with circlets of sleigh-bells affixed to the ankles."

With Dylan's autobiography as with his songs, stories are built in these layers; fragments are cobbled together to create a whole that's greater than the sum of its parts. In the end, "facts" are never really as important as the essential truths in Dylan's music.

There are some things we *do* know about Dylan: He was born as Robert Zimmerman in Duluth, Minnesota, on May 24, 1941; he grew up in the tight-knit Jewish community in Hibbing, his mother's hometown. After graduating high school in 1959, he enrolled at the University of Minnesota but only lasted one year. While he was there, he tapped into the burgeoning folk scene and began consistently using the stage name Bob Dylan. Having been a rock and roller, Dylan's musical trajectory changed around this time when he was introduced to the music of Woody Guthrie, which, in Dylan's words, "made my head spin."

In January 1961, he arrived in New York City determined to do two things: perform in Greenwich Village, the center of America's folk music revival, and meet Woody Guthrie. By the end of his first week, he'd done both.

Dylan probably got to the city January 23, the day the front page of the *New York Times* proclaimed it the "coldest winter in seventeen years," a line Dylan would borrow for one of his earliest compositions, "Talkin' New York."

In *No Direction Home*, Martin Scorsese's documentary on Dylan's early career, the singer remembers that first day: "I took the subway down to the Village. I went to the Cafe Wha?, I looked out at the crowd, and I most likely asked from the stage 'Does anybody know where a couple of people could stay tonight?'"

Singer-songwriter Fred Neil presided over the bar's eclectic all-day lineup. Dylan showed his chops by backing up Neil and singer Karen Dalton on the harmonica and was hired to "blow my lungs out for a dollar a day."

Immersing himself in the music scene, Dylan soaked up everything he heard, from live acts in the bars and coffee houses south of Washington Square to the records he'd spin at Izzy Young's Folklore Center down the street from Cafe Wha?. In the meantime he continued to embellish his back story. In *No Direction Home*, Izzy Young recalls Dylan telling him, "I was born in Duluth, Minnesota, in 1941, moved to Gallup, New Mexico; then until now lived in Iowa, South Dakota, Kansas, North Dakota (for a little bit). Started playing in carnivals when I was fourteen, with guitar and piano. . . ."

Later, newspapers picked up the fake biography, writing about the cowboy singer from Gallup. Stretching all the way back to the city's Dutch pioneers, people have come to New York to reinvent themselves, to cast off their old identities and strike out in new directions. Dylan's fanciful back story may have been an extreme case, but it was effective.

In 1962, Dylan recorded his first album, simply titled *Bob Dylan*. It included thirteen tracks, most of them traditional folk and blues numbers except the sardonic autobiography of "Talkin' New York," and "Song to Woody," an elegy to his hero. The tune to "Song to Woody" is borrowed from Guthrie's "1913 Massacre," and the words were written one afternoon at the Mills Bar on Bleecker Street, a local hangout.

As Dylan's repertoire of cover songs and originals grew, he landed better gigs, playing at Gerde's Folk City and the Gaslight, a basement dive just down MacDougal Street from Cafe Wha? that had become a popular spot in the late 1950s for Beat poetry readings. In 1963, Dylan's second album, *The Freewheelin' Bob Dylan*, reversed the formula of the first—though heavily influenced by older folk songs, all but two numbers were Dylan's own compositions, leading off with what would become an anthem, and perhaps his best known song, "Blowin' in the Wind." Three weeks later, Peter, Paul, and Mary would release their own version of that song, which would soar to the top of the charts. Almost instantly, Dylan was a star.

So was MacDougal Street. As the *New York Times* pointed out in August 1963, MacDougal Street by this point had "sightseeing buses sometimes bumper-to-bumper . . . driving through the block [while] guides point out the coffeeshops by name."

Folk music was everywhere, from the basement stage at the Gaslight to old speakeasies like the Fat Black Pussycat to prestigious venues like Carnegie Hall, where Dylan performed in October 1963. In the same way that tourists had flocked to the Village in the first decades of the century to see a "real bohemian," now they were drawn to MacDougal Street to hear Dylan, Dave Von Ronk, Joan Baez, Doc Watson, Tiny Tim, Peter, Paul, and Mary— bar hopping around the streets of the Village, you could hear dozens of great musicians in just one night.

A month before *Freewheelin*'s debut, ABC television had launched the television show *Hootenanny* to capitalize on the folk music craze. When worried Greenwich Village residents found out that Robert Moses had decided that there would be no midway at the impending 1964 World's Fair, they complained to the *New York Times* that MacDougal Street would now obviously become the busiest tourist destination in the entire city.

Yet despite his growing fame, Dylan could still hang out on Bleecker Street, drinking coffee all day, and scribbling lyrics in his notebooks. It was a moment between renown and anonymity that he would never enjoy again.

One rainy afternoon in October, I'm standing outside Cafe Wha? with a pair of clients. I make this stop early on my Dylan walks because—unlike many Dylan sites—it's still there. It sits across from the famed Minetta Tavern, and if you block out the other buildings, it could almost be 1961 again.

I've started my tour in nearby Washington Square Park, which has been attracting buskers and other musicians since Jane Jacobs and Shirley Hayes kicked out vehicular traffic in 1959; however, on this gray day, the inclement weather has chased most of them away. Then, just as we finish looking at Cafe Wha?, the heavens open. My clients are a wonderfully gung-ho male couple from Toronto; as the rain pelts harder, their enthusiasm wanes, and we take the opportunity to duck into Caffe Reggio just up the street. A fixture on MacDougal Street since 1927, Reggio is a great reminder of the important imprint of the Italian-American community in the Village south of Washington Square. Without the proliferation of cafes in the area, the folk movement (and Beat poetry scene before it) might never have gotten off the ground.

Sitting by the window at the cafe, we're at a table that Dylan could easily have occupied fifty years ago. Like us, he would have stared out across the street at Louisa May Alcott's house, the spot where she wrote *Little Women*. I peer south, and can see the green awning of the nail salon at 110 MacDougal, above which would have been Izzy Young's Folklore Center. A couple of doors down from that, in the basement, was the Gaslight.

At the mention of the Gaslight, my companions perk up.

"Might we go in there?" one asks, but I shake my head.

"It's been a succession of bars, but I think it's between tenants now. There's still a Kettle of Fish over on Christopher Street, but it's not the one Dylan knew. There's no more Folklore Center, no more Gerde's Folk City, no more Fat Black Pussycat."

In advance, I try to warn people what they will and won't see of early '60s New York on this tour, but I can still tell that they are disappointed. However, the rain is letting up, so I encourage them to drink up.

"What I can show you is this," I say, pulling out the album cover for *The Freewheelin' Bob Dylan*. "If you want, you can stand in the middle of the street and re-create this scene."

I've rarely had anyone turn down this offer. If Dylan is your God, *Freewheelin'* is your Old Testament. Sometimes people hesitate—perhaps fearing it's too cheesy—but not these two. They're already up and ready to go.

At the time *Freewheelin'* was recorded, Dylan had moved into his own place, a small apartment on the third floor of 161 West Fourth Street—in the heart of the Village—which he shared with his girlfriend Suze Rotolo. Columbia Records dispatched a staff photographer, Don Hunstein, to shoot the album cover. After some awkward photos inside the apartment of Dylan strumming the guitar, Hunstein suggested a change of venue. Despite the freezing cold, Bob and Suze were asked to walk down Jones Street—just around the corner—while Hunstein snapped photos. Bob shoved his hands in his pockets to keep warm and Suze wore a coat over her sweater; it felt so bulky that she later recalled that she looked "like an Italian sausage."

Back at Columbia's offices, someone sifted through Hunstein's contact sheets and picked the cover image, a shot of Dylan with a half-smile on his face and Rotolo holding onto him for warmth. As Rotolo rightly notes, "it is one of those cultural markers that influenced the look of album covers precisely because of its casual, down-home spontaneity."

To get to Jones Street, we have to pass Dylan and Rotolo's apartment—today upstairs from a sex shop—and my companions dutifully stop to take pictures. When we turn onto Jones Street, I gesture at a building on the west side of the street with a diamond pattern on the facade. Then I show them the same building on the album cover.

Once they are in position they hand me two cell phones and a camera to capture the moment. Luckily, Jones Street is one of those Village byways that sees little traffic, so I can take multiple shots until they've got the image just right. As we walk to our next stop, I can see that both of them are already sharing the image with the world via Facebook.

I wonder what Dylan thinks of all this hero worship. Does he ever stumble upon these images online? (The idea of Bob trolling Facebook is odd, but who knows.) What does he think when he finds a picture of two middle-aged Canadian men, ecstatic to be walking the spots that he walked? For all I know he's searched "Bob Dylan Walking Tour" on the web and found my own website, promising to open a small window on the singer's world. Or maybe he pays no attention at all.

———

As Dylan's fame grew, his privacy diminished, and New York seemed an increasingly smaller place to him. He broke up with Suze Rotolo and began dating Joan Baez, a much bigger celebrity than he was at the time. In her song "Diamonds and Rust," she remembered them staying in the "crummy" Hotel Earle; it's now the Washington Square Hotel and guests can even request to stay in Baez and Dylan's room.

Dylan eventually met and married Sara Lownds, and in 1965 they moved into the Hotel Chelsea more or less full time. By the mid-sixties, the Chelsea had become a hub for creative people as diverse as Arthur Miller, Arthur C. Clarke, Leonard Cohen, and members of Andy Warhol's entourage. It was here that Dylan worked on the beginning of *Blonde on Blonde,* the double album that some consider his masterpiece. When he sings of the heat pipes coughing in "Visions of Johanna," it could well be the hotel's antiquated boiler he's talking about. Ten years later in "Sara," he reminds his soon-to-be-ex-wife that he wrote the side-long ballad "Sad-Eyed Lady of the Lowlands" for her while staying at the Chelsea Hotel.

In rapid succession from 1964 to 1966, Dylan "went electric" at the Newport Folk Festival; wrote and recorded "Like a Rolling Stone"—still widely considered rock music's greatest achievement; and recorded the Nashville-tinged *Blonde on Blonde,* a poetic work of staggering ambition. He had gone from being an unknown folk singer in a basement club to the "Voice of a Generation" to a traitor to the cause to a rock and roll superstar with lightning speed. It was little wonder that he then wanted to retreat.

In 1965, Dylan moved to Woodstock, New York, where, on July 29, 1966, he crashed his motorcycle, snapping multiple vertebrae.

Or, he didn't.

To this day, Dylan's guarded privacy and penchant for storytelling make some believe that he either never crashed at all, or exaggerated his injuries. Whatever the truth, Dylan retreated from public view and when he returned his musical output—the sparse *John Wesley Harding,* the pure country of *Nashville Skyline,* the confounding *Self Portrait*—seemed designed to kill the old Bob Dylan once and for all. Maybe once no one cared about him anymore, he could safely return to normalcy.

For Dylan, normalcy meant MacDougal Street. In 1969, Dylan moved into 94 MacDougal on a quiet block south of Bleecker Street, hoping to recapture the spirit of what had brought him to New York in the first place. The house, one of a row constructed in the 1840s, is part of a charming landmark district; in the 1920s the houses along MacDougal and Sullivan Streets were renovated as a middle-class development, and all share a large, common garden, which is hidden from view. In fact, when I bring visitors to the house, it's a significant letdown. The house has little outward architectural charm and I am forced to merely describe the private gardens. A blank facade hiding hidden treasures—did Dylan buy the house as metaphor?

All I can point out are the garbage cans; Dylan might have hoped that coming back to the Village would reclaim some of the anonymity he'd enjoyed at the beginning of the decade, but he was now much too famous for that. Self-proclaimed "garbologist" A. J. Weberman would pick through Dylan's trash cans looking for scraps of information that might unlock the secrets of Dylan's songs. When Dylan grew fed up with this, he chased Weberman down and beat him up.

As I talk about the house, red double-decker tour buses stream across nearby Bleecker Street; sometimes my clients and I will hear the bus guide pointing out that this was where Dylan lived, with all "the other bohemians and beatniks."

The guides make it seem like the neighborhood is *still* filled with hippies and Beat poets, but even by the time Dylan was moving back to the area in 1969, it had already inexorably changed. Washington Square drew more Vietnam War protestors than folk singers; the clubs along MacDougal had closed, moved, or changed management. Only the old coffee houses—Cafe Reggio, Le Figaro, Cafe Lanza across from Dylan's new house—seemed unchanged.

While Le Figaro, a major Beat hangout, is now gone, Lanza and Reggio soldier on. Even though Dylan never got back his anonymity when he returned here, I wonder if he took comfort in the fact that some things resolutely stayed the same. In some ways, that's the secret to New York's success: sure, a Starbucks opens, but it's in an 1830s townhouse that's next to an Italian restaurant from the 1930s. On some blocks, the squeeze of corporate franchising feels more intense, but really only in places where the city comes in—a la Robert Moses—and bulldozes everything in its path do the connections to the past disappear.

While living at 94 MacDougal Street, Dylan wrote and recorded *New Morning*, which began as a collaboration with Archibald MacLeish on the play *Scratch*. Dylan and MacLeish parted ways after Dylan had composed only three songs for the play, including one that was to become a standard, "Time Passes Slowly." This was probably just as well for Dylan: *Scratch* closed after just three days, but *New Morning* was hailed as a comeback.

Though he resumed performing publicly at a 1968 Woody Guthrie tribute concert, he made few public appearances and after *New Morning* didn't release an album other than his soundtrack to *Pat Garrett and Billy the Kid* for three years—an eternity considering the quantity of his output in the 1960s. In 1973, he and his band—*The* Band—prepared a new album (*Planet Waves*) and a sold-out, double-billed tour of stadiums. The tour was closely followed by *Blood on the Tracks,* an album often ranked among his best. The fame Dylan had been dodging crept back into his life.

He began hanging out at the Bottom Line on West Fourth Street (now gone) and the Bitter End and Other End, clubs on Bleecker Street, where he absorbed new music—and that of old friends. Sometimes, he'd spontaneously take the stage. Slowly, an idea hatched in Dylan's mind—a traveling show, almost like a carnival, of musicians playing small towns and intimate venues—the exact opposite of his tour with The Band. In 1975, in the wake of the album *Desire* and the official release of a long-bootlegged collaboration with The Band from the '60s called *The Basement Tapes,* Dylan launched the Rolling Thunder Revue. Joining him were Joan Baez, Roger McGuinn of the Byrds, Allen Ginsberg as resident poet, playwright Sam Shepard, and dozens of other musicians and hangers-on. It was a fertile, maniacal period in Dylan's life.

Though Dylan comes and goes from the city to this day—rumors swirl that he has a place on Striver's Row in Harlem—the Rolling Thunder Review and his time at 94 MacDougal marked the last time that he called New York home.

~

The New York that Dylan left in the mid-1970s was a very different place than the one he'd driven into from Minnesota fifteen years earlier. For one thing, the city was quickly running out of money. Crime had been on the rise since the middle of 1960s and by the late '70s was reaching epic proportions. In 1977, the city was plunged into a blackout that sparked looting; meanwhile, serial killer David "Son of Sam" Berkowitz was on the loose. It wasn't a good time to be a New Yorker, and it's hard to blame people like Dylan—and so many others—for jettisoning the city in favor of safer, sunnier climes.

Dylan, however, was undergoing much bigger changes than just moving out of New York. In 1978, he had a vision of Jesus and became a born-again Christian. He released two albums of Christian-influenced music—*Slow Train Coming* and *Saved*—followed by the overtly fundamentalist *Shot of Love* and the more secular (though still, in my mind, covertly fundamentalist) *Infidels. Infidels* was the first Dylan album I bought with my own money and I wore out the grooves playing it on my lousy Sears turntable.

One New York Dylan show I remember fondly was at the Roseland Ballroom in midtown in 1993. Roseland is a small space and since the show was general admission, I'd arrived early enough to secure a great location on the floor, right next to the raised platform that was going to serve as the VIP section. It was quite a crowd—Bruce Springsteen and Neil Young were both there (and joined Dylan for the encores)—but I was most interested in the fact that standing about five feet away from me was Allen Ginsberg.

The Beat poets were a crucial influence on the Village folk scene. Indeed, there might never have been a Village folk scene if the Beats hadn't paved the way. Places like the Gaslight and Kettle of Fish on MacDougal Street that were staples of the folk circuit first drew audiences because of the Beat poets like Ginsberg, Gregory Corso, and Jack Kerouac. Dylan and Ginsberg became close friends in the early '60s, and Dylan later credited the Beats for much of his musical development: "I came out of the wilderness and just naturally fell in with the Beat scene. . . . It was Jack Kerouac, Ginsberg, Corso, Ferlinghetti . . . it had just as big an impact on me as Elvis Presley."

Which means that standing five feet away from Allen Ginsberg meant I was standing five feet away from the Beat's version of Elvis Presley. Cool.

I recall standing in the cavernous interior of Madison Square Garden; Dylan played "Yea Heavy and a Bottle of Bread!" a song from *The Basement Tapes* so obscure that only a handful of us recognized it.

"That was a request, of course," Dylan said with a sly smile at the end. To this day, I wonder who had the clout to request that song—and have it played.

The first time I'd seen Dylan at Madison Square Garden was as the centerpiece of his own thirtieth anniversary show in 1992, dubbed "Bob Fest" by Neil Young. Even today, when celebrities flock together for concerts at the drop of a hat, something about this night seemed otherworldly. To have Young, Eric Clapton, George Harrison, Johnny and June Carter Cash, The Band, Willie Nelson, and so many more all together on one stage was magical enough.

But the best part came at the end. Dylan walked out on stage with just his acoustic guitar and sang "Song to Woody." It's easy to knock Dylan's singing style—David Bowie called it a "voice of sand and glue"—but on this night, he hit every note, and every word just hung there. It had been thirty years since he'd rolled into town to meet Guthrie and get discovered. Here he was the dean of American songwriting, singing this song as if he were sitting on the side of Guthrie's bed at Brooklyn State Hospital.

It also marked a radical shift in Dylan's output. Just ten days after the concert, Dylan would release *Good as I Been to You,* an album of traditional folk and blues songs—the very songs that he'd peppered his set with at the Gaslight and Cafe Wha?. Another traditional album, *World Gone Wrong,* followed before Dylan catapulted back into the spotlight with *Time Out of Mind* in 1997 and began a series of albums, steeped in American roots music, that have been critically praised and some of the best-selling work of his career.

Alas, due to technical difficulties (Dylan's guitar wasn't properly plugged into the soundboard) the version of "Song to Woody" from that night didn't make it onto the show's souvenir album and seems to have disappeared. It's been over two decades since that concert and my own memory of it is fading. Dylan has released eight studio albums, multiple installations in his "Bootleg" series, live albums, compilations, and one weird Christmas album in the meantime. He's also been on his "Never Ending Tour" (a term Dylan himself doesn't really like) since the late 1980s, playing over a hundred dates a year even though he's now in his early seventies.

But when I hear the opening licks of "Song to Woody," I'm transported to Madison Square Garden in 1992, and sometimes—if I'm lucky—to Greenwich Village in 1962, where an American icon was born.

The New York skyline at dusk.

CHAPTER 19

New York Stories:
Martin Scorsese and Woody Allen

ASK PEOPLE TO NAME THEIR FAVORITE NEW YORK MOVIE and you'll get some intriguing answers: *Ghostbusters, The Sweet Smell of Success, Saturday Night Fever, When Harry Met Sally, The Warriors, Teenage Mutant Ninja Turtles* (I'm not kidding), *Do the Right Thing,* a surprising number of votes for *Serendipity*—the list goes on and on.

On tours of Central Park, people will stop me as we pass underneath one of Vaux and Olmsted's stone bridges and ask, "Is this where Kevin meets the pigeon lady in *Home Alone 2?*" (It's not—that was a soundstage.) On tours of the Lower East Side, I'm always amazed at how many people still remember the pickle shop from *Crossing Delancey*. When I stop to point out the Empire State Building, it immediately evokes fond memories for many people of *An Affair to Remember* (or *Sleepless in Seattle*).

For many visitors and transplants, their first experiences of New York are shaped by film. Sure, there are famous TV spots, but it's at the movies where the city really makes a lasting impression. This is true even for native New Yorkers—seeing familiar, ordinary places up on the big screen elevates them and, by extension, the viewer. Woody Allen, growing up in Brooklyn, knew Manhattan not from real life—but from the glamorous depictions in the films he would go see every week.

For me, certain iconic scenes stand out because they stir up memories of New York's past: that incredible opening sequence to *West Side Story* filmed in San Juan Hill on the Upper West Side; the "New York, New York" number with Frank Sinatra and Gene Kelly from *On the Town;* the chase scene under the elevated subway tracks in Bensonhurst in *The French Connection;* the view of Greenwich Village backyards as seen from Jimmy Stewart's apartment (filmed on a set, but authentic nonetheless) in Hitchcock's *Rear Window*.

But when people ask me what films evoke the best sense of the "real" New York—the past and present—I always point them to the works of Martin Scorsese and Woody Allen. From Scorsese's 1967 debut *Who's That Knocking at My Door?* to Allen's 2013 meditation on collapse, *Blue Jasmine,* from the thugs of the nineteenth century in *Gangs of New York* to the halcyon world of the 1940s in *Radio Days,* these two directors have imbued their films with a sense of what it is to be a New Yorker. While on one level, Scorsese's *Mean Streets* seems to have little in common with Allen's *Manhattan,* in fact, both men share similar backgrounds, influences, and ability to brilliantly use the city as a character itself.

Martin Scorsese was born in Corona, Queens, in 1942, but his family moved to Elizabeth Street in Little Italy when he was young. Scorsese recalled that his father had been able to get the house in Queens because he was "assisted by a crime family," but when those criminal connections proved too much for the landlord, they were forced to move back in with family in Manhattan.

Living first with his grandparents at 241 Elizabeth Street and then at No. 253 just up the block, the streets of Little Italy formed young Scorsese's entire world. He went to church at St. Patrick's Old Cathedral on Mott

Street; he attended the private school next door. His only excursions out of the neighborhood—both literally and figuratively—were to movie theaters on Sixth Avenue, 14th Street, or 42nd Street with his father. Later, when he started classes at New York University, Scorsese was unfamiliar with the area—he'd simply never been in that part of Greenwich Village, even though it was just a half-mile from his home.

Movies filled and expanded Scorsese's world. Plagued with asthma that kept him indoors, he would repeatedly watch the week's "Million Dollar Movie," soaking in everything from westerns to Italian cinema. "I love movies," Scorsese said in a 1975 interview. "It's my whole life and that's it."

Scorsese began studying film at NYU in 1960—when the French New Wave was in vogue—and was deeply influenced by his teacher, Haig Manoogian, who co-produced Scorsese's student film, *I Call First*—which was later shaped into his first feature, *Who's That Knocking at My Door?* That film and its follow-up, *Mean Streets,* both starring the then-unknown Harvey Keitel, depicted the Elizabeth Street world that Scorsese had grown up with. The opening shot of *Who's That Knocking* shows a tenement apartment—complete with hallway transoms—straight out of Jacob Riis. Scorsese's characters circle the neighborhood, going to restaurants, Italian social clubs, and church. They have families, but they share a kinship of the street.

Mean Streets centers around Keitel as Charlie and Robert De Niro as Johnny Boy, brothers in arms trapped in the claustrophobic blocks surrounding old St. Patrick's. They eat, drink, and chase girls. Charlie tries to collect on bad debts for his uncle, a local Mafia capo, while Johnny Boy prefers not to work, instead borrowing "money all over this neighborhood, left and right from everybody," and never paying them back. In a memorable sequence, Charlie and Johnny Boy patrol the streets of Little Italy, at one point picking up garbage can lids to become impromptu gladiators. Their lives are stunted: by circumstance, by geography, by money, and by the overarching guilt of being Catholic.

Scorsese's next film, the documentary *Italianamerican,* offers an insight into Scorsese's own upbringing as the son of Italian immigrants. Scorsese interviews his parents in their tenement apartment. His mother, Catherine, shares her secrets for making pasta with meatballs; his father, Charles, talks about growing up in the neighborhood—going to Yonah Schimmel's for knishes, and being hired to light the stoves of Jewish families on the Sabbath since they couldn't do any work.

His parents' matter-of-fact attitudes mirror those of the people I've talked to who grew up in Little Italy or the Lower East Side: *Two families living in a tiny three-room apartment? That was life.* I once had a client who was passed through the air shaft from one tenement to another when he needed babysitting. People are mortified when I tell this story, but the guy said it with a shrug that seemed to say: *So what—that's what we did.*

Walking the streets of Little Italy today, the world of Scorsese's childhood—and his earliest films—seems hard to find. The block of Elizabeth Street where Scorsese grew up is now part of Nolita ("North of Little Italy"), an area of trendy clothing stores and sidewalk cafes. The tenements are still there, as is Yonah Schimmel's on nearby Houston Street, but the number of Italians, year by year, grows thinner. *Mean Streets* opens with the San Gennaro festival, where Scorsese was able to shoot after his father paid off the festival's organizers. Today, the festival still thrives, but there are ongoing conflicts between the non-Italian residents of Mulberry Street and the supporters of the street fair.

There is still a Little Italy, of course, mostly on the blocks of Mulberry south of Kenmare Street. But few of the restaurants that cater to the tourist trade are very old; many don't even date back to the *Mean Streets* era. A few reminders of the immigrant neighborhood survive: on Grand Street, Alleva, the city's oldest cheese shop, is still going strong after more than a century; nearby, John Jovino's gun shop (outside of which Keitel and De Niro have their garbage-lid fight) is a neighborhood landmark. But if Scorsese were to make *Mean Streets* today, would he shoot it on Mulberry Street? Or in order to achieve authenticity, would he have to build acres of set, as he did for 2002's *Gangs of New York,* somewhere on a soundstage?

After *Mean Streets,* Scorsese's next New York picture—which some critics argue remains his best—was *Taxi Driver,* the exploration into the troubled mind of cabbie Travis Bickle, played by De Niro. Describing the film as having "a rage in it that I saw in my grandparents," Scorsese has long identified the film as a very personal work, calling it a reflection of "my state of mind." I hope that's not entirely true, as Travis Bickle's state of mind is a frightening thing to behold.

The film remains a remarkable portrait of New York in the mid-1970s: The rain-soaked streets of Times Square still reflect countless neon signs, but that's about the only continuity. *Taxi Driver's* Times Square is pimps and hustlers and porno theaters. Though Scorsese sets up Bickle as an outsider from the beginning, it's the scene at the XXX Lyric Theater on 42nd Street—where De Niro takes Cybill Shepherd on a date to a dirty movie—where Bickle's antisocial personality comes to the forefront.

The stretch of 42nd Street that is home to the Lyric wasn't always squalid; the theaters—some of the oldest in Times Square—were built around the time New York's first subway lines opened in 1904. However, after World War II, most of the legitimate theaters couldn't make a profit, and one by one they became movie houses (some of which Scorsese frequented as a boy). As Times Square grew seedier, the movie theaters switched to showing pornography. By the time of *Taxi Driver*, 42nd Street was a place that tourists seldom ventured after dark.

What a change to walk these blocks at night now—the sidewalks are so jammed with tourists, costumed street performers soliciting tips for photographs, and hucksters trying to get me to see a comedy show, that I can barely move. The Lyric, the porno theater from *Taxi Driver*, still stands; it's now the Foxwoods Theatre, home to such big-budget Broadway shows as *Spider Man: Turn Off the Dark*.

Between Broadway houses, movie multiplexes, Madame Tussaud's wax museum, and the overall carnival feeling, it's a wonder they just don't shut down 42nd Street altogether and give it over to the pedestrians. Under the Bloomberg administration, the city closed portions of Times Square to vehicular traffic and made the city more accommodating to walkers and bikers. If that isn't the single biggest repudiation of Robert Moses, I don't know what is. Or, as Travis Bickle might say, a real rain has finally come down and washed his world away.

Though Times Square's transformation is extraordinary, I'm also interested in the more subtle ways the city has changed since the 1970s. To find a less conspicuous place to see those changes, I search out the site of *Taxi Driver*'s climax, the tenement where Jodie Foster's character, Iris, works as a teenage prostitute. The building still stands on East 13th Street, and it's cheerier in real life than it appears in the movie even though it's a faceless tenement like so many on these East Village blocks. What's jarring is the construction project down the street, a new apartment building calling itself The Jefferson. On the scaffolding, signs advertise it as THE BIRTHPLACE OF COOL, and an ORIGINAL BOHEMIAN ENCLAVE. The gulf between the cheap rents in the *Taxi Driver* tenement and prices at the Jefferson—where studio apartments start at $850,000—is staggering.

Around the same time that *Taxi Driver* was being hailed for plumbing the psychological darkness of New York's streets, Woody Allen was starting work on *Annie Hall*, which would earn him two Oscars and make him a household name. The film places its characters in neighborhoods that seem the opposite of those in *Mean Streets* and *Taxi Driver*. But in the same way that Lillian Wald and Caroline Astor inhabited different worlds within the same city, so do Travis Bickle and Annie Hall.

⟶⟵

Woody Allen was born Allen Konigsberg in Midwood, Brooklyn, in 1935. Though he would draw on his own childhood for the characters Alvy Singer in *Annie Hall* and Little Joe in *Radio Days*, neither movie was autobiography. Knowing that doesn't lessen how much I love the image of him growing up underneath a roller coaster as Alvy does in *Annie Hall*.

Like Scorsese, Allen's childhood was centered on going to the movies. As he recalled to Eric Lax in *Conversations with Woody Allen*:

> [S]o much of my life revolved around [movie houses] in the neighborhood. You'd go there on your dates, you'd go there to meet girls, you'd go there to pick up girls, you'd go there to see films. . . . It was a whole other world. You had this feeling of entering a temple in a certain way. . . . It was a paradise.

Allen began writing jokes for newspaper columns while a teenager, adopting a pseudonym so that his classmates wouldn't find out. He graduated to writing jokes for television, including for the great Sid Caesar, and doing stand-up. He wrote and starred in his first film, *What's New Pussycat?* in 1965, vowing afterward to direct his future projects himself. For the next ten years, Allen worked steadily, but didn't make a film focused on New York.

All that changed in 1977 with *Annie Hall*, where Allen traded the slapstick of *Sleeper* and *Take the Money and Run* for more grounded romantic comedy, creating the tale of two New Yorkers—Alvy Singer and Annie Hall—who come together and split apart over the course of the film. Unlike the grit of Scorsese's Lower East Side and Times Square locales, *Annie Hall*'s New York revolves around the Upper East Side.

Allen moved to a Fifth Avenue duplex in 1970, and once he started making movies in the city, Upper East Siders became constant characters. Even to New Yorkers, there's sometimes a false sense that the neighborhood is all pre-war apartment buildings, swanky cocktail parties, and upscale restaurants. Allen depicts that neighborhood—sometimes to devastating effect, as in *Blue Jasmine*—but as *Annie Hall* shows, there's another Upper East Side too.

After an opening flashback to the Coney Island of Alvy's youth, *Annie Hall* moves to the present day with a fantastic tracking shot of Allen and

Tony Roberts walking along East 66th Street between Second Avenue and Third Avenue as they head to the Beekman Theater. This isn't the Upper East Side of mansions and Museum Mile. Here, the architecture is more utilitarian, with giant glazed white-brick apartments that were trendy after World War II; this was the Upper East Side for secretaries and middle managers, the new New Yorkers coming to take advantage of the post-war boom.

While Travis Bickle in *Taxi Driver* has more freedom to roam the city because of his cab, he's still in many ways as trapped by circumstance as the characters from *Mean Streets.* Woody Allen's characters, by contrast, are able to take advantage of what the city has to offer. Alvy and Annie meet because they both play tennis at the same club near South Street Seaport. Later, they drive out to the Hamptons. They go for walks in Greenwich Village; they dine on the Upper West Side. These are people whose education and economic privilege open up the city for them.

One thing Allen's characters rarely seem to do, however, is ride the subway—which, especially in *Annie Hall*—would have ruined the illusion of New York as the domain of Marshall McLuhan–quoting, tennis-playing intellectuals. Woody Allen movies are like Edith Wharton novels in this regard. Both paint telling portraits of a society—high and low—that's devoid of public transit. In the late 1970s of *Annie Hall*, one step through the subway turnstiles brought you to another world, a place much closer to Travis Bickle's universe.

Over the years, Allen has drawn criticism for the lack of diversity in his casting and settings; few African-American characters appear in his films ("I don't know the black experience well enough to really write about it," said Allen) and even the director's leading ladies have critiqued his writing for women. In the end, the world of *Annie Hall* is actually as compartmentalized as that in *Taxi Driver*—it is just a very different compartment. Directors like Scorsese and Allen are experts in their own milieu; luckily, we have gifted directors like Spike Lee and the late Nora Ephron whose films show New York from other points of view.

Two years after the Oscar-winning success of *Annie Hall,* Allen explored similar themes in the film that some critics regard even more highly, *Manhattan.* Here was Allen's true valentine to New York, especially in the now-famous black-and-white opening montage. His character, Isaac, narrates, "'Chapter One. He adored New York City. He idolized it all out of proportion.' No, make that: 'He romanticized it all out of proportion. . . .'" After more false starts, Isaac finally says, "New York was his town. And it always would be." On cue, fireworks blast over the skyline.

Beyond the magical opening scene, the film again makes good use of sites around the city: The characters dine at Elaine's and the Russian Tea Room; Allen and Diane Keaton hide out in the Hayden Planetarium and discuss art at the Guggenheim and the Museum of Modern Art.

So many of these places are gone. The planetarium was torn down and replaced by the new Rose Center for Earth and Space at the Museum of Natural History—a definite upgrade. But I miss the old MoMA that Allen shows here. The new museum reeks of efficiency, but the renovations destroyed most of its character.

In truth, watching all these old Scorsese and Allen movies is certain to trigger a sigh of nostalgia in any New Yorker—even in those who didn't know the city then. Something as mundane as seeing the old black-on-yellow street signs can stir up a fondness for a city where everything is doomed to be replaced.

Movies are like time capsules. Certainly, they create false realities—to capture *Manhattan*'s iconic scene set against the backdrop of the Queens-boro Bridge, Allen's crew had to import a park bench—but they also pre-serve moments in time, often inadvertently. In 1988, Scorsese and Allen both participated in the anthology film *New York Stories*. Who knew when Allen superimposed his character's mother's disembodied head over the World Trade Center in "Oedipus Wrecks" that films like his would turn out to be our best medium for keeping our memories of those towers alive?

❧

While Woody Allen was receiving commercial and critical respect for *Annie Hall* and *Manhattan*, Martin Scorsese veered in a completely different direc-tion, paying homage to both the city *and* big-budget Hollywood musicals by making *New York, New York*. A critical and commercial flop, the film starred Robert De Niro and Liza Minnelli as sparring lovers and musicians. At least we got something lasting out of it: Kander and Ebb's "Theme from *New York, New York*," the city's unofficial anthem. From sporting events to the ball drop in Times Square on New Year's Eve, the song (best known in Frank Sinatra's version) embodies the four centuries of striving that have defined the city. Even in Peter Stuyvesant's day, I bet there were immigrants, fresh off the boat, thinking, *If I can make it there, I can make it anywhere.* Certainly that's how I like to imagine Johannes Nevius.

Scorsese bounced back with *Raging Bull* (a film set in New York but not really about the city), one of his greatest achievements. The dark comedy *The King of Comedy* followed, the story of deranged comic Rupert Pupkin (De Niro) and his attempt to kidnap a famous talk show host (Jerry Lewis) to help his own career. Filmed mainly at night, *King of Comedy* is a strange mix of the psychotic energy of *Taxi Driver* and the artifice of *New York, New York*. Rupert, as part of his fantasy, has mockups of Sardi's restaurant and Jerry's television studio built in his basement. These don't just reflect his mental state, but mirror the artifice inherent in movie making. Is the New York on screen real? Or just a fantasy?

More successful was Scorsese's 1985 dark comedy *After Hours*, in which Griffin Dunne's Paul Hackett is thrust into a Kafka-meets-Hitchcock-meets-*Wizard of Oz* world of Soho after dark. It had been ten years since Scorsese had filmed *Taxi Driver*, and *After Hours* explored loneliness and isolation from the point of view of a victim of circumstance, an everyman just looking for a good time.

This was the first Scorsese film I saw on the big screen and I was instantly intrigued—not so much by the story, which was funny and unsettling, but with the sense that what I was seeing was New York. It was so dark and foreign, a place where artists in their underwear made papier-mâché sculptures and bouncers at clubs quoted Kafka. It was the sort of place I wanted to move to. Meanwhile, on screen, Paul—like Dorothy in *The Wizard of Oz*—only wished to go home. He just couldn't figure out how to escape.

By this time, Woody Allen had fallen into his pattern of basically writing and directing a film every year. His next landmark film came in 1986 with *Hannah and Her Sisters*, which grossed $85 million and won Academy Awards for stars Michael Caine and Dianne Wiest (as well as a writing Oscar for Allen).

The narrative is connected together by three Thanksgivings set in the apartment of Hannah (Mia Farrow) and which were filmed in Farrow's own Central Park West high rise. (Though Allen and Farrow were together at the time, he lived in his own place on the Fifth Avenue side of the park.) Hannah's sister Lee lives in a Soho loft with her artist boyfriend, Frederick, and begins an affair with Hannah's husband, Elliot (Michael Caine). The contrast between the pre-war hominess of Hannah and Elliot's Upper West Side apartment and the graffiti-strewn blocks of Soho could not have been clearer. Like Scorsese's Paul Hackett, Elliot finds himself thrust into another world; the difference is that Elliot wants to be there and finds himself inevitably drawn back in by Lee, even when he vows to stay away. Eventually he is forced to go home to Hannah, and re-embraces the security of their marriage.

As a tour guide, one of my favorite scenes is early in the film when Holly (Dianne Wiest) and her friend April (Carrie Fisher) are being wooed by David, an architect played by Sam Waterston. When they ask him what his favorite buildings are, David offers to show them. They pile into his car—of course—and head off to see David's (and Allen's?) favorite New York landmarks. To the average filmgoer, it's a perfectly pleasant survey of a lot of Gilded Age and Art Deco architecture; to a tour guide, it's ridiculous. Who would go visit the Ansonia, hop over to the Graybar Building at Grand Central Terminal, then back up to Seventh Avenue for the riotously ornate Alwyn Court? *And do it driving?*

David's list of buildings contains some real New York gems, including the New York Yacht Club and Pomander Walk. He ends on East 62nd Street, admiring the home of Edith and Ernesto Fabbri; Edith was the great-granddaughter of Cornelius Vanderbilt, and the house is appropriately overwrought. Two doors down, David points to Percival Goodman's Fifth Avenue Synagogue, a modernist temple from the late 1950s.

I've always found the contrast between the Fabbri house and the synagogue fascinating, but Holly, David, and April find the newer building banal. Even if the other buildings on David's list don't reflect Allen's own personal picks, David's reaction to the synagogue certainly mirrors Allen's own dismay about, as he later remarked, "new buildings that are built with no regard to the context they're in."

Allen's rejection of the newer, edgier art in favor of an older, rosier world came to its apex in the unapologetically sentimental *Radio Days* from 1987, which is probably my favorite film of his. Set in the Rockaways (a stand-in for Long Beach, Long Island, where Allen lived some as a child), the film is a series of vignettes about how radio was central to the lives of people like Allen and his family when he was a boy. Film, of course, was key in Allen's development as an artist, but it was radio—from serialized adventures to big band concerts to breaking news—that provided the hum of everyday existence.

When I went out to the Rockaways to explore Jacob Riis Park, I stopped by the block where *Radio Days* was filmed, to see a preserved corner of 1940s New York. Only on reaching the block did I realize how much set dressing had been done to transform the street. Today, assisted living facilities and homes with signs that warn RESIDENTS ONLY line the block. Underemployed men hung out on the sidewalks and sat on the stoops, wondering why

I was there. I retreated to the other end of the block, where traffic whizzed by and I turned the corner. It was a reminder of how often reality just can't measure up to the magic of the big screen.

In 1990, Martin Scorsese returned to New York for *Goodfellas,* an exploration of the world of the Mafia that had been on the fringes of *Raging Bull* and *Mean Streets.* The film, based on the true story of mobster-turned-informant Henry Hill, was a compelling look at what Scorsese called the "dangerous seduction" of joining an organized crime family. The film's most famous shot—maybe Scorsese's best in any film—was the single-take tracking shot of Ray Liotta's Hill and his girlfriend, Karen (Lorraine Bracco) entering the Copacabana from the service entrance. The camera follows Henry and Karen down the stairs, through the kitchen, and into the nightclub, never wavering. A special table is set for them; other mobsters send over champagne. Henry, if just for this one moment, is the center of the universe—or, as Scorsese said, "it was like being in the court of the kings."

A few years later, Scorsese's *The Age of Innocence* was his first attempt at a true historical drama, and he does a stunning job of keeping his contemporary film grounded in the world of the 1870s. As I mentioned in the Edith Wharton chapter, Scorsese used the National Arts Club as one of his sets for *Age of Innocence;* around the same time, there seemed to be a flurry of Hollywood activity on Gramercy Park. Robert Redford used the club for *Quiz Show,* then Woody Allen came for *Manhattan Murder Mystery.* I never came face to face with either Scorsese or Allen during their shoots, though I did pass Woody on the street when he was filming his 2003 comedy *Anything Else.* In fact, because Allen is so prolific, it's hard *not* to run into one of his shooting locations every now and then. It's almost a rite of passage for transplants to the city to have their first Woody Allen sighting. Once you've seen Woody, you're a real New Yorker.

I was leading a tour when I saw Allen on the Upper East Side, and actually missed out on the opportunity to be in the background of *Anything Else* because of a real rarity: an obnoxious client. Our customers are, almost by definition, decent people—if you're interested in paying to walk around for two hours listening to me talk about history and architecture, you're probably a nice person who wants to be there.

Well, this guy wanted to be there—but he also wanted to punctuate every comment he made by socking me in the arm. As we walked up Madison Avenue, we were approached by a production assistant from Woody

Allen's crew, who told us we'd be in the shot and to just walk normally and not look at the camera.

As we continued walking, my client slowed down and stared directly at the camera—specifically so he could ruin the take. His desire to not follow directions meant he'd lost his chance to see himself on the big screen—and mine too, of course. He was very proud of himself; he probably punched me in the arm.

———

In general, Woody Allen's films, even popular ones, don't make people call up and say, "Can you give me a tour?" Indeed, only one film has ever done that—and it continues to do it to this day: Martin Scorsese's *Gangs of New York*.

This is a blessing and a bit of a curse. I'm happy for the work, and glad the film has spurred interest in nineteenth-century immigrant New York. However, just as Herbert Asbury's book on which the movie was based played fast and loose with history, so did Scorsese and his screenwriters. This was their right—Scorsese wasn't making a documentary, after all. He was filming a big-budget story of love, gang warfare, and revenge set against a historical backdrop.

Still, people are dismayed when I tell them that Tyler Anbinder, the most prominent scholar of the Five Points era, has argued that the most notorious gang in the book and film, the Dead Rabbits, may not have actually existed. A hallmark of touring the Five Points today isn't pointing out the things that did happen there, it's talking about the things that didn't.

Some might disagree, but I really think it's better than no history at all, and I never fault people for developing an interest in their own history, even if that history isn't entirely real. One of my most recent tours in the Five Points was an Irish-American mother and daughter who were inspired by the film to learn about their heritage. After a decade of research, they finally stumbled upon an address of their ancestor, a tenement on Mott Street.

"Isn't that Chinatown?" the mother asked as we ascended the hill from Columbus Park to the old Church of the Transfiguration.

"Yes," I replied. "Chinatown today. Little Italy a couple of generations ago." I pointed to a list of names on the church exterior of men who'd died in World War I. All were Italian except for three Irish surnames.

"A generation before World War I," I continued, "this was one of the largest churches in the world. Thousands of Irish Catholics called this church home. Maybe even your great-great-great grandparents."

We continued north on Mott Street toward the address they'd given me. I cautioned them that the house wouldn't likely be standing. Much of the architecture along this stretch of Mott is old, but not that old.

We passed 65 Mott Street, considered by many to be the oldest tenement left in the city, and paused to talk about what life would have been like in this building during the Civil War.

"So my ancestor would have known this building?" the daughter asked.

"Yes," I replied. "This was definitely here." I pointed out a few more structures that, just from the outside, looked like they might be the right time frame. We kept going north, past Canal Street and into the section of Mott that was once all Italian.

Finally, we came to a building near Kenmare Street—the only street in the neighborhood named for a place in Ireland—and paused outside a rundown brick building. It had obviously once been a townhouse, a reminder of when Mott Street had housed middle-class families as well as immigrants. The age of a house like this can be tough to judge from the outside, but to my surprise, it looked like it could easily have been their ancestor's home. They were thrilled.

When Scorsese made *Gangs of New York*, he built a meticulous re-creation of the Five Points on a set at *Cinecittà*, outside Rome, Italy. Too much of the actual neighborhood—particularly the "vile rookeries" that Jacob Riis once wrote so vividly about—had been destroyed over time to make filming in the area possible.

But Five Points isn't really gone. For one thing, it lives on in Riis's photos, and Asbury's book and Scorsese's film, and my tour.

I looked around to take in my bearings. Scorsese must have walked past this house a thousand times growing up, and here it still stands. Around the corner was Bayard's Mount, where Alexander Hamilton's artillery company defended the city. A twenty-minute walk up the Bowery was Peter Stuyvesant's private chapel where his remains lie to this day; I'd be visiting them with another group later that afternoon.

But this moment wasn't about Scorsese or Hamilton or Stuyvesant or me; it was about this mother and daughter. They handed me a camera to capture them in front of their great-great-great grandparent's home. For all the vivid depictions of Irish street life in *Gangs of New York*, the Gilded Age in *The Age of Innocence*, the grand era of radio in *Radio Days*, or the fireworks in *Manhattan*, this humble, broken-down townhouse had done these filmmakers one better.

It had, for a moment, brought the past back to life.

Maps

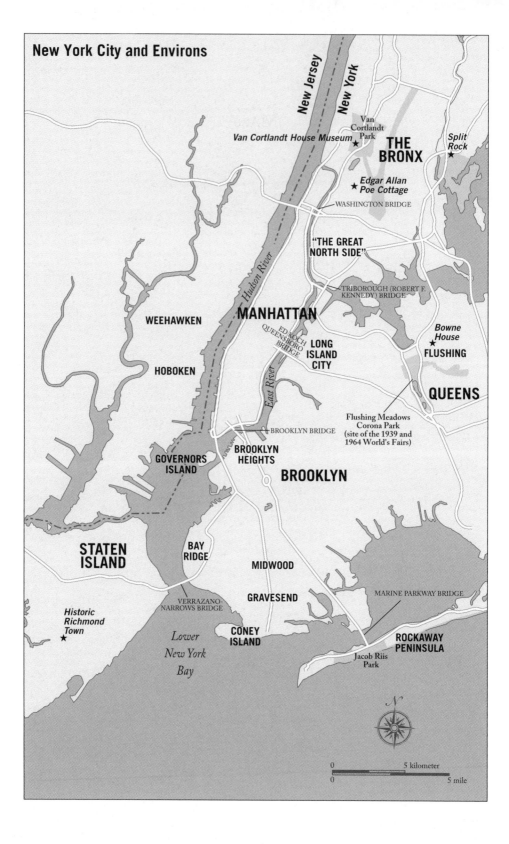

New York City and Environs

New Jersey

New York

Van Cortlandt House Museum ★

Van Cortlandt Park

THE BRONX

Split Rock ★

Edgar Allan Poe Cottage ★

Hudson River

WASHINGTON BRIDGE

"THE GREAT NORTH SIDE"

TRIBOROUGH (ROBERT F. KENNEDY) BRIDGE

WEEHAWKEN

MANHATTAN

ED KOCH QUEENSBORO BRIDGE

LONG ISLAND CITY

Bowne House ★

FLUSHING

HOBOKEN

East River

QUEENS

Flushing Meadows Corona Park (site of the 1939 and 1964 World's Fairs)

BROOKLYN BRIDGE

GOVERNORS ISLAND

BROOKLYN HEIGHTS

BROOKLYN

STATEN ISLAND

BAY RIDGE

MIDWOOD

MARINE PARKWAY BRIDGE

GRAVESEND

Historic Richmond Town ★

VERRAZANO-NARROWS BRIDGE

CONEY ISLAND

Lower New York Bay

ROCKAWAY PENINSULA

Jacob Riis Park

N

0   5 kilometer
0   5 mile

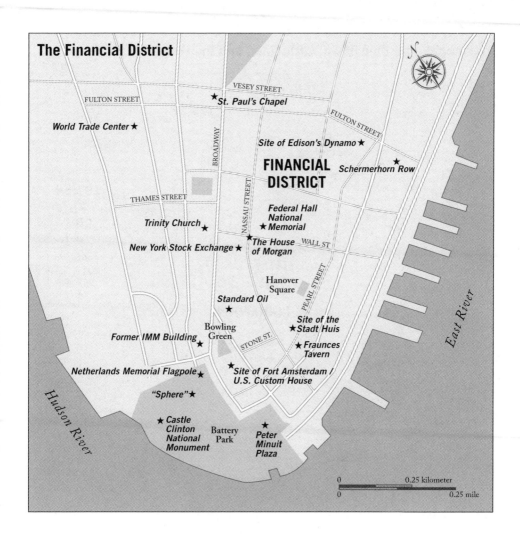

The Financial District

VESEY STREET

FULTON STREET

★ St. Paul's Chapel

World Trade Center ★

FULTON STREET

BROADWAY

Site of Edison's Dynamo ★

FINANCIAL
DISTRICT

Schermerhorn Row ★

NASSAU STREET

THAMES STREET

Federal Hall
National
★ Memorial

Trinity Church ★

New York Stock Exchange ★

The House
of Morgan

WALL ST

★

Hanover
Square

PEARL STREET

Standard Oil
★

Bowling
Green

Former IMM Building ★

STONE ST.

Site of the
★ Stadt Huis

★ Fraunces
Tavern

Netherlands Memorial Flagpole ★

★ Site of Fort Amsterdam /
U.S. Custom House

"Sphere" ★

★ Castle
Clinton
National
Monument

Battery
Park

★
Peter
Minuit
Plaza

East River

Hudson River

0   0.25 kilometer

0   0.25 mile

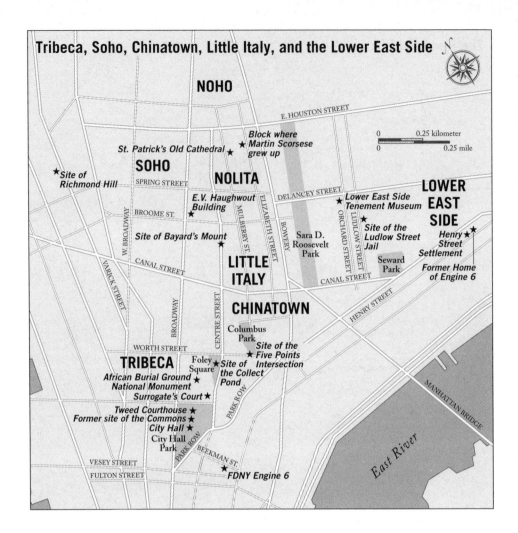

Tribeca, Soho, Chinatown, Little Italy, and the Lower East Side

NOHO

E. HOUSTON STREET

0   0.25 kilometer

0   0.25 mile

Block where
★ Martin Scorsese
grew up

St. Patrick's Old Cathedral ★

SOHO

★ Site of
Richmond Hill

SPRING STREET

NOLITA

DELANCEY STREET

LOWER
EAST
SIDE

E.V. Haughwout
Building ★

★ Lower East Side
Tenement Museum

BROOME ST.

W. BROADWAY

MULBERRY ST.

ELIZABETH STREET

BOWERY

ORCHARD STREET

LUDLOW STREET

★ Site of the
Ludlow Street
Jail

Henry ★
Street
Settlement

Site of Bayard's Mount ★

CANAL STREET

Sara D.
Roosevelt
Park

LITTLE
ITALY

Seward
Park

Former Home
of Engine 6

VARICK STREET

BROADWAY

CENTRE STREET

CANAL STREET

HENRY STREET

CHINATOWN

Columbus
Park

★ Site of the
★ Five Points

WORTH STREET

Foley ★ Site of Intersection
Square the Collect
Pond

TRIBECA

African Burial Ground ★
National Monument
Surrogate's Court ★

PARK ROW

Tweed Courthouse ★
Former site of the Commons ★
City Hall ★

City Hall
Park

PARK ROW

BEEKMAN ST.

East River

MANHATTAN BRIDGE

VESEY STREET

FULTON STREET

★ FDNY Engine 6

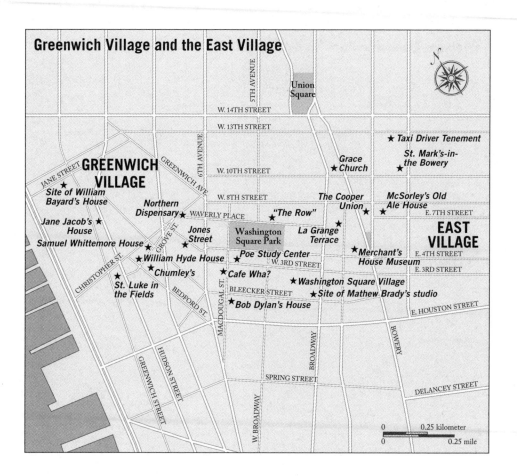

Greenwich Village and the East Village

Union Square

W. 14TH STREET

W. 13TH STREET

5TH AVENUE

6TH AVENUE

★ Taxi Driver Tenement

GREENWICH
VILLAGE

Grace
★ Church

St. Mark's-in-
the Bowery
★

JANE STREET

GREENWICH AVE

W. 10TH STREET

★
Site of William
Bayard's House

Northern
Dispensary ★ WAVERLY PLACE

W. 8TH STREET

The Cooper
Union ★

McSorley's Old
Ale House
★
E. 7TH STREET

"The Row"
★

EAST
VILLAGE

Jane Jacob's ★
House

Samuel Whittemore House ★

Jones
Street

Washington
Square Park

La Grange
Terrace
★

E. 4TH STREET

★ William Hyde House ★

GROVE ST.

Poe Study Center
W. 3RD STREET

★ Merchant's
House Museum

E. 3RD STREET

★ Chumley's

★ Cafe Wha?

CHRISTOPHER ST.

St. Luke in
the Fields
★

BEDFORD ST.

MACDOUGAL ST.

BLEECKER STREET

★ Washington Square Village

★ Site of Mathew Brady's studio

★ Bob Dylan's House

E. HOUSTON STREET

HUDSON STREET

GREENWICH STREET

BROADWAY

BOWERY

SPRING STREET

W. BROADWAY

DELANCEY STREET

0   0.25 kilometer

0   0.25 mile

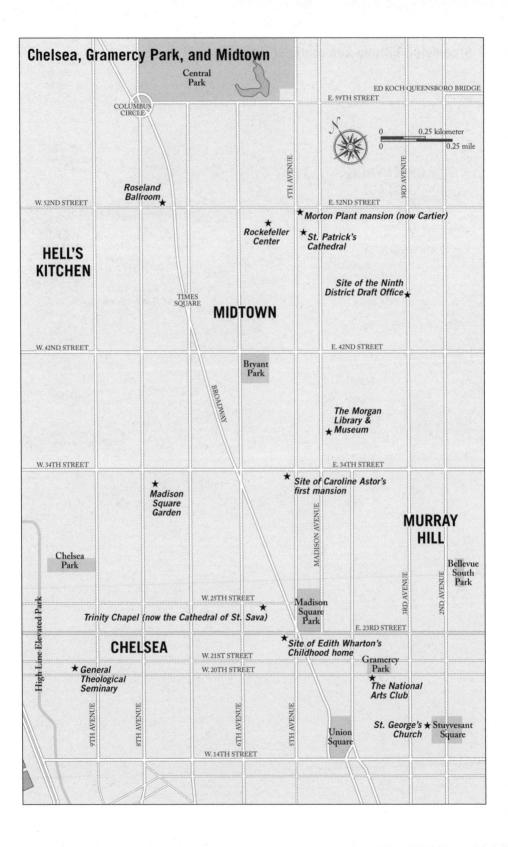

Chelsea, Gramercy Park, and Midtown

Central Park

COLUMBUS CIRCLE

ED KOCH QUEENSBORO BRIDGE

E. 59TH STREET

N

0   0.25 kilometer

0   0.25 mile

5TH AVENUE

3RD AVENUE

W. 52ND STREET

Roseland Ballroom ★

E. 52ND STREET

★ Morton Plant mansion (now Cartier)

★ Rockefeller Center

★ St. Patrick's Cathedral

HELL'S KITCHEN

Site of the Ninth District Draft Office ★

TIMES SQUARE

MIDTOWN

W. 42ND STREET

E. 42ND STREET

BROADWAY

Bryant Park

The Morgan Library & ★ Museum

W. 34TH STREET

E. 34TH STREET

★ Madison Square Garden

★ Site of Caroline Astor's first mansion

MADISON AVENUE

MURRAY HILL

Chelsea Park

Bellevue South Park

3RD AVENUE

2ND AVENUE

High Line Elevated Park

W. 25TH STREET

Madison Square Park

Trinity Chapel (now the Cathedral of St. Sava) ★

E. 23RD STREET

CHELSEA

★ Site of Edith Wharton's Childhood home

W. 21ST STREET

Gramercy Park

W. 20TH STREET

★ General Theological Seminary

★ The National Arts Club

9TH AVENUE

8TH AVENUE

6TH AVENUE

5TH AVENUE

St. George's ★ Stuyvesant Church   Square

Union Square

W. 14TH STREET

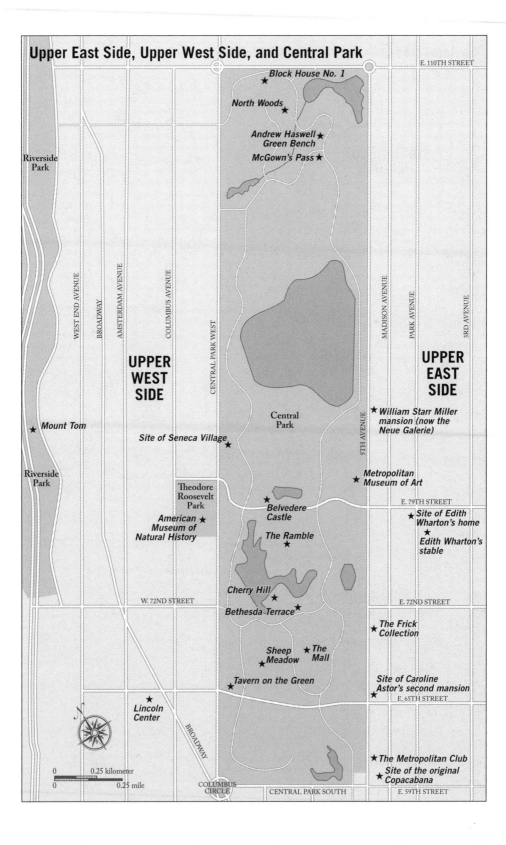

Upper East Side, Upper West Side, and Central Park

Block House No. 1 ★

North Woods ★

Andrew Haswell ★
Green Bench

McGown's Pass ★

Riverside
Park

E. 110TH STREET

WEST END AVENUE

BROADWAY

AMSTERDAM AVENUE

COLUMBUS AVENUE

CENTRAL PARK WEST

MADISON AVENUE

PARK AVENUE

3RD AVENUE

5TH AVENUE

**UPPER
WEST
SIDE**

**UPPER
EAST
SIDE**

Central
Park

★ Mount Tom

Site of Seneca Village ★

★ William Starr Miller
mansion (now the
Neue Galerie)

Theodore
Roosevelt
Park

Metropolitan ★
Museum of Art

Riverside
Park

American ★
Museum of
Natural History

Belvedere ★
Castle

E. 79TH STREET

★ Site of Edith
Wharton's home

★
Edith Wharton's
stable

The Ramble ★

Cherry Hill ★

Bethesda Terrace ★

W. 72ND STREET

E. 72ND STREET

★ The Frick
Collection

Sheep ★ ★ The
Meadow   Mall

Tavern on the Green ★

Site of Caroline
Astor's second mansion ★

★ Lincoln
Center

BROADWAY

E. 65TH STREET

★ The Metropolitan Club

★ Site of the original
Copacabana

N

0   0.25 kilometer

0   0.25 mile

COLUMBUS
CIRCLE

CENTRAL PARK SOUTH

E. 59TH STREET

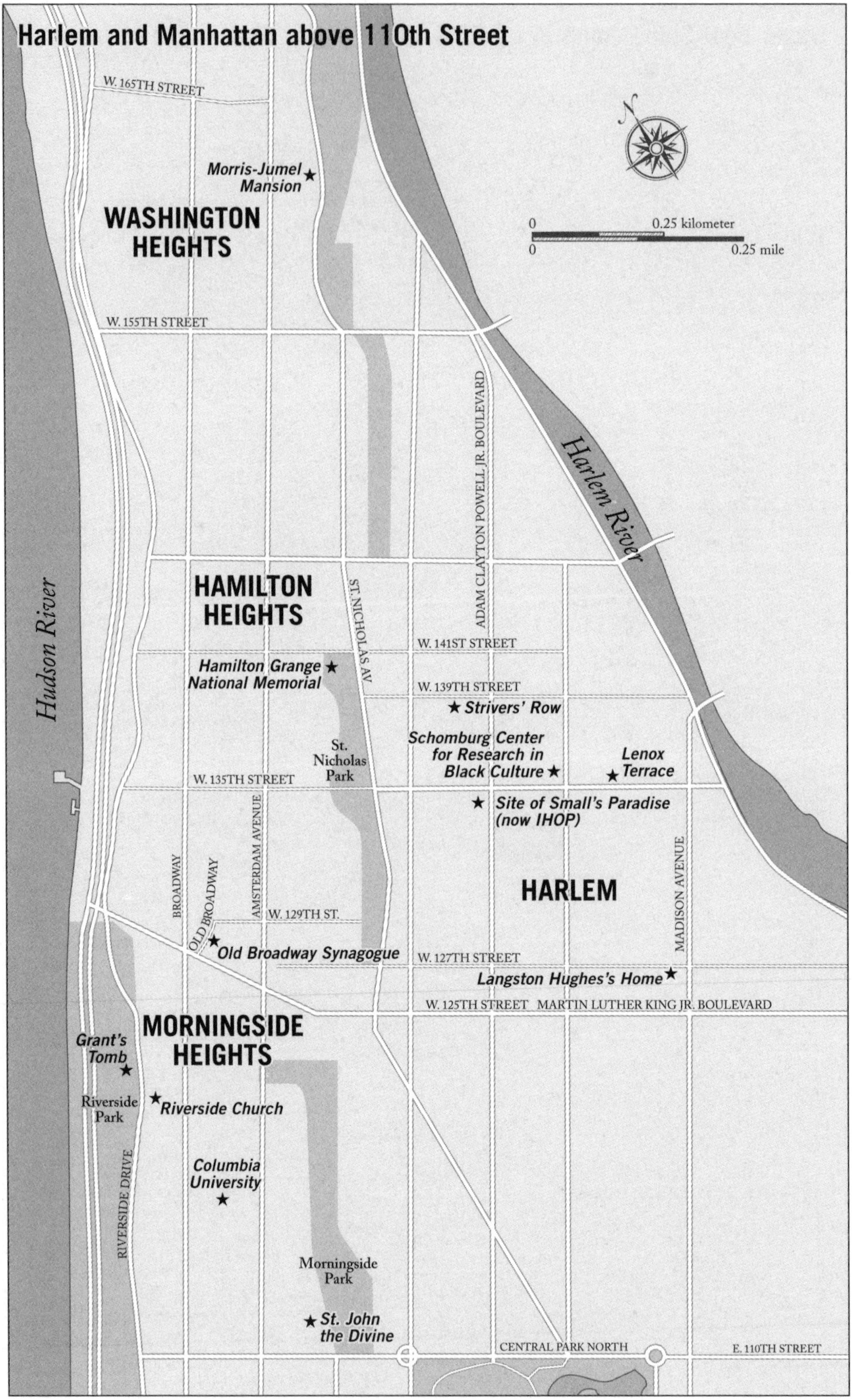

Harlem and Manhattan above 110th Street

W. 165TH STREET

Morris-Jumel ★
Mansion

WASHINGTON
HEIGHTS

W. 155TH STREET

0   0.25 kilometer

0   0.25 mile

Hudson River

ADAM CLAYTON POWELL JR. BOULEVARD

Harlem River

HAMILTON
HEIGHTS

ST. NICHOLAS AV.

W. 141ST STREET

Hamilton Grange ★
National Memorial

W. 139TH STREET

★ *Strivers' Row*

*Schomburg Center
for Research in
Black Culture* ★

*Lenox
★ Terrace*

St.
Nicholas
Park

W. 135TH STREET

★ *Site of Small's Paradise
(now IHOP)*

BROADWAY

OLD BROADWAY

AMSTERDAM AVENUE

MADISON AVENUE

HARLEM

W. 129TH ST.

★
Old Broadway Synagogue

W. 127TH STREET

Langston Hughes's Home ★

W. 125TH STREET MARTIN LUTHER KING JR. BOULEVARD

*Grant's
Tomb*
★

MORNINGSIDE
HEIGHTS

Riverside
Park

★ *Riverside Church*

RIVERSIDE DRIVE

*Columbia
University*
★

Morningside
Park

★ *St. John
the Divine*

CENTRAL PARK NORTH   E. 110TH STREET

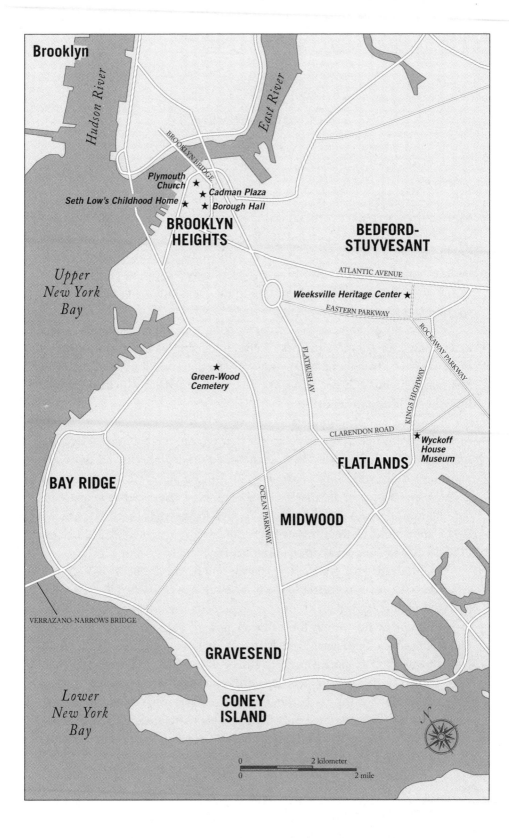

Brooklyn

Hudson River

East River

BROOKLYN BRIDGE

Plymouth Church ★
★ *Cadman Plaza*
Seth Low's Childhood Home ★ ★ *Borough Hall*

BROOKLYN HEIGHTS

BEDFORD-STUYVESANT

Upper New York Bay

ATLANTIC AVENUE

Weeksville Heritage Center ★

EASTERN PARKWAY

ROCKAWAY PARKWAY

FLATBUSH AV

★ *Green-Wood Cemetery*

KINGS HIGHWAY

CLARENDON ROAD

★ *Wyckoff House Museum*

FLATLANDS

BAY RIDGE

OCEAN PARKWAY

MIDWOOD

VERRAZANO-NARROWS BRIDGE

GRAVESEND

Lower New York Bay

CONEY ISLAND

N

0   2 kilometer
0   2 mile

ACKNOWLEDGMENTS

MANY THANKS TO EVERYONE WHO HAS HELPED this book along all the many stages of its creation. A special debt of gratitude to our agent, Joy Tutela, of the David Black Literary Agency, for all her hard work taking this book from outline to reality. Thanks also to everyone at Lyons Press, in particular our adroit editor, Jon Sternfeld, whose important contributions to this book are too numerous to mention.

We are always appreciative of our walking tour clients, some of whom make cameo appearances in these pages, for giving us the opportunity to share what we love about New York with them. A word of thanks to the Spartans, who not only come tour with us twice a year, but who demonstrate the value of lifelong friendship.

As you've probably surmised, we love to "pet two cats with one hand" (if we may continue in our quest to get that phrase into common usage) by running and exploring New York at the same time. Not only did our early morning outings with Spike allow us to investigate places we wanted to talk about, many important discussions on how to shape the narrative helped fuel our long runs. Special thanks to everyone who logged miles with us, particularly Candy Stahl, Cathy Fitzpatrick, Sarah Martinez, and Kelly McKinney. (Thanks also to Mrs. Spike for lending her husband to us so much.)

Our gratitude goes out to all our family and friends for being so enthusiastic about the book, particularly the Cafe a la Plage coffee klatch, who were generous with ideas and words of encouragement at all stages of the project, including during our search for a title. A note of appreciation to Marlowe Greenberg, Nick Scharlatt, Tom Mitchell, and the Foothold Technology family for all their support. Thanks to Robert Doernberg and Stephen Klym, who pitched in on short notice during the proposal writing phase; and to Kathleen O'Connor for her continued support. We are grateful to Andrew Zeitler for his feedback on some of the chapters after we'd looked at them too long, and to Sarah Parrish for both putting us up and putting up with us.

Thanks to John Antonides for his hospitality, and to Laura Auricchio, who helped with some research quandaries. Also helpful were Misato Takemori, who assisted in our quest to find the Poe Mantel, and Robert Pusilo and Paul Richards Lemma of Authentiques, who are always generous with their time as we sift through old images of New York. Heather Herrera and Joy Gannon warrant a mention for always being their cheery, enthusiastic selves. The seed of the idea for this book was actually planted during a trip to London, so thanks to Kenna and Neil Roberts for making that happen.

NOTES ON SOURCES

Though some of the books we've consulted are out of print, most can be found at used bookstores, libraries, or as e-books online. Because we write about a number of historic sites, it has been invaluable to be able to access online the nominations for the National Register of Historic Places (nps .gov/NR) and designation reports for New York City's Landmarks Preservation Commission (nyc.gov/html/lpc/html/forms/reports.shtml). We've consulted online newspaper archives, most significantly the *New York Times* (nytimes.com) and Old Fulton NY Post Cards (fultonhistory.com), which contain thousands of newspapers.

There are a number of blogs dedicated to New York history. Two that deserve special mention are Tom Miller's "Daytonian in Manhattan" (daytonianinmanhattan.blogspot.com) and Kevin Walsh's "Forgotten New York" (forgotten-ny.com), which are great resources for architectural and historical musings.

On that same note, our own blog can be found at footprintsinnewyork .com; each week, we highlight an aspect of the city's history, often tied to one of the places or people in this book.

Chapter 1: Shadows of Shadows: Peter Stuyvesant and the Dutch Frontier
The best book about New Amsterdam is Jaap Jacobs's *The Colony of New Netherland: A Dutch Settlement in Seventeenth-Century America*. Russell Shorto's *The Island at the Center of the World: The Epic Story of Dutch Manhattan and the Forgotten Colony That Shaped America* focuses on the fight for sovereignty between Peter Stuyvesant and Adriaen van der Donck; that book is good, but even better is Henri A. and Barbara Van der Zee's *A Sweet and Alien Land: The Story of Dutch New York*, which captures what life was like in seventeenth-century Manhattan. Also recommended is Henry H. Kessler and Eugene Rachlis's *Peter Stuyvesant and His New York: A Biography of a Man and a City*.

Our beer and brandy exchange rates are based on prices quoted in Mike Dash's *Tulipomania: The Story of the World's Most Coveted Flower and the Extraordinary Passions It Aroused*.

Seventeenth-century sources include Adriaen Van der Donck's *Description of New Netherland*, the *Narratives of New Netherland, 1609–1664* (edited by J. Franklin Jameson), and the various government documents translated into English and published as *The Records of New Amsterdam, 1653–1674* (edited by Berthold Fernow and Edmund Bailey O'Callaghan), the source of the quote about one quarter of the city being "turned into taverns." O'Callaghan also edited *Documents Relative to the Colonial History of the State of New York*, where the quote about Stuyvesant being "like a father over his children," can be found. Some of these documents have been more accurately re-translated recently by Charles Gehring at the New Netherland Project (nnp.org). The quote from Robert Juet's journal about "red cassocks" is in *Half Moon: Henry Hudson and the Voyage that Redrew the Map of the New World* by Douglas Hunter.

Johannes Nevius's biography appears in *Joannes Nevius and His Descendants* by A. V. D. Honeyman; Honeyman's more outlandish claims should be ignored. Peter Claesen's house is open to visitors (wyckoffassociation.org); details of his life can be found in Morton Wagman's "The Rise of Pieter Claessen Wyckoff: Social Mobility on the Colonial Frontier," in *New York History* (Vol. 53, No. 1, January 1972). The Schenck house in the Brooklyn Museum has recently been restored (brooklynmuseum.org). For those interested in a stiff drink, all the libations at the Dead Rabbit are historically sourced (deadrabbitnyc.com).

The best book probably ever written about New York City also deals extensively with New Amsterdam, I. N. Phelps Stokes's seven-volume *Iconography of Manhattan Island, 1498–1909*. All New York historians are in Stokes's debt.

Chapter 2: The Dissenters

In addition to general works about New Netherland (see Chapter 1), a few books tackle religious tolerance (and intolerance) in the period, including *Religion in New Netherland: A History of the Development of the Religious Conditions in the Province of New Netherland, 1623–1664* by Frederick J. Zwierlein, and *New Netherland and the Dutch Origins of American Religious Liberty* by Evan Haefeli. We also consulted *The First Prejudice: Religious Tolerance and Intolerance in Early America* edited by Chris Beneke and Christopher S. Grenda (source of the Johannes Polhemus quote), and the 1901 publication, *Ecclesiastical Records, State of New York* (Vol. 1), for Rev. Megapolensis's firsthand account of the Quakers in New Amsterdam.

Anne Hutchinson is the subject of *American Jezebel: The Uncommon Life of Anne Hutchinson, the Woman Who Defied the Puritans* by Eve LaPlante. The lives of Hutchinson and Lady Deborah Moody are also surveyed in *Four Women in a Violent Time: Anne Hutchinson (1591–1643), Mary Dyer (1591?–1660), Lady Deborah Moody (1600–1659), Penelope Stout (1622–1732)* by Deborah Crawford. More on Moody and the founding of Gravesend can be also be found in *First Founders: American Puritans and Puritanism in an Atlantic World* by Francis J. Bremer. Those interested in old Dutch architecture should read Maud Esther

Dilliard's *Old Dutch Houses of Brooklyn*—keeping in mind that it's not always correct. More recently, Joseph Ditta wrote the neighborhood survey *Gravesend, Brooklyn: Then and Now.*

There's never been a good biography of John Bowne, though the *Journal of John Bowne, 1650–1694* has been reprinted many times. We appreciated talking to members of the Religious Society of Friends in Flushing and the architectural team renovating John and Hannah Bowne's house (bownehouse.org).

Chapter 3: The DeLanceys and New York's Lost Century

Though the English Colonial period is among the least talked about in New York history, there are a few excellent sources: *Merchants and Empire: Trading in Colonial New York* by Cathy Matson; *Before the Melting Pot: Society and Culture in Colonial New York City, 1664–1730* by Joyce D. Goodfriend (the source of Charles Lodwick's "too great a mixture of nations" quote); *Stubborn for Liberty: The Dutch in New York* by Alice P. Kenney; and *Privilege and Prerogative: New York's Provincial Elite, 1710–1776* by Mary Lou Lustig, which covers James DeLancey's role in the Zenger trial.

For the DeLancey family, we consulted Katharine Greider's *The Archaeology of Home: An Epic Set on a Thousand Square Feet of the Lower East Side*, which focuses on James DeLancey (the one-time owner of the land on which Greider's house was built). Greider is the source of the "handsome American" quote. We also looked at D. A. Story's genealogy *The DeLanceys: A Romance of a Great Family, with Notes on Allied Families*, and Stokes's *Iconography* (see Chapter 1). For background on Fraunces Tavern see *A Sketch of Fraunces Tavern and Those Connected with Its History* by Henry Russell Drowne.

Leisler's Rebellion: A Study of Democracy in New York, 1664–1720 by Jerome R. Reich is a thorough discussion of the events; Ralph J. Caliendo summarizes them in *New York City Mayors, Part I: The Mayors Before 1898*. The politics of the era are laid out in *The Lord Cornbury Scandal: The Politics of Reputation in British America* by Patricia U. Bonomi. Regarding Stephen DeLancey's piracy, see Greider, as well as *The Urban Crucible: The Northern Seaports and the Origins of the American Revolution* by Gary B. Nash.

For the alleged 1741 slave revolt, we consulted *New York Burning: Liberty, Slavery, and Conspiracy in Eighteenth-Century Manhattan* by Jill Lepore, a fascinating study of this deplorable event, and *The Great New York Conspiracy of 1741: Slavery, Crime, and Colonial Law* by Peter Charles Hoffer. See also *Slavery in New York*, edited by Ira Berlin and Leslie M. Harris, and *In the Shadow of Slavery: African Americans in New York City, 1626–1863* by Leslie M. Harris. The archaeological reports of the African Burial Ground are all available at gsa.gov/portal/content/249941. For the story of another colonial family's complicated relationship to slavery, Mac Griswold's *The Manor: Three Centuries at a Slave Plantation on Long Island* is a must-read.

Chapter 4: Alexander Hamilton: The Life and Death of a Patriot

The most authoritative recent biography is Ron Chernow's *Alexander Hamilton* (which, among other things, is where we found out about the five hundred prostitutes that patrolled Holy Ground near King's College). Other good biographies include *Alexander Hamilton: A Life* by Willard Sterne Randall (source of the Hercules Mulligan quote about "notwithstanding the firing"); *Alexander Hamilton, American* by Richard Brookhiser; *Alexander Hamilton: America's Forgotten Founder* by Joseph A. Murray (source for the "all of London was afloat" quote); and John C. Hamilton's hagiography of his father, *The Life of Alexander Hamilton.* John Trumbull's recollection of seeing Hamiton and Burr together before the duel comes from *Founding Brothers: The Revolutionary Generation* by Joseph J. Ellis.

For background on New York in the Revolution, see *1776* by David McCullough; *The Battle for New York: The City at the Heart of the American Revolution* by Barnet Schecter; and *Divided Loyalties: How the American Revolution Came to New York* by Richard M. Ketchum.

Aaron Burr's perspective on the events at Weehawken is in David O. Stewart's *American Emperor: Aaron Burr's Challenge to Jefferson's America;* the best books on the Burr/Hamilton rivalry are Thomas Fleming's *Duel: Alexander Hamilton, Aaron Burr, and the Future of America,* and *A Fatal Friendship: Alexander Hamilton and Aaron Burr* by Arnold Rogow (source of the "If I had read Sterne more" quote). To learn more about Harlem during Hamilton's era, see *Harlem: The Four Hundred Year History from Dutch Village to Capital of Black America* by Jonathan Gill.

Chapter 5: DeWitt Clinton and the Making of the Modern City

Evan Cornog's biography of DeWitt Clinton, *The Birth of Empire: DeWitt Clinton and the American Experience, 1769–1828,* is the best source on New York's most important mayor, though it barely mentions the Manhattan street grid or War of 1812. A good capsule biography of Clinton can be found in Caliendo's *New York City Mayors* (see Chapter 3).

The Erie Canal medal box made from "wood brought from Erie" is in the New-York Historical Society (nyhistory.org).

The quote about "vesting too much power in the multitude" comes from Jabez D. Hammond's 1842 *History of Political Parties in the State of New-York, from the Ratification of the Federal Constitution to December, 1840.*

To tour City Hall, make reservations at nyc.gov/html/artcom/html/tours/tours .shtml.

To read more about the causes of War of 1812, consult *The Encyclopedia of the War of 1812: A Political, Social, and Military History* edited by Spencer Tucker, et al. The firsthand account of John Pierce's "mangled body, raised on a platform" is from James Stuart's 1833 memoir, *Three Years in North America.*

For more information on the Manhattan street grid, Marguerite Holloway's biography of John Randel Jr., *The Measure of Manhattan: The Tumultuous Career and Surprising Legacy of John Randel, Jr., Cartographer, Surveyor, Inventor*, and *The Greatest Grid: The Master Plan of Manhattan, 1811–2011*, edited by Hilary Ballon, are overflowing with good information. (The quotes from the commissioners' plan and from Clement Clarke Moore can be found in Ballon.) When talking about the side effects of the grid, our data about private carriage ownership comes from *The Park and the People: A History of Central Park* by Roy Rosenzweig and Elizabeth Blackmar. We also benefited from reading "The Evolution of New York" by Thomas A. Janvier in the June 1893 issue of *Harper's New Monthly Magazine.*

Chapter 6: Gertrude Tredwell: At Home in Greenwich Village
Mary L. Knapp's *An Old Merchant's House: Life at Home in New York City 1835–1865* is a great history of Seabury Tredwell's East Fourth Street home and the best book we've read on domestic life in nineteenth-century New York.

We consulted Henry James's *Washington Square,* and the film *The Heiress* directed by William Wyler. Mona Simpson's "Can She Be Loved? On 'Washington Square'" in the June 3, 2013 issue of the *New Yorker* provides the source for James's story; more details are in *Fanny Kemble: A Performed Life* by Deirdre David.

A good contemporary source on single womanhood is the 1852 tract *"Single Blessedness" or Single Ladies and Gentlemen Against the Slanders of the Pulpit, the Press, and the Lecture-Room.* We also consulted *Women and Marriage in Nineteenth-Century England* by Joan Perkin, and *Mothers and Daughters in Nineteenth-Century America: The Biosocial Construction of Femininity* by Nancy M. Theriot.

The Randall Farm and Sailors' Snug Harbor are the subject of *The Sailors' Snug Harbor: A History* by Gerald J. Barry. Luther S. Harris's *Around Washington Square: An Illustrated History of Greenwich Village* details how the area went from graveyard to park. Also good is *It Happened on Washington Square* by Emily Kies Folpe, source of Alexander Hamilton's "at great expense" quote. The line about how "kin benefited in proportion to their consanguinity" comes from Edith Wharton's "False Dawn," in *Old New York.* We also consulted *A Century of Banking in New York, 1822–1922* by Henry W. Lanier (source of the "hotel of rough boards" quote), Eric Homberger's *Mrs. Astor's New York: Money and Social Power in the Gilded Age,* Charles Lockwood's *Manhattan Moves Uptown: An Illustrated History,* and Talbot Hamlin's *Greek Revival Architecture in America.*

Chapter 7: "A Ghastly Poverty": Edgar Allan Poe
There are almost as many Poe biographies as there are Poe stories and poems; we found Peter Ackroyd's recent *Poe: A Life Cut Short* to be the best compact overview of his life. We also consulted *Edgar A. Poe: A Biography: Mournful and Never-Ending Remembrance* by Kenneth Silverman, *Edgar Allan Poe: A Critical Biography* by Arthur Hobson Quinn, and *Edgar Allan Poe: The Man* by Mary E. Phillips from 1926 (this is out of print, but has the best overview of every place Poe lived in New York). The

"Raven Room" at the Brennan farmhouse is described in *The Life of Edgar Allan Poe* by William F. Gill, and the *Critical Companion to Edgar Allan Poe: A Literary Reference to His Life and Work* by Dawn B. Sova. The story of the Poe mantel can be found in Benjamin Waldman's "Ghost Upon the Floor," in *Columbia* magazine (Fall 2011). Poe's letters—including the heartbreaking missive to George W. Eveleth we quote here—can be found in Quinn. Edward Valentine's memory of chasing down Poe comes from *Edgar Allan Poe in Richmond* by Keshia A. Case, et al.

Poe's ghost is talked about in a host of books about New York, including *Ghosts of New York City* by Therese Lanigan-Schmidt and *New York City Ghost Stories* by Charles J. Adams III. The story of Mary Rogers—who became Poe's Marie Rogêt—is best told in Daniel Stashower's *The Beautiful Cigar Girl: Mary Rogers, Edgar Allan Poe, and the Invention of Murder*. Our knowledge of this period was also informed by Eric Homberger's *Scenes from the Life of a City: Corruption and Conscience in Old New York*, and *Recollections of a New York Chief of Police* by George W. Walling.

Poe's own work has been anthologized countless times; being in the public domain, it is freely available online.

Chapter 8: The Birth of Central Park

The best books about Central Park are *The Park and the People: A History of Central Park* by Roy Rosenzweig and Elizabeth Blackmar; *Central Park, An American Masterpiece: A Comprehensive History of the Nation's First Urban Park* by Sara Cedar Miller; and *Creating Central Park* by Morrison H. Heckscher. We also consulted Henry Hope Reed and Sophia Duckworth's somewhat cranky 1967 history *Central Park: A History and a Guide*.

For Calvert Vaux, Francis R. Kowsky's *Country, Park, and City: The Architecture and Life of Calvert Vaux* is the must-read (and source for our quote about Horace Greeley thinking they'd "let it alone a good deal more"). William Alex's *Calvert Vaux, Architect and Planner* is a beautiful survey of why Vaux was the best Victorian Gothic architect in America. Urban historian Witold Rybczynski's *A Clearing in the Distance: Frederick Law Olmsted and America in the Nineteenth Century* (source of the "republican art idea" quote), and Justin Martin's *Genius of Place: The Life of Frederick Law Olmsted* are the best of the Olmsted books, though Olmsted's own *Walks and Talks of an American Farmer in England* is an edifying read. The quote about "harmonizing and refining influence" comes from *Frederick Law Olmsted: The Passion of a Public Artist* by Melvin Kalfus. The nature of leisure in Central Park is covered in *Sport in Industrial America, 1850–1920* by Steven A. Riess.

We also consulted Olmsted and Vaux's annual reports, in which they justify what they've recently built and beg for money. Their winning Greensward Plan is housed at the Arsenal in Central Park and well worth seeing in person.

Andrew Jackson Downing's idea that "every laborer is a possible gentleman" comes from "The New-York Park," in *The Horticulturalist and Journal of Rural Art and Rural Taste* (Vol. 6, 1851), which Downing edited.

We also consulted *William Cullen Bryant: Author of America* by Gilbert H. Muller, as well as the *Annual Report of the American Scenic and Historic Preservation Society* (1912) which discusses the creation of Bryant Park. Bryant's "New Public Park" editorial is reprinted in *Power for Sanity: Selected Editorials of William Cullen Bryant, 1829–1861*. His death is related in James Grant Wilson's *Memorial History of the City of New-York, from its First Settlement to the Year 1892*. Asher Durand's *Kindred Spirits* is the subject of *Kindred Spirits: Asher B. Durand and the American Landscape* by the San Diego Museum of Art, and also plays a key role in Bill Bryson's *A Walk in the Woods: Rediscovering America on the Appalachian Trail*.

Chapter 9: Abraham Lincoln and the Civil War

The best survey of the New York City Draft Riots is Barnet Schecter's *The Devil's Own Work: The Civil War Draft Riots and the Fight to Reconstruct America*. Also worth seeking out: Iver Bernstein's *The New York City Draft Riots: Their Significance for American Society and Politics in the Age of the Civil War*, and Joel Tyler Headley's *The Great Riots of New York, 1712–1873*, a firsthand account of the riots. George Templeton Strong's diary—available in print and online—provides insight into privileged New Yorkers' views on the war. Fernando Wood's quote about "our aggrieved brethren of the Slave States" is from *Fernando Wood of New York* by Samuel Augustus Pleasants.

To find out about Henry Ward Beecher and the Plymouth Church, we consulted *The Most Famous Man in America: The Biography of Henry Ward Beecher* by Debby Applegate. Eastman Johnson's depiction of Pinky is considered in *Seeing High and Low: Representing Social Conflict in American Visual Culture* edited by Patricia Johnston.

Lincoln's visit to the Plymouth Church and the Cooper Union Speech is the subject of Harold Holzer's *Lincoln and New York*. We also read the firsthand account of Lincoln's visit (originally published in the *New-York Evening Post*) in *The Living Age* (Vol. 85, No. 1094, May 20, 1865). Mary Todd Lincoln's many trips to New York are detailed in *Mary Todd Lincoln's Travels* by Wayne Calhoun Temple. The details of John Wilkes Booth in New York can be found in *American Brutus: John Wilkes Booth and the Lincoln Conspiracies* by Michael W. Kauffman. For the Confederate plot to burn the city, see *A Vast and Fiendish Plot: The Confederate Attack on New York City* by Clint Johnson.

Our knowledge of the role that black New Yorkers played in the draft riots and into the African-American community at Weeksville was not only deepened by our guide at the Weeksville Heritage Center (weeksvillesociety.org), but also by reading *In the Shadow of Slavery* by Leslie M. Harris (see Chapter 3), *Black Gotham: A Family History of African-Americans in Nineteenth-Century New York City* by Carla L. Peterson, and *African American Freedom Journey in New York and Related Sites, 1823–1870: Freedom Knows No Color* by Harry Bradshaw Matthews.

Chapter 10: Boss Tweed

The best biography of Boss Tweed is Kenneth D. Ackerman's *Boss Tweed: The Corrupt Pol Who Conceived the Soul of Modern New York*. Also worth a look are Denis Tilden Lynch's *Boss Tweed: The Story of a Grim Generation* from 1927, and Leo Hershkowitz's *Tweed's New York: Another Look*, though Hershkowitz downplays the Tweed Ring's criminality. Tweed's testimony can be found in the *Report of the Special Committee of the Board of Aldermen Appointed to Investigate the "Ring" Frauds, Together with the Testimony Elicited During the Investigation*, issued January 4, 1898. The quote about "fire laddies" acquiring "social prestige" comes from Robert Ernst's *Immigrant Life in New York City: 1825–1863*.

We toured the Tweed Courthouse (nyc.gov/html/artcom/html/tours/tours .shtml), but those interested in the architectural history of the building are best off reading *Leopold Eidlitz: Architecture and Idealism in the Gilded Age* by Kathryn E. Holliday. A summary of the courthouse frauds can be found in *King of Heists: The Sensational Bank Robbery of 1878 That Shocked America* by J. North Conway. John Davenport's *The Election Frauds of New York City and Their Prevention* details how Tammany Hall stole elections. The implementation of the Tweed Charter of 1870 is chronicled in *History of the United States: From the Compromise of 1850 to the McKinley-Bryan Campaign of 1896* (Vol. VII) by James F. Rhodes.

Thomas Nast's cartoons—and his influence on political cartooning—is the subject of *Doomed by Cartoon: How Cartoonist Thomas Nast and the* New York Times *Brought Down Boss Tweed and His Ring of Thieves* by John Adler and Draper Hill; the definitive biography is *Thomas Nast: The Father of Modern Political Cartoons* by Fiona Deans Halloran. For Jacob Wrey Mould—architect of Tavern on the Green and Bethesda Terrace—see the books on Central Park listed in Chapter 8. Tavern on the Green's history is chronicled in *Tavern on the Green: 125 Recipes For Good Times, Celebrating The New York Legend* by Jennifer Oz LeRoy and Kay LeRoy, the former proprietors. The quote about Peter Sweeny's "general onslaught on every grove, shrubbery and tree" is from the "Reports of Central Park Commissioners and Other Documents, 1865–1871," reprinted in the *National Quarterly Review* (Vol. 22, No. 44, 1871). Mould's horse trough is talked about in "The Daily Plant," the newsletter of the New York City Parks Department (Vol. 21, No. 4377, August 6, 2006).

Nathaniel Parker Willis's "On Furnishing a House," was included in his collection *The Rag-Bag: A Collection of Ephemera*. Tilden and the controversial election of 1876 are the subject of *Centennial Crisis: The Disputed Election of 1876* by William H. Rehnquist.

Chapter 11: Mrs. Astor and Mrs. Wharton: Tales of the Gilded Age

Edith Wharton's New York novels are the single best way to get a feel for the social mores of the Gilded Age. The most famous are *House of Mirth* and *The Age of Innocence*, though we also recommend *The Custom of the Country*, and the novellas in *Old New York*. Wharton's short stories set in New York, including "Mrs. Manstey's View" and "After Holbein," are anthologized in *The New York Stories of Edith Wharton*.

For Wharton's biography, see Hermione Lee's *Edith Wharton*, Shari Benstock's *No Gifts from Chance: A Biography of Edith Wharton*, and *The Two Lives of Edith Wharton: The Woman and Her Work* by Grace Kellogg Griffith, as well as Wharton's autobiographies, *A Backward Glance* and the fragmentary *Life & I*, which can be found in *Edith Wharton: Novellas and Other Writings*. We also consulted Maureen E. Montgomery's *Displaying Women: Spectacles of Leisure in Edith Wharton's New York*. Analogs between historical figures and Wharton characters are found in the *Dictionary of Real People and Places in Fiction* by M. C. Rintoul.

Caroline Webster Schermerhorn Astor is the subject of Eric Homberger's *Mrs. Astor's New York: Money and Social Power in the Gilded Age* as well as *The First Four Hundred: New York in the Gilded Age* by Jerry E. Patterson. Grace Church and its sexton, Isaac Hull Brown, come up in most discussions of high society; Brown's quote about controlling "Society above Fiftieth Street" can be found in Carl Carmer's *My Kind of Country: Favorite Writings About New York*. Details of the pew auction can be found in Homberger, in the dissertation *Women, Wealth, and Power: New York City, 1860–1900* by Florence W. Asher, and in the diary of ex-mayor Philip Hone. Herman Melville's "The Two Temples," long out of print, is available now as an e-book. *Gilded City: Scandal and Sensation in Turn-of-the-Century New York* by M. H. Dunlop chronicles Grace Church's role in opulent Gilded Age weddings. Ward McAllister, Brown's successor, wrote *Society as I Have Found It* in 1890, a fascinating insight into how he thought society should be governed.

Two good books on Gilded-Age mansions are *Manhattan Moves Uptown: An Illustrated History* by Charles Lockwood, and *Empty Mansions: The Mysterious Life of Huguette Clark and the Spending of a Great American Fortune* by Bill Dedman and Paul Clark Newell Jr. Edith Wharton's nonfiction design primer, *The Decoration of Houses* (written with Ogden Codman Jr.), sheds light on the taste of the time; also worth seeking out is "Edith Wharton's Houses," by Alexandra Lange, posted on the *New Yorker*'s "Page-Turner" blog on May 23, 2012.

Chapter 12: How the Other Half Lived

The best way to understand Jacob Riis is to read his two most important books, *How the Other Half Lives: Studies Among the Tenements of New York* and *The Making of an American*. (The latter is harder to find in print, but freely available online.) A good biography of Riis is *Jacob Riis: Reporter and Reformer* by Janet B. Pascal.

Similarly, Lillian Wald's autobiography, *The House on Henry Street,* provides insight into contemporary life on the Lower East Side. Wald's key role in public health nursing is chronicled in "Bringing Care to the People: Lillian Wald's Legacy to Public Health Nursing" by Karen Buhler-Wilkerson in *American Journal of Public Health* (Vol. 83, No. 12, 1993).

Riis and Wald's influence on city planning (and the building of Columbus Park) are discussed in *Transformations of Urban and Suburban Landscapes: Perspectives from Philosophy, Geography, and Architecture* edited by Gary Backhaus and John Murungi.

Firsthand recollections of growing up on the Lower East Side (including Robert Leslie's) can be found in *You Must Remember This: An Oral History of Manhattan from the 1890s to World War II* by Jeff Kisseloff.

The Lower East Side Tenement Museum is best experienced firsthand; the tours are always small groups and they do a terrific job illuminating immigrant life (tenement.org). If you can't go in person, architectural historian Andrew Dolkart's *Biography of a Tenement House in New York City: An Architectural History of 97 Orchard Street* is a thorough history. Jane Ziegelman's *97 Orchard: An Edible History of Five Immigrant Families in One New York Tenement* tells the story of the building through the foods that were cooked there. *A History of Housing in New York City* by Richard Plunz considers tenement house laws; another good resource is *The Encyclopedia of Housing* (Second Edition) edited by Andrew T. Carswell. The Jacob Riis housing project is discussed in Philip Lopate's *Waterfront: A Walk Around Manhattan* and in *The Universitas Project: Solutions for a Post-Technological Society* edited by Emilio Ambasz, et al.

Chapter 13: Seth Low: From the Brooklyn Bridge to the Big City

Seth Low is such a critical New Yorker that it is surprising that there aren't more biographies of him. In 1925, his nephew, Benjamin R .C. Low, wrote the odd, little biography *Seth Low.* Better is Gerald Kurland's *Seth Low: The Reformer in an Urban and Industrial Age* from 1971. Low's role as Columbia's president is detailed in *Stand, Columbia: A History of Columbia University in the City of New York, 1754–2004* by Robert A. McCaughey.

The best history of the Brooklyn Bridge is David McCullough's *The Great Bridge: The Epic Story of the Building of the Brooklyn Bridge.* David M. Scobey's *Empire City: The Making and Meaning of the New York City Landscape* summarizes the importance of connecting Brooklyn to Manhattan. The remarks from the Brooklyn Bridge opening ceremony were published in 1883 as *Opening Ceremonies of the New York and Brooklyn Bridge: May 24, 1883.*

For a history of Columbia's move uptown, see Andrew S. Dolkart's *Morningside Heights: A History of Its Architecture and Development*, which also pointed us to the criticisms of the campus in *The Architectural Record.*

Andrew Haswell Green is the subject of Michael Rubbinaccio's *New York's Father is Murdered!: The Life and Death of Andrew Haswell Green* (less sensational than its title suggests) and Anita Klutch's dissertation *Andrew Haswell Green: The Father of Greater New York and His Dual Vision of a Cultivated and Consolidated Metropolis.* A good source for the history of five-borough consolidation is Richardson Dilworth's *The Urban Origins of Suburban Autonomy,* which describes the reluctance of some outer-borough residents to join New York City. The history of the Washington Bridge is detailed in *The Bronx: In Bits and Pieces* by Bill Twomey; Ralph J. Caliendo's *New York City Mayors* (see Chapter 3) also chronicles the annexation of the Bronx.

Seth Low's role in consolidation (and running for mayor of the city) is nicely summarized in Edwin G. Burrows and Mike Wallace's *Gotham: A History of New York City to 1898.* To read about those same events without the filter of history, Daniel Van Pelt's 1898 *History of the Greater New York: New York to the Consolidation* provides a firsthand account.

The history of the New York City Marathon is told in *A Race Like No Other: 26.2 Miles Through the Streets of New York* by Liz Robbins. (The critique of "citizens who appear to be running around in their underwear" is in *Miss Manners' Guide to Excruciatingly Correct Behavior* by Judith Martin.) A good discussion of John Rochester Thomas's Surrogate's Courthouse can be found in *The Architectural Guidebook to New York City* by Francis Morrone.

To find out more about Improv Everywhere and what they do, visit improveverywhere.com. (Our rainy night is chronicled in "The Camera Flash Experiment.")

Chapter 14: The City of Morgan

Two biographies of J. Pierpont Morgan stand out: Ron Chernow's *The House of Morgan: An American Banking Dynasty and the Rise of Modern Finance* and Jean Strouse's *Morgan: American Financier,* both of which paint vivid portraits of the financier and his world. Most of the sites in this chapter are discussed by one or both of these works. Morgan's "damn the expense" command to Stanford White comes from Strouse. The description of Morgan's painting of a "young fey woman" is from Chernow.

The Morgan bank bombing is the centerpiece of Beverly Gage's *The Day Wall Street Exploded: A Story of America in its First Age of Terror.* To find out more about electrifying Lower Manhattan, check out *The Power Makers: Steam, Electricity, and the Men Who Invented Modern America* by Maury Klein and *Edison: Inventing the Century* by Neil Baldwin.

Morgan's role at St. George's Church is touched on in William S. Rainsford's *The Story of a Varied Life: An Autobiography,* and in the *History of Saint George's Church in the City of New York, 1752–1811–1911* by Henry Anstice. The architectural history of Morgan's library can be found in *The Making of the Morgan: From Charles McKim to Renzo Piano* by Paul S. Byard. A good perspective on the

Panic of 1907 can be found in *Hetty: The Genius and Madness of America's First Female Tycoon* by Charles Slack.

Morgan's role as a trustee and benefactor of the American Museum of Natural History—and the theft of the Star of India—is covered in *Dinosaurs in the Attic: An Excursion into the American Museum of Natural History* by Douglas J. Preston. The story of Morgan's Vermeer is told in *The Robber Barons* by Matthew Josephson.

Andrew S. Dolkart's *Morningside Heights: A History of Its Architecture and Development* is the single best history of the building of the Episcopal Cathedral of St. John the Divine and Morgan's role in it.

Chapter 15: The Liberators: Harlem, Greenwich Village, and the American Left
Many books cover Greenwich Village's role as "America's Left Bank." The encyclopedic *The Village: 400 Years of Beats and Bohemians, Radicals and Rogues, A History of Greenwich Village* by John Strausbaugh is a good place to start. Other works we used: *Around Washington Square* by Luther S. Harris (see Chapter 6); *Republic of Dreams: Greenwich Village, The American Bohemia, 1910–1960* by Ross Wetzsteon (source of the "fun, truth, beauty" quote); *Greenwich Village, 1920–1930: A Comment on American Civilization in the Post-War Years* by Caroline F. Ware; and *The Improper Bohemians: A Re-Creation of Greenwich Village in its Heyday* by Allen Churchill. The song "Down in Old Greenwich Village" is anthologized in *New York Sings: 400 Years of the Empire State in Song* by Jerry Silverman. For a general overview of the period, we consulted David Wallace's *Capital of the World: A Portrait of New York City in the Roaring Twenties*.

For the history of Prohibition see Daniel Okrent's *Last Call: The Rise and Fall of Prohibition*, and Michael A. Lerner's *Dry Manhattan: Prohibition in New York City*. In *Drink: A Cultural History of Alcohol* Iain Gately notes that New York had 32,000 speakeasies during Prohibition. Surprisingly, the best details of Lee Chumley's life and his speakeasy are found in *Haunted Greenwich Village: Bohemian Banshees, Spooky Sites, and Gonzo Ghost Walks* by Tom Ogden.

Max Eastman is the subject of only one biography, *The Last Romantic: A Life of Max Eastman* by William L. O'Neill. Eastman and Mabel Dodge are covered in *Up from Communism* by John P. Diggins and *All-Night Party: The Women of Bohemian Greenwich Village and Harlem, 1913–1930* by Andrea Barnet. Most issues of *The Liberator* are available online at marxists.org.

Claude McKay's own works—particularly *Home to Harlem* and the autobiography *A Long Way from Home*—provide valuable insights into Harlem in the 1920s and 1930s; McKay's influence is detailed in *The Cambridge Companion to the Modernist Novel* edited by Morag Shiach. We also consulted *Claude McKay: Rebel Sojourner in the Harlem Renaissance, A Biography* by Wayne F. Cooper, and *Claude McKay: A Black Poet's Struggle for Identity* by Tyrone Tillery.

We looked at Langston Hughes's autobiography (*I Wonder as I Wander: An Autobiographical Journey*), his exchange of letters with Carl Van Vechten (collected in *Remember Me to Harlem: The Letters of Langston Hughes and Carl Van Vechten*,

1925–1964, edited by Emily Bernard), and Arnold Rampersad's biography *The Life of Langston Hughes: Volume I, 1902–1941: I, Too, Sing America.* However, Hughes's poetry and prose—such as *The Collected Poems of Langston Hughes* and *The Way of White Folks*—are the best way to understand his political convictions. Other resources include *Socialist Joy in the Writing of Langston Hughes* by Jonathan Scott; *Communists in Harlem During the Depression* by Mark Naison; and *New Negro, Old Left: African-American Writing and Communism Between the Wars* by William J. Maxwell.

Kathleen Drowne's *Spirits of Defiance: National Prohibition and Jazz Age Literature, 1920–1933,* and Steven Watson's *The Harlem Renaissance: Hub of African-American Culture, 1920–1930* both consider the importance of speakeasy culture. (The story of Eastman and McKay being turned away from Ned's is found in Drowne.) Alain Locke's *The New Negro: An Interpretation* and Van Vechten's *Nigger Heaven* are worth seeking out for anyone interested in the roots of the Harlem Renaissance. (Due to its title, the latter—though still in print—can be hard to find.) Van Vechten's influence is detailed in "*Nigger Heaven* and the Harlem Renaissance" by Robert F. Worth in *African American Review* (Vol. 29, No. 3, 1995). *Encyclopedia of the Harlem Renaissance* edited by Cary D. Wintz and Paul Finkelman covers everything from musicians to politicians, along with the key places associated with the era. Hilary Ballon's *New York's Pennsylvania Stations* considers the causes of the exodus of African Americans from the Tenderloin district to Harlem.

Chapter 16: Peace through Trade: The Rockefellers and the Modern City

It's amazing that John D. Rockefeller Jr. hasn't been the subject of a major biography. In 1956, family confidant Raymond B. Fosdick wrote the hagiographic *John D. Rockefeller, Jr.: A Portrait.* Better is the 1976 multigenerational biography of Junior, his father, and his five sons, *The Rockefellers: An American Dynasty,* by Peter Collier and David Horowitz.

The details of the Ludlow Massacre can be found in *Blood Passion: The Ludlow Massacre and Class War in the American West* by Scott Martelle. For the building of Riverside Church, see Andrew S. Dolkart's *Morningside Heights: A History of Its Architecture and Development,* and the church's official *History of the Riverside Church in the City of New York,* edited by Larry G. Murphy.

The best history of Rockefeller Center is Daniel Okrent's *Great Fortune: The Epic of Rockefeller Center;* also worth seeking out is *The Art of Rockefeller Center* by Christine Roussel. The symbolic implications of the art at the Center are touched on in *Classical Mythology: A Very Short Introduction* by Helen Morales. The Rockefellers' contributions to the arts in general are the subject of *America's Medicis: The Rockefellers and Their Astonishing Cultural Legacy* by Suzanne Loebl.

David Rockefeller's role in building the World Trade Center is detailed in *City in the Sky: The Rise and Fall of the World Trade Center* by James Glanz and Eric Lipton, and in *Divided We Stand: A Biography of New York's World Trade Center* by

Eric Darton. The destruction of the complex has been covered in too many books to mention, but the recent *Battle for Ground Zero: Inside the Political Struggle to Rebuild the World Trade Center* by Elizabeth Greenspan proved valuable in our research. The story of the "Sphere" sculpture is told, in part, in the documentary *Koenig's Sphere: The German Sculptor Fritz Koenig at Ground Zero* directed by Percy Adlon.

Chapter 17: The Battle for New York: Jane Jacobs vs. Robert Moses

Robert Caro's monumental biography of Robert Moses, *The Power Broker: Robert Moses and the Fall of New York,* is the first place to start in any examination of Moses's life. However, as Hilary Ballon and Kenneth T. Jackson point out in *Robert Moses and the Modern City: The Transformation of New York,* Caro doesn't always get the details right. Their book also provides a thorough catalog of Moses's achievements, detailing the building of every swimming pool, beach, and housing project built under his watch.

Jane Jacobs, by contrast, is best approached first through her own work: the groundbreaking *Death and Life of Great American Cities,* as well as her articles, the most important of which, "Downtown Is for People," was published in *Fortune* magazine in April 1958 (and is available online). Also worth reading is "Jane Jacobs Was Right: Gradual Redevelopment Does Promote Community" by Eric Jaffe published on *Atlantic* magazine's Atlantic Cities blog on March 8, 2013. Jacobs's line about the "idiotic assumption" behind the planning of Lincoln Center can be found in *The American City: What Works, What Doesn't* by Alexander Garvin.

The fights between Moses and Jacobs are the subject of *The Battle for Gotham: New York in the Shadow of Robert Moses and Jane Jacobs* by Roberta Brandes Gratz, and *Wrestling with Moses: How Jane Jacobs Took on New York's Master Builder and Transformed the American City* by Anthony Flint (source of Moses's line that "cities are created by and for traffic").

Chapter 18: "City Like a Web": Bob Dylan and MacDougal Street

Bob Dylan's early years in Greenwich Village fill pages in just about every biography of the singer. Start with his autobiography, *Chronicles: Volume One,* which, as Scott Warmuth argues in "Bob Charlatan: Deconstructing Dylan's *Chronicles, Volume One*" (*New Haven Review,* No. 6, 2008) needs to be taken with a grain of salt. In Martin Scorsese's documentary *No Direction Home,* he interviews Dylan at length, and it is probably Dylan's best first-person account of the era. Other valuable sources are Suze Rotolo's autobiography, *A Freewheelin' Time: A Memoir of Greenwich Village in the Sixties;* David Hajdu's *Positively 4th Street: The Lives and Times of Joan Baez, Bob Dylan, Mimi Baez Fariña, and Richard Fariña;* and June Skinner Sawyers's *Bob Dylan: New York,* which chronicles the singer's associations with the city. Sean Wilentz's *Bob Dylan in America* also contains information on Dylan's Greenwich Village years (and the "naturally fell in with the Beat scene" quote). To read more about the influence of the Beat poets on the folk movement, see *Beat Culture: Lifestyles, Icons, and Impact* edited by William Lawlor.

Chapter 19: New York Stories: Martin Scorsese and Woody Allen

If we had to whittle it down to five must-see New York movies for Martin Scorsese and Woody Allen (an almost impossible task), they'd be: *Taxi Driver, After Hours, GoodFellas, Age of Innocence,* and *Gangs of New York* (Scorsese) and *Annie Hall, Manhattan, Hannah and Her Sisters, Radio Days,* and *Blue Jasmine* (Allen). Obviously we talk about many more films in this chapter, and they are all worthwhile. In particular, Scorsese's documentary about his parents, *Italianamerican*, is hard to find but worth the search. Anyone interested in movies filmed in the city should consult Richard Alleman's *New York, The Movie Lover's Guide: The Ultimate Insider's Tour of Movie New York.*

Both Scorsese and Allen have sat down for extensive interviews about their lives and films. Richard Schickel's *Conversations with Scorsese,* and *Scorsese on Scorsese,* edited by David Thompson and Ian Christie, are the best for hearing Scorsese discuss his vision and influences. We'd also recommend *Martin Scorsese's America* by Ellis Cashmore. For Allen, Eric Lax's *Conversations with Woody Allen: His Films, the Movies, and Moviemaking* is a terrific resource, as is *Woody Allen on Woody Allen,* conversations he had with Stig Bjorkman. In researching *Radio Days,* Thierry De Navacelle's *Woody Allen on Location*—a diary of shooting the film— proved insightful. The quote about Woody Allen and people of color comes from *A Companion to Woody Allen,* edited by Peter J. Bailey and Sam B. Girgus. We also consulted "The Art of Humor No. 1, Woody Allen," by Michiko Kakutani in *The Paris Review* (No. 136, Fall 1995). Scorsese's comments that *Taxi Driver* is his "state of mind" come from Robert B. Weide's film *Woody Allen: A Documentary.*

Elaborate shooting scripts were published for Scorsese's historical dramas featuring illustrations, interviews, essays, and stills from the films. *The Age of Innocence: A Portrait of the Film Based on the Novel by Edith Wharton* and *Martin Scorsese's Gangs of New York: Making the Movie* both illuminate Scorsese's historical influences.

Photo Credits

Page 1: From *The Memorial History of the City of New-York,* edited by James Grant Wilson (New York: 1892). Page 171: Postcard publisher unknown, ca. 1907. Page 184: Postcard © 1896, J. S. Johnston, New York. Page 226: Postcard published by Frank E. Cooper, New York (date unknown). Page 254: Photograph by the authors.

LIBRARY OF CONGRESS
(PRINTS & PHOTOGRAPHS DIVISION)

Page 62: LC-D416-445. Page 91: LC-DIG-pga-01678. Page 105: LC-DIG-pga-00646. Page 120: LC-USZ62-5803. Page 138: LC-USZ62-117137. Page 154: LC-USZ62-29408. Page 198: LCUSZ62-94188.

Historic American Buildings Survey
Page 15: HABS NY, 41-FLUSH, 1–12. Page 27: HABS NY, 31-NEYO, 128–1. Page 78: HABS NY, 31-NEYO, 30–7.

Detroit Publishing Company Collection
Page 44: LC-D416-445.

Carl Van Vechten Collection
Page 212: LC-USZ62-42503.

NYWT&S Collection
Page 239 (left): C. M. Stieglitz, LC-USZ62-136079. Page 239 (right): Phil Sanziola, LC-USZ62-137838.

Carol M. Highsmith Archive
Page 265: Carol M. Highsmith, LC-DIG-highsm-13922.

INDEX

(Italicized page numbers indicate illustrations.)

abolition, 122, 123–24
Adams, John, 45, 47, 54
African Americans, 110, 111, 124, 130–31, 135, 218–24. *See also* slaves and slavery
African Burial and National Monument, 38–39
Allen, Woody, 266, 269–72, 273–75, 275–76
American Anarchist Fighters, 201–2
American Progress (Sert), 234
American Revolution, 34, 45–51, 60
"Ancestral Libation Chamber" (Leon), 38, 39
animal anti-cruelty laws, 146
Arthur, Chester, 186
Articles of Capitulation, 25
Asbury, Herbert, 176
Astor, Caroline Webster Schermerhorn, 156, 157, 158, 160–67
Astor, John Jacob, 75, 82, 96, 157
Astor, John Jacob, III, 161
Astor, John Jacob, IV, 161, 211
Astor, William B., Jr., 157, 161
Astor, William Waldorf, 161
Auboyneau, Prince, 36

Baez, Joan, 259–60, 262
Battery Park, 10, 237–38, 242–43

Bayard, Judith, 6, 58
Bayard's Mount, 47, 50, 277
Beat culture, 263
Beaver Path, 29
Beecher, Henry Ward, 122, 123–24, 135
Belvedere Castle, 115, 145
Berkowitz, David "Son of Sam," 262
Bethesda Terrace, 16, 115, 116
Big Six (fire company), 139, 141, 144
Block, Adriaen, 3
Block House No. 1, 70–71, 111
Bloomingdale Road (Broadway), 74–75, 99
blue laws, 114
bohemianism, 213–16, 218
Booth, John Wilkes, 96, 117, 128, 132–34
Borglum, Gutzon, 135
Bottle Alley, 175–76
Bow Bridge, 115
Bowery, 47, 52, 70, 74
Bowling Green (park), 10, 45–46, 49, 200
Bowne, Hannah, 24, 26
Bowne, John, 12, 24–25, 26
Brady, Mathew, 112, *120,* 125, 126
Brewster, Mary, 180
British Empire Building, *226,* 233, 234
Broadway, 9–10, 74–75, 99, 155
Bronx, 191, 192, 241
Brooklyn, 10, 50, 130–31, 185–86, 187, 188, 191–95

Brooklyn-Battery Bridge, 69, 242, 243
Brooklyn Bridge, 137, 184, *184,* 184–87, 191, 197
Brooklyn City Hall, 185
Brown, Isaac Hull, 155, 156, 158, 169
Bryant, William Cullen, 92, 106–10
Bryant Park, 109
Burns Coffee House, 28, 33, 40
Burr, Aaron, 43, 48, 50, 51, 53–58, 59–60, 61
Burton, Mary, 37, 39

Cafe Reggio, 258, 261
Cafe Wha?, *254, 255,* 256, 258
Carnegie, Andrew, 165
Castle Clinton, 65, 69–70, 242–43
Castle Garden Immigrant Landing Depot, 69
Castle Williams, 64–65, 69
Central Park, *105,* 105–18, 135, 145–47, 194
Century Association, 108
Chelsea, 75, 76
Chelsea Hotel, 260
Chester, Sam, 134
Chinatown, 171–72, 173, 181–82, 276
Chumley's, 216–17
Church of the Pilgrims, 123
City College, 220
City Hall, 66–67, 185, 196
Civil War, 121–22, 129–35, 142

Claesen, Pieter and Grietje, 10–12

Clark, Cyrus, 97

Clark, W. A., 165

Clemm, Maria, 93, 98, 99, 100, 101

Cleveland, Grover, 186, 189

Clinton, DeWitt, *62,* 63–76, 86–87, 153, 197

Clinton, George, 34, 55, 65, 67

Cloisters, 235

Codman, Ogden, 166

Colden, Cadwallader, 45

Cole, Thomas, 109

Collect Pond, 38, 47, 140

Colorado Fuel and Iron (CFI), 227–28

Columbia University (*formerly* King's College), 45, 46, 99, 189–91

Columbus Park (*formerly* Mulberry Bend Park), *171,* 171–73

Committee to Save the West Village, *239,* 250

Communism, 219, 223, 224

Coney Island, 197, 247

Connolly, Richard, 144, 145, 148, 149

Consolidation of Greater New York, The (Weinert), 197

Cooper, Charles D., 55

Cooper, Peter, 126, 127

Cooper-Hewitt National Design Museum, 165

Cooper Union Address, 125, 126–27

Copeland, William, 148

Corbin, Margaret, 50

Cosby, William, 34–35

Cotton, John, 19

Cram, Ralph Adams, 210

Davis, James E., 66

Davis, Noah, 149, 150

Dead Rabbit tavern, 13

Death and Life of Great American Cities, The (Jacobs), 240, 244–45, 250

Death of President Lincoln (Currier & Ives), 132

Declaration of Independence, 48–49, 86

DeLancey, Etienne (Stephen), *27,* 27–34, 36, 39–41

DeLancey, James, 30, 33, 34–35, 37–38, 40

DeLancey, Oliver, 33, 40

DeLancey, Othello, 37–38

Dell, Floyd, 217

Dodge, Mabel, 215

Donck, Adriaen van der, 3, 6–7

Dongan, Thomas, 30

Downing, Andrew Jackson, 106, 107, 111

draft, military, 121–22, 129–30, 142

dueling, 43, 47, 56, 57, 59

Dutch colonial history, 1–14, 15–26

Dutch Reformed Church, 16

Dutch West India Company, 3, 5–7, 9, 25

Dylan, Bob, 255–64

E. V. Haughwout cast-iron store, 126, 128, 252, 253

Eastman, Max, 215–19

Economy Candy, 181

Edison, Thomas, 202–3

Edson, Franklin, 186, 187

Eidlitz, Leopold, 143, 148

1811 Commissioners' Plan ("The Grid"), 71–76, 86, 110, 251

Einstein, Albert, 230–31

Eisenhower, Dwight D., 190

elevators, passenger, 126

Ellis Island, 69

Emancipation Proclamation, 130, 132

Embury, Aymar, II, 248

Empire State Building, 161, 234

English colonial history, 9, 25, 27–31. *See also* American Revolution

Erie Canal, 63–65

Fabbri, Edith and Ernesto, 274

Fairchild, Charles, 137, 152

Fat Black Pussycat, 257, 258

Federal Hall, 67

Federal Hall National Memorial, 201

Federal Reserve, 206

Fifth Avenue mansions, 164–66

Fifth Avenue Synagogue, 274

fires, 36–37, 84, 111, 133–34

First Anglo-Dutch War, 2–3, 8–9

First Roumanian-American Congregation, 181

Fitzgerald, F. Scott, 216, 221

Five Points, 96, 137, 140, 147, 173, 276–77

Flushing, 9, 12, *15,* 15–16, 18, 23–26, 193

Flushing Remonstrance, 23–24

Fort Amsterdam, 10, 18

Fort George, 36, 45, 46

Fort Orange (*now* Albany), 3

Fort Tryon Park, 50, 235

Fort Wood, 65, 70

Fosdick, Harry Emerson, 229

Fosdick, Raymond, 229

Four Continents (Lentelli), 234

Fox, George, 17, 26, 231

Fraunces Tavern, *27*, 34, 40, 41, 46, 51, 54
Freewheelin' Bob Dylan, The (album), 257, 258–59
French, Daniel Chester, 234
Frick, Henry Clay, and Frick Collection, 166
Friends (television show), 63, 81–82

Gangs of New York (Asbury), 176
Gardiner, Julia, 82
Garvey, Andrew, 143, 148
Gaslight, 257, 258, 263
General Electric, 203
George III, King of England, 46, 49
Gerde's Folk City, 257, 258
Gilbert, Cass, 73, 200
Gilded Age, 143, 156–70
Ginsberg, Allen, 262, 263
Goerck, Casimir, 72
Gold, Michael, 218
Gotham Court, 175, 176
Governors Island, 3, 64, 69
Grace Episcopal Church, 155–58
Grange, The, 52, 56–57, 58–60
Grant, Ulysses S., 134–35, 144, 211
Gravesend, 9, 18, 21–22, 25
Great Fire of 1835, 84
Greek Revival architecture, 82–83
Greeley, Horace, 106, 107, 127, 152
Green, Andrew Haswell, 106, 108, 113, 117, 149, 189, 191–93, 194, 196
Greenwich Village, 58, 79–82, 94–96, 213–19, 249–52, 256–64, 266, 271
Green-Wood Cemetery, 152, 153

Grid, The, 71–76, 86, 110, 251
Griswold, Rufus, 92, 101–2
Guthrie, Woody, 256, 263

Hall, Oakey, 144, 145
Halleck, Fitz-Greene, 92
Hamilton, Alexander, 43–61, *44*, 67, 80, 99
Hamilton, Eliza Schuyler, 51, 56, 58, 59, 61, 99
Hamilton, John C., 56–57
Hamilton, Philip, 56
Hamilton Grange National Memorial, 52, 56–57, 58–60
Hanover Square, 28, 29
Harlem, 47, 50, 75, 213, 219–23, 243–44
Harlem Renaissance, 213, 218, 219, 221–23
Hayden Planetarium, 272
Hayes, Shirley, 249, 258
Hearts of Oak militia, 46–47
Heerman, Augustijn, 7
Heins, George, 210
Heiress, The (movie), 77, 89
Hemingway, Ernest, 216
Henry Street Settlement, 180, 181, 182
heresy, 18, 22–23, 24
High Bridge, 195
High Line, 76
Historic Richmond Town, 41–42
Hodgson, Robert, 18, 22–23
Holland House, 235
Hone, Philip, 86–87, 156–57, 197
Horgan & Slattery, 196
Horsmanden, Daniel, 37, 38
Hosack, David, 57, 58, 59
House of Morgan, 201–3, 205
How the Other Half Lives (Riis), 175–76, 179, 180

Hudson, Henry, 3
Hudson River School, 110
Hughes, Langston, *212*, 219, 221, 222, 223–24
Hunt, Richard Morris, 213–14
Hunter, Robert, 35
Hunterfly Houses, 131
Hurricane Sandy, 183, 188
Hutchinson, Anne, 19–20, 22
Hyde, William, house of, 81–82, 88

immigrants, 96, 140–41, 144, 171–73, 175–77, 180, 267–68
Improv Everywhere, 184–85
Ingoldesby, Richard, 30–31
Interchurch World Movement, 229
International Building, 235
International Mercantile Marine (IMM), 200
International Workers of the World (IWW), 217, 228
Irving, Washington, 9, *91*, 91–92, 103

J. P. Morgan & Co., 201–3, 205
Jacob Riis Park, 247–48
Jacobs, Jane, 76, *239*, 240, 243–44, 246, 248–53
James, Henry, 77, 79, 88
Jefferson, Thomas, 53, 54–55, 65, 67, 68
Jewish Museum, 165
Jews, 23–24, 176–77, 180, 220
Johnson, Eastman, 123–24
Johnson, Fenton, 217–18
Johnson, James Weldon, 217
Jones, George Frederic, 157, 159

Jones, Lucretia Rhinelander, 157, 158, 159
Jones, Mary Harris "Mother," 228
Jones, Mary Mason, 158
Jones Beach, 241, 247

Kellum, John, 142, 143
Kieft, Willem, 5–6, 19–20, 23
Kindred Spirits (Durand), 109–10, 208
King, David, 220
Kings Bridge, 195
Kirk, William, 243–44

Lady Moody House, 21
Lady Moody Triangle, 22
Lady Writing (Vermeer), 209
La Farge, John, 149
LaFarge Hotel, 133–34
Lafayette, Marquis de, 67, 69
Lafayette Place, 82–83
Lafayette Theater, 222–23
La Grange Terrace, 82–83
La Guardia, Fiorello, 67, 242
La Maison Francaise, *226,* 233, 234
Landmarks Preservation Commission, 93–95, 252–53
Lee, Robert E., 211
Leisler, Jacob, 30–31
L'Enfant, Pierre, 67, 74
Leon, Rodney, 38, 39
Lewis, Sinclair, 214
Liberator, The, 215, 217–18, 224
Limelight nightclub, 205
Lincoln, Abraham, *120,* 122–36, 193, 224
Lincoln, Mary Todd, 128–29, 132, 155
Lincoln Center, 244, 245–47
Lind, Jenny, 69
Lindsay, John, 251, 252

Little Germany, 137
Little Italy, 171–72, 173, 266–68, 276
Little Owl restaurant, 81, 82
Livingston, Brockholst, 54
Livingston, Edward, 66
Locke, Alain, 221
Lodwick, Charles, 27
Long Island, 3, 18, 241
Loss, Frederica, 103
Lovelace Tavern, 29
Low, Seth, 186–87, 188–91, 193–94, 196, 197, 203
Lower East Side Tenement Museum, 176, 177
Lower Manhattan Expressway (Lomex), 240, 249, 250–53
Low Library, 190
Lownds, Sara, 260
Ludlow Massacre, 228–29
Lynes, Stephen, 148
Lyric Theater (*now* Foxwoods Theater), 268–69

MacDougal Street, 214, 257, 260–62, 263
Madison Square, 86
Madison Square Garden, 207, 263
Mall, the, 114, 116, 117, 133
Manhattan, 1–5, 7, 13, 14, 18, 24, 26, 27, 28, 43, 47, 50, 112, 187, 195–96
Manhattan Bridge, 140, 251
Manhattan Company, 53–54
Marble Palace, 125, 128
Marcy, William L., 144
Marine Parkway Bridge, 248
Masses, The, 215, 217, 224
McAllister, Ward, 161, 169
McCarren Park pool, 247
McEntee, Jervis, 112

McGown's Pass, 70, 108, 110
McKay, Claude, 218, 219, 220
McKim, Charles, 190, 205
McSorley's Old Ale House, 127–28
Megapolensis, Johannes, 17–18
Melville, Herman, 156
Merchant's House Museum, 77–79, *78,* 83–86, 90
Mersereau, William, 41
Metropolitan Club, 206–7
Metropolitan Hotel, 128
Metropolitan Museum of Art, 83, 108, 137, 147, 161, 199, 208–9
Metropolitan Opera, 232, 245–46
Mey, Cornelius, 3
Miller, William Starr, 166
Minetta Tavern, 258
Minuit, Peter, 3–4, 13–14
Mitchel, John Purroy, 117
Moody, Deborah, 20–22
Moody, Henry, 20, 21
Moore, Clement Clarke, 73, 75–76, 81
Morgan, Amelia Sturges, 208–9
Morgan, J. Pierpont, *198,* 199–211, 229
Morgan, Jack, 201, 202
Morgan Library, 199, 205, 206
Morningside Heights, 189–90, 209, 230
Morris, Lewis, 35
Morris-Jumel Mansion, 50
Morton, Levi P., 194
Moses, Robert, 69, 118, 146, *239,* 239–53, 257, 264
Mould, Jacob Wrey, 112, 115, 137, 139, 145, 146–47, 208
Mount Tom, 97, 98

movie locations, 163, 173, 190, 217, 247, 265–77
Mulligan, Hercules, 46
Murphy, Jack "Murph the Surf," 208
Murphy's Tavern, 4
Museum of Modern Art, 235, 272
Museum of Natural History, 147, 199, 208

Nast, Thomas, *138*, 140–41, 144–45, 150, 151, 153
National Arts Club, 149, 163, 275
Native Americans, 3–6, 9, 14, 19–20
42nd Street, 268–69
Neil, Fred, 256
Netherlands Memorial Flagpole, 4
Neue Gallery, 166
Nevius, Adriaentje, 7, 9, 12
Nevius, Avon M., 9
Nevius, Johannes, 2–3, 7, 8, 9, 12, 272
New Amersfoort (Flatlands), 10
New Amsterdam, *1*, 1–26, 30
New Haarlem (*renamed* New Lancaster), 47
New Netherland (Dutch colony), 1–2, 9, 25
New York Aquarium, 69, 243, 248
New York Central Railroad, 211
New York City
  crime, 183, 252, 262
  five-borough consolidation, 187, 189, 191–97
  name change, 30
  as nation's capital, 51, 52, 67–68
  nighttime skyline views of, *265, 272*

oldest buildings in, 1, 10–12, 16, 24, 29, 31, 50, 127, 130, 268, 277
  population statistics, 71, 140, 173, 187, 194–95
  rental rates, median, 183
  urban development, 71–76, 239–53, 244–45
New York City Marathon, 73–74, 195–96
New-York (Evening) Post, 55, 106–7, 182
New York Public Library, 109, 196
New York State Council of Parks, 241
New York State Theater, 245
New York University, 93–95
New York Weekly Journal, 35
New York Yacht Club, 274
Nick Moore's Tavern, 103–4
Nicolls, Richard, 25, 30
9/11 attacks, 28, 46, 66, 141, 195, 237–38
Nine Men, 6–7
Nolita, 268
Northern Dispensary, 96
North Woods, 116, 118
Nude Descending a Staircase (Duchamp), 166

Old Broadway Synagogue, 75
Olmsted, Frederick Law, 71, 76, 106, 111, 112–18, 145
O'Neill, Eugene, 214, 217
Orme, Caroline Astor, 165
O'Rourke, Matthew, 148
Otis, Elisha, 126
Outdoor Recreation League, 173

Palazzo d'Italia, 235
Panic of 1907, 205–6
Payne, Daniel, 102, 103
Pearl Street, 29

Pendleton, Nathaniel, 56, 57
Peter Minuit Plaza, 5, 13
pew rents, 156–57, 204
Philharmonic Hall (*now* Avery Fisher Hall), 245
Phyfe, Duncan, 84
Piano, Renzo, 205
Piccirilli, Attilio, 235
Pierce, Franklin, 110
Pilat, Ignaz, 116
Pinky (Rose Ward), 123–24
pirates and piracy, 33, 80
Plant, Morton F., 164–65
playgrounds, first public, 181
Plymouth Church, 122–23, 124, 128, 135–36
Poe, Edgar Allen, 92–104
Poe, Virginia, 94, 98, 100–101
Polhemus, Johannes, 12, 13, 23
Pomander Walk, 274
Prohibition, 214, 216
Pujo, Arsene, 206

Quakers, *15*, 15–18, 22–25, 26
Queen Elizabeth II Garden, 28
Queens, 15, 191, 192, 193, 195, 241, 266

Radio City Music Hall, 235
Rainsford, William, 204
Ramble, 115, 116
Randel, John, Jr., 72–73, 74, 86
Reed, John, 214, 215, 217, 221
Renwick, James, 155
Reservoir Square, 109
Reynolds, James, 53
Reynolds, Maria, 53
Richmond Hill, 48, 95, 96

Riis, Jacob, 169, 172, 173, 174–77, 179, 180, 182–83, 247, 277

riots and rebellions, 28, 30–31, 35, 121–22, 129–31, 151

Riverside Church, 230–31, 232

Riverside Park, 97, 135

Robertson, Hugh Sterling, 232–33

Rockaway Beach, 247

Rockaways, 248, 274–75

Rockefeller, David, 234, 236–37

Rockefeller, John D., 221, 225

Rockefeller, John D., III, 234, 245

Rockefeller, John D., Jr., 182, 203, 225, 227–30, 232–35

Rockefeller, Nelson, 234, 235–36, 237

Rockefeller Center, 225, *226*, 232–35

Roebling, Emily, 186, 197

Roebling, John, 186

Roebling, Washington, 186–87

Rogers, Mary, 102–4

Rolling Thunder Revue, 262

Roosevelt, Franklin D., 182, 241, 242

Roosevelt, Theodore, 134

Roseland Ballroom, 263

Row, the, 87–88

Rumsey playfield, 239

Sabbath observance, 6, 114

Sailors' Snug Harbor, 80, 87

Sands, Gulielma, 54

Sanger, Margaret, 214

San Juan Hill, 244, 247, 266

Schenck, Jan Martense, 12

Schermerhorn, Abraham and Helen, 157

Schomburg Center for Research in Black Culture, 224

Scorsese, Martin, 163, 173, 256, 266–69, 272–73, 275, 276–77

Seagram Building, 236

Seneca Village, 110, 111

Seward, William, 122, 148

Seward Park, 173–74, 181

Seymour, Horatio, 144

Shakespeare, William, 117, 118, 133

Sheep Meadow, 116, 145–46

Sherman, William Tecumseh, 135

Sherman Antitrust Act, 225

Sinclair, Upton, 215, 228

slaves and slavery, 28, 29–30, 33, 35–39, 40, 122, 123–24, 126, 220

Society of Friends, *15*, 15–18, 22–25, 26

Soho, 240, 246, 250–53, 273

Sons of Liberty, 28, 40, 45, 49

South Street Seaport, 188, 271

speakeasies, 214, 215–17, 257

Sphere (Koenig), 237–38

St. George's Church, 203–5

St. John the Divine, 190–91, 209–11, 229–30

St. Luke in the Fields, 81

St. Mark's-in-the-Bowery, 1, 12, 25, 277

St. Patrick's Cathedral, 155, 164

St. Patrick's Old Cathedral, 266–67

St. Paul's Chapel, 46, 52, 200

Stadt Huis, 7–8, 18, 29, 67

Stamp Act, 45

Standard Oil, 225, 227

Star of India, 208

Staten Island, 12, 41–42, 87–88, 191, 195, 248

Stebbins, Emma, 115, 171

Stevens, Henry Leyden, 159, 169

Stevenson van Cortlandt, Oloff, 4

Stewart, A. T., 125, 128, 155

Stowe, Harriet Beecher, 124

Striver's Row, 220, 222, 262

Strong, George Templeton, 130

Strong, William K., 194

Stuyvesant, Peter, 1–2, 6–9, 11, 12, 13, 16–17, 18, 22–24, 25, 26, 197, 203, 231, 277

Stuyvesant Square, 204

subways, 32, 195–96, 197, 220, 248, 269, 271

Surrogate's Courthouse, 196–97

Sweeny, Peter B., 144, 145, 152

Tammany Hall, 128, 137, 141, 142, 143–44, 149, 192, 194

Tavern on the Green, 139, 146, 195

Tayler, John, 55

Temple Emanu-El, 148, 164

Tenderloin, 220

tenements, 175–82, 247

Tenth Street Studio, 213–14

Terry, Rose, 123

Thomas, John Rochester, 196

Thomson-Houston Electric Company, 203

Tiffany, Louis Comfort, 152

Tilden, Samuel J., 137, 149–50, 151–52, 163

Times Square, 268–69

Titanic (ship), 200, 211

Title I housing, 244, 247, 249

Todd, Charlie, 184–85
trains, elevated, 137,
    192, 195
Tredwell, Gertrude, 77–79,
    78, 83–86, 88–90
Tredwell, Seabury, 77–79,
    78, 83–84, 96
Triborough Bridge and
    Tunnel Authority, 241
Trinity Chapel (Saint
    Sava's), 159–61
Trinity Church, 46, 52,
    60–61
Triumph of Avarice, The
    (tapestry), 205
Trotsky, Leon, 218
Trumbull, John, *44,* 54
Twain, Mark, 156
Tweed, William M. "Boss,"
    63, 137–53, *138,* 168, 242
Tweed Courthouse,
    142–43, 148

Union Club, 206–7
United Copper Company,
    205–6
United Nations, 236
Upjohn, Richard, 160
urban development, 71–76,
    244–45. *See also* Moses,
    Robert

Van Buren, Martin, 12
Van Cortlandt, Augustus, 32
Van Cortlandt House,
    31–33, 41–42
Van Cortlandt Park, 31
Van Dam, Rip, 34–35
Vanderbilt, Cornelius, II,
    164, 165, 207, 274
Van Vechten, Carl, *212,* 221
Van Wyck, Robert A., 194
Varick, Caesar, 36

Vaux, Calvert, 71, 106, 108,
    111–18, 137, 145, 149,
    172, 192, 208
Verrazano-Narrows
    Bridge, 248
Viele, Egbert, 111–12, 113

Wagner, Robert, 250
Wald, Lillian, 169, 173–74,
    179–81, 182–83
Walker, Jimmy, 239
Walloons, 3, 13
Walton, Louis, 88–89
Wampage, 20
Warburg, Felix, 165
Ward, JQA, 133, 135
Ware, James, 178
War of 1812, 68–71
Warren, Peter, 37, 80
Washington, George, 32, 34,
    48, 50, 51, 60, 67
Washington Bridge, 192
*Washington Irving and His
    Friends at Sunnyside*
    (Schussele), 91, *91*
Washington Square, 79–80,
    86–87, 88, 207, 239,
    249–52, 258, 261
Washington Square (James),
    77, 79, 88, 89
Washington Square Arch,
    79, 207
Washington Square
    Hotel, 260
Washington Square
    Village, 250
watering troughs, 146–47
Water Street, 13
water systems and supply,
    53–54, 82, 109
Watson, James, 147–48
Waugh, Dorothy, 17–18
Weehawken, 43, 52, 56,
    57–58

Weeks, Levi, 54
Weeksville, 130–32
Welles, Orson, 222–23
Wharton, Edith Newbold
    Jones, 80, *154,* 157–60,
    162–63, 167–70, 179,
    206, 207, 252, 271
Wharton, Teddy, 158,
    159–60, 168
White, Stanford, 79, 206,
    207, 222
White Horse Tavern,
    252, 253
White Star Line, 200
Whitney, Gertrude
    Vanderbilt, 26, 203, 214
Whitney Museum of
    American Art, 214
Whittemore, Samuel, home
    of, 95–96, 217
Willis, Nathaniel Parker,
    92, 99
Winter: The Skating Pond
    (Currier & Ives),
    105, 114
Winter Garden Theater
    fire, 133
Winthrop, John, 19, 20
Witherhead, Mary, 17–18
Wood, Fernando, 112, 129
World's Fair 1939, 234, 236
World Trade Center, 65,
    236–38. *See also* 9/11
    attacks
World War I, 168, 217
Wyckoff House Museum,
    10–12

yellow fever, 79–81

Zenger, John Peter, 35